fornication:
THE RED HOT
CHILI PEPPERS
STORY

fornication:
THE RED HOT CHILI PEPPERS

JEFF APTER

STORY

OMNIBUS PRESS

LONDON / NEW YORK / PARIS / SYDNEY / COPENHAGEN / BERLIN / MADRID / TOKYO

Exclusive Distributors
Music Sales Limited,
8/9 Frith Street,
London W1D 3JB, UK.

Music Sales Corporation,
257 Park Avenue South,
New York, NY 10010, USA.

Macmillan Distribution Services,
53 Park West Drive,
Derrimut, Vic 3030,
Australia.

To the Music Trade only:
Music Sales Limited,
8/9 Frith Street,
London W1D 3JB, UK.

Every effort has been made to trace the copyright holders of the photographs in this
book but one or two were unreachable. We would be grateful if the photographers
concerned would contact us.

Printed by Mackays of Chatham plc, Chatham, Kent.

A catalogue record for this book is available from the British Library.

Visit Omnibus Press on the web at www.omnibuspress.com

Contents

To Diana,
for everything, once again

OPENING

The Mild Ones
West Palm Beach, Florida, June 2003

THIS surely can't be right. This is supposed to be the backstage area at a crazy, wild, sexy rock'n'roll show. A Red Hot Chili Peppers show, no less, a celebration of the music of a band that revelled in playing nude with only a single tube sock dangling between them and a charge of indecent exposure. This is also the same group – now minus one deceased member – that thumbed their noses at one of rock's most iconic bands and images by posing with the very same socks on cocks for the cover of their 1988 *Abbey Road* EP.

It's a band whose lead singer, Anthony Kiedis, not only penned a song by the name 'Sir Psycho Sexy', but spent many years living up to the tag. Kiedis has also gone by the name "Antwan the Swan", because of what he once referred to as his "magic wand". Kiedis' name has been linked with actresses Jennifer Aniston and Ione Skye and supermodel Heidi Klum, plus pop stars Madonna and Sporty Spice, amongst many others. He's lived so large that even eternal teenager, Rolling Stone Mick Jagger, would have had trouble keeping up with him. And this is a band whose drummer, Chad Smith – one Chili Pepper who isn't an addict-on-the-mend – has no problem spawning children (he's the father of three), but for the life of him can't maintain a relationship with any of their three mothers. It's a band whose exuberant, gap-toothed, sweet-natured bassist, the now 40-year-old Michael Balzary (aka Flea), still can't keep his trousers on once he hits the stage and plugs in. He usually prefers to pound his bass while dressed in Y-fronts, often less. It's also a band that in its turbulent 20-year life has lost a founding member, Hillel Slovak, to heroin, and miraculously saved a second, John Frusciante, from the same pointless demise. A band that has nearly enough former members to make up a football team. A band that has had not just one major commercial and critical rebirth, but two, a near impossibility in an increasingly fickle musical world.

And here they are backstage, pre show, in the midst of another hugely successful tour and album stretch, with incense burning and tofu on the menu. *By The Way*, their eighth long-player, has already shifted eight million copies and rising worldwide, with reviews praising its rich musical tapestry, comparing it to everyone from The Beatles to Beach Boy mastermind Brian Wilson. *Rolling Stone* magazine declared it "a near perfect balance of gutter-grime and high art aspiration". It's a supremely strong follow-up to 1999's 12-million-plus-selling *Californication*, an album that rescued the band from a seemingly unstoppable slide into rock'n'roll insignificance. There's a lot to celebrate – so where are the frantic, horny, anything-goes groupies with heliumated breasts? Where are the drugs? Where is the booze? Where are the dwarves? What the hell's going on?

Picture this: Flea is seated with tour manager Louis Mathieu and his assistant Gage Freeman. They're playing Boggle, the chosen sport of indolent middle America, while being serenaded by soothing classical music. Flea looks up, his luminous blue eyes not quite hiding a steely intent. "This is a very serious Boggle tournament," he insists. "I am the current Boggle champion." He's hoping that maybe his 14-year-old daughter Clara – whose name is tattooed on his left arm, right next to Jimi Hendrix – will join him soon. If she can take the time out from her all-girl band, that is.

The best word to describe Flea in 2003 is beatific. The words "God" and "gratitude" dot his sentences; he says a silent prayer before every meal. Although not tied to one formal religion, Flea now believes that, "God, of course, is the most important part in everybody."

Kiedis is nearby, in an amiable bear hug with his father, John, who's better known to all as Blackie Dammett, B-grade actor, former Hollywood scenester and the self-proclaimed "Editor and Chief Potentate" of the band's fan club organisation, Rockinfreakapotamus Peoplehood, Inc, a tag swiped from Kiedis' nickname for the band's breakthrough 1989 album, *Mother's Milk*.

The Kiedis' relationship is soap-opera worthy. There have been long periods of separation, reconciliations, recriminations, hero worship – even a stretch when the teenage Kiedis shared a Hollywood home with his father, where they lived and partied like two bachelors on the prowl. Kiedis senior introduced his son to dope, Hollywood wannabes, party girls and the rock stars who hung out with him at Rodney Bingenheimer's notorious English Disco, LA's coolest dive at the time. The Kiedis home was an open house where the sight of a naked woman – sometimes several – was absolutely nothing to be alarmed about. Kiedis' father even helped his son lose his virginity, when he was aged 12. Son repaid father many years later by buying him a sprawling six-and-a-half-acre lakeside property in Michigan. So exactly how does Kiedis remember his Hollywood youth? "Fights, drugs and lots of guys and girls getting crazy."

But today the Kiedises look more like two guys hanging out at a ball game. Then Kiedis the younger excuses himself and talks with the band's nurse, who is preparing an injection of ozone – the closest thing to drugs backstage at a 2003 Red Hot Chili Peppers show. Kiedis settles into a comfortable chair, while the nurse preps him for a fix and photographer Anton Corbijn sets up a shot that will appear in *Rolling Stone* magazine. In the article that accompanied the shot, Kiedis revealed how the *By The Way* track 'Can't Stop' sings the praises of being treated with ozone. "It's a gas that our nurse administers through the vein. Clears the body of viruses and bacteria. New medicine on the cutting edge," he declared.

While Kiedis slides into his ozone haze, Chad Smith – tall, built as if he were carved from stone – nurses his six-year-old son Justin. Now in his 15th year with the band, Smith was also born in Michigan. And despite the huge amounts of cash the band generates – handy, considering his hefty monthly maintenance payments – he's still a blue-collar guy right down to his trademark baseball cap, which covers his greying hair. Whereas the rest of the band prefer a ceremonial mug of chamomile tea before hitting the stage, Smith is more likely to knock back a Heineken or six. Smith is enormously proud of his son, who has decided that he, too, is keen on the drummer's stool. "He loves going to our concerts because, he says, 'I really like your friends in the band,'" Smith smiles. "So innocent."

Nearby is Chili Pepper guitarist John Frusciante, an almost Christ-like figure with his mane of dark hair and shaggy beard. Frusciante is a dazzling six-string maestro and the most cosmically inclined member of a band that makes no effort to deny its wholegrain, brotherly-love-for-all Californian roots. Frusciante, of course, shouldn't be here at all. And that's not because he doesn't belong in the group – those who know the band and their history quietly believe that the richly gifted Frusciante is now the creative muscle of the Chili Peppers. He sprinkled musical fairydust all over *By The Way*, not just with his guitar, but by sweetening their funk-rock sound with heavenly harmonies and sun-kissed melodies.

No, the thing is that Frusciante shouldn't even be alive. He's survived the same rampant heroin addiction that killed Hillel Slovak, the band's original guitarist, and almost claimed Kiedis. Frusciante's addiction ran so deep that once, while on the nod, he burned down his own house in the Hollywood Hills. He even resigned his cherished spot in the band, during 1992 – mid-world tour, no less – citing exhaustion and a fervent distaste for stardom. ("When I see pictures of myself back then," Frusciante now admits, "I just want to strangle the person.") He then went home and sank into a downward spiral that only ended when Flea, his close friend – no, make that equal parts mentor and punk-soul brother – visited him in hospital and talked him into rejoining the band. Flea then convinced Kiedis, who was dealing with his own relapse into smack, that Frusciante was essential to the survival of the band. Several jams later the toned, bronzed frontman agreed. That was prior to 1999's *Californication* album and the resulting Chili Peppers rebirth.

There are a few tell-tale signs of Frusciante's life in hell. Nowadays he generally chooses to wear long sleeves, which hide the ugly scars of skin grafts that he underwent to repair the bruises and abscesses on his arms brought about by years of seriously dodgy injection techniques. Oh and his dentures – set him back $US150,000 and replaced the blackened stumps of teeth that heroin and neglect had rotted away – don't quite fit right. Though he mightn't be as buff or tanned as his outdoors-loving bandmates, the lean and wiry Frusciante still looks in the best shape of his life. He's sharing a table with his grandparents and his father and is beaming with a hard-won happiness.

"My grandfather hasn't seen me play guitar since we used to play Italian songs when I was 12 years old," he says in his slightly slack-jawed style (another reminder of his hard times). "I was so happy that my grandparents decided to come to the show."

Soon Frusciante will quietly retire to a backstage room where he'll play along to favourite records and then twist himself into a strange hunched form. He'll stay that way for 45 minutes.

4

"It's this sort of Tai Chi thing that my doctor friend showed me," he explains. "You start sweating, you focus on your breathing."

Then, just before going on, Frusciante and Flea will join up for a session of Ashtanga yoga in the backstage meditation room (an essential at every Peppers show). It's their exercise of choice. They keep their yoga mats backstage at all times, in case of cosmic emergencies.

When the call comes from their stage manager that it's showtime, the four long-time pals and musical brothers form a huddle backstage. It's a ritual they've stuck with since the early days of the band: they form a circle of four, lock their hands and swing their arms in small circles, urging each other to play the best fucking show of their lives.

Their bond is genuine. As teens, all the band members, bar Smith, suffered the problems and insecurities brought about by divorced parents and broken homes and itinerant lifestyles. Flea was born in Melbourne, Australia, but at the age of six wound up in Los Angeles via New York; Kiedis drifted from the Mid-west to California; Frusciante was born in New York but moved to California, bouncing between his divorced parents; Smith wandered from Michigan to Los Angeles after playing drums at one too many wet T-shirt competitions. Despite some attempts at domestic bliss, none of the band are currently married.

The Red Hot Chili Peppers started out as friends, were pulled apart by drugs and ego and found their salvation through music. The only true, permanent bond in their lives is the band.

When the stage lights dim, the Californicators plug in and the body-rocking sounds of 'By The Way' fill the arena, sending the Chili Bowl – the good-natured moshpit situated stage front at every Chili Peppers show – into joyful convulsions. It's another sweet victory for this enormously successful, hugely influential band, enough to validate their 20-year-long rollercoaster ride of love, drugs, sex, death, rock'n'roll and despair, many times over.

CHAPTER ONE

"We would be friends forever, for better, for worse, for everything in the universe."

TYPICALLY, most Los Angelenos opt to drive, but if you're in the mood for public transport, Fairfax High School is a short ride on the number 217 bus. It'll set you back less than two dollars. The bus will pick you up on Hollywood Boulevard, heading west. Then it takes a left on Fairfax, turning towards the south. It's best to jump off at Melrose, because the school, better known to locals as "Fax City", is right at the corner of Melrose and Fairfax. It's about a mile west of La Brea, home to the mysterious tar pits, whose asphalt deposits prove – despite what modern-day Hollywood might have you thinking – that there was life here before liposuction was invented. (Somewhere between eight and 40,000 years ago, in fact.) Fairfax High is about two miles south of Hollywood Boulevard; nearby is the CBS TV centre and the famous Farmer's Market.

While the formerly art deco Fairfax High School might now look pretty innocuous from the street, it could well be the rock'n'roll high school that New York punks The Ramones dreamt about in their 1979 anthem. Legendary B-film producer Roger Corman had the same dream in his film *Rock'n'roll High School*, which starred the very same Ramones. Except Corman called his school Vince Lombardi High.

Slash, the human hairball who bled riffs for Guns N' Roses in the Eighties and early Nineties, was a Fairfax High graduate. Jackson Five siblings Jermaine and Marlon were also students. And if the school's gym looks strangely familiar, that's because it was used as the backdrop for Nirvana's riotous 'Smells Like Teen Spirit' video, the song that broke down the wall between "alternative" and mainstream music in 1992. (The clip's comely cheerleaders, however, weren't from Fairfax High; they were hired extras.)

But well before Slash, the Jacksons, Nirvana and the founding members of The Red Hot Chili Peppers slouched around the halls of Fairfax High, this was a very different landscape. When the school was built in 1924, Los Angeles was the USA's biggest agricultural county. Accordingly, Fax City was dubbed an Agricultural & Mechanical school; the main focus for the 28-acre campus were such agrarian concerns as forestry, landscape gardening, agronomy and architecture. LA's Jewish community – which nearly doubled during the school's first decade – started to move into the area and it fast became the city's Jewish heartland. Such concerns as Canter's Deli and Solomon's Book Store now found homes on Fairfax Avenue; trade was very good.

But it wasn't all about business. If you had a few hours to spare – and didn't mind the lung damage – you could check out the midget car racing at Gilmore Stadium (which is now the CBS TV site). Or if you wanted to commune with nature, you could wander through the corn, strawberry and cauliflower fields that flourished in the spot where Westwood now sprawls.

Early on, amidst Fairfax High's predominantly Jewish student body, there was a smattering of Asians, even a few African-Americans. And gradually the school moved away from all things agrarian and started to develop a reputation as an artistic haven, in part due to its proximity to Hollywood. Movie industry parents could raise their children here because the school – whose motto is "Never say die, say do" – provided the right kind of creative, arts-oriented education. (Today, however, the school motto sits alongside a placard that warns: "SEE A WEAPON AT SCHOOL? SAVE A LIFE – TELL SOMEONE.")

Larry Gelbart, from the class of 1945, who went on to create the hit TV show *M.A.S.H.*, remembers the school as "a West Point for actors". Ricardo Montalban was a graduate. So was child star Mickey Rooney. Later on, actors Timothy Hutton, David Janssen and David Arquette would spend their teen years shuffling about the school's corridors, dreaming of nearby Hollywood. (All this might explain why Fairfax High currently appears in the "Celebrity Schools" section of on-line site "The Ultimate Guide To Celebrities And Hollywood".) Actress Demi Moore is a famous Fairfax High dropout – her classmates included Sharona Alperin, the object of under-age desire in The Knack's 'My Sharona' – likewise the late singer/songwriter Warren 'Werewolves Of London' Zevon. Unlike Moore, comedians Byron

Allen and Rip Taylor managed to graduate from Fairfax High. As did Jerry Leiber, an alumnus of the Class of '55.

Fledgling songwriter Leiber, who had grown up on the very black side of Baltimore before moving to California with his family, was amazed by Fairfax's diversity. "I thought it was paradise," he said. "There were black people, Mexicans, Asians. Where I came from was very black and white." Years later, Anthony Kiedis would also be impressed by the school's inter-racial blend. "The racial mix was so varied – European and Soviet and American and African and Latin countries – and it was so harmonious. I'm very proud that we went to that school together and experienced that life. It's where we got our substance."

A year after graduating, in cahoots with fellow tunesmith and Fairfax graduate Mike Stoller, Jerry Leiber wrote a barrelhouse blues rave-up called 'Hound Dog', originally cut by Willie Mae "Big Mama" Thornton in 1952. Four years later it was a runaway hit for an acne-scarred, pelvis-shaking kid from Tupelo called Elvis Presley. In those Tin Pan Alley times – where the words "singer" and "song-writer" were mutually exclusive – Leiber and Stoller became a hot property. The songs then poured out of the Fax City pair, including such hits for The King as 'Jailhouse Rock', 'King Creole' and 'Baby I Don't Care', along with hits for others that included 'Searchin'', 'Yakety Yak' and 'Poison Ivy'.

Phil Spector was another Fairfax High graduate. Short, savvy and driven by the kind of manic energy that could light up a city, Spector was born in The Bronx, the son of first generation Russian-Jew immigrants. He had shifted to the west coast with his sister and mother in 1952, three years after Spector's father had gassed himself to death in his car. The man who would create the ground-breaking (and window-rattling) Wall of Sound production style, and who crafted hits for Ike & Tina Turner, The Righteous Brothers and The Ronettes – as well as mixing The Beatles' *Let It Be* and producing albums for George Harrison and John Lennon – got his first taste of music at Fairfax High. It was here that he fell for both R&B and the finger-poppin' sounds of West Coast jazz. And it was at Fairfax that Spector learned how to play piano and guitar. By 1960 he was in New York, re-uniting with fellow Fairfax graduates Leiber and Stoller, co-writing the massive hit 'Spanish Harlem'.

A kid called Herb Alpert could also be seen roaming the corridors of

Fairfax High. This was long before he fronted the Tijuana Brass, who hit big with 'The Lonely Bull' in 1962 and 'A Taste Of Honey' three years later, or established A&M Records, the home of easy-listeners The Carpenters and Carole King, and, later on, Janet Jackson. (In a move that might just qualify him as the most successful of all Fairfax High graduates, Alpert and partner Jerry Moss sold A&M in 1990 for a reported $US500 million plus.)

Jan Berry and Dean Torrence, a pair of squeaky clean Californian kids, fresh from nearby Emerson Junior High, were also students at Fairfax. Berry and Torrance were a couple of years younger than Alpert. That was back before they shortened their names to Jan & Dean and put their surfside harmonies on such songs as 'Dead Man's Curve', 'The Little Old Lady From Pasadena' and 'Surf City', a tune co-written by their buddy, Beach Boy Brian Wilson. Alpert became Jan & Dean's manager in the late Fifties, guiding them through the most chart-bound stretch of their short career.

By the mid-Sixties, Fairfax High School's Honour Roll was starting to resemble a rock'n'roll hall of fame.

The area's Jewish population may have peaked during the Fifties and Sixties, but Fairfax High changed radically when the February 9, 1971, Sylmar earthquake destroyed nearby Los Angeles High, a minority-heavy school. Fairfax, having been "earthquake proofed" in 1969, was only slightly damaged by the quake, which killed 14 Los Angelenos and caused millions of dollars worth of damage.

While Los Angeles High was being rebuilt, the two schools began a special schedule whereby Fairfax kids used the campus for half a day, Los Angeles High kids the other half. The cultural climate of the school changed; drugs could be scored on campus and an iron fence had to be built around the grounds to prevent students from absconding during the day. Not long after, a racial integration programme meant that students were bussed into Fairfax from other, less harmonious or affluent sections of LA. Angry anti-Vietnam War demonstrations also left their mark on the school and its students.

As one former Fairfax High graduate and teacher told me, "There was quite a lot of 'white flight' from the neighbourhood during the Sixties and Seventies."

By the time Anthony Kiedis, Michael Balzary, Jack Irons and Hillel

Slovak (the latter pair being Jewish themselves) enrolled at Fairfax High in 1977, the school was approximately 40 per cent white and the campus wasn't quite the creative breeding ground it had been in the previous three decades. And just like so many Los Angelenos, only one of these 15-year-olds – Jack Irons – could actually call California their true home.

Not much happens in Grand Rapids, Michigan, especially during the eight icy months of every year, when the lakes freeze over and the city's two main pleasures are ice skating and central heating. A big chill was the first sight that greeted Anthony Kiedis when he was born in Grand Rapids' St Mary's Hospital, on November 1, 1962. The Kiedis family were living near Plaster Creek, but his father, John, had a much bigger dream. He knew there was a lot more to life than Grand Rapids, home to the largest Dutch population in the USA (Kiedis' grandfather, however, was Lithuanian) and – until the late Seventies – the furniture-building capital of America. Anthony's father was a sharp-dressed man with a handlebar moustache and long hair, who wore snakeskin boots, rainbow-coloured suits and a winning grin. His grand plan was to become an actor in Hollywood. Anthony's mother, Margaret Elizabeth Idema (aka Peggy Idema), worked as a secretary at a law firm and was far more level-headed than her husband.

Years later, when asked about the relationship he shared with his mother, Kiedis was full of praise. "With a lot of my friends," he said, "we talk so much trash about our parents, but my own mom has been a pillar of stability and consistency in the lives of everybody around her. She and I have always been tight.

"When I was growing up, my mother was the perfect picture of unconditional love and worked her ass off to support me for about 10 years," he said in 1994. "She instilled qualities in me that I'm very grateful for."

Every bit the doting son, Kiedis even thought that his mother resembled Sixties Mouseketeer Annette Funicello.

While Kiedis would inherit his father's virtually insatiable love for women, he insists that his mother's "genuineness" rubbed off on him as well. In 1992 he told *Rolling Stone*'s David Fricke how, "At a pretty early age I fell in love with a girl and stayed with her for three years. So it wasn't like I was destined to do the same thing my father was doing."

Well, yes and no. In 1964, John Kiedis was accepted at UCLA, and with his wife and child in tow, loaded up a U-Haul trailer, hitched it to their Corvair, and headed west. He enrolled in the university's film department; he even shot a black-and-white film there, called *The Hooligans*, starring a two-year-old Anthony.

But the Kiedis marriage wasn't built to last; Margaret and John were quickly divorced. Faster than a cold snap, she and Anthony were back living in Grand Rapids.

By then John Kiedis had rechristened himself Blackie Dammett, after the crime writer Dashiell Hammett, who was later to become one of Anthony's favourite authors. And he was living large in Hollywood. He became a regular at Rodney Bingenheimer's English Disco on Sunset Boulevard, a famous LA hang-out for such stars as David Bowie, Iggy Pop, T. Rex and Led Zeppelin and attendant under-age groupies. Legendary scenester Bingenheimer must have been an inspiration for the ambitious Dammett; he was an object lesson in how to make it in LA pop culture society. (Bingenheimer, however, doesn't remember Dammett that well, recalling only "that he used to come to my English Disco".)

As a child, Bingenheimer was a stand-in for future Monkee Davy Jones; he then became a regular when *The Monkees'* TV show became a nationwide smash. His circle of pals included members of The Byrds and The Beatles; he was tight with Elvis Presley and Sonny Bono. Bingenheimer even helped snag gender-bending Englishman David Bowie a record deal in America with RCA. Bowie responded by declaring Bingenheimer "an island of Anglo nowness". He was a man worth knowing.

Back in sleepy, snowy Grand Rapids, Anthony would receive parcels from his Hollywood-based father. They'd contain love beads, posters of Bob Dylan, T-shirts and assorted ephemera. He was dazzled. "I thought, wow, this guy is tapped into another planet; I felt like I was opening a world of magic."

He'd also receive letters and phone calls from his dad, filling him in on his TV and film auditions, and listing the superstars he was meeting. He dropped such names as Alice Cooper, Lou Reed and John Lennon; Dammett did publicity work for the stars, running the West Coast office of the New York-based The Image Group whose clients included Cooper, Reed and the infamous New York Dolls. His father was also hanging out with Led Zeppelin and The Who, but didn't mention this in his updates to his son. (In a strange case of art imitating life, Dammett would go on to play a drug dealer in the 1987 movie *Lethal Weapon*; Anthony would do likewise in the 1991 film *Point Break*.) Even though Anthony wasn't quite sure who these people were, they sounded like the epitome of coolness. You sure didn't meet many guys called Alice Cooper in Grand Rapids.

Every summer, Anthony would visit his father and, not surprisingly, his attraction for the LA lifestyle started to develop. When he was "about eight", his father took him to his first rock show – a double-header of Deep Purple and Rod Stewart. Life was sweet.

Dammett had allegedly studied acting under Lee Strasberg, Michael V. Gazzo and Harvey Lembeck, and he did actually have some success. He scored bit parts – usually playing the token bad guy – in such TV shows as *Charlie's Angels*, *Starsky & Hutch*, *Trapper John MD* and *Alfred Hitchcock Presents* (and later on, *Hill Street Blues*, plus the genre-defining films *Meatballs II*, *Doctor Detroit*, *Woman In Red*, *Lethal Weapon* and *52 Pick-Up*).

Dammett even claims to have co-written the screenplay for the Olivia Newton-John vehicle *Xanadu*, as he would explain on the Chili Peppers' website. "I was a screenwriter at MGM," he wrote, "and my partners and I wrote a screenplay about Utopia that the studio heads declined to make."

The regular reports of his father's fast life in Tinsel Town were too much for his bored son to take; Kiedis poured all his frustrations into schoolyard punch-ups.

He was enrolled at Grand Rapids' Brookside Elementary, a school that attempted to integrate deaf and mentally retarded children into mainstream education. It was a successful scheme, apparently. The current Communications Director of Grand Rapids Public Schools told me that, "We are quite proud that all of our schools have a history of integrated classrooms, meaning regular education and special education students attending classes together." Kiedis became what he called the "self-appointed defender of these kids". When his guardian role led to numerous fights, Kiedis was expelled more than once. His mother – stoic as always – supported him, despite the interruptions to his education.

"My mother was always OK with it," he said in 1994. "It was important to know somebody would stand behind me for doing what I believed in."

But it was really Margaret who was fighting the losing battle. In 1973, when Anthony was 11, she finally relented and let him move to Hollywood to live with Blackie. His life was about to change completely and irreversibly.

Anthony Kiedis would describe his father as "your basic semi-subversive underground hooligan playboy womaniser type of character – but he was an outlaw in the beautiful sense of the word." But even in 1973, as he settled into his father's Hollywood apartment, Anthony wasn't too concerned about the long-term effects of their relationship; all he knew was that this definitely wasn't Grand Rapids. In keeping with Margaret's instructions, Blackie ensured that her brown-eyed boy Anthony attended school and kept out of trouble, but that didn't mean that her ex-husband curbed his own lifestyle. Hollywood fringe-dwellers drifted in and out of the Dammett apartment, as did a seemingly endless procession of beautiful women, all of whom Blackie intended to bed (and sometimes did). More than once Anthony woke up to find a naked woman wandering about the house.

Father and son began clubbing in earnest, hanging out together at the legendary Corral club in Topanga Canyon, formerly a regular gig for The Eagles and The Stone Poneys, where Kiedis would spend his nights dancing with women twice his age. Or they could be found at The Rainbow Bar and Grill, an experience that Kiedis would go on to describe as being "a 12-year-old boy in a club full of sodomising adults".

"My dad was my hero and my idol [when I was] a young teenager," Kiedis told *The Washington Post* in 1990. "I wanted to be just like him." When Blackie grew his hair to his waist, his son did likewise; when he reverted to a shorter, slicked-back style, Kiedis followed suit. Kiedis admits that his father "had a constant turnover of girlfriends", although he insists that Blackie's intentions were without malice, if not entirely honourable. "It wasn't that he was this cold-hearted user of people. He just had this insatiable desire to meet all of the beautiful girls in the world."

But as his name implied, Blackie had a dark side. Kim Fowley was a major player on the LA scene during the Sixties and Seventies, whose path would occasionally cross with Dammett. Fowley was every inch the rock'n'roll renaissance man: at various times he was a songwriter, producer (he worked with Gene Vincent, Warren Zevon, Jonathan Richman and the Modern Lovers, Helen Reddy and dozens of others), manager, publisher, consultant and scenemaker. Fowley was a self-described "Frankenstein, Cro-Magnon, sub-human, oversized, over-boned human", a true product of Hollywood, just like Dammett.

"There's been a version of Blackie Dammett for the past 10,000 years," he roared down the phone from his home on the fringes of LA. "They're called camp followers. Later on they were called fringe players. They were even called groupies. They were also called a type, not a talent. When you see Blackie Dammett, you see a guy who should have been in every Martin Scorsese movie ever made. He reeks of evil from head to toe: black hair, black shirt, black pants, black shoes, black heart, black soul. He's got the darkness down; he's a very compelling guy visually. His physical presence is that illuminating.

"He has a personality that's just as diabolical as his inner self. He's an unsavoury character to be sure. But Hollywood is crawling with these people; I myself am like that."

Jack Sherman, who would play guitar for the Chili Peppers on their first, self-titled album, has similar recollections of Dammett. "I think of [him as] this spooky Hollywood character; this vampire," he told me. "I'm an understanding and broad-minded person, [but] I was just horrified about the relationship they had. He would have been a bad guy in my book. There's some creepy stuff there, for sure."

"Blackie is a person to me that always ran hot and cold," said Keith Barry, a close friend of the band's since high school. "He's the kind of guy who's never been terribly warm to me. When we were kids, most of the stuff that Anthony and I did together was not around his father."

"He was a character all right," said Lindy Goetz, who would manage the Peppers from their beginning until 1998. "A Hollywood character. I liked Blackie a lot – and my dad sure didn't do that kind of stuff for me."

Kim Fowley readily admits that he and Dammett wouldn't go out of their way to speak to each other, but one incident still bothers him, more than 30 years on.

"One day at a big Hollywood party there was a really attractive woman and she was by herself and Blackie Dammett was there," Fowley recalled. "He had this bandage over his forehead; he'd obviously had some kind of mishap. And he was really being aggressive towards this girl, who wasn't into it, didn't want to hear about it and was frightened by the blackness of Blackie. The bandage was the cherry on the cake.

"She couldn't get away from him. Now, I'm a womaniser and a horror story, too. I looked at her and I looked at him and walked over and said, 'Let her go, leave her alone, or I will take this bottle of beer and smash it over your forehead, you piece of shit, and you'll be disfigured and you won't be good enough to get any work if you were good enough to get any. Back away, motherfucker!' That reptile backed away and the girl just took off. Then I said, 'OK, Blackie, fucker, you wanna go to the door of death?' He didn't want to go to the door of death.

"That's the only time Blackie Dammett and I ever communicated. I saw him since then; he kept his distance, I kept my distance. I understand the need for dirty sex and all that, but it has to be consensual. If someone's not into it, it's really wrong."

Even as a pre-teen, Kiedis developed a natural confidence with women, a skill that would do him no harm in his role as the lead singer of a rock'n'roll band. Fowley believes that he inherited this self-assurance from the long nights (and early mornings) he spent clubbing with Dammett.

"Blackie was very much into having Anthony ride shotgun with him. He would go to all the parties and all the clubs and he learned how to be magnetic and walk in a room and deal with women and bad guys and life in general, on a superficial, George Raft-gangster level. He was good to his boy; he hauled the kid around so he got a look at the street life. I'm sure he draws on it every day in his music and his persona."

Kiedis completely embraced the LA lifestyle and his father's wild ways. Not only did they share Anthony's first joint, but Blackie helped the 12-year-old – with a quarter of a Quaalude buzzing through his system at the time – lose his virginity.

The lucky lady was an 18-year-old redhead who happened to be dating Blackie at the time. As Kiedis recalled during a very revealing essay that he wrote in *Details For Men* magazine, she treated him like a prince. "Never before have I felt my mind, body and spirit come together in an erotic effort that transcended the bullshit and suffering of life," he wrote. "The possibilities, combinations and innuendos seemed infinite, and at the age of 12, so did life."

"The whole picture out here [in LA] was just a natural high," Kiedis said when asked about his and Blackie's bachelor-pad days. "The costumes that people were wearing, the music that people were making, the art that people were making – I loved it.

"The first time I smoked pot, I was with my Dad, and to me it just seemed like I'd landed in this magical kingdom where anything was possible. I got stoned, and my father had a girl over at the house, and she didn't have her shirt on. I said to myself, 'How lucky could a boy be?' At the time, I thought I was the luckiest kid on the block."

So how does Blackie Hammett remember these fast times? "Back then, I was working with Alice Cooper and John Lennon and I was quite the crazy maniac. So he [Anthony] grew up in kind of a wild and hectic environment."

Of course the downside was the impermanence of all these relationships and the conflict that Anthony Kiedis would later experience with those who didn't necessarily share his free-spirited upbringing. "Having a semi-maniacal womaniser for a father has its disadvantages," Kiedis understated in *Details For Men*.

"From age 11 to 16 . . . we lived like brothers, which was very beautiful but also very sad. A lot of things happened during that time that would be major contributors to the illnesses and psychotic episodes of my young-adult life."

"You pattern yourself after your parent at that age," Kiedis also said, "and what this life showed me was that more was always better. That lifestyle can set you up for a pattern to never really find your soul mate."

But those dilemmas were way in the future. In the mid-Seventies, Anthony Kiedis had many more women to meet – and he was set to begin his time at Fairfax High.

As strange as the combination now seems, the 12-year-old Kiedis did find a role model in Sonny Bono, one half of the famous team of Sonny & Cher and co-songwriter of their worldwide 1965 smash, 'I Got You Babe'. Bono was once a songwriter for Fairfax High graduate Phil Spector; he met his future wife Cher in 1963 when she was singing back-up vocals at a Spector-produced session. Much later, Bono was to become a member of the US House of Representatives, but when he befriended Anthony Kiedis during the Seventies, he was busy dealing with the stress of his separation from Cher (the couple officially split in 1974).

A close friend of Dammett's girlfriend Connie, Bono offered Anthony the kind of comfort and stability that wasn't exactly Dammett's specialty. More often than not Anthony could be found at the Bono household, hanging out with Bono's daughter, Chastity.

"As a kid," Bono told *Rolling Stone* in 1995, "Tony was really delightful and he had this tremendous imagination. [Chastity] was much younger than he was, but he would always invent these games to play with her."

"Anthony and I fondly remember long-time friend Sonny Bono," Dammett spelled out in one of his Chili Peppers fan club letters. "Sonny adored little Tony and took him along on their whirlwind showbiz ride as well as their vacations, which ironically included skiing at Tahoe, where Sonny tragically died.

"We even used Sonny's Bel Air address to get Anthony into a better Junior High School [Emerson in Westwood] and Sonny spent as much time bailing him out of the principal's office as I did."

"We took a liking to each other," Kiedis recalled, "and he used to take me on different trips that my father might not have been able to afford."

Even though Hillel Slovak only lived there for five years of his short life, the contrast between Haifa, Israel, and Los Angeles, California, couldn't have been more extreme. He was born in Israel's third largest city (and its northern capital) on April 13, 1962. Haifa is located 90 miles from Jerusalem, 60 miles from Tel Aviv, and is bordered to the north east by the medieval fortress city of Acre. Directly north lies Rosh Hanikra, which is both a majestic white cliff and the checkpoint on the Israel/Lebanon border. The bustling city, whose university boasts the most pluralistic student body in the country, lies on a broad natural bay between the Mediterranean Sea and the Carmel mountain. As picturesque as it is, life changed – not just in Haifa, but all of Israel and the Middle East – when the Arab-Israeli Six Days War erupted on June 5, 1967 and Israel attacked Egypt, Syria and Jordan. Though they were on the aggressor's side, by then the Slovak family had moved to the United States; first to The Bronx in New York and then Los Angeles. The Slovaks' intentions were simple, according to Hillel's brother James. "My parents left Israel to come to the US to start a great life."

"He was very proud of his heritage," Michael Balzary recalled in 1992, when asked about Slovak's Jewish roots.

Kiedis' first impression of Slovak, who enrolled at Fairfax High School in 1977 – around the time that his parents' marriage broke down – was slightly less dignified. He remembered him as this "kind of funny looking kid, real skinny with long hair and big lips". A photo of Slovak from the time reveals a very typical LA teenager; his hair – almost a Jewfro – was an unruly mess, and there was a hint of wildness in his gaze. And his true calling was the guitar.

By the time Balzary walked through the front gate of Fairfax High School, also in 1977, he'd quite literally travelled halfway across the world – and had crammed a lot of living into his short life. He was born in Burwood, a suburb of Melbourne, Australia, on October 16, 1962; his family's roots were Irish/Hungarian. His great-great grandfather had come to Australia in 1850 on board the *Runnymede*, from Bombay, in search of gold. The Balzarys had eventually settled in Melbourne, the southernmost mainland state capital in Australia, the city where his 80-something grandmother still lives, along with various other members of clan Balzary. As a young boy, Michael Balzary was convinced that he was Superman and could fly. He would wear his red cape like a badge of honour. "He was always very active," his father Mick Balzary would tell me.

But the bassist-in-the-making wasn't destined to spend much time flying around his hometown in pursuit of truth and/or justice. His father Mick worked as a Customs Officer, and in March 1967 was posted to New York. The family – Michael and his sister Karen, who was two years older than Michael, their mother Patricia, who was also Australian, and Mick – settled in Rye in Westchester County, having sailed on the *Oriana* from Melbourne to the US west coast and then flown to New York. Mick would alternate between working in nearby Manhattan and travelling with his job. During 1971, the Balzary marriage became, in the words of Mick Balzary, "a bit shaky" and Patricia left to live with Walter Urban, Jr, who was a jazz musician, a bassist. Michael and Karen moved with her.

Mick Balzary's US tenure was due to end in August 1971, and he had a tough decision to make: should he push his case and return with the children to Australia, or leave without them? He knew nothing of Urban, Jr – "At the time I said, 'Don't bring him near me, I'll clean him up'" – but both children had just started school in Rye. "I could have taken the kids with me," Mick Balzary told me, "but I thought, 'Bugger it,' I didn't want to disrupt their schooling. You can't just drag kids all around the place; they'd settled into that lifestyle and I don't think it would have been proper to attempt to pull it to pieces." It was while Michael was attending school in suburban Rye that a rumour developed that he was at least part Aboriginal, which stuck with him into adulthood. His father laughs at the suggestion, explaining that to tone down their Australian accents for their American schoolmates, Michael and Karen "used to talk gibberish and tell kids they were speaking Aboriginal."

The Balzarys weren't a hugely musical lot, although Patricia took some guitar lessons while living in Rye and Mick once blew the cornet in a jazz band. Michael's grandparents also had a Sunday night ritual of playing the piano. It was a different story with Walter Urban, Jr, who Patricia married not long after her former husband headed back to Australia. Michael Balzary would recall his parents hosting all-day barbecues, which turned into marathon jam sessions. "All the jazz guys [friends of Urban, Jr's] would just hang out and blow. I was, like, seven years old when that started happening and I would just roll around the floor in laughter. I could get the greatest feeling I'd ever had listening to them, just being amazed by the whole mystery of how the hell that could happen."

Although the first instrument that appealed to him was the drums, at the age of nine he'd started playing the trumpet. By the time that Michael, Karen, their mother and Urban, Jr, moved to Los Angeles in 1973, he was proficient and confident enough to sit in on his step-father's jams. Unlike typical teenagers of the early and mid-Seventies, Balzary had no interest in rock'n'roll; his early heroes were jazz players. But that wasn't a great surprise given the environment in which he grew up. "I [had] heard rock music," he told *Rolling Stone*'s Kim Neely in 1994, "but it sounded stupid to me. Obviously I wasn't listening to the fly music." So rather than bounce around the house air-guitaring to Kiss or Aerosmith, Balzary was tuning into such jazz giants as Miles

Davis, Dizzy Gillespie, Louis Armstrong and Ornette Coleman. He even made the acquaintance of Dominic Calicchio, who was the founder of the last surviving trumpet manufacturer that made their instruments by hand. When Calicchio's biography was published, there was a photo included of him with a small boy standing by his side, nursing a trumpet, smiling broadly. Who would have thought that the kid with the horn would go on to become the blue-haired, clothing-optional bassist of one of the most successful funk-rock outfits of the last 20 years?

Balzary's mother, Patricia, was sympathetic to her son's love of jazz (which ranked even above his love of basketball). So sympathetic, in fact, that she even managed to get him backstage at a Dizzy Gillespie show when Balzary was 12. Almost 30 years down the line, speaking with *Spin* magazine, Balzary still gushed with excitement when asked about meeting the be-bop master.

"I snuck backstage," he recalled, "and there's Dizzy, holding his trumpet, talking to someone. I run up to him and I'm like [looks up excitedly] 'Mr Gillespie'. And I can't even talk. I'm in awe. And he just puts his arm around me and hugs me real tight, so my head's kind of in his armpit. He smiles and just holds me there for, like, five minutes while he talks. I'm just frozen in joy – oh my God, oh my God, oh my God."

But just like his future friend and bandmate Kiedis, Balzary was having real trouble at home. Not only had his birth family fallen apart when he was eight, but his stepfather was an angry, aggressive man. His alcoholism didn't help, either. Back in Australia, Mick Balzary would receive letters from his son, spelling out the drama. "I knew a bit about that [Urban, Jr's alcoholism]," Mick Balzary told me. "At one stage Pat wanted the children to come back to me. I didn't know if it was a cop-out [on her part] but I subsequently found out that he was an alcoholic. He had big problems, which upset me. I was between a rock and a hard place. Those problems reflected on the teenage life of my kids."

Michael has even stated that Urban, Jr was involved in "shoot-outs" with the cops (his birth father knew nothing of this); terrified, he would sleep in the backyard of the family house. The only respite for him and his sister were the occasional visits with their father in Australia, or trips to Canada, where they would meet up with their father and his new wife, whose sister lived in Montreal.

"I was raised in a very violent, alcoholic household," Balzary said. "I grew up being terrified of my parents, particularly my father figures. It caused [me] a lot of trouble in later life.

"[Later in life] I wrestled with aggression and fear which originated from my childhood. I come from a pretty dysfunctional family; there were always fights and misery. There was a lot of things I had to deal with that kids shouldn't have to deal with." (In 1995, Urban, Jr admitted that alcohol was the main cause of his erratic behaviour; he dried out in the mid-Seventies.)

There was always a room for him at home, but the pre-teen Michael was spending more and more time away from his family, wandering the streets, sometimes not bothering to return for days. It was inevitable that drugs soon became as much a part of his life as jazz, basketball and his trumpet playing. Balzary has admitted to experimenting with drugs at the age of 11, and he kept up the habit for another 20 years. "I did heroin, cocaine, psychedelics and I smoked pot every day," he said. "God, I smoked so much pot."

It was around this time that Balzary also formed his first band, an extremely loose-knit group of schoolmates who would gather in the Balzary house and play after school. The trouble was that they only knew one piece of music: Henry Mancini's 'Theme From The Pink Panther'. This outfit didn't last too long.

By the time he entered Bancroft Junior High and then Fairfax High, Balzary was a quiet kid, an outsider because of his strange accent – part Australian, part American – and his love of jazz music. He had wild curly hair, deep blue eyes and a nervous scowl. It didn't help his state of mind that he had to deal with this Californian dude called Jack Irons, who would pass notes around the class at Bancroft Junior High, mercilessly taking the piss out of the new kid with the weird way of speaking.

Balzary did find a friend in Keith Barry, later to be known as "Tree". A relocated New Yorker, also from a broken home, Barry would become Balzary's closest friend for life. When they first met at Bancroft Junior High, music – especially jazz – was their shared passion, although, as Barry recalled, it wasn't too long after they met that Balzary started "moving towards the rock thing". At the time Barry was playing the guitar; he soon moved on to viola, which he would one day use on several Chili Peppers recordings. He and Balzary played together in the school band and orchestra, both at Bancroft Junior and then at Fairfax High, performing what Barry describes as "typical music department stuff".

"We were hanging around wherever the music guys were," Barry told me. "More than that, we had something in common, the misfit thing. Both of us were really not part of cliques at school."

Flea fondly remembers music and music class. "[It was] the one discipline that I had when I was a kid – definitely the most stable part of my life. I loved going to music class."

He may have been a fringe-dweller, but Balzary did manage to lose his virginity at 14, in a group-sex scenario. The fact that the girl in question was wasted on Quaaludes and a quart of whisky definitely helped the first-timer lose his cherry. "It wasn't a good situation," he would admit when asked about his first time. "That's all I'm going to say about it."

Just like Hillel Slovak, future Red Hot Chili Peppers drummer Jack Irons was also Jewish. His grandparents had left their native Jerusalem when Jack's father was three. His biggest concern when growing up in Los Angeles was the acquisition of a decent drum kit. By the age of 11 he'd drive his family absolutely crazy by banging out a rhythm to whatever was playing on the radio, using the family cutlery as drumsticks.

He and his buddy, Hillel Slovak, were music obsessives. They'd become especially tight when, in 1975, Slovak's parents allowed the future Chili Peppers guitarist to invite a small group of school friends over to the family house for his 13th birthday party. Jack Irons was one of these invitees. Irons also spent a lot of time hanging about the music room, both at Bancroft Junior and Fairfax High.

As Keith Barry remembered, "Jack was a music department geek like Michael and me. He played drums in the [school] band and orchestra." Irons was also a member of the Student League at Fairfax High. By 1977, when Slovak and Irons entered Fairfax High School, there was one band that mattered for the duo: Kiss. In an indirect way, the Kiss tribute act that Irons and Slovak formed would become the starting point for the Red Hot Chili Peppers.

But at the same time, there were rumblings in the musical underground – suburban heroes such as Kiss (or Anthony Kiedis' Michigan homeboys, Grand Funk Railroad) were fast becoming dinosaurs. People had begun talking about punk, a sound that was as raw as an open wound. Something about this primal noise made perfect sense, because in the mid-Seventies, the pop charts – especially in the music biz hotspots of the USA and the UK – were a sad and desolate place for anyone in search of music with grit. In the UK, Swedish popsters Abba were in the midst of a stretch of hits not seen since The Beatles; ex *Starsky & Hutch* hunk David Soul was crooning 'Don't Give Up On Us Baby'; Leo Sayer, Andy Gibb, Barry Manilow and Shaun Cassidy were dressing badly and laying on the soft-focus, sickly-sweet pop with a trowel. Acts such as Boney M were bringing Eurotrash pop to the mainstream. KC & The Sunshine Band were kicking off their 'Boogie Shoes'. The flare-trousered, high-harmonising Bee Gees and the whole *Saturday Night Fever* phenomenon was just a few spins of the mirror ball into the future.

As for rock'n'roll in the mid-Seventies, it seemed as though soft had become the new loud. Prog rock, the favoured form of Genesis, Emerson, Lake & Palmer and Yes, was losing its appeal. The bombastic heavy metal of Led Zeppelin, Black Sabbath and Deep Purple was also in decline. Hard-working Peter Frampton was the new golden-haired boy, while such West Coast acts as The Eagles strummed and harmonised their way into the charts. Only David Bowie seemed to offer a viable alternative, but his camp manner was a turn-off for red-blooded US rockers. The birth of punk rock was both an inevitability and a necessity. Something was needed, urgently, to wash away all this cocaine-dulled blandness – and as for the wardrobe, well, only a bonfire could set that right.

As with most revolutions, there's heated debate as to the location of punk's ground zero. Some would say it was in Sex, the Chelsea boutique that was run by Vivienne Westwood and her partner Malcolm McLaren (who would one day offer his services to the Chili Peppers as a producer). In the early Seventies, McLaren was on the lookout for a band of fringe-dwellers to be the mouthpieces for his vaguely formed anarchist and Situationist ideas. He encountered the New York Dolls on a trip to New York in 1973 and became their manager two years later, presiding over a doomed attempt to resuscitate their career. The Dolls split up but there was something about them, their anarchy, their attitude, that stuck in McLaren's psyche and which he drew on towards the end of 1975 when he assembled The Sex Pistols, fronted by an irate green-toothed Irishman by the name of Johnny Lydon (aka Johnny Rotten).

Through savvy manipulation of the media – the word "fuck" can go a long way when used shrewdly – and a trail of trashed concert halls and cancelled shows, The Sex Pistols became the hottest band in the UK. By June 1977, which by a happy coincidence was the Queen's Jubilee Year, their 'God Save The Queen' hit number two in the UK charts behind former Faces belter Rod Stewart's far more "acceptable" ballad 'I Don't Want To Talk About It'. There are many who believe that the Pistols outsold Stewart but pressure from the establishment was brought to bear to prevent their anti-monarchist anthem from reaching the top spot.

British punk had its roots in pub rock, a beer-and-sweat style of playing perfected by such bands as Kilburn & The High Roads, Dr Feelgood and Brinsley Schwarz, all of whom were skilled musicians. But many of those who came in the wake of The Sex Pistols – The Clash, The Jam, The Damned, The Buzzcocks, Generation X (featuring a very young Billy Idol), relocated Australians The Saints – were not so accomplished, at least not at first. All that was needed were a few chords, a riff that would tear the paint from the walls and lyrics that screamed discontent at everything from the government to the royal family, from life on the dole to the cheap release of sniffing glue. The chant was "no future" and the rock establishment – Mick Jagger, Robert Plant, Paul McCartney, *et al* – were written off as boring old farts.

As John Dougan wrote in his essay *Punk Music*: "Dismissed by the short-sighted as crude anti-musicality, punk dared to place itself in direct confrontation with the then-ruling rock hegemony: generally 30-something pop stars content to reinvent and regurgitate clichés in a sort of stylistic stasis, a dire situation exacerbated by the tightly controlled mid-to-late Seventies FM programming style known as AOR [album-oriented rock]."

It's likely that American punk preceded the UK revolution, although it didn't have the same media impact as it had in Britain. Rock historian and journalist Lenny Kaye – soon to become guitarist for punk-poet rebel Patti Smith – collected songs from America's thriving Sixties underground in the legendary *Nuggets* set, which included such proto-punk LA acts as The Seeds and The Electric Prunes. During the late Sixties and early Seventies, the Lou Reed-fronted Velvet Underground and The Stooges, led by a writhing, frothing, cursing madman going by the name of Iggy Pop, peddled hard riffs and even harder lyrics. Pop screamed "I wanna be your dog" – and truly meant it. Reed was probably the first rock'n'roll songwriter to choose heroin abuse and sado-masochism as his leitmotif. Neither band made much of a commercial impact during their short, fiery careers – their albums were under-promoted and were usually fast-tracked to the bargain bins – but their influence on future punk rockers was enormous.

In 1974, when Hilly Kristal threw open the doors of New York club CBGBs (as in "country bluegrass blues", the music he had intended to showcase at his club), he could just about smell the change on the wind, if the stink from The Bowery weren't so intense. CBGBs was situated directly beneath a flophouse, in a neighbourhood that Kristal described as "a drab, ugly and unsavoury place", where punters had to step over snoring winos or mugging victims in order to enter the toilet-sized club. But Kristal recognised the potential of his venue as a home for the new punk music being thrashed out by New York bands like Television, The Ramones and Johnny Thunder & The Heartbreakers.

"The height of the disco era brought an increasing dissatisfaction among rock musicians and their fans," he wrote in his potted history of the club. "The formula-driven disco music and the long-drawn-out solos and other complexities in much of the rock of the late Sixties and early Seventies encouraged a lot of disgruntled rock enthusiasts to seek the sounds of simple high energy rock'n'roll, which seemed to take shape right here at CBGBs. We called this music 'street music' and later 'punk'." (Although the term "punk" had been used by *Creem* magazine writers Lester Bangs and Dave Marsh in the early Seventies.)

Kristal offered the bands willing to play at CBGBs a simple deal: he kept the money taken over the bar, they pocketed most of the "door money" (cover charge) to pay for their expenses. By 1976, he'd organised deals with "sister" clubs in Boston (The Rathskeller) and Philadelphia (The Hot Club), whereby bands could be assured of bookings in three different cities. By the end of 1976 such punk heroes as Richard Hell & The Voidoids, Blondie, Talking Heads, The Feelies and The Dictators had become regulars at CBGBs. And then there were The

Dead Boys (who came with a recommendation from Joey Ramone), who, in Kristal's words, "epitomised what a punk band should be: they were loud, raw, crass, with super high energy." The Ramones, of course, were the poster punks for CBGBs, although they actually had more chart success in the UK.

Punk started to take hold on the US west coast just as Kiedis, Balzary, Slovak and Irons got ready for Fairfax High. Rodney Bingenheimer's radio show, "Rodney on the ROQ", had been broadcast on LA's KROQ-FM since late 1976; within months he was pushing the music of such punk bands as The Ramones, The Sex Pistols and The Clash. Though not all these acts had record releases in the States as yet, LA's Bomp Records stocked up on imported 45s, and lined their walls with posters of the new punk stars: Johnny Rotten, Sid Vicious, Joe Strummer and others. *Slash* fanzine started spreading the punk gospel, while Gary Panter's *Jimbo* comics captured the mood of the LA scene. And such clubs as The Troubadour and The Starwood dabbled with hardcore bills, although punk was briefly banned from the latter in July 1977, when The Weirdos played a July 4th show and celebrated America's independence by burning the American flag. Slam dancing became the accepted punk mating ritual at LA club The Fleetwood; it was then introduced to the non-punk world via an *LA Times* piece entitled THE SLAM.

The article's wary tone increased mainstream concern in much the same way that Elvis Presley's swivelling hips had freaked out middle America back in the Fifties. But whereas Presley was dismissed as some kind of Satan-spawned sex maniac, punk rockers and slam dancers were cast as violent lunatics – and probably criminals. No wonder the movement stayed underground.

If there was a home of punk in LA, it was The Masque, which was underground in the most literal sense; it occupied a formerly vacant basement beneath The Hollywood Center at Hollywood and Chero-kee. Though the venue was shut down for a while, in the midst of the punk explosion – the LAPD had slapped a padlock on the front door by mid-1978 – it was still a breeding ground for such LA bands as The Spastics, The Germs (featuring Pat Smear, later of Nirvana and The Foo Fighters) and X, a trio who would drop in and out of the Chili Peppers' trajectory for many years to come.

Pleasant Gehman was a journalist/performer/poet/scenester who documented the LA punk scene in her diaries. Her take on LA was as lucid an account as exists. "The late Seventies Hollywood punk-rock scene was a small and insular hotbed of activity," she wrote, "where bands formed, peaked and broke up in the space of a few months, many without ever being recorded. Lyrical themes were the usual bleatings of youth: angst, suburban alienation, drug experimentation, lefty politicisms and rebellion, all tempered by a prodigious consumption of alcoholic beverages, along with various mind-altering substances, usually bought with panhandled change." When not documenting the short-lived scene, Gehman and Darby Crash, the vocalist of The Germs, would splatter themselves and their shirts with anything colourful – paint, motor oil, ketchup, steak sauce – then, once the shirts had dried, they'd compose stories on them and then wear them on stage. As you do.

This scene full of fringe dwellers was tailor-made for a rebel with a hedonistic streak such as Anthony Kiedis. But there was also a new sound coming out of New York that turned him on every bit as much as punk: it was called "hip-hop" or "rap". (The terms are interchangeable, although hip-hop is used as much to define such elements of rap culture as streetwear, breakdancing, turntablism and graffiti art as it is the music itself.)

Hip-hop tracks were like musical mosaics, mixing up "found sounds", usually samples of other songs or ambient noise, with looped drum tracks, guitar riffs, basslines and turntable scratching. South Bronx DJs Kool Herc (as in Hercules), Lovebug Starski (a marked improvement on his birth name, which was Kevin Smith) and others were taking the lead from such Jamaican sound-system DJs as Lee Perry and U-Roy, who would talk ("toast") over the top of rhythm tracks. They started to craft an Americanised version of the style in the early Seventies.

The Sugarhill Gang's 'Rapper's Delight', which emerged in the summer of 1979 and reached number six in the UK charts in December, is widely regarded as the song which brought hip-hop out of New York's clubs and house parties and into the fringes of mainstream pop culture. The song itself was a happy accident. Husband-and-wife team Sylvia and Joe Robinson – who ran an independent label called All Platinum – were in debt and on their way out of the music business, when they attended a Harlem party thrown by Sylvia's sister. There they heard guests "spitting" rhymes over the instrumental breaks in disco records. Sylvia was impressed and hired her son Joey as a talent scout. Together they rounded up Master Gee (aka Guy O'Brien), Big Bank Hank (aka Henry Jackson) and Wonder Mike (aka Michael Wright) to rap over a rhythm track taken from Chic's 'Good Times'. 'Rapper's Delight' sold over two million copies in the USA alone – and not only did it reach the UK Top 10, but the song was also a hit in Israel, South Africa and other countries not exactly known as hot-beds of hip-hop culture.

Of all the early rappers, Grandmaster Flash (aka Joseph Saddler) had the biggest impact on the teenaged Anthony Kiedis. Grandmaster Flash started out by spinning records at Bronx block parties, dances and parks. By day he studied electronics. The key elements of his style were "cutting" between tracks precisely on the beat, turning records by hand to make the needle repeat brief lengths of groove ("back-spinning") and manipulating turntable speeds. Once he mastered his idiosyncratic style he began working with rappers, first Kurtis Blow and then The Furious Five, an outfit who could both rap and break-dance. Inspired by Sugarhill's 'Rapper's Delight', they cut 'Superrappin'' in 1979, followed by such ground-breaking cut-and-paste tracks as 1981's 'The Adventures Of Grandmaster Flash On The Wheels Of Steel', which blended snatches of Chic's 'Good Times' (again), Blondie's 'Rapture' (the first white rap–cum–pop hit) and Queen's 'Another One Bites The Dust'. Cautionary tales of ghetto life and drug abuse, such as 1982's 'The Message' and 1983's 'White Lines', soon followed.

Not only were these tracks hits, but they made rap much more than a New York sensation. Urban music fans all over America (and else-where) were wising up to the potential that rap music offered: just like punk, you didn't need to be a conservatory-skilled muso to make a hot record – a fact that wasn't lost on Kiedis. "I heard Grandmaster Flash and it dawned on me: I can write poetry and this is my chance to get into a band. I had no training or experience as a singer, but I knew I could hang with the rap. It all kind of took off from there."

And given that America was now under the control of B-grade actor Ronald Reagan, rap had the potential to spell out the system's failings in a way that punk hadn't quite achieved that side of the Atlantic. The highly politicised Clash might have been stars in the USA, but their fervent music was a reaction to the straitjacket of Thatcherism and the

British class system, which was a mystery to most alienated American teenagers.

To Anthony Kiedis, rap music was a revelation. It helped him to realise that technique wasn't necessarily everything. He now had the firm belief "that I could do something musical without being Marvin Gaye". And when he checked out Grandmaster Flash & The Furious Five live in the early Eighties, Kiedis believed he'd seen his future.

"It was mind-blowing," he said. "I subconsciously vowed I would somehow create that type of energy to entertain others. I didn't have a clue how to write a song or sing, but I thought I could probably figure out how to tell a story in rhythm."

But that was all in the years to come. In the mid-Seventies at Bancroft Junior High everyone was checking out one very strange Kiss tribute act.

Ever since they roared out of the New York suburbs in 1970, Kiss were as unavoidable as death and taxes. Gene Simmons and Paul Stanley were the original members; they found drummer Peter Criss through an ad in *Rolling Stone*; then Ace Frehley responded to another ad, this time in liberal bible *The Village Voice*, seeking a guitarist with "flash and balls". Hidden behind full-face make-up, Kiss were the perfect comic-book rock'n'roll creation: they were mysterious (no one knew what they really looked like); Simmons breathed fire and drooled blood on stage (hey, it was just like the circus) and they rocked like mother-fuckers, especially on such early anthems as 'Rock And Roll All Nite'. Their 1975 in-concert set, *Alive*, was essential listening in male teenage bedrooms from Alaska to Australia. Hated by critics who considered them a pantomime act, their records sold in the millions. Between 1976 and 1979 the group released six platinum-selling albums and became an unstoppable force – especially when the Kiss Army (their fan club) started spreading the rock'n'roll word according to apostles Simmons, Frehley, Stanley and Criss. As the band barnstormed across America, their manager, Bill Aucoin, estimated it was costing $US10,000 per night just to keep them on the road (pyrotechnics weren't cheap).

Amongst the Kiss Army's brethren were Jack Irons and Hillel Slovak. Irons had already talked his long-suffering family into buying his first drum kit, and he was now enrolled in a drum class. Slovak had picked up a guitar at the age of 13, given to him by his uncle Aron, and would lie in his darkened bedroom listening to both Kiss and Jimi Hendrix and dreaming of somehow emulating the sensuality and scope of the master's playing and the "flash and balls" of Kiss' Ace Frehley. He signed on at a neighbourhood guitar workshop not long after being given his guitar – Irons learned to play drums in the same house of music – but formal training was not exactly high on his list of priorities. Slovak wanted to make his guitar sing like Hendrix; what time did he have for the basics?

But Kiss were still the main obsession for the two friends. At home in the Slovak house on Genesee Avenue, Hillel would dress as his Kiss member of choice – sometimes Gene Simmons, sometimes Ace Frehley – and proudly pose for photographs. Aside from music, art was Slovak's other key obsession. While in class, Slovak would usually be hunched over his schoolbook, filling page after page with his richly detailed sketches of Kiss. His favourite subject was the band's bassist/ screamer/blood drooler/mad shagger Simmons. Once he defaced photos of US presidents Roosevelt, Kennedy, Truman and Washington, transforming them into a rock'n'roll Mount Rushmore. The faces he inserted were those of Kiss' Simmons, Criss, Stanley and Frehley.

Anthony Kiedis remembers the pair's love of the band. "They were two of the biggest and strongest members of the Kiss Army," he said. "They used to dress up like Kiss and lip-sync."

The two friends' devotion to Kiss bordered on the evangelical. When Kiss' seemingly never-ending tour swung into Los Angeles, the pair found out where they were staying and camped outside their hotel for several days, hoping to catch a glimpse of their comic-book rock heroes. (Imagine the bragging rights if they could spot them without their make-up!) They also checked out the local make-up retailers, pooling their cash to buy the right kind of greasepaint for their planned Kiss tribute act. Irons was able to lay his hands on some blood capsules. And he managed to locate a codpiece, complete with realistic-looking rivets.

Now fully decked out in their very own Kiss outfits, Irons, Slovak and a couple of other schoolfriends would stand in front of their classmates, including Keith Barry and several future Chili Peppers, and mime to such albums as *Kiss Alive*, *Hotter Than Hell* and *Destroyer*. It was almost as wild as being in the band.

It was during one of these mime sessions that Irons met Alain Johannes, who would become a key player in early Chili Peppers history. Just like Balzary, Kiedis and Slovak, Johannes took a very roundabout route to Los Angeles. He was the son of entertainers – his father was from Catalonia, Spain – and he had lived in Chile, Switzerland and Mexico before his family settled in LA in the late summer of 1974. He started playing guitar at the age of four; he'd even played flamenco with a touring band ("I was the third guitar from the right"). Johannes was a music veteran in comparison to Slovak and Irons. Now a fellow student, Johannes was intrigued by Irons' Kiss outfit – he'd seen the pair walking around the schoolyard – so one day in class, just out of curiosity, he reached over and punched Irons in the codpiece. He found out that it wasn't as soundly built as he'd thought.

"Jack used to be Gene Simmons and for some reason he had this big codpiece. And – I don't know what made me do it, I'd never met him before – I just kind of tested it to see if it was really a little armour piece or not. I gave him a quick punch in the crotch – and it hurt. And he's like, 'What the – who are you?'"

Irons then introduced him to Slovak. "He's the cunt who just punched me in the balls."

By the end of 1977, now all enrolled at Fairfax High, Slovak, Irons, Johannes and another friend, Todd Strasman, had formed a band called Chain Reaction. Slovak and Johannes shared guitar duties, Irons thumped the tubs and Strasman wrestled with a bass. Their very basic setlist was heavy on Kiss tunes (no surprise there), with Strasman and Johannes bringing in some Queen songs and Led Zeppelin's 'Rock And Roll'. Punk rock didn't get a look in – years later, Irons admitted he was "a late bloomer" when it came to the movement that was making some noise in the musical underground at the time. (Michael Balzary's conversion took a little longer; his first punk show was a Black Flag set-cum-riot at The Starwood in 1980. He thought the out-of-control violence was "disgusting . . . punk rock was awful".)

The centrepiece of Chain Reaction's act was their take on Queen's 'Ogre Battle', a tricky prog rock epic that was a tad too complicated for the quartet's nascent musical talents. They premiered this and their other tributes to the bands they loved at a lunchtime show at Fairfax High's Detter Court, located at the rear of the school's main auditorium, shortly before Christmas 1977. Even though Irons and Slovak were terrified – wearing Kiss outfits and miming was easy by comparison, now they actually had to play their instruments – the more musically gifted Johannes was sufficiently impressed to suggest they do it again. Chain Reaction soon became Anthem, then Anthym, when they found out that a band with the more conventional spelling already existed. The Irons family home quickly became Anthym's rehearsal studio.

While Anthym were frightening Fairfax High students with their take on 'Ogre Battle', another strange relationship was developing at "Fax City": Anthony Kiedis was about to meet Michael Balzary.

The two might have come from different planets. Balzary was an outsider who loved jazz and hated rock'n'roll. An old school friend remembered him as a quiet kid, but "something of a favourite" with teachers. Absolutely terrified of girls, Balzary was, in his own words, "either completely introverted and scared to death of people, or I was pulling down my pants and screaming at the top of my lungs." Jack Irons' insulting sketches alienated him even more.

Kiedis, meanwhile, was very much Blackie Dammett's son. Kiedis knew what was hot and what wasn't and doubted whether anyone else at Fairfax High had a clue. And how could they? None of them had gone through their early teens in the same wild way as Kiedis. How many of these guys had smoked pot with their father, or slept with the same girl, for that matter?

"I definitely came to school with a 'fuck the masses' approach," Kiedis told *Guitar Magazine*. "While everyone was wearing OP gear and listening to Led Zeppelin, it was just too common and popular for me. So I went completely against it. I dressed awkwardly and listened to David Bowie, Benny Goodman, Blondie and all this weird stuff that my dad was turning me onto – just intentionally not to be part of the masses."

"Anthony was a very notable character at Fairfax," says Keith Barry. "He was always an extrovert; that was his strength."

With the exception of theatre studies and especially English, where an astute teacher called Jill Vernon managed to hold Kiedis' attention, the 15-year-old had little time for school. After all, what could it teach him that he hadn't already learned at his father's party pad or on the streets of Hollywood? Mrs Vernon, however, encouraged Kiedis to write, a skill that would prove handy when he became the lyricist for one of the biggest rock'n'roll bands in the world.

He wrote her a valentine in the liner notes for *Out In LA*, a bits and pieces Chili Peppers collection that was released in 1994. "I was encouraged by my seventh grade teacher to write words: this is what I did. I wrote funny little poems, love letters to my girlfriend [school gymnastic team member and senior class president, Haya Handel] and spastically amusing compositions for my school."

Fairfax High would eventually pay back both Kiedis and Flea when they made the school's Honour Roll in 1999. But in general, school held few thrills for Kiedis. His photograph in the 1980 Fairfax High Yearbook reveals plenty: unlike his classmates, who were the usual assortment of puffy-haired, zitty-skinned, ungainly-looking teenagers, Kiedis exudes an unmistakable coolness, the type of composure not found in many 17-year-olds. He even gets away with a borderline mullet hairdo.

As he would one day state, "I think that I could have stopped going to school at the age of five and been a bit more articulate and intelligent and well read than I am now having been to school.

"I don't think that [school] is the ultimate decisive factor in whether or not someone becomes educated or able to speak or write. This comes from experience and self-education more than anything that I ever learned at school."

Albeit reluctantly, Kiedis showed up most days, spending the bulk of his time with Tony Sherr, his closest friend. Then one lunchtime Kiedis found his buddy caught in a headlock by Michael Balzary. The weird loner with the even weirder accent was punching Sherr wildly with his free hand.

As Balzary recalls, Kiedis walked up to the scuffle and cut very much to the chase. "He told me to let go of Tony or he'd knock my block off. He looked pretty mean, so I let go. I figured I'd better get on his good side," he added. "He looked so weird. He looked like a maniac."

Kiedis' take on their first meeting was a little less graphic. He recalled how he and Balzary "met over a friendly altercation during lunch-break". However it happened, they soon became friends.

As first encounters go, it was every bit as unlikely as the first meeting between Alain Johannes' fist and Jack Irons' Kiss codpiece.

Kiedis again: "We were drawn to each other by the forces of mischief and love and we became virtually inseparable. We were both social outcasts. We found each other and it turned out to be the longest-lasting friendship of my life."

There was a true bond between the pair, as well as a genuine love of music and the arts. When they found themselves seated together in drivers' education class, their bond became even tighter. On the occasional day that Kiedis didn't turn up at school, Balzary was completely lost, walking around the school grounds by himself, or hanging out in the music department. ("I didn't want anyone to see I was all alone.") Soon enough Sherr was out and Balzary was Kiedis' new best buddy. And the fringe dweller blossomed alongside his charismatic pal. Balzary shaved off his naturally curly tangle of hair and was bounding alongside his cooler, slightly taller classmate Kiedis like some delirious puppy.

Years later, Blackie Dammett would recall the first time that his son introduced his strange new pal. "He brought home Flea, who was about four-foot-two, to meet me. I took one look at him and said, 'I knew he [Anthony] should have gone to Beverly Hills High School.'"

Balzary would freely state how big an influence Kiedis was on his teenage life. "When we were in high school, I remember going out to the movies or something and I had this outfit that I thought was really suave and cool – these brown corduroy pants and top. And I said to Anthony, 'Hey, like my new shirt?' And he said, 'That's OK, but anybody could wear that. The thing is to wear something else that no one could wear and be totally different.'"*

Not only did Kiedis influence Balzary's troubled sense of style, he was changing his way of thinking about music. In just the same way Balzary's appearance was going through a kind of metamorphosis, so was his attitude to music. Balzary was losing his snobbery towards rock'n'roll – even though much of it remained a mystery to him. He admits that at the time he would write such names as Styx and David Bowie on the cover of his school notebook, although he had no idea who they were.

---

* Interestingly, I spoke with many members of Fairfax High's Class of 1980, from which Balzary and Kiedis – as well as Slovak and Irons – graduated. No one has any indelible memories of the pair, which only goes to show how removed they were from the school mainstream, at least until Anthym started rocking the clubs of Hollywood.

Balzary was now Mike B the Flea. Not long after he became – and to this day remains – simply Flea. The name came to him when he, Barry, Kiedis and another friend, Jon Karson, were sitting in the car-park of a DMV office, in Flea's mother's car, preparing to go on a ski trip. "Before the trip," Barry told me, "we were talking to each other about how we shouldn't refer to each other by our real names. I think that the Flea name might have already been a joke with his girlfriend. I said, 'OK, I'm Tree.'

"In retrospect, it's funny, you know, the name Flea – he's jumpy, capricious. [Whereas] I think I'm perhaps more Tree-like."

It was at this time that Kiedis, with Dammett's encouragement, started auditioning for film roles. "He was very closely associated with the thespian folk [at Fairfax High]," Keith Barry recalled. "I think that was his first calling, because of his dad. He actually did go out on calls, got headshots; he even had a stage name, Cole Dammett." In the 1980 Fairfax High Yearbook, Kiedis is listed as "Thespians VP [Vice President]". He was awarded the school's Best Actor award in the same yearbook; his Best Actress queen was one Denise Deveaux.

According to an interview with *The Washington Post* in 1990, Kiedis stated that he, just like his father, had studied acting under Lee Strasberg. Although punk rock (and soon afterwards, rap music) excited him – along with sex, Woody Allen and jumping off roofs into swimming pools (he once broke bones in his back doing just that) – Kiedis had no idea that his future lay in music. So when the chance came to audition for a role in the film *F.I.S.T.*, he went for it.

The original story, dealing with Johnny Kovak, the head of the Federal Inter-State Truckers Union, was the work of former *Rolling Stone* writer Joe Eszterhas. But by the time Kiedis scored the part of Kovak's son, the script had been reworked into a vehicle for Sylvester Stallone, hot property after the smash-hit *Rocky* films. As the public arm wrestle between Eszterhas and Stallone continued, the shoot dragged on for seven months.

When it was released in 1978, Kiedis' role was little more than a background figure hanging around the Kovak household. But he'd developed a taste for acting. His relationship with the form would resurface throughout much of his accidental career as a musician. Occasionally he would take gigs simply to pay bills, such as the time he rapped a voice-over for an Alpha Bits breakfast cereal ad in 1984.

But despite scoring the role in *F.I.S.T.*, Kiedis had a real problem with discipline, an essential quality for any apprentice actor. "I just got too crazy to handle the responsibility of being a young actor," he said in 1990.

Another performance piece that Kiedis mastered around that time – and one that would have a long-lasting and mostly negative impact on The Red Hot Chili Peppers' reputation – was the sock on cock routine. For much of their first decade together, the band's music often took second place to their reputation for disrobing and playing encores wearing only goofy grins, and tube socks on their dicks.

However, the stunt's origins were strictly off-stage. At the age of 16, Kiedis had moved out of his father's bachelor pad. At 18 he was sharing an apartment with a room-mate whose friend had a real thing for the young, wild, free-loving Kiedis. Sadly – for her – the feeling was not mutual. (Kiedis: "I wasn't really into her.") This didn't appear to be a deterrent, because she sent Kiedis a series of very pornographic cards, including one featuring a fold-out penis with a measuring stick attached. It was an invitation that effectively said: "Come and get me." One day, when she turned up at his apartment unannounced, Kiedis had a brainwave – he walked into his bedroom clothed and emerged wearing nothing more than a sock and a doofus grin.

Kiedis greeted her "as if nothing was different – casual, like a Monty Python episode. It was actually a great phallic look." The sock was worn, as he stressed, "not just over the cock, but the cock and balls. It was just a gag. And it was a good gag." Yet over time what began as a mildly shocking deterrent for a woman he didn't fancy would become a trade-mark stunt that The Red Hot Chili Peppers could have lived without.

Back in camp Anthym, the band's bassist, Todd Strasman, confessed that he wasn't as dedicated to the rock'n'roll cause as Slovak, Irons or Johannes. He had plans to become a lawyer; Anthym was just a high school dalliance. But Slovak already had a plan when Strasman quit the band: he knew that Balzary – aka Flea – was a musically gifted guy, if a little weird. He'd played trumpet in the Los Angeles Junior Philhar-monic Orchestra and in the Fairfax High marching band. Slovak had also spotted him hanging around the school's music class.

So what if he didn't actually play bass, Slovak thought: surely the guy could learn? Even his Bancroft Junior High nemesis, Jack Irons, was OK with Flea joining Anthym, especially if he turned out to be a solid player.

As Keith Barry recalled, "The personal relationship between Hillel and Michael [Flea] was more intense than the relationship between the band and Todd. I think it was Hillel who proposed that Michael become the bass player in Anthym. He thought he would be a hipper guy for the band, and he groomed him to do that. He also taught him to play bass."*

Flea and Kiedis, often with Barry for company, were in the midst of some major teenage bonding. Their new sensation was taking spur-of-the-moment road trips together. They started to behave like the late Seventies answer to *On The Road* searchers Dean Moriarty and Sal Paradise. When they were 15, they hitched up to Yosemite National Park and spent 10 days hiking through the wilds. Looking back on this journey, Flea believes this was the time when he and Kiedis first became really close. Retreating into nature was something the pair would do at regular intervals throughout their lives, often in the company of such fellow rock gods as Pearl Jam's Eddie Vedder. As Kiedis admitted, "I really like to get in among those elements."

They once hitch-hiked to the ski resort, Mammoth Mountain, in the Sierra Nevadas, where they skied by day and crashed in a conveniently empty laundry by night. Keith Barry explained how these cash-strapped teens would fund their journeys: "We used to make it happen this way – one guy would shoplift food to eat and we'd all sneak into a hotel."

Then Flea and Kiedis shaved their heads into mohawks and hid out, hobo-style, on a train that left LA bound for San Francisco. Unfortunately they were caught and tossed from the train in Santa Barbara. They decided to hitch-hike and "a large-chested woman with a beautiful voice, named Dawn" picked them up. When she pulled over an hour later, it turned out that Dawn was actually a Don. This gender-bending incident would eventually become the inspiration for the Chili Peppers song 'Deep Kick'.

---

* Flea would buy his first three basses from Barry's father, who once played in the Fifties revivalist outfit Sha Na Na. Barry remembers the first purchase, an Aspen, as "a piece of crap; a log". The next two were progressively better.

Once they'd parted ways with Dawn/Don, they hopped another train, this one loaded with beetroots, in the optimistic notion that this would be the ride that would bring them home. Wrong again. The train ground to a halt in a goods yard and the pair were soon back on the highway, dripping beet juice, trying to score that elusive ride home. That came in the shape of one mean looking Mexican with LOS VENOS A CHICOS tattooed on his neck. The car, naturally, was stolen and the driver was on the run from the law. When the Mexican ditched the hot motor, Kiedis and Flea were on the road again, laughing their asses off.

Flea and Kiedis also travelled to Michigan to stay with Kiedis' mother. The pair rode the Greyhound bus, with Flea frequently locking himself in the bathroom to jerk off to a favourite *Penthouse* magazine. The pair spent their visit "jumping off a bridge into a river and sneaking around drinking beer and smoking weed with the locals." When they borrowed Peggy's car, they drove it straight into a ditch.

Back home they were also running wild, rarely returning home, which, given the volatile nature of both their family lives, seemed a perfectly reasonable thing to do. (Although, unlike some Hollywood kids, these guys did have homes to return to at night.) Kiedis sometimes crashed on a *chaise longue* at the rear of a house shared by Barry and his father. "Anthony was the pioneer latchkey dude," said Barry.

They'd also discovered The Starwood. Kiedis and Flea, decked out in leather jackets and an assortment of bad-ass haircuts, would hang around the very same parking lot where The Spastics had been tossed by the club's security after desecrating the Stars and Stripes. Then they'd try to sneak inside and check out such seminal US punk acts as The Germs, Black Flag (fronted by an angry ball of muscle called Henry Rollins) and The Circle Jerks. Although usually turned away at the door, they'd try anything to get in: once they even turned up nude, painted in Kiedis' mother's lipstick. Nudity and streaking was a favourite preoccupation of the wild pair.

And Flea's summation of the time? "Anthony and I were street kids, basically."

Keith Barry, who was also on many of these jaunts, agrees. "We were a bit young to be out of the house and on our own."

"In the years to come [after they first met] we would share more than my imagination could conceive," Kiedis wrote in 1994. "The adventures of pleasure and pain we shared made its way directly into the music that we would one day play."

In 1978, with a campus battle of the bands not far off and Anthym bass-less, Slovak approached Flea and offered to teach him the instrument, which he quickly warmed to. They came second in the band competition, a solid start. And Flea's own playing method – the "slap and pop" style that would become his signature sound – started to develop. Flea was also working on his idiosyncratic visual style, the manic jumps, jigs, dances and head-bobbing that would become his on-stage trademark; it was a style that was inspired as much by the moves of his favourite basketballers as anything else. Flea had a natural desire to be seen, as well as heard, above the din that Anthym were creating. And as for his playing, it didn't hurt any that he came from a jazz background; he had an inbuilt sense of swing and rhythm, essential to anyone planning to hold down a rock-solid bottom end.

Flea took only one bass lesson. He walked when the teacher tried to talk him through The Eagles' mellow ballad, 'Take It Easy'. That wasn't his thing at all.

Flea preferred to learn the bass by himself, putting in long hours in his room. "He was and still is a really hard worker," Keith Barry admitted. "He has natural musicality but he's also a worker, a plugger. He dived into that [bass] thing like crazy."

The rigours of formal training were not something that held much appeal for any of the members of Anthym – Slovak wanted to play like Hendrix; Flea, Johannes and Irons just wanted to play – so they figured they'd rather learn on the fly. And they did just that, as the self-managed band started to secure gigs in and around Hollywood, with what seemed like half of the Fairfax High campus there as a ready-made audience. The only trouble was their age: club owners would have to hide the band backstage and in dressing rooms before their sets, in the fear that they'd be busted for having under-agers in their venue, let alone as the hired entertainment. But club owners also had a need for bands such as Anthym who would play whenever, pretty much wherever – and for cheap. Even with the inherent risks, it was a fair exchange.

So while Kiedis was learning his lines and trying to squeeze into frame alongside Sylvester Stallone's overgrown ego, Anthym had outgrown Fairfax High's Detter Court and were starting to become regulars at The Troubadour, The Whisky and The Starwood.

They even got the chance to open at The Orange County Fair for Oingo Boingo, an LA band that was fronted by Danny Elfman, later to become a hot Hollywood film scorer and the man who composed *The Simpsons* theme. (In a weird coincidence, the Peppers would one day cameo in the long-running TV cartoon.) But Oingo Boingo were, as one writer put it, "regarded as minor royalty in LA's neo-Nazi circle" – an offshoot of the West Coast punk scene – so the crowd wasn't there for this band of snotty schoolkids called Anthym. By the end of their short set they'd learned the new skill of dodging flying bottles, which would prove useful in the future. The bottles might have put some dents in their gear (and Johannes' skull) but they didn't damage the four teens' enthusiasm. That Monday morning, back at Fairfax High, they walked tall; the weekend's show had supplied them with some major bragging rights.

Quite possibly the most vocal Anthym fan was Anthony Kiedis. After all, that was his strange little bass-playing buddy running around the stage like a lunatic. And Kiedis had also become tight with Irons, Johannes and especially Slovak. He and the guitarist had bonded over an afternoon snack, as Kiedis would one day disclose in his characteristically grandiose, vaguely New Age-y way.

"He [Slovak] lived just two blocks from Fairfax High School, which is where we met. One day after school he invited me over for egg salad sandwiches. One afternoon was all it took for us to know that we would be friends forever, for better, for worse, for everything in the universe."

Kiedis' favourite thing at the time was the hit duo Cheech and Chong, comedy's very stoned answer to such partnerships as Abbott and Costello. The former was the Mexican-American son of a Californian cop, the latter a Chinese-Canadian with a musical past that included a stint playing in a band with a wild-haired dude called Jimi Hendrix. As Cheech & Chong they were a bong-pulling comic act from east LA whose righteously fucked-up, anti-authority routine could be heard on such albums as *Cheech & Chong's Wedding Album* and later in the hit film *Up In Smoke*. Kiedis loved them; his voice could be picked out from the Fairfax High crowd at pretty much any point in time because he'd nailed the pair's stoned Latino drawl and had decided to use it whenever he spoke.

With Flea and Slovak as his partners in rhyme, Kiedis led the trio in a series of seriously stoned classroom recitals, inspired equally by Cheech & Chong and wino boho author Charles Bukowski. They called themselves Los Faces. They became star attractions in numerous Hollywood crash pads. Flea referred to the trio – or, at least, The Faces – in the liner notes to *Out In LA*, where he wrote, with some affection, about "Anthony, Hillel and I, also known as the Faces, Fire Man, Earth Man, Wind Man, Poco, Flaco, Fuerte, Swan, Clem Phlegm, Huey Spitoon and the Israeli Cowboy". The socks-on-cocks trick that Kiedis had earlier pulled on his female admirer would also become a standard part of the Slovak, Flea and Kiedis comedy routine, usually fuelled by the right mix of booze and dope.

Years down the line, Flea would still fondly recall the time. "People would come over, we'd hang out, smoke pot and drink beer, put socks on our dicks and run around. It was just kids living together, having fun."

Slovak, Kiedis and Flea had formed a fraternal bond that would last for many years and become the key reason why the Chili Peppers survived the types of personal and professional disasters that would kill most bands stone dead. The trio had plenty in common: divorce, music, school, drugs and a wild spirit.

"We grew up in Hollywood," wrote Flea, "and we came from broken familys [sic] and we were confused kids who hadn't even begun to understand our fear yet."

They'd also started to dabble with serious drugs at this time, moving way beyond the reefer madness of Cheech & Chong. Kiedis and Slovak – and Flea to a slightly lesser extent – were up for anything, trying out acid, heroin, coke, uppers, downers, booze, whatever was going. Drummer Jack Irons looked on cautiously as the three amigos got seriously wasted on a regular basis. He was and would remain incredibly wary about the use and abuse of drugs.

Flea thought otherwise. "When I found drugs, I thought I'd found the greatest thing," he would tell *Rolling Stone*. "All you do is snort this shit up your nose or stick this needle in your arm and you're a fucking genius."

Barry, Kiedis and Flea shared an apartment, known as the Formosa

Pad, not long after finishing high school. As Barry told me, much of their food was provided by shoplifting and breaking and entering.

"I used to go into people's houses and rob them," stated Flea in 1996, who felt such guilt that he actually tried to contact people he'd robbed and "set it straight for my own sanity". They would also shop-lift to raise drug money. And drugs were on tap at the Formosa Pad.

"It was wild," Barry recalled. "We were pretty young people."

However, such events that were going down at the Formosa Pad weren't that uncommon in Hollywood at the time, as Barry explained. "Of course drugs were endemic in the youth culture in that geographic area, so the kids of Hollywood had a lot of exposure to and were very susceptible to taking drugs. It was a very common thing among kids at that time and place. We tried pot and then went through everything: acid, coke, heroin."

Typically, it was Kiedis who led the way when it came to drug experimentation, being the first of the group to shoot up. "Anthony was the trailblazer as far as trying this stuff," Barry agreed. "Anthony and I tried injecting cocaine first; I would have been 16, 17. Pretty tough stuff.

"Here's the thing about it, that seems amusing to me in retrospect: we started with the injecting of cocaine and of course that's one of the worst possible things you could do in medical terms; the ravaging, the terribleness of it. It's immediately addictive and you'll instantly do as much as you can possibly obtain. [With] heroin, you have to really work on it to get your jones; you're not instantly addicted. But the word heroin is taboo. So when Anthony took that trip, and found someone to score heroin from, and told us, we were like aghast, because of the word heroin. I remember thinking that he would instantly die."

Barry vividly recalls Kiedis' introduction to smack. "The connection came over and we all watched as he [Kiedis] was the first guy to try it. His reports were favourable, so we all followed suit.

"I think that he has this predisposition [towards drugs]. I also think that he had some initial experience with his father beforehand; that may have whetted his appetite for it."

As Barry sees it, events at the Formosa Pad played a huge role in the drug-related dramas that would hinder the Peppers' progress for many years, even killing one of the band's members. "It was really a game of Russian Roulette," he said. "A certain number would pay the ultimate price. Others would keep paying for years, with endless relapses and rehabs and binges and what have you. Only a certain fraction would come through relatively unscathed, like Flea and me. No one could have predicted who would have been in that fraction.

"Of course it didn't seem so terrible at that time."

By the time they were 18, Slovak, Kiedis and Flea were sharing another Hollywood crash pad, on Wilton and Franklin, with, as Flea recalled, "a couple of Frenchmen of dubious distinction named Fab and Joel". While the sun set over the City of Angels, Flea would take his trumpet up to the roof of the apartment and blow, man, blow. As he played, he couldn't help but think that life was good. He was no longer a fringe dweller, he was in a band that was developing a serious following, and the drugs were working. The world seemed full of possibilities.

CHAPTER TWO

"No pubes! I told you guys no pubes!"

IF Anthony Kiedis' biggest effect on the teenage Flea was bringing the jazz-loving introvert out of his shell, Hillel Slovak was having an equally significant impact on both Kiedis and Flea. He was opening their minds to the endless possibilities of music. In particular he'd performed a magical transformation act on Flea, the self-confessed jazz snob who'd dismissed his first punk show as "disgusting". Now in their shared Hollywood house, Slovak took control of the stereo, spinning cutting-edge punk records as well as classic rock staples. Both Kiedis and Flea were willing students at Slovak's master class in rock'n'roll appreciation.

"Hillel was a huge influence on my life," Flea would write in *Behind The Sun*, a book compiled by Slovak's brother James. "I never would have begun to play the bass [without his influence]. I looked up to him, I loved the way his hair fell on his shoulders and the way he slung his red Messenger guitar around like a rock stud."

According to Flea, "I [had] heard rock music, but it sounded stupid to me. When I met Hillel, he started playing lots of rock music for me, and I got into Led Zeppelin and Jimi Hendrix. And for rock music the Sixties was without a doubt the most innovative, expressive time. To me the greatest thing that happened after that was punk rock. You can't be a relevant rock musician today without knowing punk rock and understanding it.

"The beautiful thing about punk rock," he continued, "was the intensity, the energy. And punk deflated the whole bloated rock-star thing. I think that musicians who didn't pay attention to punk have a gap in their knowledge that makes it difficult to communicate in this day and age."

Many Peppers insiders, including guitarist Jack Sherman, acknowledge how big an influence Slovak was on the musical development of Kiedis and Flea. Sherman isn't convinced, however, that the pair embraced punk as completely as Slovak. "This whole thing they were on about punk – they were enjoying it probably like anyone at that age – but they're not punk, they're Hollywood," he told me. "They were into punk [more] as some kind of mission statement, this badge of honour."*

Another big influence on their musical intake was a Fairfax High friend called Dondi Bastone, who, like Kiedis, was the son of an actor. He would introduce Kiedis, Flea and Slovak – plus Keith Barry, who spent a lot of time with the future Chili Peppers – to the more radical music of the time, which could only be heard on the *Rodney On The ROQ* programme.

"It was a very, very ripe time," Barry remembered. "Dondi was a tremendous collector and connoisseur of music. I don't think we thought at the time how significant some of the things that we were checking out were – Talking Heads, Gang Of Four. [But] we didn't need the radio, we had Dondi."

Flea's punk initiation was complete when Slovak talked him into attending the last-ever show by iconic LA screamers The Germs, at The Starwood, on December 3, 1980. From that day onwards, Flea would go on to profess his pure, unreserved love for the band, although he was ejected from the gig even before they'd demolished their first number, 'Circle One'. (Flea even tried to force-feed The Germs to future manager Lindy Goetz and convert him to punk. Goetz responded by holding his hands over his ears and screaming, "What the fuck is that?") Just four days after The Starwood gig, Germs frontman Darby Crash was dead from a heroin OD. It was the first time that the Peppers' world would be rocked by the drug that ended so many rock stars' lives.

"Nothing will ever be like Hillel, Flea and Anthony as a trio," Kiedis told *Rolling Stone* in 1994. "That's impossible. That was a time in our

---

* Further proof of this is an early Peppers gig in LA with punk heroes Suicidal Tendencies. Kiedis failed to show, insisting that he had stopped to help the victim of a road crash. Sherman felt that the singer was simply too scared to front at what he called "a true hardcore show". Keith Barry sang for the band that night. But Kiedis was often a "no show" in the band's early days – at one gig in Long Beach a three-man Chili Peppers even invited audience members to sing for them.

lives both musically and personally that will never be repeated."

Flea agreed. "Growing up, we didn't come from standard functional families. Our parents divorced when we were kids and we left home young. So our friends were our family. We were so close; we did everything together. First sex, first drugs, first time listening to Gang Of Four or Echo & The Bunnymen. First time looking at a Basquiat painting. All the most intimate experiences I had."

Flea, Slovak, Kiedis, Johannes and Irons had all graduated from Fairfax High in July 1980. Now they had to make a decision that they'd been neatly sidestepping during their high times in Anthym and Los Faces: what would they do next? For Flea and Slovak, it was a no-brainer, because they wanted to make music the main priority in their lives. Playing in Anthym was sexy and dynamic and exciting – and women were starting to pay them some attention, too.

Now that he was in a band, Flea figured, "Girls wouldn't think I was just a freaky-looking weirdo with skinny legs."

Maybe they could even make some kind of living out of playing rock.

As for college, that held absolutely no interest for them. So why bother enrolling? Irons and Johannes were under some parental pressure to at least experience further education – although, just like their bandmates, they believed that music was very clearly their calling – so they both enrolled at Northbridge College before moving on to a Valley college. Johannes had vague plans to become an architect, but that was more his family's wishes than his life goal.

Taking a cue from his father almost 20 years earlier, Kiedis enrolled at UCLA. However, unlike Dammett, who enrolled at the college's film school, Kiedis signed on as a political science major, even though he had the feeling that words and writing were what he really wanted to explore. Not only had he been influenced by Fairfax High's quiet achiever, Mrs Vernon, but Blackie Dammett maintained a reasonable library in his home and encouraged his son to read as much as possible.

But by 1981, Kiedis and UCLA went their separate ways, despite his very light schedule as a political science freshman. His only real connection was with writing classes; the rest of his studies seemed redundant. As it turns out, in his brief stay at UCLA, Anthony Kiedis didn't actually enrol in a single political science course. As he surmised in 1993, "I just got sick of going to school because it was a very stilting and unpleasant atmosphere to spend my time in. I think it's more of a self-propelled desire to want to experience life first-hand that really adds to [the] growth of somebody's intellect."

He should have already known this, of course, because this was exactly the same reaction he had had to formal education when he was in high school.

All this talk of the school of life was fine in theory, but what next for Kiedis? Given his love of language, it made perfect sense when Flea asked him to get more involved with Anthym's live shows. Over a few bongs one night he proposed that Kiedis could MC their shows, adding some "colour" to their gigs. The role was pretty straightforward: Kiedis would warm up the audience before the band came on, spitting out jokes and sparring verbally with the crowd, many of whom he already knew from high school. It all came very naturally to the flamboyant "Swan", Fairfax High's leading thespian.

As Kiedis warmed to his role, he began to interject a standard sign-off at the end of his intro. Standing centre-stage, he'd declare: "Cal Worthington* calls them the hottest rockers in LA. Their parents call them crazy and the girls call them all the time. But I call them like I see them, and I call them . . . ANTHYM!"

Then Slovak, Flea, Johannes and Irons would bound on stage and launch into their opening track while Kiedis joined his girlfriend Haya Handel in the crowd, throwing himself about like the relatively harmless lunatic that the Fairfax High alumni-heavy crowd knew him to be. The MC'ing gig was fun and the attention felt just fine, but maybe Kiedis could get even more involved with the band. He just wasn't quite sure how.

In order to pay the bills, Kiedis had taken a job at a small Hollywood film company. And soon enough he'd broken up with Handel, his partner of the last three years, as he continued his very own sexual revolution that had been set in motion by his father. Johannes and Irons had taken Kiedis' lead, too, both dropping out of college. So, along with Flea and Slovak, they turned their complete attention to Anthym. But there was a problem: the band's name.

---

* A cheesy Californian car salesman, usually seen on late-night TV ads in the company of cows or dogs.

Johannes, in particular, had been getting heavily into what became known as no wave – the missing link between the last gasps of punk rock and the synthetic, airblown sounds of new wave. No wave was predominantly a New York state of mind; it was a harsh, aggressive, guitar-powered style of rock'n'roll with artier, more musical inclinations than its predecessor punk. Its key players included such acts as Teenage Jesus & The Jerks (featuring no wave figureheads Lydia Lunch and James Chance), DNA and James White & The Blacks. Then there were serious weirdos The Residents, who loved nothing better than performing while dressed as giant eyeballs. By basing themselves in San Francisco, The Residents were bringing no wave to the west coast.

Another key influence on Anthym's fast-developing style were rock eccentrics Captain Beefheart & The Magic Band (whose one-time drummer, Cliff Martinez, would become a Red Hot Chili Pepper). Beefheart (aka Don Van Vliet) was a true American original, an artist with an amazing, octave-jumping vocal range and a freewheeling musical scope that willingly embraced everything from jazz to rock and Delta blues. This sonic melting pot was topped off with his absurdist lyrics. Beefheart was the guiding light for Anthym, who were searching for some mysterious amalgam of the music that they loved: rock'n'roll, punk, jazz (Flea now had dual roles on trumpet and bass) and no wave.

Johannes described their sound at the time as "very quirky hard rock; all adrenalin and testosterone." Anthym's new name – What Is This – summed up their stylistic collision perfectly.

Kiedis, meanwhile, was making some musical discoveries of his own. First he'd fallen under the stone-cold-rhymin' spell of Grandmaster Flash, then he was going crazy for a band called Defunkt. Formed in 1978 and based in New York, Defunkt was fronted by trumpeter Joseph Bowie, whose bloodline absolutely oozed musicality. His father was a music teacher while his brothers, Byron and Lester, were a big band arranger and trumpet player respectively. Though Defunkt only lasted five years, their efforts at fusing big band jazz with more contemporary dance grooves and punk's kinetic energy were both dynamic in concert and truly revolutionary conceptually.

Kiedis was mad about their self-titled debut album from 1980 and started talking up its merits like some kind of funky evangelist. He constantly played it to his buddies in What Is This.

When Flea could wrest control of the stereo from his buddy Kiedis, he spun new discs from punk acts The Brainiacs, Big Boys and Konk, in addition to such group faves as Hendrix and Sly & The Family Stone. But Defunkt truly was What Is This' new sensation.

"That band [Defunkt] was kind of inspirational in getting the Red Hot Chili Peppers to form," Kiedis would reveal in 1989. "We used to put Defunkt on and go absolutely berserk."

Kiedis would play Defunkt and "spin around the house. I thought how wonderful it would be to make other people feel the way I feel."

For the five friends, Defunkt represented the missing musical link, because they now had the funk. Now all they had to do was add it to their musical melting pot of rock, punk, jazz and rap.

But Flea had begun to wonder what musical possibilities lay outside of What Is This. His first freelancing gig, however, was hardly inspiring. He played congas for a cheap disco act who pulled off note perfect covers of the hits of the day, with a selection chosen from the work of Rick Dees, Linda Ronstadt and others. Then he and Slovak moved up a notch, auditioning for New York-based saxophonist James White.

White (aka James Chance) was a member of Teenage Jesus & The Jerks, the no wave act fronted by Lydia Lunch that had a real impact on the fledgling What Is This. Born in Milwaukee, White had the same anything-goes musical mindset as Captain Beefheart, liberally mixing up jazz, funk and post-punk imagery. And his original horn section had morphed into Defunkt, which gave him even more credibility points. If Flea and Slovak were going to moonlight, they couldn't have picked a better boss.

But although they were both offered spots in his band, Flea and Slovak rejected the work, despite some healthy jams. They knew that as hired hands they would have little or no say in the creative direction of the music they were playing. But it couldn't have hurt the pair's confidence to know that a player as well regarded and influential as James White could want these two skinny dudes in his band. And jamming was a blast. So while Slovak returned to What Is This, Flea discovered Fear (the band that is, not the creeping sensation).

Along with Black Flag and The Circle Jerks, Fear formed the strangest link in the unholy trinity that was LA hardcore. They were fronted by sometime actor Lee Ving, whose murky past is rumoured to have included active service in the Vietnam war. Ving was a punk provocateur, more than happy to serve it up, both lyrically and physically, to gays, women and anyone else who annoyed him on a given day. (He later played tough guys in such films as *Flashdance* and *Streets Of Fire*.) As their second drummer, Spit Stix figured, "Dead Kennedys thought we were fascists, homophobes thought we were gay, lesbians thought we were misogynists."

When they formed in 1977, Ving was backed by the perfectly named Johnny Backbeat (on drums, of course), bassist Derf Scratch and guitarist Philo Cramer. In 1978 they issued their debut single, a valentine to the City of Angels called 'I Love Livin' In The City'. Fear were just about the most confrontational of all the post-punk bands to slither out of LA. Blood was spilled as freely as beer at their shows – and make no mistake: Fear, especially Ving, loved beer. At the Stardust Ballroom, a huge skinhead almost killed Scratch. At a Starwood show, a Fear fan stabbed a bouncer. Not long after that the club banned all punk acts.

Word of the band started to spread outside Fear's hometown. By 1981, with Blues Brother John Belushi's seal of approval, the band rocked *Saturday Night Live*'s Halloween special. Not the kind of guy to miss making an impact, Ving invited some skinhead slam-dancing buddies on-stage; they set about wrecking the set while spitting out some juicy profanities (although one punk's war cry of "Fuck you, New York!" was heard only after the cameras were turned off).

Fear also made a blazing cameo in Penelope Spheeris' punku-mentary, *The Decline Of Western Civilization*, along with X, Black Flag and The Circle Jerks. Their appearance in the well-received doco proved that Lee Ving was tough, smart – and funny.

"I wish you wouldn't bite so hard when I come, OK?" Ving snarls at one heckler during a live set in the film. "You only spit as good as you suck, shithead," he tells another.

Flea had first caught the band in action at a new Hollywood venue called Club Lingerie, during the summer of 1981. He stumbled away impressed. "They were really tight, fast and aggressive," he said. "They blew my mind."

By the time of their 1982 Yuletide single, 'Fuck Christmas', Scratch had been temporarily replaced by Eric Drew Feldman, an erstwhile Captain Beefheart member. When he heard that Scratch had left – Feldman was just a stand-in – Flea applied for the gig. It didn't hurt

Flea's aspirations that he was related to one CC Smith, who was a friend of Fear drummer Spit Stix.

Flea approached the gig with his usual give-it-all-you've-got aggression. When he found out that Fear were looking for a permanent replacement for Scratch, Flea made a call and announced that he was their new bassist. Spit Stix remembers that the band were concerned by his lack of playing experience, but they were so taken by his energy and brassiness "that we just had to try him out".

"He showed up to our rehearsal hall with his bass in hand and [guitarist] Philo asked him if he had brought his rig. Flea said, 'I thought we were just going to jam?' Philo and I sort of looked at each other with our eyebrows up, but then Flea pulled this tiny, open-backed guitar amp out of his beat-up Volkswagen. Then Philo said, 'You did bring your rig.' I think he thought we were junkies or something."

Stix and the band were sold on the pint-sized excitement machine as soon as he started playing. He remembers Flea's audition well, mainly because he was "jumping in the air and shaking his head around wildly". He got the job.

In a Slash Records promo shot of the band at the time, he was known as 'The Flea'.

Of course it wasn't a huge surprise when Flea soon discovered that he and Fear came from somewhat different musical worlds. Flea's playing was shaped by jazzy invention; Fear dealt in sonic savagery. But he did his best to adapt, playing with a plectrum for the first time in his life, something he wouldn't do again until 2002. His idea of conforming was to bounce around the stage with even more mad energy than the rest of the band, inspired, as he would reveal, by Fear's "attack-orientated punk rock energy". Shit, he figured, if his playing wasn't right for Fear, at least he could look the part.

However, Spit Stix doesn't recall the union between Flea and Fear as being that uncomfortable. "He fitted just fine," he told me. "Flea was a showman and was rough around the edges."

Flea stuck it out in Fear for longer than expected, in part because it was, as he would confess, "the first band that I was in that made any money and that people came to see." What Is This may have been big men on campus, but they simply didn't have the firepower and punk-rock appeal of Lee Ving and Fear. The band's manic live power would have a lasting influence on his wildly physical style of bass-humping.

"I was a crazy kid and they were older and more mature than me," Flea mused many years later. "I was never really comfortable in that band, never could really be myself, but it was a great learning experience and that first record they made is great – outside of the rampant homophobia. Musically it's an innovative and exciting record."

Stix and Flea became tight, bonding especially well during the lengthy hours that they spent crammed into the band's tiny tour bus. On one occasion, as Stix told me, the band were returning from a gig in San Francisco and the two were having such a good time that "Flea laughed so hard that the peanuts and beer he was consuming came out of his nose."

After all, they were the two junior members of the band.

During that same San Fran trip, Flea made a lasting impression on a group of women that he was trying to convert to the punk rock world. The way Stix read the situation, it was a perfect example of Flea being "proud of his manhood" – it was also a reminder of the trouble he often had expressing himself without coming off like a certifiable lunatic.

"Across the street from the [San Fran] punk club Mabuhay Gardens was a heavy metal club," he recalled. "In those days, few good-looking girls liked punk. Flea tried to persuade some of the cute girls across the street into liking punk by dropping his pants, grabbing his big business and saying, 'Hey girls, look at this.'" Amazingly, Flea and Fear struck out with the women.

"No," Stix laughed, "it didn't work."

Anthony Kiedis would also drift in and out of the Fear radar, sometimes checking in on the progress of his buddy Flea. The Chili Peppers mightn't have started to burn up the Hollywood clubs just yet, but Kiedis, as Stix recalls, still knew how to charm women. Sometimes to Stix's own misfortune.

"I was in the China Club in Hollywood one night," he remembered, "talking to this cute girl, hoping for the best. Anthony walked up to us and asked the young lady if she wanted to go fuck in the bathroom. She did."

Flea would tell *Alternative Press* writer Jason Pettigrew that after two years with the band, he said "fuck it" and quit Fear. "It was kind of mutual; they didn't want me and the [still unborn] Chili Peppers were much closer to my heart. They [Fear] rejected me."

Stix doesn't recall his departure as being quite that clear-cut. His bandmate had actually been encouraging Flea not only to work on his music outside of the band, but had advised him to quit Fear, because, as he recalls, "Lee [Ving] didn't put his or my songs on the Fear live set list."

The couple of dozen shows that he'd played with the band were a great education for Flea. Not only did it tighten his playing but it gave him a rough idea as to how the live music industry worked. He also earned a few dollars along the way.

"Fear was an exercise in entertainment and musical discipline for Flea, I think," Stix said to me when asked about the band's impact on his playing and career. "He always had – and kept – his own funky, muscular style. I don't think that Fear took full advantage of his talents."

Just like the Chili Peppers a few years down the line, Fear's musical chops weren't given anywhere near as much attention as their obsession with on-stage mayhem and anarchy – but they could play. "I've always been a big fan of Miles Davis, John Coltrane, Sonny Rollins, Roland Kirk, Charlie Parker, Django Reinhardt, McCoy Tyner on the piano, Archie Shepp, Beaver Harris," Ving would tell *Austin Chronicle* reporter Tim Stegall, when asked to namecheck his musical influences. Stegall would go on to surmise that Fear were "not as moronic as their pose".

Working with Fear also helped Flea secure some rent-paying film work in Penelope Spheeris' feature film *Suburbia*, her follow-up project to the rockumentary *The Decline Of Western Civilization*, where Fear had burned very brightly. The film dealt with a seemingly safe, secure middle-class suburb, where – surprise, surprise – things are not as they seem. Mixing professional actors and amateurs, Spheeris cast Flea (billed as "Mike B The Flea") as Razzle, who spent most of the film toting around a pet rat, a very clear mark of his "punkness". The film was a commercial and critical failure, although live footage of LA punks TSOL was a brief highpoint. And Flea did get to meet cartoonist Gary Panter at the film's premiere. Panter would go on to play a key role in the visual style of the Chili Peppers' early albums.

Having quit Fear and unable to secure any more film work, Flea had taken a temporary position as an attendant at an animal's morgue, where he became an expert at exterminating dog and cat corpses. But Flea had also gained enough confidence in his role as Fear bassman to audition for Public Image Limited (aka PiL), the post-Sex Pistols band fronted by John Lydon (the erstwhile Johnny Rotten), despite Stix's advice that he should concentrate on his own music.

PiL were originally conceived by Lydon as an "anti rock'n'roll" band; they were one of the best and most influential of all the post-punk outfits. And Flea had some seriously big size 10s to fill – his predecessor in the band was Jah Wobble, whose dub-like basslines played a key role in the outfit's subversive wall of sound.

When Lydon sacked Wobble in 1980, he'd continued *sans* bass for their next album, 1981's *Flowers Of Romance*. But with a tour of Australia and Japan looming large, Lydon had changed his way of thinking about bassists. Flea fronted for a rehearsal in Pasadena and jammed for 30 minutes with drummer Martin Atkins, who was bowled over by the spindly bassman's skills.

But just as he had done with James White, Flea knocked back the offer of the job, despite Atkins' insistence that he was the chosen one. As it turns out, he really just showed up for the chance to jam with one of his favourite players. And again just like his James White experience, Flea wasn't convinced that he was the right guy merely to be a hired hand: his time in Fear had proved that.

"Fuck that," he thought as he drove back to LA, "I'm not going to be a sideman."

It was 1983 and Flea was returning to his old Fairfax High buddies. What he didn't know was that the accidental creation of The Red Hot Chili Peppers was about to happen.

The early signs weren't good for the year in rock 1983. Music fans in the UK recovered from their New Year's hangover to learn that former Genesis drummer and all-round nice guy, Phil Collins, had climbed to the top of the charts with his bland-as-butter take on The Supremes' 'You Can't Hurry Love'. The situation wasn't much rosier in the USA – their first number one for 1983 was the sugary treat 'The Girl Is Mine', a duet between Paul McCartney and his new-found buddy, Michael Jackson.

The prognosis didn't improve over the next few months. In the UK, with the new romantic movement in full puffy-sleeved swing, such airbrushed popsters as Kajagoogoo and The Thompson Twins were pumping out hits like 'Too Shy' and 'Hold Me Now'. Michael Jackson ruled charts and airwaves on both sides of the Atlantic with his *Thriller* album. Smooth soul-pop duo Daryl Hall & John Oates were in the midst of a record-breaking chart run, as was the Boy George-fronted Culture Club. Duran Duran and Tears For Fears were striking a multi-platinum balance of sleek, chilly production and perfect hair. Men At Work and Rick Springfield were big stars, likewise Belle Stars and Buck's Fizz.

As for dissent in the ranks, there were just a few ripples. Punk vets The Clash made a surprise appearance in the US charts when their 'Rock The Casbah' snuck into the Top 10 during January. U2 made their chart debut with the storming anthem 'New Year's Day'. Rocka-billy rebels The Stray Cats dropped their self-referential swansong, 'Stray Cat Strut', before imploding. Echo & The Bunnymen's big-haired vocalist, Ian McCulloch, crooned the lament of 'The Cutter'. And there was also the platinum-plus return of horny soulman Marvin Gaye, whose '(Sexual) Healing' was a runaway hit in early 1983.

As for rap, it was in the process of being watered down for mass appeal. Hip-hop groundbreaker Grandmaster Flash may have made an impact with 'The Message' in the latter half of 1982, but Brit hitmakers Wham! had now given the new form a serious sanitising with their god-awful 'Wham! Rap'. The sing-songy Musical Youth weren't helping the cause much themselves, thanks to their G-rated singalong about life in the 'hood, 'Pass The Duchie'. The edgier, angrier hip-hop of Ice Cube, NWA and Public Enemy was still a sound under develop-ment – and it appeared that rock'n'roll had retired guitars in exchange for cavernous drum sounds and flabby synths. Even David Bowie was fusing Carlos Alomar's space-age riffs with the wind-tunnel production of a track like 'Let's Dance'. When a band of studio cats called Toto walked away from the 1983 Grammys with an armful of silverware – they scored five awards in all – rock may as well have been pronounced dead. Technology was taking over.

No wonder Kiedis, Flea and Slovak were wigging out to Defunkt's punk-funk fury; the genre-defying band were unlike anything that the trio was hearing on the radio when they were hanging out in their Hollywood funhouse.

If there was a new groove in the early Eighties, however, it was happening on their TV set. Music Television (aka MTV) aired its first clip, the Buggles' 'Video Killed The Radio Star', on August 1, 1981 and effectively opened up a new world of possibilities. Bands big on visual appeal – the nascent Red Hot Chili Peppers included, of course – were tailor-made for this new 24/7 medium: why just hear music when you can watch it, too? Duran Duran, Prince, Van Halen, Michael Jackson, Cyndi Lauper and dozens of others became even bigger stars thanks to the visual exposure MTV provided. And acts as diverse as Tina Turner, Robert Palmer and ZZ Top worked out ways to resuscitate their careers via must-see clips on MTV. It was more than the perfect medium for couch potatoes and agoraphobics; MTV gave hungry music fans even more connectivity to the artists they loved. A great clip was now every bit as effective as a great song.

Despite its early emphasis on the safer acts dominating the charts in the early Eighties, such as Journey and REO Speedwagon, MTV changed the music industry forever, not just in such areas as promotion (record companies now had an extra medium to flog the product) but by adding a visual element to music. A band didn't simply go into the studio and cut a single; they now had to shoot a video as well. Labels could then repackage the clips and sell them alongside albums and singles.

Any act hoping to coax a few bucks out of the music machine had to consider the way they looked, not just how they played. "Haircut" bands such as Duran Duran and Spandau Ballet took charge. Stadium-filling metal act Van Halen just got bigger, mainly because they had a ready-made excitement machine in singer David Lee Roth, who smirked his way through a succession of high rotation, soft-core clips. Image was virtually everything and the savvier players in the pop market, including Madonna and Michael Jackson, got on board via such ground-breaking, budget-busting clips as 'Material Girl' and 'Thriller'. Jackson's clip for 'Beat It' cost a then record $US70,000, required 150 extras and even featured choreography – and then choreographers Toni Basil and Paula Abdul become MTV stars themselves.

It would take The Red Hot Chili Peppers several years to become MTV darlings, but there's no denying the medium's impact on their success. Watching in their lounge room, through a cloud of dope smoke, Kiedis, Slovak and Flea knew that most of the music sucked, but they were smart enough to figure out that the band that looks good had an even bigger chance of success in this strange new MTV age.

MTV, however, had very little in common with LA punk band Neighborhood Voices, who were fronted by one Gary Allen. By the time he became a friend of Anthony Kiedis and a drug buddy of Slovak's, Allen – aka the "Funky Diva" – had gone solo, taking a radical about-turn from the raw power of punk. He had been readying a costumed cabaret lip-sync routine, which he planned to premiere at LA's Rhythm Lounge club in April 1983. Allen asked Kiedis if he could put together some kind of one-off piece to get the crowd in the mood for his show. Being a natural extrovert with vaguely defined artistic plans, Kiedis readily agreed. All he now needed was some kind of act to fit with what Allen was referring to only as "a night of weirdness".

A few days later, Kiedis and Flea were in their lounge room, along with Irons (or Jackie I, as Flea had nicknamed the drummer). It was a week since Kiedis had seen Grandmaster Flash perform, and he still felt as though he'd witnessed the second coming. He'd been so inspired by the New York hip-hop master that he had been madly scribbling lyrics ever since the show. On this spring day, Kiedis was playing Defunkt yet again, when Flea started to play along to one of the band's bottomless basslines. Kiedis had a flash of inspiration: he had exactly the right rap to link with the bassline Flea was pumping out. He was going to call the piece 'Out in LA'. It was perfect for Gary Allen's big night in.

Flea quite readily refers to 'Out in LA''s bassline as being born of Defunkt. While he would rather not call it outright plagiarism, he has said, "Well, it's not a steal, but more of a feeling."

The way Kiedis saw it, "I'd rather feel that steal."

The rest of the tune was based around what Flea would simply call, "some funky jam – straight from our hearts – which became our first song."

And as for Kiedis' rap, it was a roughly formed ode to both his tight group of buddies and the city that would populate so many Chili Peppers songs. Because he knew both his pals and the city so well, the words came to Kiedis very easily. In fact, the lyric virtually wrote itself, because they'd already lived the song in the many Hollywood crash pads that these 24-hour party people had occupied.

Keidis wrote of how he and his Chili Pepper band-mates were like brothers, living out their cool lifestyles in Los Angeles alongside six million others.

He tried the introductory salvo out on Flea and Irons, who nodded their approval. Kiedis smiled and kept writing, documenting his strange relationship with his adopted hometown. He wrote about the city's seemingly endless supply of wild women ("a bunch of bad chicks") and the "chumps" that he constantly encountered. But more than anything, he wanted to express his love for LA, ideally using the most direct language possible. When he declared that, "I still get my kicks," it was a handy understatement, given his lifestyle at the time.

It wasn't Shakespeare. Hell, these lyrics were hardly worthy of some second-rate Sunset Strip sleaze rock act. But Kiedis loved the way the words flowed. When they were mixed with Flea's borrowed bassline, the blend was pretty damned righteous. So righteous, in fact, that Kiedis decided to squeeze in a reference to his Fax City sidekick during the next verse, when he mentioned his "best friend" Flea. But Kiedis had other pals to mention, including another Hollywood crashpad local, Keith "Tree" Barry. He deserved a line or two, too, as did the man writing the rhyme himself. So Kiedis memorialised himself in rhyme. He was "Antwan the Swan, from the pretty fish pond."

By this point Kiedis was psyched; not only did he mention himself but he'd also thrown a little sexual bragging into the mix. He decided to amp up that side of the rhyme just a bit further when he scrawled the next few lines; they basically amounted to a boast that the Swan loved women not by the dozens, but by the hundreds.

This was a rhyme that his old man, Blackie Dammett, would absolutely love – especially when the band got around to recording a demo of the song, because Kiedis substituted the word "fuck" for "love".

Kiedis was truly warming to this lyric-writing caper now and by the time he'd returned to the rap's refrain about his brothers living amongst six million others in LA, all he needed was some kind of sign-off to bring his rap home. When he scrawled down pretty much the first thing that entered his head – the party cry of "Step out!" – the song was complete.

The rest of this makeshift – and at the time nameless – outfit were pretty impressed, both with Kiedis' rap and the funky jam that they'd worked out to accompany it. Flea, in particular, was ecstatic.

"When friends hang out and truly love each other," he would write of the 'Out In LA' period, "cool shit ends up flowing down the river."

Still, when the Fax City four of Kiedis, Flea, Slovak and Irons got together pre-show, they had no real idea as to how Gary Allen's crowd would respond. After all, this fledgling line-up only knew the one song. When Allen pushed them for a band name – because, he explained, he had to have something for the posters advertising the gig – they came up with a tag almost as attention-grabbing as Kiedis' 'Out In LA' rap. It was a name that seemed to say everything and in fact revealed nothing about this mock combo they'd just formed. They were now officially called, at least for this one-off show, Tony Flow And The Miraculously Majestic Masters Of Mayhem. And they were ready to rock the Rhythm Lounge like a motherfucker.

Tony Flow And The Miraculously Majestic Masters Of Mayhem's sole show is one of those rare, historically noteworthy gigs that only the biggest (and luckiest) bands have in their career. It was the perfect blend of good songs (well, one good song in their case), even better drugs and precise timing. And, of course, it was one of those shows that, apparently, every scenester from the Hollywood Hills to the Sunset Strip attended. And yet there were only a couple of hundred people in the room on Melrose.

Like so much of The Red Hot Chili Peppers' life and career, the Tony Flow show was an unplanned accident that simply exploded and set the band on a trajectory that they couldn't have anticipated. The Red Hot Chili Peppers' career was one that hinged upon accidents: some happy, some otherwise.

"It started as a joke," the band has said more than once about the Tony Flow gig. In fact they've repeated this mantra so many times that it might just be the truth.

Keith Barry, who MC'ed the show, agreed. "The first Chili Peppers show was a lark," he told me. "Anthony, who was more a word painter than a narrative writer, wrote a rap, 'Out In LA', which they performed. And there was also a great deal of physicality, gymnastics, spontaneity, stuff like that."

As for the show itself, well, if you blinked you would have missed it. Nicely fired up on a tab of acid, the very under-rehearsed Fax City four marched single file across Melrose Avenue and onto the Rhythm Lounge's stage. The plan was simple: they plugged in, pulled off some syncopated dance moves and then tore through 'Out In LA'. When the song ended, they watched in complete shock as the crowd went nuts.

Anthony Kiedis described both the show and the crowd's response as "complete anarchy and mayhem – and we destroyed the whole stage."

Flea's recollection of the one-song, three-minute-long set is equally effusive. "We got our choreography together and rocked that shit at the Rhythm Lounge and we all knew deep in our assholes that this was the real deal."

Gary Allen's cabaret mime routine had no chance, because Tony Flow were suddenly the hottest ticket in town on the strength of one song. And the crowd didn't seem to be too offended that the quartet couldn't fulfil their fervent request for an encore. There was a simple reason for that, because, as Kiedis frankly admitted, "We didn't have one."

The Rhythm Lounge's savvy owner – who paid the band the princely sum of $US50 – could spot a crowd-pulling act when he paid for one. So he asked Tony Flow And The Miraculously Majestic Masters Of Mayhem back for an encore performance the next week. "But have two songs this time," he insisted.

When the quartet returned to the Rhythm Lounge, they'd not only learned another song, but they'd gained a new name: The Red Hot Chili Peppers. As with most rock'n'roll folklore, the source of the band's name remains a mystery. Kiedis insists the tag came to him when he was walking in the Hollywood Hills and he chanced upon "a psychedelic bush that had band names on it". (While there's no evidence of said mystery bush, the band's toxic levels of drug consumption at the time could explain a lot about his so-called discovery.) The more likely explanation, however, is that their name is a bastardisation of several lesser-known acts, such as Seventies British country-rock act Chilli Willi & The Red Hot Peppers, which included future members of Elvis Costello's Attractions and no wavers Snakefinger. And jazz great Jelly Roll Morton also had a combo called The Red Hot Peppers, something that Flea would have been well aware of. Their Hot Peppers sessions, recorded in 1926, were a key moment in the evolution of jazz.

Whatever its roots, the name sounded just about perfect: there was a fiery quality to their music that the Rhythm Lounge crowd seemed to love.

By the time of their return gig, the band were well and truly prepared – they now had two songs, 'Out In LA' and 'Get Up And Jump'. At this rate they'd have a full set somewhere around the end of the decade. By the time of their third and fourth engagements, the quartet had fleshed out their repertoire to include what they were referring to as "campfire" songs, which the Peppers opted to perform a cappella. 'She'll Be Coming Round The Mountain', however, wasn't destined to be a Chili Peppers staple for much longer.

The band kept jamming songs in their apartment by day and rocking the Rhythm Lounge by night. According to Keith Barry, "This went on until they had about nine songs, and they played those for months." Soon enough, the word had started to spread: these Red Hot Chili Peppers were one of the hottest new bands in LA.

"People loved it," said Flea. "We didn't even know what we were doing, it just happened by its own force. We just started playing and it exploded. The music was unheard of. No one was doing anything like that."

Once his acid-addled brain had calmed down, Flea's observation made perfect sense. Despite the band's raw, unformed sound, their sonic melting pot of funk, rap, punk and sweaty sexuality was something brand new. And it couldn't have been further removed from what ruled the charts and box office at the time, be it the airblown synth-pop of A Flock Of Seagulls, Culture Club's 'Do You Really Want To Hurt Me', or the frat boy cheesiness of Tom Cruise's hit flick *Risky Business*. By comparison, the Red Hot Chili Peppers seemed real and dirty and damned funky – even if their dance moves weren't going to give Michael Jackson any sleepless nights.

But it was still an accident, an uncharted collision of the music that they were then soaking up like a sponge.

The way Kiedis sees it, "Nothing's ever been conscious [about the Chili Peppers], especially at that point, because we were pretty high most of the time."

While the interest in the band was great news for the Peppers, it was about to create some serious issues with their brothers in What Is This. After all, they shared two of the Peppers, Hillel Slovak and Jack Irons.

"The response to the beginning of the Chili Peppers was big," said Keith Barry. "It was instantly bigger than What Is This, who'd been working for so long. What Is This was a different concept, it was all about the music and the songs. The Chili Peppers was not all about the songs; it was about stagecraft and performance, more so than the songs."

Next up for the Chili Peppers was their biggest gig yet. They were booked to warm up the crowd for New York rappers Run-DMC at

The Mix, a club operating out of the old punk haven, The Stardust. Flea's former band, Fear, were also on the bill, along with The Circle Jerks. Within a few months, the Peppers had graduated from busting moves and rhymes in front of a few hundred startled punters at the Rhythm Lounge to this 3,500-strong gig. And the crowd at The Mix didn't really mind that the headliners, Run-DMC, were so busy with their other three LA shows that night that they didn't make the gig. Music industry operators were already talking about the Peppers after just a handful of shows.

While the Chili Peppers' reputation was growing, some things didn't change, notably the band's off-stage lifestyle. It was a wilder-than-usual time for the band-under-development, as Flea would relate in the liner notes to the 2003 reissue of the band's first, self-titled album.

"We had gotten kinda popular in Hollywood after our first few shows for doin' our own thing our own way and getting into the La Dee Da [section] in the *LA Weekly* for being partying freaks out at the [club] Zero til dawn all the time, rubbing body parts with the Hollywood underground elite."

Kiedis and Flea were the two members of the group who just couldn't live fast enough; their "anything goes" attitude was intensifying as they started to earn a few dollars, especially when it came to drug-taking (Slovak wasn't far behind). Flea, who was now sporting a pink mohawk, also had trouble controlling his mouth, such as the time he was walking in his neighbourhood and gave the finger to what he called a group of "redneck guys". They stopped, turned around and promptly beat the stuffing out of the mouthy bassist.

By the time he returned home, "seeing stars and all bloody", his housemate and bandmate, Slovak, took one look at his friend and was ready to kick a little redneck ass.

"I walked in the door," Flea remembered, "and Hillel was stirring a big pot of lentils. He was like, 'What happened?' and he was holding up this lentil spoon and I said, 'Oh man, these guys kicked my ass,' and he was like, 'Let's go get them.' And he just looked so skinny and he had lentils and I was like, 'Dude, forget it, there's nothing we can do.'"

Clearly the band that plays together fights together – or at least that was the case until the Chili Peppers' light started to shine more brightly than that of What Is This. It was the first real rift between this

Californian band of brothers. It was hard for Slovak and Irons – now members of both bands – to accept that this joke band called The Red Hot Chili Peppers had suddenly become a hot property in LA; already record label talent scouts had been spotted trying to blend into the crowds at their shows. What Is This were a far more serious outfit, they'd been playing for much longer than the Peppers – and they definitely weren't formed for a one-off show and a laugh. What they lacked was the Chili Peppers' wild sexuality and their open invitation to have a good time all the time. According to Alain Johannes, "We weren't quite as outlandish onstage; we were more serious musically."

The four friends – Kiedis, Slovak, Flea and Irons – were starting to understand the fickle nature of both music and the music business: credibility didn't always count when you had a human firebrand for a lead singer and a truly distinctive – if raw and unformed – sound. It also didn't hurt that the usually shirtless Kiedis was starting to get some serious attention from female fans.

Through the autumn of 1983, the Chili Peppers secured a residency at the LA club Cathay de Grand. What Is This and the Peppers even shared a bill in September at Club Lingerie, which was unusual, because they typically made every effort to avoid conflicting schedules, allowing Irons and Slovak to work with both bands.

It was at a Club Lingerie Chili Peppers show that *LA Times* music critic, Robert Hilburn, turned up to see this much-talked-about new band. He wasn't wildly impressed by what he saw. The Chili Peppers remain convinced that Hilburn's negative take on the band put them on the outer with music critics for much of their career. Over the years they would find it much harder to score positive reviews than sell records and fill venues.

According to Flea, "Robert Hilburn came to see us . . . and we said a bunch of obnoxious things and he hated us. And because he hates us, it's like we don't exist." Interestingly, Hilburn – still a very influential and eloquent voice at the *LA Times* – doesn't recall the specific show, but insists that a far better relationship now exists between him and the band.

"I remember vaguely thinking they were silly at the time," he told me, "but I don't remember what I said. I have exchanged very nice emails with Flea since that article – he's really a charming guy."

Another LA-based writer, Harvey Kubernik, who was then writing for UK mag *Melody Maker,* was equally uninspired by their early shows. "I saw the band at the Music Machine in west LA a couple of times in the early Eighties," he told me. "I really wasn't that impressed. It was raw, but did not seem that original. There was mild applause."

At the time of Hilburn's negative review, tension was really building in the What Is This camp. It was inevitable that, given the attention that the Chili Peppers were now receiving, Irons and Slovak would soon have to make a decision as to which band they favoured.

As Flea read the situation, "All of a sudden people were starting to take us seriously – management, lawyers trying to get us contracts and shit."

Amongst these interested players was Mark "Rooster" Richardson, a journeyman studio engineer. He'd made a career out of surfacing at the right place at the most interesting times. When he was based in New York during the mid-Seventies, he spotted the first wave of US punk bands, including Patti Smith, Television and The Ramones. In 1976 he was in London when The Sex Pistols stormed, kicking and screaming, out of Malcolm McLaren's Sex boutique, snarling, "God save the Queen/ She ain't no human being." Back Stateside, he'd engineered and produced *No Regrets*, the album by San Fran bar band SVT, which included ex-Jefferson Airplane bassist Jack Casady. He'd also engineered the self-titled LP from Georgia-based four piece The Brains, a record notable mainly for the original version of 'Money Changes Everything', soon to be a smash hit for Cyndi Lauper.

Richardson was steered in the Peppers' direction by a friend, a director who had worked with Blackie Dammett. He checked them out at what he later referred to as "this strange bar in LA, not at all the sort of place you'd expect to find a band like The Red Hot Chili Peppers playing." Richardson was blown away by the band's dangerous energy and Kiedis' sexual bravado; he saw their potential and knew he had to get involved with them somehow. He met the band and within days had organised some time for them at Bijou Studios.

As the Chili Peppers prepared themselves for their debut studio experience, they were booked for a show at The Kit Kat Club. It was a show that would have a huge impact on the band's party boy rep for years to come.

Even for a group as sexually liberated as the Chili Peppers, this was one weird gig. As soon as they launched into their standard opener, 'Out In LA' – one of the maybe half a dozen songs that made up their set – semi-naked dancers gyrated around them, greedily steering the crowd's attention away from their music. When their set was over, the Peppers were struggling to come up with a tactic to regain the crowd's interest and leave some kind of lasting impression.

It was then that Kiedis remembered his old "sock on cock" stunt. Slovak, Irons, Kiedis and Flea quickly agreed that it was the perfect routine; after all, this was a strip club. Quickly, they stripped off, attached socks and returned to the stage for their regular encore, a barn-storming take on Jimi Hendrix's 'Fire'. "And brother, let me tell you," Kiedis would recount, "when we came out of that little dressing room backstage, we were levitating with nervous energy. I could not find my feet on the stage. We just had this look in our eyes like we were from outer space."

"It was a spontaneous thing to do that," observed Keith Barry, "and it became a signature thing for the band."

The club patrons were stunned, likewise the dancers. But The Kit Kat Club's manager wasn't so enthralled. According to Flea, afterwards he raced up to the band screaming, "No pubes! I told you guys no pubes!"

The idea that pubic hair was a no-show zone in a strip club was something that hadn't occurred to the high-flying four. Not that they cared, because they laughed themselves all the way home after the show. But as they packed away their gear, they were met by Lindy Goetz, who was a friend of Richardson's then brother-in-law. A former drummer – "as close as I could get to being a rock star," he told me – Goetz was a keen music industry player, having worked in promotions with such labels as MCA and Mercury; he'd also spent time with Screen Gems EMI before setting up his own production company. He'd spent 12 years in the business.

"I knew the inner workings of a record company," he told me. Goetz could see the raw potential in the Peppers as soon as they hit the Kit Kat stage – even before they strapped on their socks. "They were painted green," he recalled, laughing, "like worms or something. And they were out of their fucking minds." Goetz proposed managing the band on the spot and they agreed.

The Kit Kat show was a handy education for the band, who learned that there was nothing more effective than flashing some flesh to make an impact on a jaded audience. But as the Peppers would also learn, they would fast become known mainly for all the wrong reasons: now there was just as much interest in their dick-swinging antics as their music. Kiedis may have started talking up the band's sex-funk style, but to many The Red Hot Chili Peppers were LA knuckleheads who shocked as much as rocked. Regardless, the local music press were fast becoming big fans.

What they needed to rectify this perception problem were some recorded songs. So their next stop was the Bijou Studios, where they were helped out by Spit Stix, Flea's former bandmate in Fear, who'd kept in touch with Flea after they both left Lee Ving's gang of anarchists.

Of course the band needed more than Richardson and Goetz's zeal (and Stix's assistance) to help cut these demos. They needed some cash. Kiedis had by now moved on from his job at the film company and was employed at a computer graphics operation. His workmates were, as Flea would describe, "these meticulously anal retentive gay guys who cruised Santa Monica Boulevard for boys". Kiedis managed to coerce some money from his employers and the band were ready to (Flea's words again) "get our shit on tape".

Flea had approached Stix about helping out on the demos; at the time he was working on his own music in Studio 9, a low-rent, 16-track studio in Hollywood. Stix was an LA player; he'd heard about his buddy Flea and the Chili Peppers and had checked them out both on stage and in rehearsal. He loved what he called "the dark funk element of the early line-up". And, admittedly, he had nothing else going on right then.

"I was free," he admitted.

He assisted with production for the session, where the band spat out five raw, rocking demos – 'Green Heaven', 'Out In LA', 'Get Up And Jump', 'Sex Rap' and 'Baby Appeal'. All these songs, bar 'Sex Rap', would appear on their upcoming debut album. Much later, these demos (with the exception of 'Baby Appeal') would turn up in their more natural form on the *Out In LA* collection of outtakes and Peppers ephemera.

Typically, it wasn't all work when the band started to lay down the demos. Stix recalled how one night he was intensely focused on mixing the tracks when he overheard this strange squeaking sound coming from somewhere nearby. As it turned out, it definitely wasn't some resident studio rodent.

He laughs when he recalls what he saw. "I turned down the music to see what it was and looked up to see Flea's naked body humping the control room window from out in the studio."

And this time he'd dispensed with a sock on his cock.

Stix, sadly, had little to do with the rapidly rising Chili Peppers after helping with their first studio session. He did help them secure their EMI record deal, and for a time assisted with sound and lighting at their early shows, but he and the band fell out of contact after that.

"As you might think," he admitted to me, "I was a little disappointed when I wasn't used beyond the first demos."

When it came to the demos themselves, the five tracks were definitely works in progress. There was little in the way of tunes, but that was to some level offset by the quartet's barely restrained energy. 'Get Up And Jump' was a ramshackle funky jam – clearly a firestarter when taken live – that was elevated by Flea's lightning-fingered basslines and some slithery playing from Slovak. As far as Kiedis' vocals were concerned, it was as though he was trying to spit out as many words as humanly possible in the song's two minutes and 36 seconds. He sang as if every lungful of oxygen were his last. His breathless, virtually indecipherable rap was punctuated by such Pulitzer Prize-worthy lines as, "Say what? You got a pumpkin in your pants?"

Grandmaster Flash might have turned Kiedis on to hip-hop, but this wasn't 'The Message' by any stretch.

As for the lyrics in 'Green Heaven' – a stoner's anthem that was almost Cheech & Chong-worthy – Flea was sufficiently thrilled to write that, "I was so in love with Anthony's words . . . they used to make us laugh like shit." In fact, Flea was so inspired by his buddy's work that he would telephone his friends and read the lyrics to them. Once he even called his mother and recited the lyrics of 'Green Heaven' to her over the phone. Admittedly, the lyric is a far cry from 'Jump''s "pumpkins in pants", as Kiedis somehow finds the breath to squeeze in references to the Ku Klux Klan, L Ron Hubbard, dolphins, corrupt politicians, VD, smack and The Three Stooges. And he also manages to construct a cop-baiting rhyme that makes mention of beating black ass, which was guaranteed to rile the LAPD. It was one of the first times Kiedis had sung of anything other than his studliness; he was now writing about tough living in his adopted hometown of Los Angeles, a theme he'd revisit many times over the years.

"Our sound and our energy is fairly unique to a specific area of Los Angeles – Hollywood," Kiedis would explain. "The growing up experience in Hollywood is very intense because there is so much going on there, so much beauty and tragedy at the same time, that the sensory input is phenomenal."

As for the rest of the demos, their Rhythm Club favourite, 'Out In LA', was another punk-funk jam in overdrive, powered by herky-jerky rhythms and the band's ferocious drive. It was as though they were bursting out of their skins as they played, which explained why they'd become such a hot live ticket virtually overnight. That zeal didn't quite transfer to the studio – apart from 'Green Heaven' there was a marked sameness to the songs – but the demos were good enough to motivate Goetz to jump in his car and start shopping the band to the major labels.

The band were equally excited by their first studio session. Flea experienced what he would call a "beautiful feeling" on the day of recording. "I distinctly remember looking over at Hillel, the messiah, and feeling like I was floating." (Helped no doubt by the copious amounts of weed he and the band were consuming at the time.)

"There was really nothing else like this music at the time – or ever for that matter, not to stroke myself too much," Flea would add. "It came out of pure love, which is the most powerful thing in the world. I'm sure this demo tape is the best recording I was ever a part of."

Kiedis agreed. "The finest recordings we ever did was our first demo tape. That captured some of the more intense Red Hot feel."

Drummer Irons' reflections were, typically, more measured and less fantastical than his bandmates, although he would admit that "the demo tapes definitely had something that the later records didn't."

Twenty years later, Keith Barry isn't so sure. He's not entirely convinced that the band has ever accurately captured their live energy on tape. "I always thought that the best of the Chili Peppers was the stagecraft, the antics, the spontaneity. I'm not sure they've ever translated that into the studio," he told me.

By the time they had the tape in their hands, Kiedis, Flea and Slovak had moved base again. They were now living at what the trio called "the Land of Lee", in a part of town known as "Pot Alley", where dealers shifted dime bags downstairs. (Eventually the Peppers had to leave because Flea burned down the kitchen and their pet kittens crapped all over the apartment.) They'd play their demo to anyone who would stop and listen. At one point they even hitched a ride in the back of a truck to New York, in the hope that their demo would swing them some live work.

"We couldn't get gigs," Kiedis said, "so we just went out into the parks and played our music there out of a boom box. The first thing we noticed was that little kids started dancing. That was a little revelation right there."

Flea would also recall how children seemed to particularly take to the Chili Peppers. "Ya know," he would say, "baby appeal."

Lindy Goetz, meanwhile, continued shopping around their demo, taking meetings with any label that would listen to him. Finding them a deal, however, wasn't that easy. "Some labels were interested but the band was just so weird," he says.

Finally, by November 1983, Goetz had helped stitch up a seven album/seven year deal with Enigma, a subsidiary of EMI America. The Chili Peppers were exactly six months old.

This was a brave new world for the Chili Peppers, whose goals in 1984 were more about survival than global domination. In fact, Flea's biggest ambition at the time was filling Perkins Palace, a 2,000 capacity venue in LA. "I thought, 'One day, if I could just be in a band that could play there, that would be the ultimate.' I never dreamed The Red Hot Chili Peppers would become a pop band."

Kiedis' goals were even less grand: he just wanted to eat on a regular basis. "For years," he said, "Flea and I roamed around the city not having any idea how we were going to go about eating lunch or dinner. When we first hooked up with our manager, we said, 'If you want to manage us, you have to make sure that we eat every day.' That was the big thing. We never had money of our own or houses or cars or anything like that."

Flea backs that up, recalling in the liner notes for their reissued debut album how he and Kiedis would call Goetz, insisting that they needed to have a business meeting, ideally "at that Chinese restaurant for some of that mushu duck". His next request would be for weed.

"We actually really liked Lindy," Flea insisted. "It wasn't like he was a mark or anything. We were just hungry."

Goetz, a very good-natured man, agrees. "I could see that they needed someone to take them out for lunch – and dinner."

It was only when the band met up with Enigma's Jamie Cohen that the gravity of the situation sank in. In typical Flea fashion, his first response to seeing Cohen was to scream the words of The Sex Pistols' inflammatory anthem 'EMI' straight to his face. When Cohen presented Flea with both a tolerant grin and a handshake, the punky bassman had an awakening. "It really dawned on me that we were gonna make a record. It was kind of shocking."

The band wouldn't end up fulfilling their seven album contract with the label, and their split would not be amicable, but signing with EMI America at the time made reasonable sense. A division of Capitol Records, the American home of The Beatles' enormously profitable back catalogue, EMI America had recently hit the jackpot with David Bowie's latest album, *Let's Dance*, which – despite its now dated production – had resurrected both The Thin White Duke and his career.

Enigma was the edgier side of the EMI corporate machine. During the label's life it was home to not just the Chili Peppers, who were definitely an unknown quantity commercially, but such unclassifiable (and commercially unpredictable) acts as Wire, Keith Levene (a former member of both The Clash and John Lydon's PiL), Red Flag and Renegade Soundwave. And EMI was also the UK label for strident anti-capitalists the Gang Of Four, whose leader Andy Gill was about to become entangled in the Chili Peppers' life, if only for a short time.

In hindsight, Goetz could see that the label just didn't understand the magic of the Peppers. "They weren't bad boys, they were wild boys," he explained. "It was fun. They were The Three Stooges of rock. EMI were a nice bunch of guys, but they didn't have a clue. They could sell Richard Marx, sure – but I don't really think they liked the guys in the band. Slash would have been a better label, possibly."

As they were swept up in the excitement of signing the deal, the Chili Peppers had continued delaying the inevitable showdown with What Is This, their sonic soulmates. Irons and Slovak had a crucial decision to make: do they stick with these rough yet undeniably hot Peppers, or fulfil their more serious musical ambitions with What Is This? That decision became especially urgent when MCA Records – the American label to heavyweights The Who and Elton John – signed the band.

The way Alain Johannes read the situation, Slovak and Irons actually wanted to stay and play with both bands, an arrangement that he is sure both Flea and Kiedis would have agreed to. Johannes, however, told his sometimes bandmates that this kind of split arrangement wouldn't work out, especially now that both bands had record deals. There would also be the more complex business complications of royalty overrides and release agreements to work through. Irons and Slovak reluctantly agreed and remained in What Is This.

Irons' take on the decision was that it was all about loyalty: after all, they'd been with Anthym and then What Is This since their time at Fairfax High.

Flea had a surprisingly well-balanced take on the drama that was unfolding. "So when the Chili Peppers got offered a record contract, What Is This got offered a record contract. And Jack and Hillel had been playing for at least six years. So what were they supposed to do: go with the joke band that got a deal after six months, or with the band they dedicated themselves to for six years? So they went with What Is This, which is completely understandable."

Keith Barry could see the tension developing between this tight group of friends. "It became apparent that the Chili Peppers were going to have some work, make a record, do this stuff. With Jack and Hillel and Alain there was this great deal of loyalty; they'd worked together for a long, long time and so a choice had to be made. Jack and Hillel chose to do What Is This and Flea chose to do the Chili Peppers with Anthony. I think that strained relationships a lot for a while."

Kiedis' response to the departure of Slovak and Irons was much less composed. He was gutted. The Chili Peppers were about to go into the studio and half the band – his two buddies, no less – were walking out. He went home and cried.

"I cried because I was so happy to finally be in a band and to be strutting my flesh around town, and for my friends to fall out like that . . . I thought we were over. I was emotionally devastated."

EMI America were aware of the sudden crisis within the band, but also needed to get rolling with their new signing. After all, who knew how hot the Peppers would be in a few months' time? They gave Kiedis and Flea a couple of months to recruit and regroup; they needed them in the studio by early 1984. The pair quickly put out the word that they needed a new guitarist and drummer – and needed them very quickly. First up they hired drummer Cliff Martinez.

Martinez's path to the Chili Peppers was long and twisted. A native of Columbus, Ohio, he'd first drummed in a variety of Top 40 cover bands. It was a time in his life that Martinez would recall by saying, "The apex of a musician's career would be to play Vegas. My good gigs were playing Ramada Inns, 10 Neil Diamond cover songs a night." Several years older than the other Peppers, Martinez had moved to LA in 1976. Soon after arriving he enrolled in the Dick Grove Music School; he then played in a combo peddling George Benson covers. His punk rock conversion came very much by chance. It was 1980 and he and the Benson wannabes were rehearsing at the very low-rent Wiltshire Fine Arts building, when an ungodly racket started to ooze through the walls.

"Everybody stopped playing and held their noses," he would recall. "We wanted to see what was making this awful cacophony."

Luckily, the adjacent room had a window. Inside was LA punk band The Screamers, notable mainly for the maniacal onslaught of vocalist Tomata du Plenty.

"Tomata's face was beet red," says Martinez. "I thought the music was an affront. It was threatening to me; I hated it. Then I saw how sincere and how passionate they were about it, and I just turned on a dime. I went from hating it to loving it. And that's when I started checking out punk rock."

Gigs with The Tenants, The Weirdos, The Dickies and Lydia Lunch soon followed. Martinez was briefly a member of Captain Beefheart's band, thumping the tubs on 1982's *Ice Cream For Crow*, the last album Beefheart made before retiring to the desert to paint. While Martinez admired Beefheart's music, he wasn't especially taken by the man.

"He was a real abusive tyrant, always blaming me for 'psychic interference'. He would get really angry: 'Man, he's puttin' tinfoil in my radar!'"

Martinez was a friend of Flea's, who invited him to join the Peppers without the need for an audition. At the time, Martinez was playing in an outfit called 2 Balls And A Bat, which comprised two drummers, a guitarist, a drum machine and a four-track tape player. "It was self-indulgent, arty and weird," he recalled. Martinez was a Peppers fan, but he also felt that by joining the band he would be able to sharpen his funk-drumming chops.

"I loved funk music and hadn't played in a band that was into that heavily," he told me. "I thought it would be a big adjustment. It was a style that I wanted to be good at, but I didn't think it was my strong suit at the time."

Dozens of hopeful guitarists auditioned for Slovak's former role, and they eventually hired Jack Sherman, a guitarist of Russian/Jewish heritage. Born in Florida, Sherman had an itinerant youth – his father was an electrical engineer – having lived in New Jersey, Allentown in Pennsylvania, Rochester, New York and then San Diego. He'd played in such little-known outfits as Andy & The Rattlesnakes and new wavers All Night, before playing band leader in Toni & The Movers, who were fronted by belter Toni Childs. He'd also toured with legendary rootsman John Hiatt in 1982, and then Graham Parker, and had opened for Oingo Boingo, the LA outfit who once shared a bill with Fax City hopefuls Anthym.

Sherman was part of LA's burgeoning new wave scene in the late Seventies and early Eighties, as was his sister, a singer/songwriter with the stage name of Gail Warning. It was Gail who tipped off Sherman to the Chili Peppers' vacancy. Speaking in 2004, Sherman still vividly remembers his Peppers' audition, and the warning signs he feels he should have noticed from the get-go. For starters, there was no Anthony Kiedis. And the audition was held in deepest Hollywood, at what he calls a "crash pad-cum-rehearsal room" at the rear of the house of Addie Brik, who was Hillel Slovak's girlfriend.

"We're jamming in the key of E, the requisite funk jam," Sherman recalled. "And Flea's shaking his head from side to side violently, he's pounding the bass, he's in maniac mode – I didn't know whether to stare with my mouth hanging open or keep playing my guitar. It was so intense. I thought, 'This is somewhat appealing,' even though it wasn't anything new. It was pretty minimalistic."

After what he thought was a successful jam, Sherman didn't hear from the band for a couple of weeks, so he called Flea back and was invited along for a follow-up jam. This was even more forebidding than his first Peppers encounter. Lindy Goetz was there, and after another roof-raising jam in the key of E, he approached Sherman. "How in the world do you play like that?" he asked him.

"Then Flea came up and said, 'It's going to be hard keeping up with you man.' I had a feeling I'd be invited to join this band, but aren't we

74

brothers, don't we collaborate? What did that mean? He should have said, 'Hey man, you sound great.' Maybe that was his way of saying that, but I think it was a red flag."

Sherman still accepted the offer to become a Pepper, a move that he has ambivalent feelings about even today. He readily admits that the fact that the Peppers had a record deal "was a huge incentive in my joining the band".

Many years later, Lindy Goetz could see the mistake the band made in hiring Sherman. "Jack was an amazingly talented player, a schooled player, but not a Chili Pepper. He just didn't fit. He shouldn't have been in the band, but we were desperate."

The musical fit wasn't especially tight, and Sherman already had some reservations about these Red Hot Chili Peppers, but he and Martinez were ready and available, and the Peppers really needed to seize the moment (and EMI's cash) and start recording. Sherman and Cliff Martinez – soon to be nicknamed The Phantom, for his ability to mysteriously disappear after gigs – were hired.

Kiedis called a band meeting and spelled out the Peppers' mission statement to the new recruits. "What we set out to do," he told them, "is to be complete and utter perpetrators of hardcore, bone-crunching mayhem sex things from heaven."

But both Kiedis and Flea had uncertainties; how could these two guys fit into a musical brotherhood that had taken root seven years back in the music room of Fairfax High? As Kiedis admitted, "To try and describe that [game plan] to another musician, and have it mean something, is nearly impossible unless you've grown up with that person." His words would prove to be very true.

CHAPTER THREE

"That's homo!"

IN theory, the recruitment of former Gang Of Four guitarist Andy Gill to produce the Chili Peppers' debut album made perfect sense. Like the Chili Peppers, The Gang Of Four's mission was to merge danceable rhythms with hard-edged, uncompromising rock'n'roll. There was more than one George Clinton/Parliament/Funkadelic record in the collections of these guys from the north of England, even if they had to share shelf space with weighty tomes on politics and social upheaval. There was also the underlying influence of dub-reggae in the sound of The Gang Of Four, along with a certain pop sensibility, which possibly stemmed from the fact that their bassist, Dave Allen, was a veteran of disco cover bands.

Named as much for their fraternal bond as a nod to the counter-revolutionary faction led by the widow of Mao Tse-Tung, The Gang Of Four emerged from Leeds University in 1977 (with the exception of Allen, who answered a bassist-wanted ad in the music papers). They were peers of such British bands as The Mekons, The Au Pairs and The Fall – and the voice of frontman Jon King had the same flat, rambling tone as The Fall's Mark E Smith. The influence of their fellow post-punkers was undeniable.

Like many of their contemporaries, The Gang Of Four wanted you to dance (or at least twitch uncontrollably) and think at the same time. But unlike most bands who were searching for the missing link between the physical and the political, they were able to fuse the two without too much pain, most successfully in such early songs as 'Love Like Anthrax' and 'Damaged Goods', and their 1979 long-playing debut, *Entertainment!*

But there was one crucial difference in outlook between the Chili Peppers and Andy Gill's Gang Of Four, a difference that would become painfully clear once band and producer convened in the studio. The Gang Of Four were as cerebral as they were physical – one critic accurately described their music as "neo-Marxist funk". The only Marx that interested the Red Hot Chili Peppers was the family of Groucho, Chico and Harpo. While Andy Gill was a serious, studious middle-class Brit, Flea and Kiedis, in particular, were Hollywood punks who wanted to rock hard, party even harder and get higher than the sun.

Andy Gill's slash-and-burn style of guitar playing formed a key part of The Gang Of Four's sound. Revered US music writer Greil Marcus noted how "his instrument spat out chords like sparks". Gill also knew when to play nothing, often choosing extended silences in deference to the deeply funky rhythms of bassist Allen and drummer Hugo Burnham. Gill also co-wrote most of the band's lyrics with King.

He once produced a seemingly innocuous line – "the rubbers that you hide in your top pocket", from the song 'At Home He's A Tourist' – that led to the band being dropped from the influential *Top Of The Pops* TV show. And in keeping with punk's DIY spirit, Gill also co-designed much of the band's hilarious cover art.

By the time of their third album, 1982's *Songs Of The Free*, Allen had left the band to form the funkier, less intense Shriekback, while Gill, King and Burnham soldiered on. But when they recorded 1983's *Hard* with American engineering/production vets Ron and Howard Albert (who had worked with The Allman Brothers Band, Aretha Franklin and Crosby, Stills & Nash, amongst others), Gill and King found themselves drummer-less. They were cheekily re-christened The Gang Of Two. The band folded in 1984, playing their final show at a college campus north of San Francisco. It was a long way from Leeds University.

When working on their final album, the band had begun to tinker with drum machines, beat-keeping devices that were then considered cutting-edge technology.* The use of drum machines was a problem that Gill would soon have to address when he worked with The Red Hot Chili Peppers; he wanted to use new technology, they wanted to

---

* British Goth doomsters, The Sisters Of Mercy, were so enamoured of their drum machine that they treated it like another member of the band. They named it Doktor Avalanche.

keep it funky and organic. Looking back almost 20 years after the recording of what would become *The Red Hot Chili Peppers*, Gill acknowledges that the album "sounds of its time", but defends himself against long-standing accusations from Flea and Kiedis who believed that he was trying to make a hit record by using whatever was required.

"I don't think it's a fair observation," he told me.

Guitarist Jack Sherman agrees, going so far as to admit that he was involved in a pre-production meeting with Gill where the idea of using drum machines was floated. There were no objections raised.

"Why didn't they [Kiedis and Flea] say 'thank you, no thank you' and move on?" he asked. "They didn't realise that they had any power; they didn't realise they had any choices. Was it because he was the only producer available?"

Completely unaware of the serious confrontation that lay ahead of them, Kiedis and Flea, in particular, were thrilled by the prospect of working with Gill, as was drummer Martinez. They were big fans of The Gang Of Four's first two albums, *Entertainment!* and 1981's *Solid Gold*. Flea, in particular, was very public about his love for the albums, which he'd first heard when sharing the Formosa Pad with Kiedis and Keith Barry.

"We loved and looked up to Andy Gill so much," Flea would declare, "and those first couple of Gang Of Four records he made definitely stand up as some of the great all-time rock records [and] definitely [were a] big influence on us. Those are great records."

Gill's bass-playing partner, David Allen, was probably an even bigger personal influence on Flea. When they finally met, during the 1992 Lollapalooza tour, Flea confessed that his own bass playing technique owed a huge debt to the chops that he "borrowed" from The Gang Of Four's first two albums.[*]

So there was no debate when EMI and Lindy Goetz spoke about working with Gill. And there were also corporate links between The Gang Of Four, who were signed to EMI in the UK, and the Chili Peppers, who were with Enigma, a part of EMI America. This made the deal much easier to close – although Jack Sherman played a wild

---

[*] Having said that – and without taking too much away from Allen – generously praising the work of others is a specialty of Flea's.

card at the time by suggesting that the band approach Jimmy Page to work on the album, even though his idea was rejected. The Doors' keyboardist Ray Manzarek had also met with the band, backstage at The Whisky in LA, with a view to producing the album, but nothing came of that either.

Although Lindy Goetz remembers otherwise, Gill insists that the connection between him and the band was untouched by the greedy hands of business. Kiedis and Flea were huge fans and wanted to hang with one of their idols. It was that simple.

"Flea and Anthony told me many times that The Gang Of Four song 'Not Great Men' was the most central song for them getting into music and forming a band. I think the fact that The Gang Of Four rocked and was rhythmic, funky, whatever, blew their minds."

As for studio experience, Gill had been involved with the production on the first two Gang Of Four albums, so he clearly wasn't new to the game. Still, there were uncertainties. Gill had resisted the temptation to officially relocate to the USA, but did spend a lot of time in the States. He also had American management. But even though The Gang Of Four had made some impression Stateside, he was an unknown quantity there as a freelance producer.

"I had no conscious thoughts of trying to break America," he told me. "I just went where it was interesting and where it was happening."

With the exception of the time they'd spent making demos with Spit Stix, the band were studio virgins. Wisely, they set themselves simple goals: they wanted to make an album that accurately reflected their on-stage urgency and anarchy. And if it became a hit in the process, then all the better. Work began on the album in the early months of 1984, with plans for a release in the third quarter of the year.

The fact that Flea and Kiedis were studio novices soon became very evident to both Gill and engineer Dave Jerden. The Chili pair had no idea as to the exact definition of a producer's role in the making of a record. Their understanding of the producer's job didn't improve as sessions for the album progressed.

According to Gill, "They saw me as a hero in the beginning of this process and they didn't quite know what to expect in the studio. They were completely green; they thought a producer just hung around and stroked their egos. Then when I started saying, 'You should do more of this and less of that,' they started going, 'Hey?'

"I've dealt with a lot of bands that were inexperienced and trying to get them to understand the [recording] process is really crucial. Sometimes you succeed better than others." This was not one of those times.

Jack Sherman described the in-studio influence of Flea and Kiedis as "destructive". "They were blowing it constantly," he told me. "I thought they were clueless." He pays tribute to Andy Gill; he's sure that without his efforts the album "would have been 14 minutes long". Sherman also defends accusations of the record sounding dated or it being geared for Eighties radio. "He [Gill] just recorded it in the sound of the day with the greatest fucking engineer in the world.

"There were good moments," Sherman adds, "they're just hard to remember."

"I had no fucking idea what we were doing in a big fancy recording studio making a big fancy record." That was Flea's assessment of their time spent cutting their self-titled debut LP. And there were problems almost from the first day that the band and Gill sat down to work through the songs in pre-production. As part of his preparation, Gill had seen the band play a Hollywood club show. While he was impressed by the sheer physicality of what he described as the "speed punk" songs they were playing, it was their more mid-tempo, slightly funkier material that excited him the most. He told the band that they should focus on those songs, which was clearly not what they had in mind.

"One of the main things that was perhaps a little contentious between us was what was the best material," Gill recalled. "To me there was no doubt that the kind of super-fast surf-punk two-minute song style was all very well, but to me it seemed kind of boring."

Gill pointed out to the band that, as far as he was concerned, such songs as 'True Men Don't Kill Coyotes' and 'Green Heaven' were far more interesting than the thrashy, apocalyptic meltdown of 'Police Helicopter'. The band were confused, because the faster they played, the crazier was the response from their fans. Surely that must be the kind of record that their followers expected from the band.

Still, Gill persevered. "I said to them, this thing here, this thing you're doing, this is what I love and this is what's going to mark you out from the crowd. If you rely on this super-fast surf-punk thing you're going to be just another west coast band with apparently dodgy politics."

The band wasn't completely sold on Gill's concept. And Gill admits that it was difficult to convince the Peppers to drop the faster, punkier material from their list of songs and concentrate on making a more balanced album. But he eventually talked them round – and then he convinced Kiedis to take singing lessons, something he sorely needed if he was to do more than yell his lungs red-raw. On stage, Kiedis could mask his vocal shortcomings with an earthy sexuality and a manic physical presence – and the band's eardrum-bursting volume – whereas in the studio Kiedis had nothing to hide his limitations.

"Yeah, there was some to-ing and fro-ing, there was a bit of, 'Yeah, but we love this shit,'" Gill said of his debates with the band during pre-production. "And the funkier kind of stuff did [eventually] get featured a lot more than what they were originally wanting – and that's what they absolutely became known for. The style and the songs that are most heavily featured on the A-side of that record went on to be more heavily developed with their second and third records. It was a route map, a blueprint, for the rest of their career."

But the conflict between Gill and Flea and Kiedis (and new recruit Sherman, as well) wasn't restricted to differences of opinion regarding musical direction. Gill's middle-class British upbringing and calm demeanour didn't sit so well with Flea and Kiedis' aggressive, 24-hour-party-people lifestyle. According to Dave Jerden, who engineered the album, "Those kids were walking testosterone." You could hardly say that about Andy Gill.

Flea would refer to Gill's "dry, holier-than-thou English way", understating how that once they started working in the studio "things didn't go as smoothly as we would of [sic] liked". Dave Jerden soon learned that he had a dual role: not only was he the album's engineer, he was the mediator in the ongoing battles between Kiedis, Flea and Gill, and the clashes between Kiedis and Sherman. It was a shock for Jerden, who was fresh from working on the What Is This' five-track debut, which had been one of the smoothest recording experiences of his career.

Like so many people who would work with the Chili Peppers, Jerden had an impressive track record. He'd been the engineer on three ground-breaking records: Brian Eno and David Byrne's *My Life In The*

Bush Of Ghosts, Talking Heads' 1980 smash, *Remain In Light* and Herbie Hancock's *Future Shock*, which included the runaway hit 'Rockit', one of the first hip-hop records to truly break through into the mainstream. All these records were powered by huge rhythms and a funky undertow, elements that were crucial to the Chili Peppers' sound and, to a lesser extent, the music of What Is This. He appeared to be the right guy for the job.

Jerden had only become involved with the two new bands by chance. He was a friend of Keith Forsey, who was Billy Idol's producer. Via a record company connection at the San Andreas label, the imprint of MCA that had signed What Is This, Forsey had recommended Jerden to work with What Is This. When Jerden learned that Alain Johannes and the rest of the band were fans of both Queen and Led Zeppelin, he couldn't sign up quickly enough.

"I knew that there was something new going on with this band," he said from his home in LA. "If you mentioned Led Zeppelin at the time that was taboo – this was the whole post-punk period. Then all of a sudden this band comes in talking about Led Zep. That's the kind of stuff I used to play when I was in bands. I was interested; Steve Moyer [an exec at the San Andreas label who'd also helped connect What Is This with Jerden] knew this and that's how it happened."

Working with What Is This had been every producer's dream. Jerden and the band spent two weeks in rehearsal at Heliotrope Studios, located in a funky, ethnic part of East Hollywood. Not only was it inexpensive to hire the rehearsal space, but Jerden could detect a real scene developing in and around the area, in part because "it was away from the flash of Sunset [Boulevard]". Soon-to-be-famous players, including various members of the band that would become Jane's Addiction, drifted in and out of the studio as What Is This readied the songs for their *Squeezed* EP. (Jerden would go on to produce and/or engineer the Addiction's two biggest albums, *Nothing's Shocking* and *Ritual de lo Habitual*.)

Jerden was particularly taken by Alain Johannes, in part because he was a Led Zeppelin fan, but also because the engineer recognised that Johannes was a major musical talent.

"This kid was an amazing player; he had an amazing musical memory. He played interesting notes and he sang great. You know, Duran Duran and Human League were on the radio, and there was punk, and here was this kid, who was obviously a talent, doing things that were so sophisticated. This was the time of Pat Benatar and they were doing this rock'n'roll thing."

Jerden was equally turned on by the guitar playing of Hillel Slovak. It also helped that Jerden, like Slovak, was a huge Jimi Hendrix devotee. He clearly had a lot in common with What Is This.

"Hillel was real quiet, a real sweet kid. And he had this thing with his playing that to me was just like Hendrix – you don't learn it, it just comes naturally. It's a real cool, liquid type of playing."

Keith Barry even compared the musical relationship between Slovak and Johannes with that of King Crimson guitarists Robert Fripp and Adrian Belew. "With one guy you can define every note, whereas the other guy is pure vibe. Alain was the chops player, Hillel provided the colour."

Yet the What Is This debut would suffer the same fate as *The Red Hot Chili Peppers* – apart from some local interest from their established fan base, no one tuned in.

Jerden summed it up simply. "The What Is This EP really didn't do anything." Nevertheless, What Is This' *Squeezed* EP would eventually leave a lasting impression many years down the line. When Jerden met such key players in the Seattle grunge/alternative scene as Alice In Chains' Jerry Cantrell and Soundgarden's Chris Cornell, they both namechecked the record as a big influence on their playing and writing. What Is This couldn't shift many units, but were destined to be a favourite of fellow musos.

Chuffed with the sessions for their EP, What Is This recommended Jerden to their Chili Pepper buddies. What they didn't know was that Jerden had already crossed paths with Kiedis and Flea, well before shifting into El Dorado Studios in early 1984. He'd encountered the punk pair holding up the bars of numerous LA clubs, when Red Hot Chili Peppers was still something that was served with tacos. He had no idea that the two wannabe scenesters would eventually get around to forming a band. "Yeah, they were always on the scene, hanging out," he said.

Jerden also recalled that, for reasons that he couldn't fathom then or now, Kiedis and Flea had taken to wearing black leather motorcycle jackets with tin teacups perched on the shoulders, like bizarre epaulettes. Flea and Kiedis would call these strange embellishments "the brothers cups". If nothing else, it helped them stand out amongst the freaks and casualties that wandered up and down Sunset like members of some lost generation. 'The Brothers Cup' also became the title of a track on their second album, *Freaky Styley*.

"It was the strangest thing," Jerden laughed when asked about their relevance. "I have no idea what the teacups meant. And they were rambunctious – they used to walk into restaurants and just hassle yuppies and scream at them. They were totally obnoxious kids; they were brats."*

When Jerden checked out the fledgling Red Hot Chili Peppers playing live, he recognised their raw, nascent talent. They were wild and loud and incredibly exciting – it felt as though anything could happen at a Chili Peppers show. But the main problem when they reached the studio, as Jerden read the situation, was that Andy Gill "wanted to do more of a dance record", whereas "people were into the Chili Peppers because they made a noise, they were wild – Flea was like an animal on stage, as was Anthony. They [Gill and the band] were fire and ice."

The band and Gill agreed to compromise and experiment with one commercially minded cut called 'Human Satellite'. As Martinez recalled, Gill had asked for "just one thing with some chord changes and a melody". The results were dreadful. "It terrified all of us," said Martinez. "It was a commercial version of ourselves that we didn't like. Everybody in the band despised it." The song was quickly ditched. Band and producer also argued over the use of brass and backing vocals, mainly because they didn't mesh with the Peppers' "punk rock aesthetic", as Martinez explained to me. "Andy was in a different headspace; he really wanted to make a commercial record."

Just like most of the Peppers, Dave Jerden was a big Gang Of Four fan, but he simply couldn't equate the implacable producer with whom he was now working and the angry, passionate music that had been generated by the hugely influential British band. However, after one particularly tense session, Jerden did change his opinion of Andy Gill. The producer was locked in a discussion with Jack Sherman and was

---

* Jack Sherman believes "the brothers cups" "was some [kind of] fashion statement. They'd bang them together violently."

having great difficulty explaining to the guitarist what he felt was required for the song they were working on. Gill decided that the only solution was to play the part himself.

"There was a solo needed," Jerden recalled, "so Andy walks over, picks up the guitar and just blasts away. Everyone sat there, stunned. He was very calm, taking all this crap from the band, then in one minute he did this amazing thing."

When pushed to sum up the entire recording experience of the Chili Peppers' debut, Jerden dismisses it as "one of the most God-awful experiences of my life". As he remembers it, Kiedis and Flea would launch constant tirades of abuse at the mild-mannered Gill. They'd sometimes lean over the recording console, with their faces pressed right up against Gill's, and scream insults and obscenities directly at him. To everyone's astonishment, Gill would continue working. Their insults just bounced off him.

"They'd be saying, 'We hate you – fuck off and die!' They treated him poorly."

Jerden was amazed by Gill's ability to stay completely calm during these abusive onslaughts. It was as if he were made of stone; he was completely unruffled by their verbal attacks, at least externally. Jerden's take on Gill was that he was "a total English gentleman. I'd be arguing with them [Kiedis and Flea] and he'd be oblivious to what was going on. He was totally together, he was amazing." Cliff Martinez agrees. "He was pretty much a gentleman, he kept a stiff upper lip. He didn't let his emotions get in the way."

But the ongoing struggle became an outright war when Jack Sherman started to side with the producer regarding the direction the album was taking. He felt that if there was anyone in the studio who knew what was needed, it was Gill. Sherman was very quickly on the outer with the already livid Kiedis and Flea.

"They did not like him," Jerden understated.

As for Gill, he remembers Kiedis and Flea as wild kids. "They were pretty out of control, yeah."

Gill recalls that there was some drug use going on in the studio during the sessions, but was sure "there was more going on out of sight of me." Martinez confirms that plenty of pot was smoked, but he doesn't know of any other use/abuse.

"I know Flea was an enthusiastic dabbler in just about everything," he told me. "[But] I never saw the evidence of Anthony's heavy drug using."

Yet Kiedis would sometimes disappear from the sessions, often for two or three days. At times he was so detached from the band that Jack Sherman admits he barely got to know Kiedis at all during his stint as a Chili Pepper. "That was one of the sad things in the band: he [Kiedis] was never around much and I never got to know him, apart from being on the receiving end of his indifference or his hostility. Whereas with Flea I could sense a more tender soul there."

Going AWOL was a bad habit that in the following years would create such serious friction between Kiedis and his fellow Peppers that the band very nearly imploded.

Gill dealt with Kiedis' drug use in typical fashion: he simply carried on. The way he read the situation, "We never fingered drugs as a problem, and when Anthony would disappear, I'd just get on with it [recording]. There was always other stuff to do; you didn't have to have the singer there all the time."

When Gill was finished for the day, he would usually retire to the bar around the corner from El Dorado Studios (which he remembers as "an old, fairly funky studio that's now a car park"). He probably wasn't too taken by the scene at the studio, anyway. El Dorado was the setting for a constant flow of human traffic, with people such as comedian Robin Williams hanging around the studio's corridors. Dave Jerden was amazed by the commotion that was going on while the Chili Peppers were trying to record. "The craziest bunch of people would hang out there," he told me.

Gill had attempted to spend some downtime with the band, but was put off by their very first social outing. Flea and Kiedis had promised to take their producer "somewhere special where you'll have the coolest food ever". Gill was intrigued and quickly agreed to get together with the pair. But the two Peppers' idea of a night of fine dining was to take Gill to Pink's, a famous LA hot dog stand. "And that was their ultimate food at the time," Gill recalled with a laugh.

But the trouble ran deeper than confusion about their individual roles, their conflict over musical direction or the band's choice of exactly what defined a great meal. Much of the problem was within the band themselves. Flea and Kiedis felt that the record wasn't an accurate document of how they sounded on stage. At one stage, a clearly frustrated Gill even suggested they hire a mobile rig and record the band's next show and release that as the album. Jack Sherman laughed at the idea. "I thought, 'God forbid! This is one of the worst live bands I've ever seen or been in.'" Kiedis and Flea's dream solution would have been to try to bring Slovak and Irons into the sessions and recapture the wild energy of the original demos that they had cut with Spit Stix. But there was no way that their label had the luxury of time or the budget to help unravel the messy legalities of trying to re-hire their two original members. The reaction of Kiedis and Flea was to behave badly and almost derail the sessions.

While Cliff "The Phantom" Martinez was loved by all – Flea spoke fondly of the man both during and after his Pepper-time; Gill felt he was "a super cool drummer" – Jack Sherman wasn't treated so well by his fellow Peppers. He was an outsider who loved funk music, wasn't hot for punk, ate macrobiotic food and admitted to being "naïve" when it came to drugs. According to Gill, Kiedis and Flea described his taste in food as "homo", a favourite, much-used insult of theirs at the time. Flea and Kiedis would tease Sherman endlessly about his "weird" eating habits and his reluctance to get wild and behave as badly as his bandmates.

"I think Jack Sherman had problems with the band on a psychological kind of level," Gill said. "Flea and Anthony picked on him a lot, just for fun, really."

Sherman remains unsure of the exact cause of his poor relationship with Kiedis and his fallings-out with Flea. "Maybe they smelled condescension because I didn't like the music they liked," he told me. "I must have had a nasty attitude or something – maybe they felt like they were looking in a mirror. I don't know."

Although it has never been recognised before, Gill insists that it was Sherman who turned Kiedis and Flea onto the joys of pure funk, which would become such an integral part of the band's sound. Martinez confirms that. Kiedis and Flea might have boasted about their love for Defunkt, but their tastes in 1984 still ran to harder-edged music, such as The Germs and Gill's own Gang Of Four. Not long after their debut was completed, Sherman would introduce the band to George Clinton – who would become a firm favourite of the Peppers, both as a funkmaster and as a mentor-cum-buddy. Clinton would eventually produce the Peppers' second album.

Gill told me that Kiedis and Flea "didn't know who George Clinton was until Jack Sherman told them."

"As far as I know they were completely ignorant of George Clinton," Sherman told me (although Martinez insists that Kiedis had played him a Clinton record at some point during his life as a Pepper). Regardless, Sherman – a huge Clinton admirer – found himself seated next to his musical hero, the Funkmeister, at New York's annual CMJ music conference, alongside Lou Reed, Nona Hendryx and Madonna. The "brothers cups", meanwhile, were elsewhere, bum-rushing the MTV set.

"I thought, 'I must make my impression on this person; he must know the depth of my interplanetary funkmanship.' I leaned over and I said, 'March To The Witch's Castle' [a track from the *Cosmic Slop* LP]. He leaned over and said, 'Man, I almost forgot that one.'" Their bond was forged on the spot.*

Kiedis' explanation was slightly different. "When we began the band we didn't know anything about Parliament/Funkadelic at all," he said in 1990. "It wasn't until after our first record, when people kept coming up to us and saying, 'You guys must be totally down with the funk,' that we looked into it, studied it and realised that it was some of the most beautiful music of the century. And that's when we started to educate ourselves to that music." No mention of Jack Sherman, though.

Back in the studio, Cliff Martinez avoided most of the conflicts. According to Sherman, "Cliff dealt with the mayhem by shutting down and putting in a pretty stiff performance and sleeping a lot. He doesn't respond well to that kind of stuff." Martinez also kept himself busy wandering the nearby streets, collecting odd bits and pieces of metal, which he'd then bring into the studio. While the arguments continued around him, he'd experiment, using his metallic collection as rhythm instruments. (He'd use some of these found instruments on his soundtrack for the film *Sex, Lies & Videotape*, which Sherman also played on.)

* When Sherman learned that the Peppers were going to work with Clinton on their second album, he made Flea and Martinez tapes of his P-Funk collection. Years later he met – and recorded with – Clinton, who would tell him: "I know what you did, and the funk knows what you did, and we thank you for making all them tapes and spreading the funk."

Get Up And Jump, clockwise from left: Hillel Slovak, Anthony Kiedis, Flea and Jack Irons. "We'd hang out, smoke pot and drink beer, put socks on our dicks and run around," Kiedis remembered. "It was just kids living together, having fun." *(Phil Nicholls)*

Red Hot Thespian: Anthony Kiedis poses for the Fairfax High School yearbook, 1980. "I think that was his first calling," said classmate Keith Barry.

Skate Mates: Flea (left), shown here with Irons and Kiedis, made an uncredited cameo in the 1986 skate-punk flick, *Thrashin'*. *(LFI)*

Peppers producer and sparring partner
Andy Gill: "We loved and looked up to
Andy Gill so much." When they worked
together, things changed.
(Robert Matheu/Retna)

Dr Funkenstein, George Clinton: He would
tell the Peppers, "If you get to the
Grammys, you do it with P-Funk." They
granted that wish in 1993. *(LFI)*

Me And My Friends: Irons, Kiedis, Flea and Slovak, 1987. *(Chris Clunn)*

The Fax City Four: Flea, Slovak, Irons and Kiedis (from left). *(LFI)*

Art Attack: When Slovak died in 1988, he was found face down on this painting; (right) his cigarette had burned a hole in the canvas. *(Courtesy of James Slovak)*

Lincoln Moronical: Flea, Kiedis, Slovak and Irons (from left) pose in front of another American icon. *(Joe Dilworth/Retna)*

Stone Cold Bush: Anthony Kiedis almost lets it all hang out. "It's a strong sense of human freedom to play nude." *(Steve Double/Retna)*

Come Together: Slovak, Kiedis, Flea and Irons cross Abbey Road, 1988. "Here's the nutty, zany guys," Flea told *Rolling Stone*, "they're at it again, they want to 'Party On Your Pussy'." *(Chris Clunn)*

Hillel Slovak: Sometimes known as The Skinny Sweaty Man In The Green Suit.
(Gary Gershoff/Retna)

Freaky Styley: Flea, Kiedis and Slovak (from left), live and loud. According to Flea, the Peppers were "too funky for white radio, too punk rockin' for black [radio]". *(LFI)*

Good Time Boy: Anthony Kiedis, aka The Swan. Band friend Spit Stix recalled that one night, "Anthony walked up and asked the young lady if she wanted to go fuck in the bathroom. She did." *(Chris Clunn)*

Knock Me Down: Hillel Slovak, not long before his overdose death. He told his girlfriend at the time, "I can handle it [heroin] but you can't." *(Frank White)*

New Punks On The Block: John Frusciante (front right) and Chad Smith (front left) with
Flea and Kiedis. "He's a very disciplined musician," Flea said of Frusciante.
"All he cares about is his guitar and his cigarettes." *(AJ Barratt/Retna)*

Martinez and Sherman would actually receive co-songwriting credits on five tracks on *The Red Hot Chili Peppers*, as did Hillel Slovak. Kiedis and Flea agreed to share the love when it came to credits (and songwriting royalties). Even Gill received a co-credit on 'Grand Pappy Du Plenty'. Their act of goodwill – mixed with a certain business naïveté – would create major problems a few years later, when Sherman took the band to court, suing them for what Flea would flippantly dismiss as "alleged emotional abuse or some bullshit". But it was far more complicated than that.

Two band partnership agreements were set up when Sherman joined. One dealt with publishing and the other with everything else band-related, including royalties earned from record sales. When those contracts were originally entered into, the agreement was that all band members would be treated equally, regardless of whether they remained in the group or for how long. This explains why there are so many multiple songwriting credits on Chili Peppers' albums, irrespective of whether one member had more input to the song. The Peppers philosophy, in principle, was this: if you jammed on the song, you got a credit.

"When I came over to Lindy's to join the band," recalled Sherman, "I said I'd do so on one condition: an absolute equal split on everything. Flea looked up and said, 'That's what Van Halen does.' [But] I realised that this wasn't conventional songwriting, that's why there's so many co-songwriting credits."

This publishing agreement was set up through the band's own Moebetoblame Music Company (named as a nod to their love of The Three Stooges). In the years to follow, it must have been increasingly hard for the band's core members, Flea and Kiedis, to swallow their original "all-for-one-and-equal-credit-for-all" arrangement. That was especially tough for Kiedis, who was the lyricist for virtually every song the band recorded.

But the band were barely a year old when they started working in El Dorado with Gill, which might explain both the undercooked vibe of the record, their erratic behaviour at the time and some of their not-quite-thought-through business decisions.

Producer Michael Beinhorn, who would go on to work with the Chili Peppers on *The Uplift Mofo Party Plan* and their breakthrough hit album *Mother's Milk*, remembers the Chili Peppers at that time as a fiery mix of untapped potential and uncontrollable chaos.

"They jumped all over the place, streaked meetings at their record company, took all kinds of crazy drugs, were complete lunatics – and liked music that no one else understood."*

"I think that the Chili Peppers initially didn't do much to dispel the notion that they were a bunch of crazy white boys trying to play some hack funk riffs and mix this up with punk rock," Beinhorn added, "but underneath it all, I felt that they had not only wild and limitless ambition but also the potential to grow artistically and do something of real lasting value."

The potential could be heard on *The Red Hot Chili Peppers*, but only if you dug deep and listened hard.

The album opened with 'True Men Don't Kill Coyotes', a track inspired by the thrill-killing of wild dogs in the Hollywood Hills. Appropriately, Kiedis didn't so much sing as bark the song's lyrics, while the rest of the band was kept to a muzzled growl in the background. Gill's cavernous production style – very much the flavour of the time – was at its most prominent here. It could have worked on a record by ABC or Tears For Fears, who were then big stars, but these Peppers needed some studio heat. Not only did the first track on the Chili Peppers' first album have more breathing space than virtually any other song they ever recorded, but it failed to generate the kind of sparks they could produce as a live band.

Regardless, Gill still sees 'True Men' as one of his favourite Chili Peppers' tracks – and certainly his favourite few minutes on the album. Even today he sometimes revisits the track. He feels that it truly captured the excitement and whiff of danger that the band could then produce. "It really soars," he told me, "and it has all the things that are good about the band – it's passionate in a way that they've lost these days."

But if Kiedis had gotten his way, the track would have turned out very differently. When Gill heard the original demo, he felt that the song needed an overlay of acoustic guitars; Sherman agreed. But the

---

* The streaking story is true – Kiedis once confessed to bursting into a conference room at EMI and running naked through a meeting because they were not allowed to attend. The suits at EMI were not impressed, complaining to Goetz.

acoustic guitar was an instrument that in post-punk 1984 horrified both Flea and Kiedis, in much the same way that they were wary of backing vocals and brass. Acoustic guitars might have belonged on an Eagles record or on something from one of those "homo" singer/songwriters, but they didn't have any place on a Red Hot Chili Peppers song. In an act that required almost military-styled manoeuvring on their part, Gill and Sherman quietly retired to a corner of the studio to work out the acoustic guitar part. Then the band's vocalist burst into the studio.

Gill picks up the story, chuckling all the way through his recollection. "Halfway through the take the door opens and Anthony is screaming, 'What's that sound?' When I said it was an acoustic guitar, he said, 'That's fucking homo!' grabbed the guitar off Jack, threw it to the ground and said, 'No fucking homo acoustic guitar on my record.'"

Guitarist and producer were stunned by his outburst, but kept working, as Gill admitted. "He fucked off about 10 minutes later and we got a take and it made it to the record. In fact, it's what makes the track."

As Sherman recalls, "Most of the good guitar playing was done while they [Kiedis and Flea] weren't there. It was guerilla recording, because they were so destructive, blowing it constantly. That was the only way I could get any parts done.

"Anything that was the 'Little Wing' side of Hendrix was homo. I was almost beaten to death for that. I was frustrated – why couldn't we have a few chord changes? If it was pretty, it was not allowed."

In fact, most of Sherman's guitar work on the album was solid. His chicken-scratch picking played a feature role during 'Baby Appeal', backing up a rap from Kiedis that tried to explain why children like the band's funk-punk explosion of sound, digging their funky spiel which makes them squeal. Kiedis concluded, "The Chili Peppers have baby appeal." Sherman mightn't have admired Kiedis as a human being or bandmate, but he could see the obvious talent in his rapping, especially on this song. "As an early rap boast," he said, "I'd throw genius at it."

The following track, 'Buckle Down', was a kind of limp electro-funk that only came to life when Cliff Brooks' lively congas kicked in. Kiedis' rap, meanwhile, was his very own watered-down take on Grandmaster Flash's 'The Message': "Don't give up the fight in life," he yelped, "You better buckle down."

If only the band themselves had wised up to this warning. As the sessions progressed, their behaviour simply got worse, especially when it came to their attitude towards Gill. The band would argue, at length, about Gill's fondness for drum machines, as if that were the root flaw of the record. But their conflicting temperaments presented an equally large problem. Kiedis and Flea weren't in control of the situation in the studio – and they weren't the kind of punks who would readily admit that they were out of their depth. The pair felt that Gill was tampering with their songs and their style.

"He thought it was necessary to use rhythm machines as our drums," Kiedis said a few years after the album was released, "because that was what was getting on the radio at the time. He took it that we had to do whatever it took to conform to the sound of the radio." (Martinez had trouble drumming to a "click track"; he still believes that it "sterilised" the band's sound.)

"It was a seriously different point of view that we had going into things," Flea added, when asked about his relationship with Gill. "Instead of ending up with a record that was hard-edged funk or namby-pamby pop-funk, we ended up with a record in between.

"We knew what we wanted," insisted Flea, "a raw fucking rocking album. But we didn't know how to go about it and we didn't go about it in the right way because we'd just burst in and say, 'We don't like this and we like that,' instead of working with him."

All their comments proved is the clarity to be found in hindsight. And as both Jerden and Gill would point out, the language they used in the studio was a little spicier than that.

As for the rest of the album, the track 'Get Up And Jump' sounded like much of the processed funk of the time: it was repetitive and chilly. This wasn't helped, of course, by the echo-chamber production. A blast of horns and some nimble-fingered fretwork from Flea did give the track a little go-forward, but you can't help but suspect the best version of 'Get Up And Jump' was delivered in front of a madly appreciative, appropriately jazzed Rhythm Club audience during one of the band's chaotic first few shows.

The slowed-down 'Why Don't You Love Me' – inspired, in part, by the Hank Williams records that Flea and his pal Bob Forrest used to spin on a regular basis – had a certain goofy charm, especially when Kiedis asked the hard question: "Why don't you love me like you used to do/ How come you treat me like a worn-out shoe?" (Kiedis actually swiped some of Williams' lyrics verbatim.) Judicious use of the three-piece horn section (trumpeter Patrick English, tenor saxophonist Kenny Flood and trombonist Phil Ranelin) spiced up a strangely quirky cut. However, the track that the band considered their defining moment up until then, 'Green Heaven', was a soggy mess in the studio, slowed down until it was almost travelling in reverse. The robotic rhythms and lack of any true aggression didn't do the track any favours.

The demo version of the track, with basic production from Fear's Spit Stix, was added to the 2003 reissue of *The Red Hot Chili Peppers*. It proves how the song might have sounded if Gill and the band had opted to use this strangely stoned original as a production template.

As for 'Mommy Where's Daddy', Flea has said that he was very proud of its white-boy funk groove, and that's a fair comment. It was the best recording on the entire album, where Sherman lays down some gut-level funk guitar which literally came out of nowhere. "In the middle of a conversation I started playing something," he remembered, "and Andy said, 'Can you play that again?' It became the intro and the outro for the song. I felt like I was channelling something." Martinez and Flea, meanwhile, kept the rhythms rock-steady, while some heavy-breathing sax, courtesy of Kenny Flood, floated in and around Kiedis' twisted, big-pimping vocal (which was "fucking brilliant," to Sherman's ears). Then the guitarist brought it home with a crisp, clean solo, by far his finest moment on record with the band. "I think the arrangement of 'Mommy Where's Daddy' is good," said the track's arranger, Keith Barry. "The horns fit the track."

The Peppers and Gill should have learned something from 'Mommy Where's Daddy': if they'd kept the rest of the album as bare-boned and simple, it could have been far more effective.

As for their signature song, 'Out In LA', on record it was a stop-start affair, a chance for each band member to kick out the jams with their own solos. But it was spoiled by Kiedis' garbled vocals. 'Police Helicopter' is so half-formed that it crashed after 70 seconds; 'You Always Sing The Same' didn't even last 20 seconds before it imploded.

But the album's instrumental finale 'Grand Pappy Du Plenty' ditched the dumbed-down funk of the previous pair of tracks and tried out some weird, spacey atmospherics. Its recording was one album session that Sherman recalls with something approaching fondness. All of the band and producer Gill had smoked some pot, while Gill and Sherman bonded over an affection for The Band (a chord from their ballad 'Whispering Pines' can be found in 'Grand Pappy'). "That was a great day," Sherman admitted to me.

The track closed the album with a suggestion that there was more to the Red Hot Chili Peppers than four white boys in Funkadelic clothing. The band knew this, too: 10 years later they used it to open their set at Woodstock 1994.

The Chili Peppers' debut record wasn't a complete failure. It did establish the basic template for their punk-funk fusion, and Kiedis' hard-rapping style was years ahead of such contenders as Mike Patton from Faith No More. It also proved they could work their way around some tricky time signatures and body-rocking rhythms. What the record needed was some real fire, but the sound of the album was cold and distant, while Kiedis' lack of a genuine singing voice meant that his white-boy raps, while innovative, wore thin very quickly. And at this early stage they weren't so much writing songs as stringing ideas around riffs and solos that had been worked up by individual members.

When reflecting on the album in the liner notes for its reissue, Flea was still disappointed by what might have been. But he was a touch more sanguine in 2003 than he was at the time of its creation.

"I used to really regret that we didn't make the record I thought we could of [sic]," he wrote, "that it could have been a classic record. But Anthony recently pointed out to me that it was all part of our learning process and had we been too good too fast we never would have continued the long and rich growing process we are still on."

The soap-opera-worthy drama that was the recording of *The Red Hot Chili Peppers* worsened when the band encouraged Gill to talk about his time with The Gang Of Four. According to Flea, Gill was not enthused about his best-known work, which came as a major shock to Flea and Kiedis. "He [said he] didn't know what he was doing with those records." That was too much for Flea to take; he didn't just study the basslines of Dave Allen, he genuinely loved those albums.

"That's disheartening," he said with some restraint, "because those are great records."

They were also records that Flea used as sonic benchmarks for the Peppers' first album. "We wanted to go for a sound like that – not as sparse but with the same raw funkness. But when we got together he wasn't into the same thing any more."

Martinez had the same startled reaction. "Andy basically renounced all their music."

The Gill vs the Peppers battle reached an unfortunate crescendo when, midway through recording, Gill was diagnosed with testicular cancer. He flew to New York for an operation to have one testicle removed, leaving Jerden in charge. Then the sessions really fell apart when the engineer collapsed with what was thought to be some kind of intestinal parasite. Instead, he turned out – not surprisingly – to be suffering the effects of extreme stress. As Gill recalled, "He told me he couldn't take it any more, these antics of Anthony and Flea. Then he called in sick."

When Jerden recovered, and with Gill still convalescing, Kiedis and Flea pulled the engineer aside and begged him to start again and re-record the album from scratch.

Jerden's response was firm. "I told them I couldn't do that."

If there was one incident that precisely captured the mess that was the recording of the Peppers' debut LP, it was the notorious "Turd In The Box" stunt. Gill was busy mixing the album – by which time Dave Jerden had actually walked out of the sessions – when Flea and Kiedis drifted in, "half interested", as Gill recalls. After a few minutes of hanging about the mixing desk, Flea told Gill that he and Kiedis were "going for a shit".

"It was like they do it together because they're brothers and they shit at the same time or something," Gill laughed.

To this bizarre revelation, he responded, "That's marvellous, bring me one back, will you?"

As the words left Gill's mouth, he knew he'd made a horrible mistake. Martinez recalls the producer banging his head on the console in horror.

"As soon as I said that, I went, 'Oh fuck, why did I say that?' Sure enough, five minutes later they walk in with a pizza tray with a pile of steaming turds on it and placed it in the middle of the mixing desk. I didn't move, I didn't say anything, but the engineer had no idea what was coming and was last seen running down Sunset Boulevard, screaming. That was exactly what happened."

In Chili Pepper legend, the "Turd In The Box" incident was almost as infamous as their "socks on cocks" stunt. Somehow, the stoic Andy Gill remained composed throughout the whole ordeal.

"When children are behaving badly," he said to me, "there's no point in losing your temper. Then you're just sinking to their level."

When Flea spoke with *Rolling Stone*'s David Fricke, reflecting on their debut LP, he explained how "our natural, spontaneous thing wasn't there. If we'd had that original line-up on the first record, I think we would have been a lot more popular a lot sooner. We would have gotten the real thing, hardcore, down on record. We were so explosive at the time – and it's not an explosive record."

This observation, of course, is in contrast to the thoughts of producer Gill, who believed that their debut album was a blueprint for much of their early career.

On reflection, Jerden can hear some merit in *The Red Hot Chili Peppers*, but doesn't think the album comes anywhere near capturing the type of electricity that the band was capable of generating. "That [playing live] was an over-the-top experience," he says. "The songs didn't represent that. I did think that they had a lot of talent and what they were doing was really hip. Anthony was rapping and no one on the west coast knew what the fuck that was. I was aware of it through working with Bill Laswell and because of people like Afrika Bambaataa. But out here there was no scene at all. Anthony was the first one doing it; he was way ahead of his time."

As Lindy Goetz admitted, "Andy did a great job, but it was impossible to capture their energy on record."

Given the intensity of his anger towards Gill during the making of the album, it's strange that Flea still went on to contribute liner notes to the 1995 reissue of The Gang Of Four's *Entertainment!* album, famously noting: "It made me laugh to hear that guy from U2 [The Edge] talk about his guitar influences being old bluesmen. I thought, 'Hey, you dipshit, what about Andy Gill?'" And while making their *One Hot Minute* album, Flea gave a song-under-development the working title 'Gang Of Four', simply "because the first part sounds like The Gang Of Four." Time, maturity – and possibly a large dose of guilt about his earlier behaviour – may have inspired Flea to show more respect to Andy Gill and his work.

Gill is now – as he was 20 years earlier – unfazed about Flea's attitude towards him. "Look, Flea is the most vocal member of the band, he's the one who shoots his mouth off the most. Over the years he's been very ambivalent about me and the record. Sometimes I read things where he speaks to the press about me. He's said, 'Andy Gill, he's a bastard and I hate that record.' Other times he says how he really wants to apologise to me – he's said that in print. But that's just Flea; it's water off a duck's back to me."

Gill has maintained what he describes as a "slim communication" with the band – the Chili Peppers turned up at a Gang Of Four reunion show at London's Brixton Academy in the mid-Nineties, and spent time backstage with Gill and the band. He and Martinez also keep in touch. And his overall assessment of Flea? "He does have a good heart but he's got a big mouth and sticks his foot in it regularly."

The Chili Peppers did manage to get some things right with their debut album. For their cover artwork, they hired Gary Panter, a native Texan who had relocated to LA and had fast become an artist-in-demand. Panter was an illustrator, painter, designer and sometimes musician, who would go on to become one of the most influential graphic artists of the late 20th century. Panter was the creator of *Jimbo*, a post-nuclear punk-rock cartoon character whose life and times had first been chronicled in *Slash*, the Seventies LA fanzine-cum-punk-bible that was essential reading for any self-respecting scenester during the city's lively but brief dalliance with punk rock.* "Flea was very nice to me always," Panter told me, "and liked Jimbo. [In fact] he is a kind of Jimbo."

Panter had become friendly with Flea after they both attended the premiere of Penelope Spheeris' 1984 movie *Suburbia*, in which Flea cameod. By that time Panter had designed cover art for a trio of Frank Zappa's late Seventies albums, *Studio Tan*, *Sleep Dirt* and *Orchestral Favorites*.

The resulting artwork that adorned the cover of *The Red Hot Chili Peppers* – a vivid, bloodshot image that burned your eyes like a punk rock take on the work of Ralph Steadman – was very indicative of the wash overlay style of paintings that Panter was working on in the early Eighties. But the cover artwork was as interesting for its wild, bug-eyed depictions of Flea and Kiedis as it was for the placement of recent

---

* *The Simpsons'* creator Matt Groening would eventually publish the *Jimbo* comics.

recruits Sherman and Martinez. They were shadowy background figures, a few steps removed from the real action. The image would prove to be prescient, especially for the increasingly unpopular Jack Sherman, whose days as a Red Hot Chili Pepper were definitely numbered.

They may have wisely chosen LA's hottest counterculture artist to design their debut's cover, but the band encountered real problems when they presented the finished record to EMI. As far as the Peppers were concerned, they had the album title ready: it was called *True Men Don't Kill Coyotes*. EMI disagreed, figuring – reasonably enough – that this relatively unknown outfit needed some kind of marketplace identity with their first release. So *The Red Hot Chili Peppers* it was going to be. The band were obviously disappointed.

But first of all the label actually had to take possession of the master tapes. When the album was completed, the label took their own sweet time paying Andy Gill, who decided the best response was to take the tapes "hostage" until he was paid. Strangely, considering their in-studio friction, Flea supported the producer, insisting that the words "PAY ANDY" be etched into the run-out groove of the vinyl album.

"At the end of the record mixing in LA," Gill recalled, "the label tried to suggest I had gone over budget and that my advances would thus be cut back. But everything we had spent had been OK'd by both Lindy Goetz and by the A&R department.

"[Eventually] I gave them the tapes, as a gesture of goodwill, and they then agreed that I was right and I was paid the full amount. The run-out groove of the album, 'PAY ANDY', was Flea's idea, to his eternal credit."

When this flare-up was combined with the disagreement over the album's title, it was the beginning of many disputes between band and label that would eventually tear them apart. Another problem occurred when the album was issued on CD – the inner sleeve of the disc was blank, with no mention of band member names or album production details.

Kiedis was incensed. "I always thought it was pretty cheesy that you just get this little sort of wispy slip of non-informational [sic] artwork."

Not that the argument over the album's title or lack of sleeve notes really mattered, given the state of popular music when *The Red Hot Chili Peppers* was finally released in August 1984. The only punk-funk revolution happening at the time was within the fertile imaginations of Kiedis and Flea – it certainly wasn't being reflected in mainstream culture. In the UK, Liverpudlian shock popsters Frankie Goes To Hollywood – a proudly gay, heavy leather, synth-pop freak show – had the Top 10 chart in a stranglehold, taking both the top spot with 'Two Tribes', and the number five position with 'Relax'. Minneapolis hit machine Prince, meanwhile, was a star on both sides of the Atlantic with his smash 'When Doves Cry'. The song was number six in the UK and number two in the USA, where it was kept off top spot only by Ray Parker, Jr's theme song to the movie *Ghostbusters*. Pop veterans also featured heavily in the charts, the charge being led by such masters of schmaltz as Lionel Richie ('Stuck On You'), Elton John ('Sad Songs') and Stevie Wonder ('I Just Called To Say I Love You'). All rock'n'roll had to offer was Bruce Springsteen's keyboard-sodden 'Dancing In The Dark' or the MTV-powered rebirth of Texan riffers ZZ Top, who'd hit big with 'Legs'. The only sign of change in the charts at the time was the appearance of Grandmaster Flash's 'White Lines (Don't Don't Do It)', which was a hit in the UK but a nonentity in the USA. The grunge and alt-rock revolution was a long way off. As far as the record-buying public was concerned, The Red Hot Chili Peppers were just another band from LA. Although college radio embraced them, what they needed was the attention of pop radio, and there was no way these Hollywood party boys belonged there in 1984.

But what they did have to offer was a video for the track 'True Men Don't Kill Coyotes', directed by Graeme Whitler. Primarily a performance video, shot on a tiny Hollywood sound stage, the clip definitely reflected its low budget: the opening shot is a cheap diorama of the Hollywood Hills, with the mythical chilli pepper bush nestled in the foreground. It's only one step removed from a Japanese sci-fi movie. Shot in day-glo colours, which was very much the MTV standard in 1984, the clip might have been short on production qualities – it was no big-screen production *à la* 'Thriller', that's for sure – but it did shine a very strong light on the band's best features: the manic on-stage vitality of Flea and Kiedis. Sure, they were lip-syncing, a necessity that the band would grow to hate, but Kiedis (who spends part of the video wearing a garbage bag on his head, for unspecified reasons) and Flea, who wears multi-coloured hair clips and a worryingly unstable expression, throw themselves around the small set like two seriously demented men on a very funky mission. And that mission was, probably, to hide the fact that the song they were promoting was adequate at best, a clunky, overcooked slice of faux-funk pop with a title that was simply too long for the average radio DJ to back announce. Yet in spite of Kiedis' uncoordinated miming, the clip was engaging enough, a fast-paced, rapid-cut introduction to The Red Hot Chili Peppers. But it was a different situation for new Peppers Sherman and Martinez. Just as in Gary Panter's album artwork, they remained background players, sporting pained expressions and truly awful outfits. (Possibly in a case of payback for his various "offences" during the album's creation, such as his "homo" acoustic guitar playing, Sherman was dressed as some kind of poor man's pimp.) Neither Sherman nor Martinez tried to keep up with Flea and Kiedis' epileptic gyrations, especially during the part of the video where the foursome ditched their instruments, splashed paint over each other and attempted a choreographed dance routine. The message may have been unintentional but it was clear enough: this was Kiedis and Flea's band. Martinez and, especially, Sherman, were hired hands.

Dave Jerden agreed with this. He told me that there was no question that the band was really built around the chemistry between Kiedis and Flea. "That's The Red Hot Chili Peppers right there," he said. That's an opinion shared by long-time manager Lindy Goetz. "The core is Anthony and Flea."

The Red Hot Chili Peppers was largely ignored on release; its reviews were restricted to LA street press and the very occasional mention in the mainstream media. *Rolling Stone* magazine didn't even acknowledge the album's existence until its 2003 reissue. The entry in *The New Rolling Stone Encyclopedia Of Rock & Roll* summed up the 11-track release in this way: "The album stiffed." What Is This' debut EP, *Squeezed*, hadn't fared much better, even though *Trouser Press* was blown away, describing the band's sound as "wild, muscular rock-funk with a demented outlook", before going on to compare them to their sonic brothers, the Chili Peppers. "Chris Hutchinson and Jack Irons ride a fearsome rhythm behemoth," they observed, "and Alain Johannes and Slovak both provide offbeat songs, unnervingly mental vocals and psycho guitar licks, making *Squeezed* a gut'n'butt-shaking experience you won't soon forget." *Trouser Press* were one of the lone voices who were also big on *The Red Hot Chili Peppers* LP, noting how the album "melds floor-shaking rhythm'n'roll to wickedly clever songs like 'True Men Don't Kill Coyotes', 'Baby Appeal' and 'Get Up And Jump'. The Chili Peppers, who aren't above a little self-obsessed boasting or earnest political protest, play a thoroughly entertaining mutation of George Clinton, Was (Not Was), Peter Wolf, Sly Stone, Kurtis Blow and Wall Of Voodoo."

Despite this odd flicker of attention, the record came and went quickly. Goetz, who during his 14 years as Peppers manager rarely missed a show, spending much of their early years in the back of the tour van, realised that word on the band would eventually spread. But they needed to get outside of LA to do that. If 30 people turned up at their first show in one city, he figured, by the time they returned for their next gig the crowd would have built to 250. "Flea thought I was working them to death," he would tell me, "but I knew it was the only way to break this band."

The band would play anywhere, usually for $200, sometimes $250, which might just cover their expenses and get them enough fuel to make the next show.

By this time Jack Sherman knew that he was a very square, health-food-eating, relatively drug-free peg in a round hole. Sherman has his suspicions that Kiedis and Flea were elbowing him aside to prepare for Hillel Slovak's return to the band. Before the album tour began, he wasn't sure if he could continue with them; he even asked a psychic for advice, who gave him the green light to continue. Then he called band attorney Eric Greenspan and asked what would happen if he quit the Peppers. "He said, 'We'll sue you,'" Sherman told me in 2004. So he had no option but to carry on, albeit briefly, as a Chili Pepper. But Sherman had a sinking feeling as soon as he climbed on board the tour van. A Peppers pal, who was at the wheel, turned to the new Pepper and asked: "Hey, Jack, have I told you about my friends who run people over for sport?"

Their first show beyond their Hollywood safety zone was in Aspen, Colorado, at the Cathay Grand Club. But they didn't really make much impact until they returned to Kiedis' hometown of Grand

Rapids in November 1984. And, as with much of the band's early career, the first impression they made was not necessarily one that would win over new fans and establish the band as serious players with funk in their hearts. In short, they pissed people off.

Blackie Dammett had set up the Grand Rapids show for his son's band by asking a favour of a promoter friend. The Peppers were locked in for a November 4 appearance at the Top Of The Rock, a small local venue that could squeeze in maybe 400 punters. Kiedis must have been understandably nervous; apart from the odd homecoming to see his mother, he'd been nowhere near Grand Rapids in almost a decade. The show, however, was a disaster. The house was only half full. And while Flea might have been Kiedis' closest ally – hell, they even crapped together – he didn't help his buddy's homecoming nerves when he responded to some hecklers, who had made their way onstage and flashed the band, by dropping his pants and doing likewise. Not surprisingly, the locals were unimpressed.

"I'd shoot a son like that," observed one concert-goer in *Grand Rapids Press*.

Jack Sherman remembers it as "an almost innocent 'nature child' reaction" that went wrong. "Imagine a party for two-year-olds," he stated, "where one just pulls down their diaper and the others go, 'Me, too!' That's how I remember it. I thought it was hysterical."

Kiedis also laughed it off. "I saved the clipping from the concert," he joked after the show. And he went on to state how his mother, who was in the crowd at the show, "liked the socks". But Peggy Idema, who had hosted the band for Thanksgiving dinner the night before, actually wasn't that thrilled by the flashing incident and the reaction that followed. She was in tears as she drove the band away from the gig, according to Sherman. The Red Hot Chili Peppers weren't seen in Grand Rapids again for some time.

"The event haunted the rest of the tour," Sherman recalled.

As word of their Grand Rapids debacle started to spread, the band would be warned repeatedly by promoters about "pulling that sort of stuff here".

After this fiasco, the Peppers picked up whatever shows they could. The response to their set at Washington's Ontario Theater was more favourable, even if the crowd didn't necessarily appreciate the way these Californians mouthed off at the audience.

"Hollywood's Red Hot Chili Peppers . . . pumped out an abrasive and nutty brand of funk and rap that eventually turned the audience against them," reported *The Washington Post*'s Joe Sasfy. "Their choppy funk was enriched by zany dancing, obscenity, squabbles with the audience and Hendrix-style guitar work."

The band continued to gig regularly throughout late 1984, head-lining their first tour, which took in much of the west coast and major Midwestern cities (Grand Rapids, Michigan, of course, didn't make their itinerary). Life in the back of a stinky, cramped tour van can be tough for the tightest of friends, so it must have been hell for Jack Sherman, whose estrangement from the band had increased since the disastrous sessions at El Dorado. Cliff Martinez also felt his pain. "It was tough being on the road, six guys in a van shoulder to shoulder for 10 hours a day – and doing drugs," the drummer said. "It was like being married to people you don't have sex with."

A review of a January 1985 show in San Francisco hinted at the gulf that had developed within the band. While the Peppers' performance was described as a "scalding, non-stop barrage of mutated urban funk", it was Kiedis ("an eye-catching presence on stage") and a "reckless" Flea who commanded the audience's attention (and sometimes their insults; heckling from both band and audience was a given at early Peppers shows). When Kiedis mounted a speaker stack towards the end of the show, dropping his trousers and flashing the crowd, Martinez remained earthbound, an "undistinguished" presence. Decked out in a shower cap, Sherman "alternated between lean rhythm parts and spare solo lines", but gave the two hottest Peppers an extremely wide berth. The stage was theirs; he was simply there to play guitar.

Kiedis found it impossible to restrain his hostility towards Sherman: at one show he pelted the guitarist with yoghurt, as some kind of state-ment about his "weird" eating habits. At a gig in New Orleans, when Flea broke a bass string (which is much more time-consuming to replace than a guitar string), Sherman stepped up to the mic to talk with the crowd, and Kiedis threw a glass of water in the guitarist's face. Sherman stormed off the stage, fuming.

Back in the tour van, when the band wanted to get wild and party, Sherman chose to sleep. He was not a big drug taker; he was more interested in the high generated by a good shot of carrot juice. While

Kiedis and Flea would hit the streets, Sherman and his room-mate Martinez would stay in and gorge on macrobiotic food. Even though Kiedis and Flea continued to rile the mild-mannered guitarist, the "freak" who was into funk music and health foods, by the end of the tour, Sherman did actually feel more like a Chili Pepper than ever. He'd survived a tough initiation. "I was 28, I'd just gotten married. I was all hale and hearty; I thought, 'You know, I could stay in this band a bit longer.' Obviously they didn't have that feeling. I feel they were trying to intimidate me out of the band because Hillel wanted back."

By February 1985, he was fired, becoming the first in a very long line of ex-Chili Peppers. His dismissal was a classic example of Kiedis and Flea's inexperience. Sherman knew that something was up when Kiedis and Flea called a meeting at his house. "I was the odd man out, I was in Santa Monica. 'Hmm, this is strange,' I thought. They show up, they say, 'You're out of the band, bye.' Half laughing, cups clanking, they run out of the front door.

"Cliff [Martinez] asks me do I want him to stay. I don't know what to do: do I cry? I'm in shock. I got into a rant, which he couldn't take any more. Then I picked up the phone and looked for the next person to play with.

"I think that was the reaction of an emotionally disabled, dysfunctional person," Sherman said of his reaction. "I had no ability to process it. Move on? That's not healthy. I didn't have the business experience to realise that I wasn't in a garage band, I was in a corporation.

"Maybe it's this – you've been abandoned by Hillel and this bad-ass drummer, Jack Irons, who've left your joke band for What Is This, and they must have felt really fucking shitty about themselves. I played the scapegoat in my family, so maybe I set myself up for this."

But there was an unusual postscript to the relationship between Jack Sherman and his erstwhile bandmates.

In 1989, Sherman was among a swag of Chili Pepper friends and acquaintances invited into Ocean Way Studios to contribute backing vocals to the anthems 'Good Time Boys' and 'Higher Ground', two standout tracks from the band's 1989 album, *Mother's Milk*. "I get down there, put on the headphones and am fucking blown away by 'Higher Ground'," he told me.

It appeared as though the band and their former guitarist had moved on from their not-so-amicable split.

But on March 12, 1993, Sherman sued the band, their manager Goetz and attorney Eric Greenspan, charging that the terms of his partnership agreement with the band were violated when he was fired in 1985. (This was the "alleged emotional abuse or some bullshit", that Flea had referred to in his liner notes for *The Red Hot Chili Peppers*.) Sherman's suit claimed that he was "treated with contempt and subject to continuous verbal abuse and ridicule and even occasional physical abuse" from Kiedis and Flea. His suit also alleged that he wasn't given the contractually mandated 10 days written notice of his sacking from the band.

Sherman also alleged that between 1985 and 1991, he'd asked Eric Greenspan several times about the status of royalties that were owed to him, but was "curtly told that the albums were still unrecouped." And he claimed that he didn't receive his slice of the $30,000 publishing advance for the band's *Freaky Styley* album, on which he was given nine co-songwriting credits. The only money he claims to have received was a cheque for $1,700, which he presumed to represent the settlement agreement he'd signed in September 1985.

It was only after Sherman had read a book called *Business & Music* that he started wondering why he didn't receive any statements outlining Chili Peppers record sales for the two albums on which he had writing credits. He then placed a call to the royalties department at Capitol Records.

"A guy answers the phone. I told him who I was and he said, 'Don't tell anyone I told you, but they've been touring on your royalties, they've been cross-collateralising your funds – you need a lawyer.' "

Sherman – who had spent some time post-Peppers in recovery groups dealing with what he referred to as "childhood stuff" – then felt prepared to further pursue his case with the band.

Greenspan dismissed Sherman's case as being "completely without merit". His official statement read: "Jack Sherman was a member of the Red Hot Chili Peppers a long time ago. Many years later and after the band became successful, he came forward with this action. This is after he received accountings – at the same time and in the same amounts – as the other band members for the records he performed on. When he asked, he was given all royalty statements for the band and their publishing company. Despite numerous requests, he has yet to tell us what he thinks he is owed." The dispute was eventually dismissed in Los

Angeles on March 22, 1994, when Superior Court Judge Stephen Lachs ruled that Sherman's case had exceeded the statute of limitations.

Sherman's attorney, Neville Johnson, had countered that the statute of limitations didn't apply here because of Sherman's "past emotional problems" and that Sherman was only now "capable of putting his business affairs in order and contesting past acts."

"My wife told me not to let that child abuse stuff get in there," Sherman admitted in 2004. "I said, 'But that's true.' That's not what killed it, it was the statute of limitations thing."

Sherman also admits that the statute of limitations could have worked in reverse if he'd pursued the band earlier. When he eventually consulted a lawyer, Sherman was told: "Had you stood up you would have been a millionaire by now. He said if I'd gone in when there was nothing there, a lawyer would have said, 'You can't throw this guy out just because you don't like him. You have to give him a little piece.' If a judge awarded me 5 per cent of the figure? Go figure.

"I just wish they hadn't been fucking me. If I had the maturity to get a lawyer in 1985 and go through the motions, end of story. Thank God I made that phone call, otherwise I would never have seen any money."

Sherman feels as though he has been "erased" from Chili Peppers history. His name is barely noted in the 2003 reissue of *The Red Hot Chili Peppers*; no photos of him appear in the *What Hits!?* collection, and he was not mentioned in the 1999 VH-1 *Behind The Music* special on the band.

"I could look at it two ways," he figures. "It's either charity because they only have horrible things to say and are sparing me, or they're trying to erase me from history.

"Andy [Gill] and I did the best job we could under duress [on the debut album]. We were collaborators in completing that record. We put in more work than they did in a maelstrom of gunfire and worse. I'm proud of that. I made that record. Can't they recognise that that beginning had value? Who was there trying to honour their concept? A total stranger, no less, getting no thanks. They tried to make no record at all, they were sabotaging the record the entire time. I don't want to be a scapegoat any more."

Hillel Slovak, meanwhile, was having troubles of his own, unsure whether his musical destiny lay with What Is This or his Chili Peppers brethren. A month before Sherman was fired, Slovak wrote in his diary about his mixed emotions (along with his revelations that he'd been consuming both freebase and heroin). But his diary entry also revealed that Jack Sherman was probably right: Kiedis and Flea were pushing for their friend to return to the Peppers.

"What will I do about memusic [sic]?" he wrote. "Very confused and filled with strife. Much pressure from all around – got to write that song, keep hearing things that I don't want to play – but am disillusioned about the business. Not sure if I can go back to the Peppers and be happy. I am afraid to spoil valued friendships. I have the best friends in the world."

According to his then girlfriend, Addie Brik, the Peppers simply offered Slovak more than What Is This. "What Is This," she admitted to me, "was a good band – but always was and sounded like Alain's band. Ultimately this wasn't what Hillel wanted. His confusion was about leaving a school friend and bandmate. Understandably it was a hard decision for him."

Flea's take on the situation was very simple. "Hillel was off somewhere making a record with What Is This and was callin' me up talking about how he was ready to come back to the fold. And that was getting me feelin' mighty fine so AK and I gave the Shermdog the axe."

The drama as it unfolded, of course, was a lot more complex than Flea's throwaway description would suggest. There's no such thing as an easy sacking, especially when songwriting royalties are involved. But regardless of who made the final persuasive phone call, by February 1985, Slovak had agreed to rejoin the band. Three of the Fax City Four were now reunited as Red Hot Chili Peppers.

CHAPTER FOUR

"The next day my shit turned snow white. I thought that was God's way of telling me, 'You can't do a lot of this.'"

GEORGE Clinton had already lived several lives by the time Jack Sherman introduced the funk-soul brother to the punk-funk upstarts. He'd been a singer, producer, band leader, hitmaker and manic performer, who'd drawn his inspiration from sources as wildly diverse as funk, soul, Detroit pop, Fifties doo-wop and the acid-drenched rock of the Sixties. He was both a major player in the African-American music world and a hugely influential figure in the broader rock'n'roll scene. And most importantly, Clinton was funky – and freaky – to the bone. His motto was "funk 'em if they can't take a joke", an attitude to which the Chili Peppers could very clearly relate.

Born in 1940 in Kannapolis, North Carolina, Clinton and family had relocated to New Jersey in the early Fifties, where he made a living straightening hair. While hanging out in the barber's backroom, he and a group of harmonising buddies formed The Parliaments, a vocal quintet who made some impact on the R&B charts. When he encountered his first bout of record company-itis and was prevented from using the band's name – it was now owned by Berry Gordy's Motown label, who had just dropped the band from their roster – Clinton disbanded The Parliaments in 1968 and gave birth to Funkadelic (although he retained the members of The Parliaments, a strategy he would use more than once in his musical life). Clinton had moonlighted in Detroit in the early Sixties, working as a songwriter and producer, and it was there that he started to warm to the idea of a band collective – hence Funkadelic.

But whereas The Parliaments played it relatively straight, Funkadelic took their R&B roots and mashed them up with the psychedelic rock of such masters as Frank Zappa. A radical new sound was born, with smooth vocal lines sharing sonic space with wailing guitar feedback and funked-up rhythms: it was as if James Brown were fronting a band starring voodoo chile Jimi Hendrix. (Key Funkadelic members Maceo Parker and Bootsy Collins had both played with the J.B.s, Brown's backing combo.)

Clinton described this revolutionary new sound as "a combination of funk and psychedelia which is gonna blow Motown away". "I knew that The Temptations and Gladys Knight & The Pips had . . . the choreography, the outfits and the tight routines," Clinton added. "So we decided to go to the other side and be the bad boys of the whole thing."

The sound was eclectic and electric, and the band generated nearly 40 R&B hits during the Seventies, along with such ground-breaking long-players as *Free Your Mind . . . And Your Ass Will Follow* (1970) and *Maggot Brain* (1971), which, as *Rolling Stone* would declare, "contains the nasty, oozing essence of Funkadelic [with] unbelievably sweet vocals and acoustic guitars [wrapped] around Clinton's disillusioned musings on the counterculture."

If Funkadelic were a spontaneous psychedelic rock ejaculation, Clinton's second band of the Seventies, Parliament (not to be confused with The Parliaments), were a funky free-for-all. Coexisting with Funkadelic and sharing the same explorer's spirit, Parliament's debut LP, *Up For The Down Stroke* (1974), was considered "the sexy R&B yin to Funkadelic's skanky metal yang". Parliament hit a hot streak with 1976's pair of albums, *Mothership Connection* and *The Clones Of Dr Funkenstein*; Clinton and his merry funkateers had reached a prolific high. Parliament's live shows were quite literally out of this world, the band arriving on the funk "mothership" and blowing minds with their freaked-out funk and wild costumes. Science fiction was colliding with Sixties acid culture – and the band's loyal fans were mad for it, just as the Chili Peppers' small band of believers lapped up their wild fusion of punk, funk and rock'n'roll.

Label hassles intervened again in 1980 when Polygram swallowed Parliament's label, Casablanca. So Clinton took the maverick approach and shut down both bands – but once again retained the players. In 1982 he signed with Capitol, both as a solo act and as the leader of the

P-Funk All-Stars, which featured – not surprisingly – former members of both Parliament and Funkadelic.

But when the Chili Peppers came calling, Clinton was embroiled in more legal hassles, this time brought about by the endless royalty problems created by working with 40 musicians, four labels and three bands over the past three decades. It was 1985 and Clinton's career needed a kickstart. The rock'n'roll crowd had begun to disregard him, while his rediscovery by generation hip-hop was still several years away. Working with a hot new band such as the Red Hot Chili Peppers offered him the chance to regain both credibility and commercial worth.

When asked about his wilderness years during the Eighties, Clinton casually dismissed his time out of the spotlight. "I went to the bathroom," he laughed. Then he added how, "We was just taking care of some legal business. [And] when there ain't no good subjects to jump on, it's hard to get inspired." Obviously the Chili Peppers represented a chance to regain the spark of inspiration that he so badly needed. And the cash would also come in handy.

If there was one legacy that Jack Sherman had left the Peppers, apart from their belated interest in health food, it was his love of Parliament/Funkadelic, whose music was embraced by the Peppers like a long-lost sibling. In much the same way that the band's decision to work with Andy Gill on their debut album was prompted by their love for The Gang Of Four, they couldn't believe their good fortune when the Funkfather agreed to produce the follow-up. This guy was a legend; surely he could help them find their true sound.

Flea, in particular, was gobsmacked. He called Clinton "the epic mythological prolific genius himself, Dr Funkenstein". To tie up the deal, Flea and manager Goetz – who had done some promo work with Clinton in the past – had met with him, flying into Detroit from LA and staying on Clinton's farm.

Flea recalled the meeting when he wrote liner notes for the reissued *Freaky Styley* in 2003. "I was mighty nervous to meet him but no one ever made me feel more comfortable more quickly – ever. He is the warmest, kindest man in the world."

Clinton's manager, Archie Ivy, recalled what the band asked of Clinton. "They said they want to be funky. We really taught them how to be funky. They lived [for a time] with George. He said, 'Look boys, you got the funk, but because you're white, you're gonna make it to the top before we do.' Give credit, not [just] to George Clinton, but to Parliament/Funkadelic."*

Manager, bassist and funkfather spent some quality time together, prior to the sessions, which were to take place first at the studio located on the Detroit farm where Clinton lived and then at Detroit's United Sound. Clinton bought Flea and Goetz tickets to an Aretha Franklin show and a bond was formed which would last long after the band's second album was wrapped.

Though it seemed like an idyllic set-up, Clinton didn't actually own the studio or the farm where the band would work before heading into United Sound, where John Lee Hooker, Aretha Franklin and Jackie Wilson had recorded. In yet another classic case of a great talent being screwed over by the music biz, it's likely that Clinton was living on the farm – which was located in Rochester, just outside Detroit – thanks only to the good graces of Armen Boladian, who owned Westbound Records, the label which had released all the early Funkadelic albums and who would be given such credits as "Supervisor" on these albums. According to Richard Kortvelesy, a reliable source when it comes to Detroit music history, it seemed that Boladian owned the property. Boladian let Clinton live there, rent-free, in exchange for unpaid royalties on Clinton songs that he had published through his Bridgeport Publishing.

Clinton used the farm-based studio primarily for recording demos and basic album tracks. He may have been known universally for his good-time-all-the-time music, but things were pretty tough for George Clinton when he connected with The Red Hot Chili Peppers.

The band, meanwhile, needed some new tunes. This time around they wanted to go into the studio much better prepared. With Slovak now officially a Chili Pepper, Kiedis and Flea shifted camp to Mexico – with a Fostex 4-track recorder in tow – in order to work up some songs, many of which had been co-written with Sherman prior to his sacking (in rehearsals that, once again, Kiedis failed to attend). Once settled south of the border, the pair struck up a sweet deal with a waiter at a

---

* Clinton would tell the band, "If you get to the Grammys, you do it with P-Funk," a wish they granted in 1993.

nearby restaurant. In exchange for the Peppers' weed, he would provide free flan and coffee every night. The change in scenery clearly worked, because while in Mexico the pair committed to tape the bare bones of such future *Freaky Styley* songs as 'American Ghost Dance' and 'Catholic School Girls Rule'.

Sweetly stoned and chuffed with their new tunes, Kiedis and Flea convened with Slovak and Martinez back in Hollywood, at a rehearsal space called Far Out, which they shared with their punk heroes The Circle Jerks. Slovak, Flea and Martinez cut out one night to play an instrumental gig under the moniker Stale Bastard, but the bulk of their time was spent shaping the songs for *Freaky Styley*, Slovak reworking Sherman's guitar parts.*

By spring, band and gear were on the road headed for Clinton-land. It was agreed that they would stay on the farm while in pre-production, which to the Peppers must have seemed like the funk motherland.

"George Clinton is amazing," Kiedis gushed. "He's the ultimate hard-core funk creator in the world, ever. If anybody ever wanted to ask you what was the greatest funk/metal ever, it would be Parliament/ Funkadelic. Their music is so great that I don't think people are even capable of understanding how great it is."

Flea was just as enthused. "George Clinton is a beautiful person," sighed the now shaven-headed bassman. "He's like a very warm man, good to be around. He's very inspirational; he's like an exploding cosmic love bomb that explodes in all directions."

Pre-production for the album took place on Clinton's farm and at a studio called Detroit On Parade, which was operated by a Clinton buddy named Navarro, a local character who Flea remembers as not being the "kind of guy you'd ever want to fuck with". The Peppers' stay on Clinton's property, however, was brief. Flea recalls that "maybe [Kiedis] smashed George's snowmobile or something", so not long after sessions began they were shipped off to what Flea described as "some condo type of thing", located in Bloomfield Hills, an upscale Detroit suburb.

Cliff Martinez, however, has vivid memories of the time spent on

---

* A band-produced demo of the track 'Nevermind', taken from these sessions, would end up on the *Out In LA* collection.

the Funkadelic farm. "It was a kick. We had our instruments set up in George's living room. Every day we'd wander out in our bathrobes and play and George would talk about arrangements." The walls in Clinton's house were adorned with gigantic Pedro Bell paintings (the artist behind many Clinton album covers); stuffed animals were scattered everywhere. And pot was virtually on tap. As Lindy Goetz recalls, "It was a wild time."

Those wild times continued when the sessions shifted to United Sound. Clinton wasn't a punctual man: the band would arrive after lunch, but their producer wouldn't roll in until early evening. Sessions would continue until early morning, when the band would head back to their condo and crash. This nocturnal lifestyle continued for the three months of recording.

But it wasn't as if the band were prisoners of Bloomfield Hills. Occasionally they'd adjourn to such downtown spots as Lili's 21. It was there that a very wasted bunch of Peppers would heckle local bands and behave in the wayward, reckless manner befitting snotty Californian punks. Kiedis and Slovak had sniffed out the local cocaine dealers and would load up on the cheap local product ("mass quantities" of the stuff, according to Kiedis). "Under the influence of said substance," Kiedis said, "we would sometimes be miserable and we would sometimes dance and be absurd."

Martinez – who remembers Detroit as "crack central, the only place where Pyrex beakers are sold next to boxes of Q-tips in gas stations" – fondly recalled one night of major indulgence. "Flea and Hillel cooked up a load of freebase from powdered coke and we lit it and inhaled it," he told me. "That was my one big drug experience. It was the first time in my life that I felt euphoric with drugs – everything was right with my life and the planet and the band. But the next day my shit turned snow white. I thought that was God's way of telling me, 'You can't do a lot of this, Cliff.'"[*]

According to one Detroit clubber, "These guys were just out of control. When other bands dropped in from out of town, the only thing they wanted to do was get up and jam. But the Peppers [thought] they were a big deal because they were from LA, because they were

---

[*] In a sad postscript, Clinton was busted in December 2003 for possession of crack cocaine.

recording out in the sticks with George Clinton – [but] who was George Clinton in 1985, man?"

In the liner notes for the album's 2003 reissue, Flea had a different take on their nocturnal adventures. "One night when we were there [in Detroit] we went to a rock club and a band was playing but when they went off stage, before they could return for their encore, we ran up and grabbed their shit and started rockin'. That was fun."

Kiedis' recollections of the night are different yet again. He remembers asking the band if they could jam, but was rejected. " 'We'd rather not have you messing with our sensitive equipment,' " he was informed. The Peppers did anyway, pulling off what Kiedis described as "the rockingest tunes that little club ever witnessed. We tore the place to pieces." The next day Detroit papers had dubbed their set "the guerrilla warfare gig".

On the same night, a wildly stoned Slovak – wearing a shiny new suit – bounced around the dance floor, "like a crazy freak", according to Flea. He was immediately christened The Skinny Sweaty Man In The Green Suit, a nickname that would stick.

Clinton's preferred working method in the studio was gentle bullying, speaking to the band members through their headphones in his low, rumbling voice. One time he stressed that Flea needed to put "more muscle" into his bass playing. If anyone else had asked the bassman to do that it could have been disastrous, but Flea sucked up his pride and played just that little bit harder, as instructed. "[Clinton's voice] was the greatest sounding thing I ever heard," Flea observed upon *Freaky Styley*'s 2003 re-release. "We'd be out there rocking and his voice would come in, 'Yeeeah git it . . . come on now! Dig deep,' and so forth."

The atmosphere in the studio was far more positive than the mood during the recording of their debut long-player. There were no turds in pizza boxes or "homo" acoustic guitars this time around – just a lot of weed being smoked and good times for all. "We had fun in the studio," Martinez stated. "George told us not to be intimidated. There was a controlled party atmosphere in the studio, with people sitting around, ready to do handclaps. I remember smoking a pile of pot and – this is awful to say – but I discovered that drugs could be a tool. I played much better, with that particular type of music, when I was stoned. I felt I played so much better than on the first record, in part because of this loose, party-type atmosphere."

It wasn't as though their wild nightlife was impeding the album's progress; in fact, it seemed the party just keep going when the band adjourned to the studio. Their new songs were evolving well under the watchful eyes (and ears) of Dr Funkenstein, despite the fact that Clinton – unlike Andy Gill – hadn't checked out the band's live act before recording with them. But he was fast becoming a Chili Peppers convert. He also steered the band in the direction of a pair of covers that would become standout tracks from *Freaky Styley* and establish a tradition for the band, who would go on to put their own spin on classics from Jimi Hendrix, The Stooges, Bob Dylan and The Ramones, even Bachman-Turner Overdrive.

One of the covers came from Sylvester Stewart (aka Sly Stone) who, like George Clinton, was a maverick. Despite operating on the fringes of the mainstream, Stone made a huge impact on the hippie and post-hippie era culture. Having moved from his native Texas to San Francisco in the Fifties, Stone was raised on the heavenly sounds of gospel, before studying the trumpet and then cutting a local hit, 'Long Time Away', at the ripe old age of 16. He was a DJ and then a record producer when he hooked up with a female trumpeter, Cynthia Robinson. Together they formed the legendary Sly & The Family Stone. By the time of their second album, 1968's *Dance To The Music*, the band's rock/pop/soul hybrid was drawing attention from both sides of America's racial divide – and when fused with the Stone's wild racial and sexual mix, the combination was pretty damned explosive. They broke out all over with an incendiary set at the 1969 Woodstock festival. Their leader's canonisation was complete when Miles Davis named Jimi Hendrix and Stone as his favourite musicians, even though drug problems, arrests, stints in rehab and a reputation as "no show Sly" damaged his legend during the latter part of his career. Stone had even guested on Funkadelic's *Electric Spanking Of War Babies* album in 1981, long after his star had faded.

For *Freaky Styley*, the Chili Peppers chose to cover 'If You Want Me To Stay', a Top 10 R&B hit from the band's 1973 album, *Fresh*, which turned out to be the Stone's final charting track. Kiedis was a fan of the song, in part because he recalled that a teammate from his junior high school football team used to sing the chorus in huddles. But the links with the music of Sly Stone were stronger than that. Kiedis could see in Sly Stone some of his own inconsistencies as a human being.

"Sly Stone is a perfect example of someone who had a very powerful message in his music that he didn't necessarily live by himself," said the man who would soon be harming his already questionable rep with a song called 'Party On Your Pussy'. "[But] I like to believe there's hope for anybody," Kiedis continued. "He's another one of my all-time favourites. And I don't think that it's ever too late for anybody to bounce back. I love him 'til the day he dies, just because he's written some of the most beautiful music ever and he played it with such conviction."

With an approving Clinton looking on, the Peppers delivered a perfectly serviceable reworking of a great song. Once Kiedis opened his mouth to sing it was clear that he was no Sly Stone, but with the Horny Horns – Fred Wesley, Maceo Parker and Benny Cowan – at his back, the Peppers couldn't miss. Some spicy, funky guitar fills from Slovak and a chorus of deep harmonies helped bring the song on home. It was one of *Freaky Styley*'s best moments, a natural high.

The second cover on *Freaky Styley* was the band's take on The Meters' 'Africa', a standout from their 1974 *Rejuvenation* album, which they renamed 'Hollywood'. The Meters were a big favourite of George Clinton, who pushed the Peppers in the direction of 'Africa'. His voice can be heard rumbling around somewhere in the midst of the track.

Formed in 1967 and fronted by Art Neville, The Meters pumped out lean, juicy R&B that was as earthy and nourishing as a plate of gumbo; they defined New Orleans funk. But they were a band with a split personality, because they were equally well known as one of New Orleans' finest backing bands. They worked on albums by Dr John, Paul McCartney & Wings, Robert Palmer and LaBelle, as well as opening for The Rolling Stones on their 1975 American and 1976 European tours.

What the Chili Peppers attempted to do with their take on 'Africa' (aka 'Hollywood') was lay claim to some deep funk roots. But hearing a shirtless, bronzed white LA dude such as Kiedis tossing out lines about "going back to the brotherland" was a bit hard to swallow. Fortunately, Clinton's good melodic sense saved the song from becoming a white-boy's notion of what funk should sound like, as he added layers of vocals from himself, studio hand Mike "Clip" Payne and others, as well as enticing some more swinging brass from the Horny Horns.

In a strange twist, the Peppers' own song, the rumbling 'Jungleman', which opened the album, accidentally borrowed a Meters song title. Flea insists there was no collective consciousness at work. "I swear to God that we had never heard the Meters' song when we wrote 'Jungleman'. It was just a wild coincidence."

The song itself showed that despite Kiedis' inability to find his own singing voice, he could still deliver an amusingly dumbed-down rap about being a jungle man who is able to have all the bush he can. And the band proved that they could recognise a serviceable groove when they uncovered one, while Hillel Slovak got one of many chances on the record to cut loose with some supernova stringwork. "Hillel was very Hendrix influenced," Martinez recalled, "and he was an open-minded guy. Jack [Sherman] could do a lot of different styles, whereas Hillel could be both a cerebral player and a bit Neanderthal."

Slovak's return to the Peppers had also improved inter-band life, according to Martinez. "Things moved much smoother with Hillel in the band. He was able to live and breathe and create without being called a fag, unlike Jack."

But you had to wonder whether Clinton and those around the band were truly confident of the quality of their songcraft. 'Africa' and 'If You Want Me To Stay', the record's pair of wisely selected covers, were placed amongst the album's first four tracks. It wasn't exactly a vote of confidence: the band were leading with aces, but they weren't *their* aces.

What is beyond dispute is the fact that *Freaky Styley* was certainly a far more testosterone-powered record than their debut. Kiedis, in particular, had his sexual mojo working during the tracks 'Sex Rap', 'Lovin' And Touchin'' and the malicious 'Blackeyed Blonde'. As for the track 'Battleship', it was actually better known as 'Blowjob Park' and had been in the band's live set as early as January 1985. Its watered-down title was the first but not last time that the band would have to modify a song name to please the legal department at EMI. Not that it mattered greatly; it was little more than a manic throwaway, a chance for the band to rock hard and bellow a borderline homophobic chant of "blowjob park" until their lungs started to bleed.

Then there was 'Catholic School Girls Rule', a blatantly X-rated meditation on the dangerous lure of teenagers in school uniforms. Lines that quote the title of the celebrated porn movie *Deep Throat* must have appealed to actor/director Dick Rude, who offered to direct a video for the track. The clip turned out exactly as you would expect, with plenty of flesh, swearing, blasphemy – and simulated blowjobs in cubicles from willing "actresses". Kiedis even got the chance to play a "ghetto Jesus" character, dragging his cross while running his discerning eyes over some seriously nubile school-agers. He looked like one happy rock dude.

The iconoclastic video, of course, wasn't destined for high rotation on MTV. Britain's Duran Duran could get away with the occasional exposed female nipple – and there was more bumping and grinding in Prince videos than a big night at the local pole dancing emporium. But the Chili Peppers simply weren't on that same commercial level. MTV didn't need to play their clips; why risk a fight with the censor? So 'Catholic School Girls Rule' remained a Chili Peppers collectible until it was packaged as part of the *Positive Mental Octopus* video set in 1990. As stupidly entertaining as the clip is, it doesn't do anything to downplay the band's worryingly misogynistic reputation. There is a very thin line between sexy and sexist, and the Chili Peppers hadn't yet worked out how it should be trodden.

The album's title track, however, had the makings of an early classic. The four-legged groove machine of Flea and drummer Martinez latched onto a sinewy, muscular riff, while Kiedis mumbled how he planned to "fuck 'em just to see the look on their face" – but unfortunately the song dried up barely a minute in. One question that the song failed to answer was whether the singer was referring to the hundreds of ripe and ready ladies that Antwan The Swan had lined up against the wall during 'Out In LA' – or was he taking aim at the critics and radio programmers that had sidestepped their debut album? Regardless of his intention, the song was proof that the band could funk things up very deeply when required.

'Brothers Cup' was another track that packed a lazy-boned groove with a classic George Clinton feel; it also featured smart, smooth interplay between Flea, Martinez, Slovak and the Horny Horns. 'Yertle The Turtle', meanwhile, displayed Kiedis' love of goofy rhymes. This was like Dr Seuss without clothes, what Kiedis would refer to as walking "the tightrope of fruitcakeitude". Flea was mad for Martinez's work on the track, praising his "stunning beats".

There was at least one track completed during these sessions that was left off the album, again in controversial circumstances. 'Millionaires Against Hunger' was the band's attempt at a rebuke to the well-intentioned but somewhat heavy-handed fund-raisers of the time, including Band Aid's 'Do They Know It's Christmas' and 'We Are The World', a monster hit that was wailed by Michael Jackson, Lionel Richie and many other platinum-plus American stars of the day. The proceeds from these songs were to be used to relieve famine in Africa. But the Peppers took a very punk rock stance regarding the situation: why didn't these mainstream stars just write a cheque, instead of setting themselves up as international saviours, hell-bent on feeding the world? EMI failed to see the humour in the song; it was left unused for five years until it found a home on the B-side of 1990's *Taste The Pain* EP. But the band must have learned something from the experience, because throughout the rest of their career they would become actively involved in raising cash for various worthy causes, without ever talking up their involvement.

Freaky Styley was a patchy record, though clearly a step in a funkier, rockier direction after the letdown that was *The Red Hot Chili Peppers*. Kiedis still had trouble deciding when he should rap and when he should croon – and his singing voice remained little more than a rusty croak, despite the lessons he'd taken during their first album. Even when he opted to rap, he was sometimes more focused on speed than coherence, which stripped his lyrics of any real punch. But Slovak was given the chance to bust loose with some blazing solos and Flea and Martinez were beginning to form a super-tight, deadly-funky rhythm unit.

And Clinton had brought enough friends into the studio to make the album something of an all-star jam, a chance for the Peppers to hang out and record with their heroes. The Horny Horns were all Parliament/Funkadelic/P-Funk insiders; likewise percussionist Larry Fratangelo and backing vocalists Steve Boyd, Gary Shider and Andre Williams. Michael "Clip" Payne, who also helped out with harmonies on the record, was another Clinton pal – and he became very tight with Flea during the making of the album. As Flea recalled, their bond was formed early in the recording process when Payne came up with the word "gloryhallastupid". That was just the kind of nonsense that appealed to the 22-year-old.

Unlike their tense studio experience with Andy Gill, the Chili Peppers walked away reasonably satisfied from the *Freaky Styley* sessions. In George Clinton they'd gained both a mentor and a fan for life, while they felt that his production had helped them come closer to capturing the real essence of the Red Hot Chili Peppers. In early interviews for the album, Kiedis, especially, was rhapsodic when asked about working with the renegade of funk.

"What he does with vocal arranging is incredible and the experience we had working with him I wouldn't trade for a penthouse suite in the Empire State Building," he said. "I'm so fortunate to have had that experience of making a record with him. It was a blessing to be able to hang out with him and learn from him."

The links between producer and singer extended beyond the studio doors, as Kiedis would reveal. Early in the sessions, before they were cast off to the condo in Bloomfield Hills, Kiedis and Clinton woke early and went fishing on a lake on Clinton's property. He hadn't done this type of bonding with his father, Blackie Dammett.

"He's got a little pond out back," Kiedis remembered fondly, "and one day he and I got up early and went out and caught breakfast."

As for Flea, he could spot the big improvement in the band's playing and also in their ability to understand the workings of the studio. In short, *Freaky Styley* sounded so much more like the Chili Peppers than their debut long-player. "I feel great about this record," he declared, "about the way we played. After we just didn't get the groove of who we were all the way on the first record, I was so happy just to hear deep groove come out of the speakers when we were recording this music."

The bassman knew this wasn't a record that radio could embrace – that was still a few years into the band's future – but he didn't seem to be too concerned. The way he viewed the album, it was simply "too funky for white radio, too punk rockin' for black [radio]". But it was a definite improvement on their debut. The band were moving in the right direction.

Most critics thought likewise. *Freaky Styley* garnered many more reviews than *The Red Hot Chili Peppers*, and most of them were favourable.

Writing in *Interview* magazine, Glenn O'Brien declared that, "The Red Hots are as hard-edged as the Stooges [and] are funkier white boys than KC & The Sunshine Band . . . [this] is the first record of the rest of your life." *Rolling Stone*'s Ira Robbins was one of the first writers to notice how the Peppers were behaving like some kind of funky United Nations, striving to integrate what were considered "black" and "white" music.

He wrote how, "After two decades of racial division, popular music is in the midst of an overdue and exciting effort to integrate itself." He went on to note how the band were "irreverent, punky rockers with a jones for rhythm and blues vernacular and a commitment to humour, variety and unbridled stylistic independence."

It was the highest praise that the band had received in their now two-album-long career.

The *AllMusic Guide* gave a thumbs-up to the album's "pure, uncut funk", claiming that with this record, "The Peppers seem fully in control of their vision to be accessible successors to P-Funk." Writer Jason Birchmeier firmly believed that the choice of George Clinton as producer was wise. He was "perhaps the most inspiring individual the Peppers could have worked with at this point in their career." *Alternative Press*, meanwhile, considered *Freaky Styley* "truly a schizo record".

Writing in Boston's *The Globe And Mail*, Liam Lacey found the band's cover of Sly Stone "interesting" and The Meters' 'Hollywood (aka Africa)' "moderately inspired". But one question remained un-answered: "Do the Chili Peppers self-destruct from excess," Lacey asked, "or start getting better?" He couldn't have known how poignant a question that was for drummer Cliff Martinez. Another Pepper was about to bite the dust.

While the *Freaky Styley* reviews were more favourable – and more widespread – than those of their debut album, the Peppers didn't shift a whole lot of units when the album appeared in September 1985. Topping the chart in the UK was David Bowie and Mick Jagger's cover of Martha And The Vandellas' 'Dancing In The Street', which was shamelessly premiered during Live Aid. Other Live Aid stars – Phil Collins, Dire Straits, Madonna and Tina Turner – were also riding high in the charts on both sides of the Atlantic. Flea's comment that his band were "too funky for white radio, too punk rockin' for black" was right on the money – and EMI were no closer to scoring them mainstream radio airplay. 'Catholic School Girls Rule' was a tough sell at a time when a syrupy remake of the already drippy 'I Got You Babe' was the song of the moment.

Lindy Goetz decided that the band should target Europe – there was a thriving "alternative" musical community on the continent, even before the term existed, and Goetz felt that EMI had a better understanding of the band there than in North America. 'Hollywood' was chosen as their first-ever release in the UK, while a video was shot to promote 'Jungleman' Stateside.

The clip pieced together some performance footage with the obligatory backstage mayhem and images of the photo shoot for the album's front cover, where the band thrashed about on trampolines while lensman Nels Israelson captured the good-natured anarchy. The band cut loose, choosing costumes that allowed them to live out a few personal fantasies. Flea regressed to his Australian childhood, strutting his stuff in super-hero tights and cape, Kiedis sported a purple pimp coat and Martinez and Slovak modelled a selection of funky hats. It captured the upbeat, party-hard mood of the album perfectly.

The band would tour from October 1985 through to March 1986, virtually without stopping for breath. Their crowd numbers had gradually started to improve, as Goetz had predicted, while the action stage front was becoming increasingly physical. Off stage, the band were as wild as ever. When asked how the band members spent their downtime, Flea shocked a reporter from *The Dallas Morning News* with an unprintable reply, which he modified to: "A lot of sex. And we play basketball, read books, get high." But rocking was their main priority for the months following the release of *Freaky Styley*.

A gang of surly upstarts calling themselves Guns N' Roses opened for the Peppers in LA towards the end of 1985, while the band readily picked up two support slots with LA heroes X during September. They also opened for Run-DMC during the same month, in San Francisco and Hollywood. On October 31 they played a Halloween show at New York venue The Ritz. East Village local Joey Ramone came backstage after a blistering set; clear evidence that the Chili Peppers were starting to be noticed by bands that they regarded as heroes.[*] Journalist Steve Roeser was backstage with The Ramones and the

---

[*] Years later the Chili Peppers would contribute to a Ramones tribute album, compiled after the deaths of Joey and Dee Dee Ramone.

Chili Peppers that night – it's actually Roeser's ticket stub that appears in the artwork of the reissued *The Red Hot Chili Peppers* album. He remembers that Flea "was particularly great on stage" that night. He also recalls that Joey Ramone was forever checking out new bands. "Joey, apparently, never stayed home and relaxed," he told me, "which perhaps is why he's no longer with us."

The Peppers kept on moving. In October they made their Pittsburgh debut at a club called The Decade and the show turned into a small-scale riot. Kiedis decided to keep the good vibes flowing even after their set had ended by demolishing an 80-pound bag of popcorn with the help of a hatchet and an enthusiastic audience. When combined with the Peppers' now obligatory "socks on cocks" routine, their frat-boy-heavy crowd – tonight coated in popcorn and sweat – went apeshit.

While Flea was talking up their live shows as "kind of like a whirlwind, tornado, hurricane, blaspheming around the stage with a hundred per cent of our energy," their crowds were equally taken by their locker-room, *Animal House*-styled antics. As the band started to discover, it was becoming increasingly hard to sell records when your fans saw you as a rock'n'roll circus act. To many the Peppers were stoned punks stumbling about with socks hanging off their dicks. The songs didn't really matter.

Kiedis didn't seem too fazed. To add to the band's party-boy image, he had taken to wearing a new stage outfit – a skimpy skirt constructed from an American flag, teamed with very serviceable tennis shoes. Some nights he chose to wear a little something beneath his skirt to maintain his modesty, other nights he opted to simply let it all hang free.

"It's very stylish," Kiedis said when asked about his punk rock spin on Old Glory. "I've even hung upside down from ceiling pipes at clubs and let the skirt fall down over my face, giving the audience a new view of my nakedness. [It's] shock value," he explained. "We do it to get people's attention. It's also a strong sense of human freedom to play nude."

By mid-December the occasional nudist and his fellow Peppers were filling Rockefeller's, a 400-capacity venue in Houston, Texas. Wisely, the venue served their drinks in plastic cups. "Whether it was to protect the band or the crowd, we're not sure," noted a reporter from the *Houston Chronicle*.

This was one of the larger cities where the band had started to make some kind of impact. Their show was well received, one reviewer noting that it contained "enough flash and trash to send a standing-room crowd home into the cold drizzle happy as loons."

While *Freaky Styley* received solid praise but few sales, and the Peppers' live reputation was spreading, their Fairfax High pals What Is This were having some brief, unexpected success. Their *Squeezed* EP had cornered a little more college radio airplay than their soulmates in the Chili Peppers. Their parent label, MCA, was sufficiently satisfied to green-light the recording of their first album, proposing Todd Rundgren as the possible producer.

Rundgren was a rock'n'roll prodigy from Philadelphia who in the late Sixties fronted The Nazz, a Beatles' loving band of power-popsters. When they split he immersed himself in cutting-edge technology and blue-eyed soul songcraft for such ground-breaking solo records as *Something/Anything* and 1978's *Hermit Of Mink Hollow*. He then produced Meat Loaf's hi-calorie hit *Bat Out Of Hell*, and worked with acts as stylistically opposed as the White Punks On Dope, The Tubes, downmarket riffers Grand Funk Railroad and apple-pie popster Shaun Cassidy. Rundgren was also an innovator in the field of rock videos. By 1981 he'd opened his own computer-video studio in Woodstock, New York, as well as undertaking occasional tours where he came on like a high-tech one-man band, playing acoustic sets to backing tapes while his computer-graphic videos flashed on a screen behind him.

But the relationship between Rundgren and the now Slovak-less What Is This (Johannes chose not to replace him, but "to just play more guitar") wasn't good. As another session dragged along fruitlessly, the band told their producer that they were going to jam on The Spinners' 'I'll Be Around', just for fun. Rundgren hit the record button and left the band alone in the studio. When MCA execs dropped by Rundgren's Bearsville Studio to check on the progress of the album, the first track that Rundgren previewed for them was the "fun" cover, which wasn't even supposed to be recorded, let alone released. The MCA staffers were wise to the commercial potential of the song (it had originally been a Top 20 US hit for The Spinners in late 1972), and made it the focus of their marketing campaign for the album. The throwaway cover became a minor hit, peaking at number 62 in August

1985, just as the Peppers were preparing to deliver *Freaky Styley*. But the rest of What Is This' self-titled album was ignored. What Is This were in as deep a hole as their band of brothers the Chili Peppers – and the two bands' membership exchange programme was about to start up again. Jack Irons was ready to rejoin the Red Hot Chili Peppers.

Cliff Martinez made just a few more appearances as a Chili Pepper – he was there for their first, brief European tour, early in 1986, where the band got the chance to reunite and jam with George Clinton, live to air on German TV. Then there was a Chicago show in February, where they supported The Beastie Boys. He also appeared with the rest of the band during their cameo on the film *Tough Guys*, which starred Kirk Douglas.*

But Martinez's time was fast running out. He was losing interest in the seemingly endless slog of touring, and Jack Irons was keen to move on from What Is This and hook up, once again, with his Fairfax High buddies. When Alain Johannes brought his girlfriend, Natasha Schneider, into What Is This, Irons read this as a clear signal that his role within the band was "lessening".

Irons then received a call from Flea, offering him the drummer's chair in the Peppers. Once he completed some final work with What Is This, Irons was free.

Cliff Martinez thus became the second in what would become a conga line of ex-Peppers over a stretch of 12 years. Unlike Jack Sherman, he was made to feel "like a permanent member" of the band. But he now admits to losing both his interest and enthusiasm for the Peppers, even though he put up some resistance when Flea – who detected the change in the drummer – asked him to leave.

"I wasn't ready and didn't really want to go," he confessed. "But a few years later I realised I should have gotten out sooner. I wasn't giving my best. They were right to give me the axe. I didn't know it, but I think I wanted to do some writing of my own. I was getting to be an unpleasant person to be around. I lost interest in the lifestyle and the music, I guess."

By March 1986, the "Fax City Four" of Kiedis, Flea, Slovak and Irons were officially reunited. It was almost as if they were reliving their

* Writing in his diary, Slovak described it as a "long and interesting day . . . Kirk kicks".

glory days as Tony Flow And The Miraculously Majestic Masters Of Mayhem. They had a short, sharp mini-tour ahead of them, including a set at *Spin* magazine's first anniversary party, but the funky four were hot to get back into the studio and record a real Red Hot Chili Peppers album.

CHAPTER FIVE

"Our music is like a bowel movement."

B Y late 1986, The Red Hot Chili Peppers were a troubled band.
Despite the seemingly neat fits with producers Andy Gill and
George Clinton, *The Red Hot Chili Peppers* and *Freaky Styley* had not
made any kind of commercial impact, each album selling around
75,000 copies. Neither release had registered on the *Billboard* Top 200
album chart. The sales meant that EMI recouped their moderate
investment in the band, but it wasn't enough to convince them that the
Peppers should suddenly be their biggest concern. In a move that
would strengthen the band's opinion that they didn't rate highly on the
list of EMI priorities, in late 1986 the company moved the Peppers to
their more specialised EMI Manhattan label.

Kiedis, who, in a statement at the time, doubted whether EMI knew
how to get the band radio airplay, was dismissive of the move. "[It] was
almost like, 'Do what you like, it's probably not going to sell anyway.'"

In the words of Michael Beinhorn, who would go on to produce
their next two albums, as far as their label was concerned, the Chili
Peppers were "this band no one there could figure out, nor do anything with."

Flea, who'd just proposed marriage to Loesha Zeviar, a recent high
school graduate eight years younger than the wild-eyed bassist (and
pregnant with his child), was equally cold when it came to business
dealings with EMI. "I felt a lotta times that the only reason they [EMI]
kept us was because they would go to [one of our] shows and see 3,000
kids going wild." He was pumping up the fact that the band at the time
were playing 1,000 capacity venues, but his concern about the label's
intentions were clear and probably justified.

Crucially, the band did have a true believer in manager Lindy Goetz.
According to engineer Dave Jerden, Goetz "stuck with them like a

dog". Goetz was frustrated that their two albums hadn't convinced many others what he held to be an undeniable truth – this band had star potential.

To LA scenester Kim Fowley, Goetz was the unsung hero of the band, and the architect of their rise. According to Fowley, "Lindy Goetz is never given any credit. He was Brian Epstein, he was Colonel Parker, he was Malcolm McLaren. [I] have nothing but good things to say about Lindy Goetz and his 25-hour-a-day belief in that band. That guy was astounding."

Erstwhile Pepper Cliff Martinez agreed. "He was always there for everything. He kept everybody's shoes tied and wiped the dribble off your chin. He was a pretty positive force. Lindy was really good at keeping it together, when there was a lot of stress, a lot of friction."

"My role was that of big brother, a friend," Goetz confessed to me. "I knew I would have a problem [breaking the band]. But we were going out there trying to conquer the world."

In some ways, Michael Beinhorn was the man least likely to work with these tattooed Californian funk-punks. Flea had referred to him as "a professional type of producer guy", which was hardly the warmest accolade. But Beinhorn's background was more detailed and credible than that slight suggested.

During the early Eighties, Beinhorn had been the keyboard player for Material, the band fronted by Bill Laswell, an outfit renowned for their intellectualised, anything-goes sense of musical experimentation. Forming the core of the band with Laswell on bass and Fred Maher on drums (who would go on to play with Lou Reed and produce records by Matthew Sweet), Beinhorn contributed to such highly regarded works as the 1981 album *Memory Serves*. They also cut the club single 'Bustin' Out' with soulful belter Nona Hendryx. After playing on Laswell's 1982 solo album, *Baselines*, and *Ambient 4: On Land*, one of Brian Eno's radical journeys into sonic stillness, Beinhorn then moved into production.

Along with engineer Dave Jerden, who'd already played his part in Chili Peppers history when he worked with Andy Gill on their 1984 debut, Beinhorn co-produced (with Bill Laswell) Herbie Hancock's Grammy-winning *Future Shock*. This was the record that generated the breakout hit, 'Rockit', a wild intermingling of hip-hop, jazz and pop.

Its inspired, innovative video collected five MTV awards in 1984. In his spare time, Beinhorn created the Ultra Analog recording format, which used two-inch tapes recorded at 7.5 ips (inches per second). But this invention was more than some audiophilic wet dream – what it did was bring out the low end of the sound spectrum, which proved extremely useful when Beinhorn began working with such rock acts as Ozzy Osbourne, Soul Asylum and, of course, The Red Hot Chili Peppers.

Beinhorn, however, wasn't the first choice of either the band or even the label when it came to a producer for the Peppers' third album. They'd already reached out to Rick Rubin, the bearded, shades-wearing former heavy rock freak. Rubin was extremely hot at the time; he'd helped bridge the gap between hip-hop and rock via such huge hits as Run-DMC's *Raising Hell* (1986) and, in the same year, produced The Beastie Boys' enormous smash *Licensed To Ill*. Born Frederick Jay Rubin on Long Island, New York, he co-founded Def Jam Records with hip-hop pioneer Russell Simmons while still studying at New York University. Rubin was 21 at the time. His first production efforts were very rock and very hardcore – in 1985 he produced Slayer's *Hell Awaits* and the next year he worked on their follow-up, *Reign In Blood*. But it was Rubin's crossover work with Run-DMC and the Beasties that piqued the Chili Peppers' interest. If he could achieve anywhere near the same success with them that he'd scored with the snotty, misogynistic New Yorkers, surely the Chili Peppers would be on their way out of the rut in which they were currently stuck.

As with much Chili Pepper history – and so much of rock'n'roll history, come to think of it – there are several versions of the first meeting between Rubin and the Chili Peppers.

Flea's recollection was that the producer, with The Beastie Boys in tow, arrived at their rehearsal room in early 1987 while the Peppers were working on getting songs together for their third album. A jam ensued, but the bassman recalls that "we did not connect with Rick. The vibe was very weird."

Rubin's recollection of the brief get-together confirmed this. "It was kind of at the height of the unhealthy version of the original line-up," he said when asked in 2002. "I remember going to a rehearsal [no mention of The Beastie Boys being with him, though]. Musically, it felt good, but the energy in the room felt dangerous and not good." He would tell Flea that the mood in the studio was "one of the most depressing feeling rooms he had ever been in".

Beinhorn's own take on the meeting, however, is slightly different. When he agreed to produce the album that would become *The Uplift Mofo Party Plan*, one of the first steps he took was to sit down with the band and ask them exactly who else they'd approached before he was hired.

"Their story on Rick Rubin," Beinhorn told me, "was that they reached out to him and he, in turn, rebuffed them as – according to them – he wished to work with bands of greater stature."

Whatever the case, the Peppers wouldn't work with Rubin until 1991's *BloodSugarSexMagik*, by which time enough drama had taken place in the Chili Peppers camp to confirm the wisdom of his decision to postpone working with them.

But the most left-field possibility as producer for the Peppers' third album was former Sex Pistols manager Malcolm McLaren. After his Johnny Rotten-fronted punk proteges had collapsed in a very ugly, very public mess in January 1978, McLaren moved on to pirate-styled pop star, Adam Ant. Then, in a typically astute, albeit self-serving move, McLaren poached Ant's backing band (for the grand sum of £1,000) and talked them into supporting a 14-year-old Burmese singer, Myant Myant Aye. Her name, purportedly, was Burmese for Cool Cool High. McLaren christened her Annabella Lwin and the band became Bow Wow Wow, whose debut single, 'C30, C60, C90, Go', appeared to encourage home-taping and therefore incensed the record industry.*

Having scored Top 10 Hits with 'Go Wild In The Country' and a remake of The Strangeloves' 'I Want Candy', Bow Wow Wow imploded in 1983, and McLaren began piecing together his own records, under the characteristically understated tag of Malcolm McLaren And The World Famous Supreme Team. He scored huge hits in both the UK mainstream chart and the US dance charts with the eccentric cut-and-paste jobs 'Buffalo Gals', 'Butterfly' and 'Double Dutch'. Cliff Martinez was still a Chili Pepper when McLaren met with him,

---

* Bow Wow Wow were Chili Peppers faves, too: Kiedis would go on to mention the band in his lyrics for 'Suck My Kiss', where he was "swimming in the sound of Bow Wow Wow". They were also namechecked during *Californication*'s 'Right On Time'.

Flea, Kiedis and band buddy Pete Weiss. The band were all for the possibility of working with McLaren. If Rick Rubin wasn't ready to make them stars, surely the man who invented The Sex Pistols could do the job.

"We loved Bow Wow Wow and The Sex Pistols," Flea recalled, "so we were psyched. I really looked to this guy as someone who could make us huge and cool and famously rad."

McLaren's meeting with the band was far stranger than having Rick Rubin and The Beastie Boys gatecrash band rehearsals. They agreed to talk in the more formal, more corporate surroundings of EMI's Hollywood office. McLaren arrived in a Rolls-Royce; his outfit for the day was magisterial white robes. He came with an assistant in tow, "a cute blond boy", as Flea remembered.

After introductions had been made, McLaren outlined his radical plan, which he was sure would give the Chili Peppers the stardom they craved. He believed that the band should perform while decked out in skate-punk gear and play simple, Chuck Berry-styled riffs. Guitarist, bassman and drummer would stay in the background, leaving centre-stage to Kiedis. To McLaren, the singer was the star and the rest of the band should not get in his way. There was also talk of a film starring the band. To say that the trio were stunned by his strategy was an under-statement. After all, weren't they supposed to be a band of brothers?

"He was going, 'Right, 'ere's wot we do,'" Flea would reveal four years later. "'Anthony, you're gonna be the star and you three can just sit at the back playing simple rock'n'roll.' That was his concept and we did not want to go for it. After that he went on speeching [sic] about how important it is to get back to the roots of rock'n'roll 'cos nothing has ever been done differently and we think we're doing it differently. But he gave this real convincing speech about being in touch with the origins of it."

"He had a vision of really altering the band, [taking] a real roots music approach," the deadpan Cliff Martinez laughed. "He said to Flea, 'You may not be able to be the majestic bass player you imagine yourself to be.' I thought, 'OK, he's dead in the water.'"

The band would go on to sing about the experience in the *Uplift Mofo* song, 'Backwoods'. But Flea, who had been dragging on a joint throughout the meeting with McLaren, had a far more immediate reaction to McLaren's bizarre idea. He fainted.

"I remember holding down the joint for a long time, just smoking it thinking I was this super cool, pot smoking artist guy," he would write in his liner notes when the *Uplift Mofo* album was reissued. "Malcolm started in on how he was gonna dress us up in his new 'skate punk' fashion . . . and I started feeling real dizzy and freaked out and [was] not the cool artist guy any more."

Once the bassist had been scraped off the floor of the EMI offices, the meeting with McLaren was over. He wasn't hired.

According to Michael Beinhorn, the other main competitor for the album's production spot was Mick Jones.* The co-founder of The Clash, Jones had left the iconic Britpunks in 1983 and taken a thinking-person's-pop twist with his new outfit, Big Audio Dynamite, who emerged in 1985 with their *This Is Big Audio Dynamite* LP. He'd recently produced the album *Westworld* from the UK post-punk outfit Theatre Of Hate. Jones was an interesting possibility for the Peppers, considering that both The Clash and Big Audio Dynamite were bands that were very aware of what was going on in the worlds of hip-hop, funk and rock. And this was exactly the kind of fusion the Peppers were trying to create.

But this didn't come to pass. The job, instead, went to the "professional type of producer guy" Beinhorn, who at that time, apart from his stint in the studio with Material and Herbie Hancock, had only produced relatively small-scale bands, including The Parachute Club and Idle Eyes. But even before being hired, Beinhorn did what George Clinton neglected to do, and developed a working knowledge of the Chili Peppers. So what if they didn't leave a sizeable impression on him?

He'd first heard them on New York college radio, although he can't recall which track was being spun. Beinhorn admits that he gave the song "some passing scrutiny" but was suitably underwhelmed. "It didn't occur to me at the time that I'd be working with them in the future – at that point I wasn't thinking in terms of whom I'd be working with down the road."

By late 1986, however, Beinhorn was hustling for production work and had set up a meeting with Michael Barakman, who was in A&R at EMI. Barakman mentioned the Chili Peppers, a band in dire need of a

---

* Dylan organist/sidekick Al Kooper was also considered at one point.

producer who could help capture their live explosiveness on record. Within a few weeks Beinhorn was on his way to New Orleans, where he checked out the Chili Peppers' live show and then travelled with them in their van to their next gig in Dallas, Texas. Beinhorn was smitten by the Peppers both as performers and as people.

"I found myself enjoying their company quite a bit," he recalled of his time in the back of the tour van, "and was very hopeful that I'd get the opportunity to work with them."

To EMI and manager Goetz the deal was this: the Chili Peppers were a troubled band under development who needed a sympathetic studio partner. Beinhorn was a fledgling producer who'd recognised the band's potential. And just like Clinton and Gill before him, he could use the work. Once Beinhorn had signed up to produce what would become *The Uplift Mofo Party Plan*, he formulated a clear strategy that outlined exactly what the band and the album (and the label, for that matter) needed and what their previous pair of albums had failed to do: this record had to bottle the intensity and mad energy of their live shows.

As Beinhorn recalls, "I enjoyed their [New Orleans] performance and it occurred to me that to capture their energy in some way on a recording would be a great boon for them."

He then picked apart both *The Red Hot Chili Peppers* and *Freaky Styley* in an attempt to isolate what mistakes shouldn't be repeated and what elements of the two albums were worth retaining. Beinhorn thought that the key problem with both these albums was an inconsistency in the areas of performance and songwriting. He thought they were patchy long-players that could have been so much better.

"I knew that I could use those inconsistencies to underscore and illuminate what I felt the band needed and help get them to the next level. I felt that in some ways they were in a creative rut and I wanted to do what I could to get them out of it."

The band were now working on fresh songs for the album in their rehearsal room; much of the new material would come out of these jams. Beinhorn was completely comfortable with this situation – given his diverse musical background, he was no stranger to improvising. "They didn't use many structural elements," he told me. "This was not much different than other creative situations I'd been in. As for being prepared, that was never a strong suit for the band. Then again, they worked up most of their structures in rehearsal."

During their first meeting and the subsequent road trip-cum-bonding session, he had picked up that there was some kind of "drug problem" within the band. His first suspicion was that it was nothing serious; maybe the band were smoking a little too much pot or doing some coke. After all, what rock band didn't imbibe a little bit? The truth, however, was that the heroin use of Kiedis and Slovak had, by this stage, reached chronic proportions, which might explain why Rick Rubin shied away from working with them – savvy players like Rubin could sniff out that kind of trouble at a thousand paces.

Still, Beinhorn wasn't quite prepared for the announcement that drummer Jack Irons made when he collected him at LAX at the start of pre-production. "When I got off the plane," Beinhorn recalled, "I was informed by Jack Irons that Anthony was a full-on raving addict and Hillel was a slightly less afflicted user. To say that the drug addiction created problems for the project was an understatement."

Jack Irons kept a wide berth when it came to hard drugs, in part because it was simply too dangerous for the drummer to dabble. He had just been diagnosed with Bipolar Manic Depressive Disorder and was on daily medication to relieve the intense anxiety attacks he was experiencing. To add narcotics to this mix could have been lethal. And the internal strife in Pepper-land brought on by drug use was only adding to his personal traumas. "I would try to avoid any situation that might trigger this [bipolar] condition," Irons would later admit. "[But] the music business seemed to be one of those situations.

"I don't think music is too far removed from someone's mental state," he would add. "I think it's very indicative. When a person feels more free and happy, they play more free and happy."

But the words "free" and "happy" were not being thrown around too liberally by the Chili Peppers at this time.

What Beinhorn (and Goetz and EMI) faced was a band that were not only struggling to rise above being hometown heroes, but were confronting their own demons: hard drugs and nervous disorders. And at the same time the band were convinced that their label felt they were little more than a source of irritation. Or, as producer Beinhorn put it, "I think we were all convinced that most of the people who were at EMI had tile grout between their ears, as well as in them." The Chili Peppers were in a mess; it was a surprise that *The Uplift Mofo Party Plan* was even made.

"I recall it as a kind of gloomy time of our career," Flea would state, looking back on the making of the album. "Drug use in the band was really beginning to make a morose stand. It began to seem ugly to me and not fun; our communication was not healthy."

The band's downward spiral intensified when "No Show" Kiedis started to miss rehearsals. He would go missing for days on end while Irons, Flea and Slovak prepared songs for the new album. It appeared that Kiedis' addiction was wooing him away from his sonic soulmates, even though Slovak's need for smack was just as strong.

Beinhorn told me how, "We would lose Anthony for weeks at a time while he'd stay at his girlfriend's house and shoot up."

Lindy Goetz confirms this, when asked about Kiedis' indulgences at the time. "Anthony was completely fucked up on drugs," he admitted.

Band and producer would call the singer at regular intervals, pleading with him to at least make an appearance at rehearsals. When he did, his stays were very short. He'd soon be back at his girlfriend's place and they'd retreat into their heroin-induced haze.

Writing one night in his diary, Slovak was clearly affected by the turmoil in the band – and was starting to question his own substance abuse problems. "Fuck drugs!" he wrote. "Music is my destiny. I want to get into the album more than anything; it's my saviour. I pray that Anthony returns to cosmic soulness and a new love and respect will happen."

Slovak, however, unlike Kiedis, didn't share his addiction with his partner. Addie Brik insists that he continually warned her off smack. "In our time together, he was adamant that I did not get involved with drugs," she said. "He said to me, 'I can handle it but you can't.' Anyone who knows about drugs knows this is exceptional behaviour beyond belief."

The same couldn't be said of Kiedis. "It was impossible to get any contribution from him whatsoever," Beinhorn stated. "When we had demos with full instrumental tracks and Anthony had to come up with lyrics and melodies, he [would] instead show up with lyrics for a song the band had cut a while before and shelved as it was mediocre. It was infuriating to everyone and I got so angry with him that I threw him out."

Beinhorn insists that he had no choice; Kiedis simply wasn't fit to work on the record. Nor was his behaviour fair to his bandmates, who knew how crucial this album was to their careers. They'd been toiling hard on their new music and Kiedis simply wasn't contributing. Beinhorn could see that, too, and figured that if no one else was willing to speak up and fire the Pepper frontman, at least temporarily, then he had to do it.

"This was just the final insult – amongst a great many others – to everyone else who'd been working so hard and had been waiting for him to do the same."

Kiedis was given a month to clean up and (hopefully) return to work. In order to do that he left LA, something he'd do every time he needed to detox. The band, meanwhile, continued working on their lyric-less, sometimes melody-less songs. Lindy Goetz does recall trying out a new singer at the time, a mysterious character called "Ron". "But it didn't last long."

When Kiedis finally returned to the city, he'd kicked his habit and announced that he was ready to work. The rest of the band were thrilled and relieved in equal parts, although it was not absolutely clear that they were in the best state of mind to start work on the album. They only had a handful of songs ready for recording and one of those was a cover, their supercharged, hip-hop influenced take on Bob Dylan's immortal 'Subterranean Homesick Blues'.

"It is difficult to say whether or not the band was prepared to make an album," Beinhorn figured. "It was, however, essential to their survival at that point."

Ready or not, by May 4, 1987, the Peppers, Beinhorn and engineer J.B. Bauerlein, who had also helped out during pre-production (and would tragically die a few years later in a motorcycle crash) had shifted into Hollywood's Capitol Studios to begin recording the third album. Flea remembers it as a time of "mishaps and nearly breaking up [plus] some good inspiring moments." He was insistent that, "It wasn't all bad, we did have a lot of fun, too." Despite all the drama during its creation, the album cost around $120,000 to record, which was relatively cheap, although Beinhorn would admit that the mixing budget was exceeded, slightly.

Not only were the band working towards creating some of their own history, but they were moving into some seriously sacred musical territory. Located in the heart of Hollywood, Capitol Studio was opened in 1956 as a recording home for the many stars that were signed to Capitol Records. It was a living, breathing shrine to some of the most significant pop music ever recorded. You could almost smell several decades' worth of music history as you walked in the front door. Legendary crooners Nat "King" Cole and Frank Sinatra had recorded there, Sinatra cutting his timeless ballad 'My Way' at Capitol. The Beach Boys, The Isley Brothers and Frank Zappa had worked there. Jazz greats Louis Armstrong and Ella Fitzgerald had cut some of their best-loved tracks at Capitol. More recently, The Beastie Boys had made their furious, testosterone-heavy racket inside its walls. The Red Hot Chili Peppers were hoping that a little of this musical magic would rub off on them.

While working with Beinhorn, Kiedis and Flea had few of the production concerns that they'd experienced with Andy Gill on their debut album. Flea's only regret about *Uplift* was what he described as "those stupid triggered drum sounds that rob the drums of their dynamics". When not finding themselves sharing a Capitol Studios urinal with former Van Halen singer "Diamond" David Lee Roth, the Peppers were, again in Flea's words, coming up "with some pretty funky shit".

"As it turns out," he would add, "*Uplift* is probably the rockingest record we ever made. I don't mean the best, though to some it might be, I just mean in terms of straight up rockin' and not giving a fuck – making some art. This record really brings the rock, funk and art in just the way we wanted to at the time. We were crazy as shit and on a highway to hell, but we did it, we pulled it off and we made a record we are proud of.

"Overall it was a strange time in our career but I really see it as being a rock solid booming and interesting record. We were the boys from Hollywood, the boys from Fairfax High. I feel very happy about the songs and it is obvious to me that we were still growing and changing at a good rate."

Given the inherent drama and baggage that the Chili Peppers took into the studio with them, it's amazing that *The Uplift Mofo Party Plan* is such a solid record, a great leap forward from its predecessors. It is also the favourite Chili Pepper LP for producer Beinhorn, despite the fact that its successor, *Mother's Milk*, was the album that truly broke the Peppers creatively and commercially. For Beinhorn, *Uplift* was a revelation both for the band and him as a producer and collaborator.

"I love the whole record. [But] it was [also] the first time that I really began to feel my oats as a producer, as an arranger/songwriter [Beinhorn would receive a co-songwriting credit on 'Behind The Sun'] and as a performer. "The whole experience was draining and exhausting," he added, "but a remarkable thing, when I hear it. It totally evokes for me that time, all the places we were when we made it, the people involved and every infinitesimal thing that was taking place at that time. There is a great sense of freedom and reckless abandon about the record which I love."

The record was also a breakthrough for Kiedis, who'd kicked the life-threatening smack habit that triggered his temporary sacking from the band. Beinhorn considered this a "personal triumph" for the wild-maned, lady-killing "Swan". He firmly believes that the album contains some of Kiedis' best word-work. But when the album was completed, a rumour started circulating that in order to try and keep Kiedis' heroin use in check, Beinhorn had moved into the same apartment block as the singer. He denies that.

"It is untrue," he insists. "Anthony was living at his girlfriend's mom's house at that time. I didn't have a car and I couldn't drive so after a few months of working with the Chili Peppers, I decided to move out to California, since I began to realise that the record we were making was going to take some time. I moved into an [available] building that was right across the street from the band's manager, Lindy Goetz.

"At some point in the process," he continued, "Anthony was staying at Lindy's house for a short time while he was trying to kick heroin and that, I suppose, is where one gets the idea that I was Anthony's neighbour. It's not like we went to each other's house to borrow sugar or something."

As for Hillel Slovak, the guitarist's own sparring match with heroin had turned into a slugfest as the sessions progressed at Capitol. Though more discreet in his drug use than Kiedis – unlike the band frontman, the guitarist would turn up when he was required – Slovak's addiction would sometimes impede the record-under-development. Beinhorn remembers that there was one telltale sign that Slovak had been using; his usually good-natured outlook would suddenly darken, as if a rain cloud had formed over his head. This was very much out of character because almost everyone who knew or worked with Slovak remembers him not just fondly but lovingly. In fact, Beinhorn considered him "one of the funniest people I have ever known", recalling a particular time when he compared the producer's role with the band with that of "Steve Martin with The Beatles". The producer was so taken by Slovak's mistake that he admitted he preferred to be compared to the Hollywood comic rather than George Martin, the buttoned-up Beatles collaborator.

Beinhorn remembered one particular session where a stoned Slovak was attempting to work on a relatively tricky guitar part. The results were disastrous. Slovak was attempting to pull off a guitar part using a voice box, which required him to insert a long plastic tube into his mouth. "Hillel was continually nodding out as he was waiting to play – and each time he nodded out, this was accompanied by a very loud gagging sound as the plastic tube kept going down his throat as he would lurch forward, very abruptly waking him. Boy, was he pissed."

The producer insists, however, that this was a rare slip-up for Slovak. "He never let it interfere with his work until *Uplift* was completed."

"Hillel would get fucked up sometimes," confirmed Lindy Goetz, "but he could still play."

If there was one song on *Uplift* that precisely captured the Chili Peppers' upgrade from funky wannabes to genuine contenders, it was 'Behind The Sun'. Opening with a sublimely simple descending bassline from Flea which merged into a crisp, clean lick from Slovak, it was by far the best thing the band had ever committed to tape. And it didn't really matter that Kiedis' eco-friendly utopian dream of a lyric was a reworking of 'Out In LA', because there was a sweetly melodic pull to the song that was irresistible. And a sitar solo from Slovak as the song headed into the sunset – with its echoes of The Beatles' George Harrison – gave it real potential as a stoner's anthem.

The song had grown out of a riff that Slovak had been tinkering with in the studio, but what it lacked was a vocal melody. That problem was rectified when the perfect melody came to Beinhorn while the band were demoing the song, hence his co-songwriting credit. The song was more about restraint and the band's emerging grasp of nuance than raw amperage and sweat. You'd never call the Chili Peppers fast learners, but their ears and minds were starting to open.

As for Kiedis' contribution to 'Behind The Sun', he was off with the dolphins. Literally. "The idea of the underwater world seems incredibly inviting to me," he said when asked to explain the song's lyric. "The dolphin or the whale has an extreme capacity for intelligence, communication, love of life, in a reasoning, rational sense. They live in peace, below the ocean. We should take a look at these other beings that we share the planet with, getting along a lot better than we are. I would very much like, at some point in my life, to write music for them to listen to."

There were several other highs on the album, not the least being Kiedis' developing skills as a rhymer. He found his flow on the opener, 'Fight Like A Brave', where he dropped an agile rap that contrasted Park Avenue with a park bench, ingeniously managing to rhyme bitchy princess along the way. In four lines he painted a vivid picture of life in the big city, while a skyscraping solo from Slovak took the song even higher. Behind them, Jack Irons pounded the skins as if he were channelling some Native American spirit. (Maybe via Kiedis, who was proudly sporting a tattoo of Chief Joseph of the Nez Percé on his shoulder.)

During the session for 'Fight Like A Brave', the band had offered Irons their own peculiar twist on team spirit while he was laying down the drum track. When Irons had trouble finding just the right groove, his bandmates knew exactly how to inspire him to drum like a brave. So as one, Slovak, Flea and Kiedis pulled out their tackle and pressed their sacks against the studio glass, while Irons searched for the perfect beat. It was a standard Chili Peppers studio ploy and this time it worked.

"They gave me 'scrotes' while I was playing to give me energy," Irons would explain. "That was the main inspiration for that song. If we're having a hard time getting a take we'll say, 'Testicles out,' and we'll get them out and it'll help us."

While the band remained clothed for their search-and-destroy rip through Dylan's 'Subterranean Homesick Blues', Kiedis dared to add his own verse to the Bobfather's amphetamine-powered prototype rap from 1965. The reprobate Kiedis throws in lines that sustain a rhyme through God willin', Bob Dylan, chillin', thrillin' and red hot killin'. Whether 'Homesick Blues' was crying out for a slap-bass, hip-hopping makeover is uncertain, but the Peppers' take on the song proved that their confidence and imagination were growing. And Slovak's voice-box solo was absolutely smoking – when he wasn't gagging on the thing, that is.

Bob Forrest was a huge Dylan fan, and he had suggested that they rework the track from the timeless *Bringing It All Back Home* album. He pulled the band aside one day at rehearsal and floated the idea. When he told them "it's a rap song," they were sold.

Having done his fair share of living outside the law, Kiedis connected with the slightly jaded, anti-authoritarian lyric of the song (as did US terrorist outfit The Weathermen, who took their name from the lines "You don't need a weatherman/ To know which way the wind blows"). "I like the whole paranoid idea of the song," Kiedis would admit. "There's always an organised form of police that's always focusing on you, especially now in LA. It's heavy in LA. When I sing that song, I mean what Bob wrote."

When asked about 'Homesick Blues', Kiedis even thought there was a hint of funk in the Dylan original. That was a first. "Well, you know," he told early band confidant Steve Roeser, "funk comes in all shapes and sizes. And I'm sure there is some brand of funk to be deciphered in [Dylan's] music. Just because he was so great, there's gotta be an element of funk, otherwise he couldn't have been so great. I just like Jimi Hendrix's versions of his songs better."

Beinhorn was won over by the band's version as soon as he heard the original demo. All he asked the band to change was the way the kick drum pattern followed the bass guitar; once that was corrected the song came together easily.

As for the rest of *Uplift*, 'Me And My Friends' was another of their energetic "band-of-brothers" shout-outs, as 'Slim Boy' Slovak, Bob Forrest and Jacky (Irons) were all namechecked by a nearly breathless Kiedis. The song would remain a set-closer for the Chili Peppers as late as their 2003 By The Way tour. For Kiedis, the track was a simple celebration of friendship.

"The communication between friends is the essence of daily life," he said at the time of the record's release. "I just love my friends. I like the idea of being able to extend my love as freely as possible. If I had a spiritual love, it would have to be unconditional love."

Within a year those bonds of friendship would be strained to breaking point when his and Slovak's rampant drug abuse took a deadly turn. But right now they were four friends making the best record of their brief careers. 'Me And My Friends' celebrated that.

Just like 'Friends', 'Backwoods' was another song that would stay in the band's live set for years. Inspired in part by their bizarre meeting with Malcolm McLaren and his plans to reshape the band as retro-rockin' skate punk dudes, the track was also a sweetly twisted paean to the roots of blues and rock, in which Kiedis and the band paid dues to Little Richard, Howlin' Wolf, Chuck Berry and Bo Diddley. Kiedis' tongue-twisting rap was a challenge for even the most adroit rappers, let alone a white boy with a minor speech impediment (Kiedis has trouble pronouncing his 's'es). But that didn't stop him, especially after he heard Slovak's riffwork for the song. "Just the nature of that guitar groove made me think a lot about the history of rock'n'roll in America," he said. "And it was kind of a feel as well, a combination of music and the backwoods of America."

There was some filler on *Uplift*, most noticeably the choppy, Zappa-esque 'Skinny Sweaty Man' – a reference to Slovak's coked-up rampage in Detroit – and the punkish 'Love Trilogy'. 'No Chump Love Sucker' was a somewhat turbocharged update of *Freaky Styley*'s 'Battleship' (aka 'Blowjob Park'). The slight 'Walkin' On Down The Road', meanwhile, was notable mainly for a Cliff Martinez co-writing credit. Unlike Jack Sherman, Martinez had maintained a serviceable relationship with his former bandmates. "Cliff was a great Chili Pepper," according to Flea.

But while 'Behind The Sun' would become the song that proved the Chili Peppers were more than drug-hungry Hollywood punks with permanent hard-ons, two cuts from *Uplift* would make more of an immediate (and lasting) impression. One was the band's first real statement of intent, while the other further perpetuated a reputation that the band would never be able to completely shake off.

'Organic Anti-Beat Box Band' came on like a band manifesto. It was a barnstorming, good-time rave-up that closed the album, kicked into action by an irresistible opening lyrical salvo where Kiedis headed back a few years in time, briefly reinventing the Chili Peppers as the "Fax City Four". Over a signature funked-up Peppers backing, Kiedis recalls the time when the Fax City Four were four young men. Even more so than he'd done with 'Out In LA' or 'The Brothers Cup', Kiedis was mythologising the Chili Peppers, setting them up as spokes-punks for LA's lost generation. We represent the Hollywood kids, he howled.

The song was a sly dig at such platinum-plus stars as The Beastie

Boys, acts whose use of technology seemed false to the Peppers. What these bands failed to do was create their own music from scratch. Like sonic bower birds, they would find the ripest possible jam and rap over the top of it, an approach which was in direct contrast with the Peppers' attitude of building a song from a raw jam. 'Organic' was also a sharp left jab in the direction of Andy Gill, whose use of drum machines had been one of the issues that the band felt had killed their working relationship while they were making *The Red Hot Chili Peppers*.

'Beat Box' was a celebration, so the band decided to turn its recording into a party. Amongst the "party vocalists" on the track were such friends and lovers as Flea's fiancée Loesha, Slovak's girlfriend Addie Brik, producer Beinhorn, band buddy Bob Forrest plus members of the LA outfit Fishbone, who'd been following closely in the Peppers' funk-punk footsteps. It was a good-natured riot, a statement that outlined exactly who the Chili Peppers were and what they were all about. In fact, the only downside was Slovak's surliness during the session; he'd taken heroin beforehand and as Beinhorn recalls, "He was especially grumpy that evening."

Slovak's take on the evening's events – 'Anti Beat-Box' was the last song recorded for the album, on June 9, 1987 – was slightly different, as he noted in one of his occasional diary entries. "We did the party vocals for 'Organic'; very fun," he wrote. "I'm high on coke – too many drugs but I really enjoyed it for the album sessions. It is getting a little bit boring, though.

"[But] it was so fun," he wrote of the entire *Uplift* sessions. "I'm so extremely proud of everybody's work – it is at times genius. Anthony's words are really something else. This is going to be a hit – it has to be – every track is soooo good."

Slovak was so smitten by 'Beat-Box' that he wouldn't leave the studio until Kiedis' vocals were finished. His presence put Kiedis "into a state of inspired excitement. We were all very tickled by how good our record was sounding. I was especially blessed because a few months earlier I had been kicked out of the band for being too wrapped up in drug addiction to rock out. This was now a time of celebration and elation."

The band would talk up 'Organic' at every opportunity. It also gave them the chance to let loose on a few favourite subjects during interviews. "Today's funk isn't very funky to me," said Flea when asked about the song's anti-technology message. "It's just too clean. Funk should be dirty music; it's not pristine, it's gotta have that dirty grungy feel. Every time I play a gig they play this song called 'Pump Up The Volume' – and they call that funk? That's not funk, man, that's a bunch of sequencers jacking off for androids – it's not for people who like to shake their ass and get down."

As usual, Kiedis would add to his friend's diatribe, but he opted to use a far more scatological turn of phrase. "The best way to describe our music is like a bowel movement," he said, "because it comes out of us very naturally and it'll always be like that."

While 'Organic' may have won the band some new devotees because of its pure funk attitude, 'Party On Your Pussy' was a very divisive Peppers mission statement. It was a track where the band trod the finest of lines between outright misogyny and free-spirited sexual liberation. The fact that the completed song resembled one big sweaty sex party was a major achievement – it was a tune that made you feel guilty *and* horny. This was slippery white boy funk, brought on home by a huge shoutalong chorus that made its point perfectly clear. "I want to party on your pussy, baby," the band and various ring-ins screamed, "I want to party on your pussy." Amongst the song's choir were Beinhorn and his girlfriend Annie Newman; her involvement suggests that maybe the song wasn't as offensive to women as many wowsers thought.

But EMI were not so sure. They insisted the song be re-titled 'Special Secret Song Inside', although the original idea was to rename the song 'Special Secret Sauce Inside', which would have been much wittier. A sticker that read – EXPLICIT LYRICS: PARENTAL ADVISORY was plastered over the top of Gary Panter's second vivid cover design for the band when the album was released.

The band were dismayed by EMI's conservatism – it was another black day in the relationship between the Peppers and their label. After all, The Red Hot Chili Peppers weren't interested in reining in their sexuality or putting a sock on their hormones. As Kiedis told one reporter, "We are always going to grow and change, but we're never going to ignore our cock and balls." But EMI were insisting they do just that. At the very least they were placing an oversized condom on the band.

As for what he called the "sexist interpretation" of 'Party On Your Pussy', Flea dismissed this as "really shallow". He insisted the song had a good heart. "It was an endearing compliment to the female race who we treat as equals and who we love very much. There is no sexist attitude in this band."

The misogynist tag would stick with the band for a long time after the release of *Uplift*, even to the extent that Flea felt 'Party' prevented the entire album receiving the airplay it deserved. He believed that the response of programmers to the album was based solely on that one track. "'Here's the nutty, zany guys,'" he said disparagingly when speaking with *Rolling Stone*. "'They're at it again, they want to "Party On Your Pussy".' Which was one song on the album." (He was conveniently overlooking the dodgy lyrics of other tracks on *Uplift*, especially those on 'Love Trilogy', where Kiedis lets rip on a sex-rap about buns and legs that spread.)

Producer Beinhorn, meanwhile, stuck by the band answering the call of their collective hard-on. "Who could be offended by a song with such endearing subject matter?" he said when asked about his response to the track. "I loved it. I do recall a friend of my father's becoming visibly upset by the song and claiming that the song was liable to promote violence towards women. I'm still trying to figure that one out."

At the time of its release in September 1987, the album's producer knew nothing about the song being retitled. He did admit to being hugely disappointed when he learned of the switch – and, justifiably, he found the new title "execrable". The relationship between EMI and The Red Hot Chili Peppers was becoming chillier with each release.

But to some extent, EMI's censoring the album was not a great shock. They were simply responding to the new mood of conservatism that was sinking its claws into most forms of mass entertainment in the mid-Eighties. The directive to censor the arts came from a group called the Parents Music Resource Centre (the PMRC), whose source was very close to the country's main source of political power, the Oval Office.

The PMRC wasn't the first collective that had attempted to censor music in the USA, but it was definitely the most powerful, well-organised – and without question, the best connected.

As early as 1954, Michigan congresswoman Ruth Thompson introduced a bill into the US House Of Representatives that would prohibit mailing any pornographic recording, although it was never made entirely clear just who would decide what was deemed to be pornographic. There were also many famous, much more public acts of censorship, the most prominent being in 1957, when the producers of *The Ed Sullivan Show* decided to shoot Elvis Presley from the waist up because his swivelling hips might inflame the passions of otherwise uninflammable women.

But even before then, in 1956, ABC Radio successfully convinced Cole Porter to water down the lyrics of 'I Get A Kick Out Of You', dropping the line "I get no kick from cocaine" and inserting "I get perfume from Spain".

Then, in 1966, there was the famous burning of Beatles records following John Lennon's inflammatory comment that the reaction of the band's fans would suggest that "we're more popular than Jesus Christ". The Fab Four became a popular target – a year later, The Beatles' 'A Day In The Life' was banned by the BBC, who claimed (justifiably, as it turned out) that the song contained explicit drug references. Lennon had more trouble with the authorities in 1969, when 30,000 copies of his and Yoko Ono's *Two Virgins* album were seized by American authorities. The Vice Squad shut down one retailer who carried the album, because it sported a nude cover image of the pair of hippie mavericks. Many US radio stations refused to spin The Beatles' 'The Ballad Of John And Yoko', because the song contained references to both Christ and the Crucifixion. Lennon's 1972 track, 'Woman Is The Nigger Of The World', received a blanket ban by virtually every radio station in the country. Lennon, of course, would be hounded by the authorities for years before finally being granted a Green Card in 1975.

In 1970, US President Richard Nixon told radio broadcasters that rock music lyrics should be screened for content and that any music containing drug references should be banned outright. Nixon's Vice-President, Spiro Agnew, condemned rock'n'roll as "blatant drug culture propaganda" and pleaded with Americans to "move hard and fast and bring it under control". This was the same President Nixon who granted a very stoned Elvis Presley a tour of the White House, where they discussed the evils of drug use.

But the PMRC – who crawled out of Washington in May 1985 – were the most prominent and influential group in the history of music censorship. It was the pet project of three powerful Washington women – Mary Elizabeth "Tipper" Gore (wife of then-Senator Al Gore, who would go on to become Bill Clinton's VP), Susan Baker, who was married to James Baker, President Reagan's treasury secretary, and Pam Howar, whose husband owned a major Washington construction company.

The song that set them off was Prince's 'Darling Nikki', a second-rate track from the Minneapolis hit machine that told the sordid story of a woman sometimes seen "masturbating with a magazine". Not only had the three women found the song in their children's record collections, but Howar's aerobics instructor sometimes played the track. They became even more incensed when they started to explore the lyrics of various heavy metal acts. The trio composed a letter that they mailed to equally well-connected friends and associates, which spoke out against "some rock groups [who] advocate satanic rituals [while] others sing of killing babies".

The artists on their hitlist included the usual suspects (Black Sabbath, AC/DC, Prince, Judas Priest, W.A.S.P. and Mötley Crue), as well as such borderline cases as Twisted Sister, Def Leppard and Madonna, along with seemingly bizarre targets, including pop queens Cyndi 'She Bop' Lauper and Sheena 'Sugar Walls' Easton. According to Gore, all of these acts represented "a sick new strain of rock music glorifying everything from forced sex to bondage and rape."

The PMRC lobbied the Recording Industry Association Of America (RIAA) and demanded that any records deemed "objectionable" should be labelled accordingly. They even set up their own rating system. An X rating would indicate explicitly sexual or violent content; O would warn of "occultist material"; D/A warned of songs dealing with drugs and alcohol. This led to a typically cutting reply from Frank Zappa, one of the PMRC's most vocal opponents, who asked whether the next batch of suggested labels would include "a large yellow J on material written or performed by Jews".*

As unreasonable as it seemed, by September 1985, the Senate Committee On Commerce, Science And Transportation sat to evaluate the PMRC's requests. The wife of the Committee's Chairman, John Danforth, was associated with the PMRC. So too was the wife of

---

* In 1986, an "explicit lyrics" sticker was slapped on Zappa's *Jazz From Hell* LP, even though the album was entirely instrumental.

Senator Hollings, who was also on the committee. It was a stacked deck from the start.

Even though the Senate committee had no real powers of legislation, by November they'd convinced 20 RIAA member labels, including EMI, to print warning stickers that advised consumers (and, most importantly, parents) of potentially "dangerous" material. Only A&M, the label owned by former Fairfax High graduate Herb Alpert, backed out of the agreement.

By the time of the release of *The Uplift Mofo Party Plan*, George Michael's relatively harmless single 'I Want Your Sex' had been banned by radio stations on both sides of the Atlantic, while the family of a 19-year-old suicide victim tried unsuccessfully to sue Ozzy Osbourne because, they claimed, his song 'Suicide Solution' had led to their son's death. The Dead Kennedys' leader, Jello Biafra, had also been arrested on suspicion of distributing pornography. The object in question was actually the cover art for the band's album *Frankenchrist*.

Given the mood of the times, it's surprising the Peppers were able to release any music at all, let alone get naked at their shows or use the words "party" and "pussy" in the same sentence. They attempted to downplay their distaste for EMI's insistence that they modify the title of 'Party On Your Pussy', but the band must have been very soured by the experience.

"It doesn't bother me at all," Kiedis replied, when asked about the new form of censorship. "Our lyrics are very explicit and if they wanna inform the buying public, I have no problems with that. [However] we love pussy and we love everything about women."

Kiedis did, however, dedicate 'Party On Your Pussy' to First Lady Barbara Bush on at least one occasion.

Yet in spite of the PMRC stickering – or maybe, in part, due to the accidental publicity it generated – *The Uplift Mofo Party Plan* was generally well received. It even became a favourite record of Aerosmith's Steve Tyler. And although the record was battling for chart space with sure-fire hitmakers Michael Jackson, Huey Lewis & The News, Madonna, Rick Astley, Whitney Houston and Prince, it actually snuck into the *Billboard* Top 200 album chart – a first for the band – peaking at number 148.

The Chili Peppers were finally starting to receive the right kind of attention and their sales were slowly building. The reviews they received for their new album were equally supportive. US mag *Paper* declared it "perhaps the hardest rock'n'rap record to date". Reviewer Steve Blush knew that the band were a very square peg in the round hole that was commercial radio at the time, "But boy, can they rock." Writing in *The Globe And Mail* newspaper, music writer Chris Dafoe asserted that "while they don't have the invention or the talent of the Parliament/Funkadelic crew [that] they look to for inspiration, the Chilis capture the spirit and mix in lots of male bonding, braggadocio and gratuitous sex, all presented as good-natured crazy fun." He was correct that the band weren't especially authentic, but they were breaking down some barriers. What they were doing was introducing their punk-funk brew to a mainly white, male audience – an audience who probably thought that George Clinton was related to the governor of Arkansas.

In his review of *Uplift*, James Healy of *The Omaha World-Herald* compared the band favourably to arch-rivals The Beastie Boys – he even figured that the "explosive anthem" 'Organic' was the Peppers' breast-beating response to the Beasties' huge hit, 'Fight For Your Right (To Party)'. He called *Uplift* an "irreverent, witty, obnoxious and loud" album, also noting (favourably) how the band shunned "trendy electronic gadgetry such as drum machines". As far as 'Party On Your Pussy' was concerned, Healy refused to buy into the censorship debate. "The track will never make Casey Kasem's American Top 40," he shrugged. "Oh well, that's the price of being on the cutting edge."

Florida's *St Petersburg Times* took a similar angle when reviewing the album. "Move over Beastie Boys," declared music writer Eric Snider. "This . . . Pacific Coast version of rock-rap-punk puts the Beasties to shame." The band would no doubt be pleased that Snider believed that 'Organic' "just about sums up the Chili Peppers' stance". Years before "keeping it real" became a rock'n'roll cliché, the Peppers were speaking out against clogging songs with technology – and their message was starting to be heard.

Writing at the time of the album's reissue in 2003, the *AllMusic Guide* went so far as to state that "in a perfect world, the Red Hot Chili Peppers' breakthrough album wouldn't have been 1989's *Mother's Milk*, but 1987's *The Uplift Mofo Party Plan*." Reviewer Bill Meredith noted, quite rightly, how this was the definitive band line-up – an observation that band manager Goetz agrees with – and the Peppers were undeniably better for that. "Slovak and Irons brought things to the Chili Peppers that no one else ever has."

As always, there were naysayers. *Rolling Stone* weren't entirely sold on the album, granting the record only a two star rating while screwing up their noses at the way the band "pummels listeners with harsh, pseudopsychedelic fretwork and hoarsely barked party-chant choruses." As for 'Party On Your Pussy', that was written off as an example of Kiedis' "locker room-humour level" of lyric writing.

Producer Beinhorn, however, made a prophetic statement when interviewed on the album's release. "There are bands which are being overlooked who will be the mainstream in a few years," he said. "They always miss this in the record industry. This is a feeling I have about a group like the Chili Peppers. To me, they're probably the best live band in the United States right now."

Touring was now as much a part of the Peppers' life as eating and breathing, and they filled much of the time between the album's September release and the end of 1987 with as many shows as they could possibly play. Hitting the road on October 21, the band had two months' worth of gigs ahead of them, with only three days of proper downtime.

Writing in his diary just a few days prior to the tour, Slovak was both optimistic about the upcoming shows and concerned for his own well-being. There was a frighteningly prophetic tone to his observations. "Been spending much time alone," he wrote, "and for the most part enjoying it . . . except for fleeting feelings of self dread and the sinking feeling that I've allowed myself to sink into a very scary and tricky place.

"These have been unusual days for me," he continued, "sometimes I feel tested. I do think of death often; not in a wishful way, just (I don't know) – it would solve things. (Cop out!) I feel in a way that my time, in a way is limited – it's not a strong premonition, perhaps just idle, strange, twisted thoughts."

Slovak wrote of his plans to exercise and eat well while on the two-month tour; he also documented his feelings about his bond with drummer Jack Irons, despite their very different lifestyles. "I feel quite close to Jack, he is a true friend. I think he, too, is as sensitive about the number of years we've shared as I am."

Now ensconced in the largest tour bus of their lives, the Peppers swept through Washington DC, Chicago, Houston and elsewhere, with funk-metal upstarts Faith No More in tow for most shows. Five days before Christmas 1987 they sweated up a storm at the "Orange County For The Needy" benefit concert in Anaheim, California, while they rounded out their roller-coaster ride of a year with a show at San Francisco's legendary Fillmore.

The Peppers were also picking up some high-profile support gigs, such as an opening set at Dallas' Bronco Bowl for U2 soundalikes The Alarm. As documented in *The Dallas Morning News*, on-stage the band were torn between the stupid and the serious. One minute they'd be confirming their hardcore cred by dedicating a song to D Boon, the frontman of Californian punks The Minutemen (Boon had died almost exactly two years before), the next they'd be sending the slam dancers into convulsions, or dumbing-down their between-song banter until the show resembled some kind of punk take on the Marx Brothers. But as reporter Russell Smith shrewdly noted, the band's music had real impact. "People who try to label the act a one-note, one-joke wonder underestimate the underlying force of the music [that] carries its own simple, instinctive power. Obnoxious but fun."

He'd summed up the Peppers' early career crisis precisely. While the band couldn't resist winding up their audience, getting nude and behaving in character as LA's crude, tattooed answer to The Beastie Boys, the Peppers desperately wanted their music to be taken seriously. But they really had no idea how to go about doing that.

And EMI didn't help their cause by failing to release 'Behind The Sun' as a single. Not only was it the album's best track but it had the potential to gain the Peppers exposure across any number of rock radio formats – and MTV coverage surely wouldn't be too far behind. Instead the song was put on hold and EMI pushed 'Fight Like A Brave' as *Uplift*'s first single.

Perversely, 'Behind The Sun' was finally released as a single in 1992, when it was used to help flog the band's *What Hits!?* set. By then the Chili Peppers had moved on from EMI and had become multi-platinum stars, thanks to the album *BloodSugarSexMagik* and its hit single, 'Under The Bridge'.

Although manager Goetz took a relatively calm stance when the song became a belated hit, there was no avoiding the fact that EMI had made a huge mistake. *Uplift* could have been a much bigger album if the label had chosen its lead single wisely. "The band and I felt this could have been our first radio track back [in 1987]," he said, blaming the "old regime" at EMI Manhattan for refusing to release the track as a single.

Producer Beinhorn was another who bemoaned the treatment the band was given by their label. "What's a couple of thousand dollars extra in promotion?" he asked when the record was released. But the money wasn't forthcoming.

'Fight Like A Brave' was packaged with a Dick Rude-directed video – he'd also worked on 'Catholic High School Girls Rule' – that did absolutely nothing to play down the band's party-boys rep. The clip brought together high-velocity performance sequences, a tribal dance around a Hollywood swimming pool and a wild LA street scene. Oh and the video closed with the band – and what could best be described as the Chili Peppers army – marching proudly through the woods, Kiedis, Flea, Slovak and Irons dressed like the bastard offspring of Sgt Pepper. The clip was a riot, no doubt, but did little to change the broader public's perception of the Chili Peppers as wild, probably psychotic, perpetrators of mayhem.

Their end of year tour was extended into the first week of 1988, as they headed deep into the Pacific Northwest, after bringing in the New Year with a typically anything-goes show in Vancouver. While Slovak was writing in his diary that he was going to make 1988 a "new, drug-free phase of my life", influential radio station KROQ had started to "spot play" 'Fight Like A Brave'.

The band's growing legend for kick-starting mayhem was given a few more column inches in late January when a free lunchtime "hullabaloo" at North Hollywood's Palomino, sponsored and promoted vigorously by an LA radio station, was shut down. About 1,000 fans tried to squeeze into the 264-capacity club, stopping lunchtime traffic. Somewhere near 30 police units had to be called in to break up the mad scramble. The band had tried playing 'Me And My Friends' and then Jack Irons started jamming on 'Them Changes', a Band Of Gypsys/Buddy Miles classic. But that was as far as they could get before the plug was pulled.

Palomino owner Bill Thomas was shocked by the reaction. "It was a bunch of maniacs getting into a frenzy," he told *The Associated Press.*

"They were stopping traffic out there. They were coming through the windows in here. The Red Hot Chili Peppers are hot but I didn't think they were that hot."

Proving that any publicity can be good publicity, interest in the Peppers kept building. They were confirmed for the cover of Britain's *New Musical Express* in the same month as the Palomino riot; there was also a Japanese tour scheduled for March. And, as far as the Fax City Four were concerned, 'Behind The Sun' was the next single due to be lifted from *Uplift Mofo*.

Despite Slovak and Kiedis' addictions, the band's future hadn't looked this bright since the time they danced like acid-addled madmen across the stage of LA's Rhythm Lounge back in 1983. But within six months they would sink into the darkest phase of their lives, a tragic place from which the band would take years to recover.

CHAPTER SIX

"Dude, your brother's dead."

G IVEN the riotous reception that they had received at their "secret" Palomino show, 1988 had the makings of a bumper year for the Red Hot Chili Peppers. The signs were all positive: they'd recorded *The Uplift Mofo Party Plan*, their best album yet, and the response to the record was more favourable than either of their first two LPs. And in Kiedis, Flea, Irons and Slovak they had what many considered to be the definitive band line-up, the perfect blend of musical empathy, tattoos, muscle and fraternal brotherhood.

As far as Flea was concerned, the creation of *Uplift Mofo* was the crucial first leg of a three-stage career journey. "When the Peppers formed," he said at the time, "we had a very important secret plan. First was to make a great record. Second step was to make a great video. And the third step was to make a great tour. We figure we've done step one with *The Uplift Mofo Party Plan*. As far as that record goes, I think it's captured the live intensity of the band and it's captured different aspects of what we play musically."

There were also indications that 1988 was going to be a banner year in rock'n'roll outside the Peppers' California enclave. Though the "alternative breakthrough" and generation grunge was still a Seattle pipe dream, the underground revolution that was launched by American college radio was starting to spread its tentacles into the mainstream. R.E.M. burst out all over with *Green*, the album that transformed America's definitive college band into the coolest guitar-rock act to be heard on mainstream radio. The Peppers' LA brothers, Jane's Addiction, released the primal, cathartic *Nothing's Shocking*, a defining moment in late 20th century shock'n'roll. Fishbone, who'd spent many hours and miles on the road with the Chili Peppers, dropped *Truth And Soul*, a record that perfectly captured their fiery mix of funk, rock and sweat. X got back to their roots with *Live At The Whisky A Go-Go*. Faith No More were moving on up with *Introduce Yourself*, which included the hit single 'We Care A Lot', a funk-punk workout that was virtually cut from the template that the Chili Peppers had crafted over the course of their first three albums. And even though they were in the midst of disbanding, Hüsker Dü's sprawling double album, *Warehouse: Songs And Stories*, was another crucial record that helped dismantle the Berlin Wall that once separated college rock acts from the mainstream.

There were even signs of rehabilitation in the pop charts. In the UK, indie-pop act The Primitives had elbowed aside the likes of Billy Ocean and Bros on their way up the ladder with their surprise hit 'Crash', while Morrissey, Prince, INXS and Terence Trent D'Arby were bringing a strong whiff of credibility into teenage bedrooms on both sides of the Atlantic. It wasn't quite the breakthrough that was kick-started by Nirvana's epochal album *Nevermind* – that was still a few years off – but it was a relief to see and hear pop stars who could actually play and write arresting, emotionally true music.

But as the Chili Peppers continued to tour, swinging through St Louis and New York during April and May, the stranglehold that heroin had over Slovak drew even tighter. The guitarist's work was at times sloppy and he became increasingly alienated from his bandmates. The groundwork that the Peppers had laid over the past four years was being eroded by his toxic lifestyle. And his bandmates were in no position to offer him guidance – Kiedis was too preoccupied with his own addiction and Jack Irons had his mental health concerns to deal with. Flea, meanwhile, was busy with his wife Loesha, and the impending birth of their child. And Flea was also devastated by the death of jazz great Chet Baker. Only a few months earlier he had met Baker and cameoed in *Let's Get Lost*, a doco that had charted the jazzman's wayward life, and a bond had formed between the two.

Slovak was less obvious in his drug abuse than Kiedis. The feeling at the time was that if heroin were going to claim the life of a Chili Pepper, the victim would be Kiedis.

"They were all afraid that I was going to die because I would just take too much too often for too long a period of time," Kiedis would confess. "Hillel was much more subtle and much more cunning in his disguise. He had everyone believing that he had it under control."

But Kiedis was coherent enough to recognise the tell-tale signs of his bandmate's addiction. "I became so familiar with the nature of addiction that I knew Hillel was in as deep as me," he said. "He was just more in denial. Hillel thought he had power over the dark side."

Alain Johannes believed that Slovak, just like Irons, was inclined towards manic-depressive behaviour. Slovak escaped his demons by using smack – and lots of it. "I think he was having problems dealing with reality in general," said Johannes.

To Addie Brik, Slovak simply lacked the skills to deal with his addiction. "I think he did not have the egotism and sustaining urge for social and professional advancement to straighten up once this poison had him hooked," she said to me. "This was where his dilemma and confusion came from. Then again he was a young man and I think I'm not mistaken in saying that young men do tend to go wild and live life to the hilt – and that is a dangerous game."

"Hillel was a nice Jewish boy," said Lindy Goetz. "He was a great guy, a friend, our brother."

This was a crucial time for the band. After the disappointment of their first two albums, *Uplift Mofo* had given them some momentum, and the shows – despite the constant demand for goofy behaviour – were now reasonably well attended. Their second European tour was only a couple of weeks away. EMI had even green-lighted a date – June 27, 1988 – for the band to begin rehearsals for their fourth album, with Michael Beinhorn again working the desk. The date would become hugely significant in Chili Peppers history, but for all the wrong reasons.

By May the band felt that Slovak's unpredictability was holding them back – the only real connection he had with the band at the time was speaking with Flea about Loesha's pregnancy. Slovak predicted that their child was going to be a girl. Flea remembers it as "one of the last things we got on about". It was clear that Slovak's addiction was pulling them apart.

"We didn't get along very well," he said a year down the line, "because of the problems he had and the problems I had, but everybody has periods in their relationship like that. And I wish I could have told him that before he died."

Kiedis also admitted that the band and their guitarist simply weren't communicating. "Hillel definitely shut us out. No matter how much you want to help somebody, because they think that they're above being needy, you can't make them do something."

When the band had reached Washington DC for a May Day show at the Bayou, with soulmates Fishbone and Thelonious Monster in tow, the crisis with Slovak was peaking. After almost every show of the tour to date he'd disappear into the night, eager to score from whomever, wherever. He had no time to hang with his buddies and conduct a post-mortem on the show. His playing was suffering, as was his relationship with his fellow Peppers. Chinese whispers had started to spread up and down Sunset about the impact that Slovak's addiction was having on his once peerless playing. The rumour-mongers said that Slovak would spend entire shows playing the one song, oblivious to his bandmates, or how he would crank his amp so high that ultimately their sound guy had to shut him down altogether, just so the rest of the band could be heard.

But on the day of their Washington show, at a club that had also been a stepping stone for such rising stars as U2 and R.E.M., Kiedis decided that he must step up and fire the band's guitarist, his old school friend. There are differing reports of exactly what happened next.

According to Fishbone's Angelo Moore, a close friend of the band and a perfectly reliable witness, he interceded and talked Kiedis out of the action he was about to take. He pulled Kiedis aside and told him why he should help his bandmate work through his ordeal, not cut him adrift.

"Bands like us are on a sinking ship," he said, looking around the room at members of the Peppers, Thelonious Monster and Fishbone. "If we're ever going to maintain a stronghold in this world of meaningless pop music, we've got to stick together."

Kiedis later related how Moore's words had a profound effect on him. "It dawned on me that we did, in fact, have to stick together if we wanted to stay alive."

Of course the unspoken subtext of Moore's declaration was this: your friend is in trouble and he needs you. Now. As a fellow addict, Kiedis understood perfectly well the lesson that Moore was relating. And according to at least one journalist who covered the Washington show, Slovak blazed brightly on stage that night. It seemed as though he was reacting physically to the personal demons he was struggling to keep in check.

"Hillel was imploding like crazy," reported *Melody Maker*, "and the effect of this was to twist that wonderfully lugubrious face into the most shocking contortions, to send the gangly limbs flying out from his body at impossible angles in a display of breathtaking uncoordination."

Backstage, after the show, the band even demonstrated a new stunt, the Hors D'Oeuvres, which involved the use of paper plates, each with a hole in the middle. Once the plate was settled on a Chili Pepper lap, wedding tackle would be manoeuvred through the hole. The result was a nasty surprise for unsuspecting dinner guests.

So, according to the official line in Chili Peppers history, Slovak stayed in the band. Yet producer Michael Beinhorn – who'd taken it upon himself to fire Kiedis during the making of *Uplift Mofo* – insists that Slovak was in fact sacked from the band around this time and that it was a key event in the freefall from which he would not recover.

"I loved Hillel," Beinhorn told me, "but he'd become increasingly despondent in the months preceding his demise. He'd been fired from the band for his heroin use after Anthony had gotten clean – this also had to do with the effect the drugs were having on his ability to play. In the interim, the band replaced him; suffice it to say, his replacement was utterly useless.

"These events," Beinhorn added, "apparently sent Hillel into an emotional tailspin from which he'd never recover."

No record exists of a guitarist taking Slovak's place at the time, at least not until the recruitment of DeWayne "Blackbyrd" McKnight in August. And Addie Brik denies her boyfriend was ever axed from the band. "Threatened, yes, but never seriously fired." Lindy Goetz's recollection backs this up. "There were some problems at times with drugs getting in the way," he said, "but I don't think we fired him. But then a lot of things are foggy to me."

Regardless of the chain of events, by the second week of May, the Chili Peppers were on their way to the Pink Pop Festival in Holland. Manager Goetz insists that by this time Slovak was clean. And Kiedis also made a vow to abstain from heroin, as he explained to a *Melody Maker* journalist when the band arrived for dates in London, Leicester and Manchester. "I [have] discontinued my career as a drug abuse professional," he told writer Carol Clerk. "I was becoming unconcerned with life and my friends and the ones I have loved.

"I hated the idea that I was lying to myself on a regular basis," he continued, "and lying to my mother and losing touch with my friends. Flea, who's probably my best friend in the band, became very disgruntled. He's constantly getting better and needs to be challenged. It got to the point where I was no longer doing that because I was using too many drugs. He told me, at one point, that he couldn't play with me any more.

"I spent some time after that regrouping my life. I'm much happier now I'm able to learn and experience life with a clear mind. My power and capacity as a singer is [sic] improving. My friendships are another of the things I live for."

Every night when the band tore through 'Me And My Friends', a live essential, the song would carry a much deeper meaning for Kiedis. It reminded him of what he had almost lost.

Kiedis had a new love in his life, actress Ione Skye, the teenage daughter of Sixties cosmic folkie Donovan. She was now living with Kiedis (who, even into his thirties, would continue dating teenagers). They had met at a party prior to the release of *Uplift Mofo*; she was still a student at Hollywood High, and was best known for her role two years earlier in the bleak teen drama *River's Edge*. Kiedis publicly declared her to be "one of the most ultimate angelic creatures on earth". She was often spotted in a dazzling Navajo jacket, a gift from Kiedis.

The Peppers even recorded a track, 'Taste The Pain', that would turn up on the soundtrack of *Say Anything*, a smart teen flick starring Skye and John Cusack.

While touring Europe, Kiedis had taken a vow of chastity in deference to their live-in relationship. He confessed that he was doing his best to fend off the attention of the many groupies that the band were now drawing. "Every night on this tour there's been an attractive female who has offered me her body," he reported. "In the past, I would've done it, and I might have enjoyed it or regretted it. But at this point, the idea of doing it makes me squeamish. Even if I did get an erection, the idea of following through would leave me very sad and sick to my stomach. I'm better off going back to my hotel room and masturbating and waking up without any regret."

Kiedis had apparently sworn off groupies, heroin, even cigarettes and alcohol, opting instead for the relief found in "basketball, solace and peace". He was living like some kind of funky monk.

Hillel Slovak, however, didn't appear for the *Melody Maker* interview until the tape recorder had just about stopped rolling, making it downstairs for breakfast "at a time when the others were finishing lunch". It served to exacerbate the already strained relationship between him and the rest of the band. At their Mean Fiddler show a couple of nights earlier, he'd disappeared from the stage mid-set, convincing many punters that the rumours of his unreliability had some basis in fact. Slovak, however, passed it off as the result of an allergic reaction to some pills he had taken. "I was hallucinating onstage," he explained. "It's the first time I've ever, ever, ever lost control. I was just backstage, freaking."

The explanation closer to the truth was that Slovak was doing his best to stay true to his vow to not shoot junk. He was probably undergoing withdrawal symptoms, a condition that is similar to an extremely wretched dose of 'flu. Slovak was in the midst of an incredibly difficult time, both physically and psychologically. He was trying to deal with a raging addiction, hang onto his place in the band and impress jaded UK audiences.

The *Melody Maker* article was named "Peace Corpse". It was an unfortunately prescient title.

Former Pepper Jack Sherman told me of a chance meeting with Kiedis and Flea around this time. He insists that his two former sparring partners were thinking about inviting him back into the band. Flea told Sherman how strange it was bumping into him, because he'd just told Kiedis, "Hillel's being a dick, let's get the Sherm back in the band." Of course, nothing came of their chance meeting.

Their brief European tour included a pit stop in Amsterdam, where the band befriended tattoo artist Henk Schiffmacher (aka Henky Penky), whose Tattoo Museum was set up in the basement of a Hell's Angel coffeehouse. It was the perfect base for the band – pot was freely available upstairs and there was a seedy vibe about the place that must have reminded them of many of the clubs they'd filled in LA over the past four years. They'd visit Schiffmacher whenever they were in the city; subsequently he and Kiedis would hit the backpacker trail together, when time allowed. Schiffmacher also had a professional relationship with the band – he was now their official inkman.

Flea had become the first tattooed Chili Pepper when he had Jimi Hendrix's image inked on his shoulder; he also had Loesha's name etched across his chest. During the recording of *Uplift Mofo*, Irons had been illustrated with a whale and a dolphin, while Kiedis acquired a dazzling portrait of the Nez Percé Indian Chief Thunder Travelling Over The Mountains (aka Chief Joseph). Later on he would be decorated with a companion piece, an image of Sioux warrior leader Sitting Bull. Kiedis didn't confine his Native American interests to his body; he would often sport an Indian headdress on stage, a favourite item in his ever-changing wardrobe. During that first Amsterdam visit, Schiffmacher began adorning Kiedis' back with a huge Indian totem image, which would require several visits to the Tattoo Museum before the masterpiece would be complete.

Back in London, the band convened on a crisp May morning for another photo shoot. The image was for the cover of an EP which would fill the hole in the market created by EMI's decision not to release their first two albums in Britain. There was now a buzz in England about these "socks-on-cocks" guys; EMI and the band needed some product out there to capitalise on it.

The *Abbey Road* EP would include four tracks – a cover of Hendrix's 'Fire', plus 'Backwoods', 'Catholic School Girls Rule' and 'Hollywood (Africa)'. But the EP would be best remembered for its iconoclastic cover image. It was also one of the last times that Hillel Slovak would be shot with the band.

The Abbey Road studio in affluent St John's Wood is London's premier rock'n'roll shrine, the location where almost all The Beatles' music was recorded. For the cover of their 1969 *Abbey Road* album, the Fab Four assembled outside the studio and strolled across a nearby pedestrian crossing, while photographer Ian MacMillan caught their image on film. The crossing and the studio subsequently became must-visit locales for diligent Beatlespotters.

The Chili Peppers' plan was slightly different. The Beatles may have worn an assortment of outfits – George was in denim, John, Ringo and Paul in suits (the latter was barefoot, too, which gave the "Paul Is Dead" whisperers some heavy ammunition) – but the Peppers had simpler tastes when it came to styling. All four wore goofy grins, track shoes and not much else, apart from the trademark dangling sock. Lensman Chris Clunn quickly snapped the cover image, while the Peppers did their best not to collapse with laughter, and avoid being nicked for public indecency.

Again, the Chili Peppers were playing up to their public image. The cover idea might have been a brilliant comic move, but it didn't do anything to downplay their reputation as the Four Stooges of rock.

The band's next move was to moan about not being taken seriously. "Europe was crazy," Jack Irons would state after the tour. "The sock thing had gotten completely out of hand, it really was demanding."

To this Kiedis added, "The thing with the socks, it's such a small part of what we're all about. It's just part of the showmanship, a joke. It's a good feeling for us to be on stage naked playing a song, but we usually only do it for an encore. The ideology and philosophy and the approach of the band is what we prefer people to focus on."

But the band continued to let the dumb times roll. They even ended the tour with an on-stage streak during a Ramones set at the Provinssirock festival in Seinajoki, Finland. Just as the New York riff machines were launching into 'Blitzkrieg Bop', four naked Cali bone-heads bounded across the stage like some kind of bizarre vaudeville act. A stunned crowd looked on.

Backstage, the Ramones' manager, Gary Kurfirst, was furious, screaming that their stunt was the "most unprofessional thing I've ever seen in my life". Most of the members of the band shared his anger, except for Joey Ramone, who'd befriended the Peppers a few years earlier at their New York show. He found their streak to be "rather amusing". His statement helped defuse a heated backstage scene.

"We loved the Ramones and that's how we show our appreciation for what they were doing," a confused Flea would explain. While the Chili Peppers might have been moving in some heavyweight rock'n'roll company, they just didn't seem able to keep their dicks in their pants.

By June, band, dicks and socks were back in LA, ready to begin rehearsals for their fourth album. But within weeks the band would be in such disarray that most observers – and many band insiders – were convinced that they would never play together again.

The band had agreed to a short break once they returned home from Europe, before heading into pre-production for their fourth album. Kiedis and Slovak worked on maintaining their drug-free lifestyle, while Flea was duty-bound with Loesha's pregnancy. Yet on Saturday, June 27, 1988, Slovak scored some smack, returned to his apartment and satisfied his craving. He overdosed and died sometime later that day. His body remained undiscovered until the following Monday, when a worried friend dropped by to check on him. The second person who knew Slovak to arrive at the death scene was Keith Barry.

"Hillel lived in an apartment complex called the Malaga Castle," he told me, his distress still evident 15 years on. "When he died, nobody in the building knew who to notify. The closest they could get was a resident of the building called Texas Terry. The closest Texas Terry could think of was to call Bob Forrest. I happened to have some equipment in my car that belonged in Bob Forrest's garage. I was in the neighbourhood and I figured I'd drop it off. I drove to Bob's place and knocked on the door and he said to me, 'Hillel's dead.' Then he said to me, 'I don't know who to tell.'"

At 8 pm that night, Slovak's brother James became the first member of his family to learn about his brother's tragic death. James was sitting in his apartment, drawing, when Forrest and Barry knocked on his door. When they declined James' invitation to enter, insisting that he come outside, Slovak knew that something terrible had happened. He was no fool; he knew that his brother was going through a tough time.

As he wrote in *Behind The Sun*, "Right then I noticed their pale white faces, as if they had seen a ghost, and I knew something was wrong. I stepped outside and one of the guys said, 'Dude, your brother's dead.' I will never forget those words for as long as I live. I yelled back, 'What are you talking about?' 'Hillel's dead, he's overdosed.'

"It was right there that my whole life changed in one second."

The three drove back to Slovak's apartment. James Slovak remembers being "in total shock and sick to my stomach". After signing the release papers for his brother's body, and speaking with the police and local coroner, he then had to tell his mother about his brother's terrible demise. But first he drove to the home of his Uncle Aron, the same relative who had given Hillel his first guitar.

"I rushed to his house in a panic, freaking out on how to tell my mom. My uncle opened the door to see my face flushed red and full of tears, unable to speak."

When they broke the news to Esther Slovak, she was overwhelmed. She had no idea that her son was using drugs, which made this dreadfully bitter pill even harder to swallow. Slovak was particularly close to his mother. Addie Brik told me how "even at such a young age, he was an old-fashioned family man in great part." Other calls were made to his Chili Pepper bandmates, who were every bit as distressed as Slovak's family. After all, he was their family, too.

A distraught Keith Barry couldn't even bear to cast eyes on his dead friend at the scene. "I had the opportunity to see Hillel there [at his apartment] and I regret not doing that."

Drug deaths are not an uncommon occurrence in the world of rock'n' roll. In order to deal with the myriad pressures of life in the spotlight, drugs had proved, for many, to be the perfect, sometimes deadly anti-dote. Heroin, alcohol and/or prescription drugs had contributed to the tragically early passing of such stars as Jimi Hendrix, Elvis Presley, The Who's Keith Moon, The Rolling Stones' Brian Jones, Janis Joplin, Tim Buckley and Doors frontman Jim Morrison. Later on it would lead to the death of Nirvana's Kurt Cobain and Layne Staley, the tormented frontman of Alice In Chains. Chronic drug abuse had dulled such supernova talents as Brian Wilson and Pink Floyd's Syd Barrett, who burned out way too young. Slovak was certainly not a musician of the stature of any of these stars, but the pressures he was under were every bit as real. Because of his chronic drug problem his place in the band was shaky at best; he'd been falling out with his bandmates, and there was the looming deadline of their fourth album to cope with. But all this history and explanation didn't soften the blow of Slovak's death.

An autopsy was performed on June 29. According to a coroner's spokesman, the results were "inconclusive", which did nothing to hide the cold, hard fact that Slovak had overdosed and died alone. His addic-tion came as a rude awakening for his mother and everyone close to him.

"When Hillel died, it was an awful shock," Michael Beinhorn told me, adding that he felt Slovak was in a "despondent" state when he died, due to his drug trauma and the effect it was having on both his playing and his relationship with his fellow Peppers. But any suggestion that a deeply depressed Slovak may have committed suicide was firmly dismissed by Keith Barry.

"My theory is that it was a bad [drug] deal," he said to me. "He'd just spent tons of money fixing his car up; who'd commit suicide after doing that? I was shocked when Hillel died," he added. "I didn't see that coming."

Lindy Goetz is convinced that Slovak's death was a tragic accident – and nothing more. "He'd cleaned up, went to Europe, came home, took a couple of weeks off and made a terrible, stupid mistake. The dose was too strong."

A memorial service for Hillel Slovak was held on June 30 at 1 pm at the all-Jewish Mount Sinai Memorial Park at Forest Lawn Drive in Hollywood Hills. He was buried on King David Drive, under a tree, looking out over Highway 101 and, beyond that, the snow-peaked Mount Baldy. He was laid to rest alongside Auschwitz survivors and octogenarians, which makes his early death seem even more tragic. His grave marker reads: "BELOVED SON, BROTHER, GRANDSON & FRIEND. HILLEL SLOVAK 1962–1988". Underneath is an image of his Fender Stratocaster guitar.

Everyone who attended the service – bandmates, friends, family – were stunned into silence. Beinhorn was amongst the group that attended the service. "I remember his funeral, with everyone standing around crying," Beinhorn said, "saying how horrible it was, how they were going to quit using junk. And you just knew that they were lying through their teeth."

Beinhorn recalls that amongst the crowd at Slovak's service were the same drug dealers who'd been feeding the guitarist's habit. He was amazed by their audacity.

As for Slovak's mother Esther, she berated Hillel's friends – and his bandmates – at the service, asking them why they'd failed to tell her that her son was using heroin. She felt outraged, impotent. According to Beinhorn, "It was awful."

Flea's father, Mick Balzary, felt that Slovak's death was a huge wake-up call to the rest of the band. "I think it gave them all a big fright. They saw what had happened to one of their schoolmates; it straightened them out a bit. It changed Michael's life."

Erstwhile Chili Pepper Cliff Martinez was equally shocked when he learned of Slovak's OD. "I had heard some rumours about erratic behaviour, but when I was in the band I wasn't aware of any drug problems. The last thing I remember about him was that he was a straight-up guy. It stunned me when he died; I didn't see the downward spiral."

Within nine months of Slovak's death, both of his grandparents also died. As his brother James recalled, his grandmother's death was completely unexpected. "She was a happy, healthy person before Hillel's death. Then my grandfather just let himself wither away and got sick and died three months after her."

Missing from the group of friends, family and drug dealers at the funeral was Anthony Kiedis, who simply couldn't face the ordeal of bidding farewell to his dead friend and bandmate. He also knew, clearly, that the body lying there could have been his. Understandably, Kiedis' absence riled many of Slovak's friends and family. Keith Barry agreed. "I think lots of people were mad at him that he wasn't at the funeral."

Within a week, James Slovak had to confront the emotionally harrowing task of clearing out his brother's apartment.

"The windows [which had been] open for a week didn't get rid of the smell of death," he related in *Behind The Sun*. Amongst his brother's possessions were his diary, letters from Kiedis and Flea and other friends, plus love letters from his various girlfriends (of whom Addie Brik – who actually recorded a rarely heard EP of songs with Slovak, Flea and Irons – was his favourite). He also found a collection of artwork that Slovak had been compiling, which included various drawings and paintings. Slovak's dead body had actually been found hunched over his final painting, a darkly coloured, deeply disturbing portrait. His lit cigarette had burned a hole in the canvas.

"Hillel Slovak," James wrote, "was not just a great musician, he was a great artist, a truly great friend to everyone who knew him. He influenced a lot of musicians and created a new sound and style.

"Heroin was Hillel's problem," he continued, "a problem he knew he had to take care of. What started off as a creative, mind-opening experience with heroin turned into an out-of-control, four-year addiction. Like so many others, he was taking medication to get off the drug, but that wasn't enough."

James Slovak went on to note how his brother had been suffering from touring burn-out and homesickness, as well as the problems brought about by not being able to discuss his drug problem with his mother. Crucially, James Slovak also admitted to being aware of his brother's addiction; a Peppers' roadie had told him on the band's return from Europe. While astounded by the revelation, Slovak wrote how he "knew it must be true".

James Slovak did eventually confront Hillel about his addiction. A reluctant Hillel confessed; he wanted to know who had ratted on him and whether his mother knew of his drug habit. When James said that he hadn't spoken with Esther, Hillel was relieved. He insisted that he'd been seeing a doctor and was taking medication, which was true. "Everything will be fine," he assured James.

"If I had the chance to change that decision, I wish I would have opened my mouth," James later admitted. "I can only wonder if it might have made a difference."

The two brothers last spoke on the day of Hillel's death. They had talked on the phone and again James raised the subject of heroin use and abuse. "Shooting heroin is like playing Russian Roulette," James told Hillel. "You could die."

After a long pause, his brother replied, "I know, I love you, bro'," before ringing off. It was the last conversation they ever had.

Hillel Slovak's influence and impact on the development – and, strangely, as it turns out, the survival – of the Red Hot Chili Peppers was enormous and remains, to this day, undeniable. Kiedis would quite readily state that "Hillel's responsible for the sound we created." He taught Flea the rudiments of playing the bass; today Flea is widely regarded as a master of the four-stringed instrument. He was a key motivator in the musical direction of Anthym and What Is This and the nascent Red Hot Chili Peppers. His Hendrix-inspired stringwork elevated both *Freaky Styley* and *The Uplift Mofo Party Plan*. And he established the freaked-out, funked-up style of playing to which every subsequent Chili Peppers guitarist would aspire. To the band's hard-core followers, he defined their sound and their shirtless, toned look. His death would also prove to be the inspiration for a selection of the band's signature songs, including 'Knock Me Down', the Peppers' first genuine hit, and 'My Lovely Man'. Flea and Keith Barry still proudly display Slovak's artwork in their homes.

While Barry acknowledges the excellence of Slovak's stringwork, he truly believes that his legacy is much larger than the handful of songs he cut with the Chili Peppers. "I think Hillel was so esteemed by his friends, was so loved by them, that that was his legacy. I think his legacy is lost on a lot of Chili Peppers fans.

"He was a brilliant artist. He lived the whole artist thing, even by the way he walked into a room. Of all these guys, I think he was the most self-assured. He really knew what he was doing. Hillel was home-grown, Hillel was funky. Brilliant guy; loved him."

"Hillel died too young; it could have been any of our circle," Flea once wrote. "We loved each other the best we knew how and tried so hard to deal with our pain. We made huge mistakes but they came from love and one mistake made one less of us. Bless his immaculate soul."

Kiedis, understandably, was a hollow man after the death of Slovak. Not only had he lost a close friend and musical soulmate, but he realised how dangerous – and potentially deadly – his own heroin habit had become. Soon after Slovak's death he talked of how, because of a working knowledge of CPR, he had actually saved a couple of friends who had overdosed. He knew he should have been there to help his bandmate and friend. He also knew that heroin chose its victims randomly; it could just as easily have been Kiedis who was found dead and alone in his apartment, face-down on his dining table.

Even as late as 1992, Kiedis would acknowledge the guilt that he felt about his friend's passing. "It should have been me," he told *Rolling Stone*'s David Fricke. "My propensity for over-the-edge indulgences was more renowned than his. When Flea got the phone call, his first reaction was, 'Anthony's dead.'"

Kiedis also admitted that his own addiction had distanced him from his friend. They may have bonded over music and drugs back at the Formosa Pad, but ultimately their toxic lifestyle pulled them apart. He felt the loss deeply, more deeply that any other event in his life to that stage. These "latchkey kids" had grown up even tighter than family. All this served to make Kiedis' absence from Slovak's memorial service even more difficult to comprehend.

"Hillel was the closest person to me in my life," he continued, "and sadly enough I don't think I can ever find that with anybody else, because I don't think it happens more than once that you get that close to somebody. But as close as we were, because we were both afflicted with this disease of drug addiction, we didn't really hang out together because we didn't like to see each other in that state."

Kiedis' immediate reaction to Slovak's overdose death was under-standable – he fell off the wagon, badly, if only for a short time. While

Slovak's friends and family grieved, Kiedis threw a few belongings in his car and headed south, trying his best to cope with his loss and give up smack forever. The only music he took with him was a compilation tape of Neil Young, and the songs of the bleakly confessional singer/songwriter turned out to be a touchstone for the haunted Chili Pepper.

"It was a tragic and turbulent time in my life," he would relate, "and I was still sort of coming to terms with my own drug addiction. I was just going there [Mexico] to clean up and get away from society."

Just like many American wanderers before him, heading south of the border provided the salvation that Kiedis required. For about a month, Kiedis holed up in a Mexican village, taking long walks, fishing, detoxing and trying to get his head around the tragedy that he'd just lived through. The Neil Young songs that he repeatedly played – 'Southern Man', 'Cowgirl In The Sand', and, especially, the devastating anti-drugs ballad 'The Needle And The Damage Done' – struck a deeply powerful chord with Kiedis.

"I had a tape player," Kiedis recalled, "and so I listened to this tape over and over and over again."

Young had also witnessed the carnage that could be brought about by heroin and his music hit Kiedis hard. His powerful message that "a junkie's life is like a setting sun" must have sunk into Kiedis' subconscious like a mantra. And Young's cautionary tales made Kiedis realise that he could possibly do more with his words than boast about his sexual athletics, or shout-out to his Hollywood buddies.

The time spent away from LA and its myriad temptations also helped Kiedis understand why he and Slovak had dived so deeply and readily into heroin addiction – and he also began to understand exactly what the impact of his friend's death would be. "As far as Hillel's death is concerned," he continued, "if anything, it got me more deeply in touch with my emotions in the spectrum of the sad, which are very valid and wonderful emotions; you know the whole roundness of sad emotions is something beautiful and wonderful to experience.

"You know I would do anything in the world for Hillel to not have died, but, accepting the fact that he's dead, sometimes going to that place of love and sadness and of missing him is a really good feeling, and that's a sort of inspiring feeling when it comes to writing."

Kiedis would tap into this sorrow for several of the songs on their next album. They would be the best tracks that the band had ever committed to tape, in part because the emotions were so authentic, so convincingly real.

When asked about his drug recovery, Kiedis accredited "good luck, good fortune, good blessings, good friends and a certain amount of inner desire to not die at a young age." What Kiedis also realised during his self-imposed exile in Mexico was that The Red Hot Chili Peppers needed to keep making music. Death may have ended a great band like Led Zeppelin, but if nothing else, it would keep alive the spirit of the Fax City Four. There was also a practical side to his decision, because the band were still contracted to EMI for at least another three years. It would be difficult, and costly, to try to extricate themselves from that legal obligation. And, frankly, what else could Kiedis do with his life? He needed a creative outlet and The Red Hot Chili Peppers provided him with one. The idea of some kind of mundane, clock-punching existence was almost enough to turn him back onto drugs.

Jack Irons' response to Slovak's death, however, was much less life-affirming than that of Anthony Kiedis. He had seen the deadly price that smack had inflicted on his bandmates and buddies and yet he felt completely unable to stop Kiedis and Slovak's downward spiral. On top of his bipolar manic depression, and his staunchly anti-drugs stance, the death of Hillel Slovak proved way too much for the drummer to handle. "Who's next?" a dismayed Irons asked himself. The only way that he could cope was to completely shut down. Flea and Lindy Goetz would try to phone Irons, but their calls were ignored, and the messages started to pile up on his answering machine. Irons became completely inert, sometimes retreating into complete silence. No one could communicate with him.

Irons' family were the only people he could trust, but they faced a traumatic decision: should they commit their son to psychiatric care? Given his history of unstable mental health, they really had no option – Irons was in freefall and needed constant care just to keep him breathing. So they had him committed.

As soon as Irons was hospitalised and became able to comprehend the situation, he knew that he not only had to leave the band, he had to ditch the entire music industry.

"In many ways," he would admit, "I think I blamed the business for what happened to Hillel.

"I thought if I freed myself from the hustle of the business," Irons said in a subsequent interview, "I might live in a little more peace."

"It [Slovak's death] was a little too difficult for him," Goetz admitted. "He was very, very close to Hillel."

When asked about Irons' departure, Flea and Kiedis would do their best to downplay the real reason why he left. At one point there was even a rumour doing the rounds that suggested Irons had chosen "health food over rock'n'roll".

"That's ridiculous," Flea said. "Jack left the band because his life was changing and he needed space to understand himself more. With the death of Hillel, he just needed to be on his own."

"I think it was too much of a painful reminder for him to stay in the band," added Kiedis. "I think he was unsure whether or not the band would be a breeding ground for future unfortunate experiences. Like maybe he considered that I might die one day and he didn't want to be involved with that."

Michael Beinhorn was – and still is – a huge admirer of Irons' drumming. "I think I learned more about drumming from watching and working with Jack Irons than I have in any other situation," he admitted to me. "I feel that he is one of the great unsung drummers."*

Anthony Kiedis finally returned to Los Angeles on August 1, 1988, five weeks after Slovak's death. While the singer was now off drugs and in a far more stable state of mind, he and Flea were once again the sum total of the Red Hot Chili Peppers. The situation was a carbon copy of the time leading up to the recording of their debut album, when Irons and Slovak opted out of the Peppers and into What Is This. Now one of their soulmates was dead and another had disappeared so deep inside himself that he could not be reached. The scenario felt strangely familiar for the pair.

---

* Irons was still hospitalised in December 1988 when he received a call from Joe Strummer, former frontman of The Clash, asking him to join his band and help out on an album he was recording in LA. Irons replied, "You do know where I am, don't you?" Two former Thelonious Monster members, Zander Schloss and Lonnie Marshall, had recommended Irons to Strummer, who was not the kind of guy that responded well to the word "no". Irons checked himself out and eventually played on what would become the *Earthquake Weather* album. He later played with Alain Johannes in an outfit called Eleven and would become a key member of grunge survivors Pearl Jam.

But rather than accept that their rock'n'roll dream was fast becoming a nightmare, Flea and Kiedis were inspired to keep the Chili Peppers moving. These two old friends, who were drawn to each other by alienation, were now united by tragedy. As Kiedis would relate, "Losing your best friend at the age of 26 is a mind- and soul-blower. But there was definitely an inspiration which came from Hillel dying, which helped sharpen the focus of the band."

Lindy Goetz called a band meeting on his boat. He told Kiedis and Flea that they could survive their loss. "I felt that we could keep this thing going. Flea and Anthony did, too. So we did. But it was a little too difficult for Jackie [Irons]."

Gradually, Kiedis started to adopt a more philosophical outlook towards the death of his bandmate and buddy. "Y'know," he said, "life is just a constant series of glorious gains and lecherous losses, and you really have to accept both to go on living with any sort of stability. And the funny thing about problems and tragedies is that you really do learn a lot from them, like it or not. And to me, life is all about learning and having a good time. That's all I'm really capable of doing while I'm here."

Their first task, however, with the rescheduled sessions for their fourth album looming, was to piece the band back together. They needed a drummer and a guitarist – and the quicker, the better. Kiedis, however, denied that he and Flea were in a state of panic.

"It wasn't a panic," he insisted, "because the most important thing wasn't, 'Well, we've got to get this record out by next year.' It was, 'Let's look at our fucking lives and see what has to be done so we don't lose another person.'

"I think we all needed time to gather our bearings," he added. "There was never any question whether we wanted to continue with the band, because we knew in our hearts that we did, and we always want to be playing as the Red Hot Chili Peppers. Hillel may be dead, we're not."

Soon enough they'd put out the word that they were in need of two new Chili Peppers. Once again their main man of funk, George Clinton, helped out, recommending a guitarist by the name of DeWayne "Blackbyrd" McKnight.

McKnight was born on April 17, 1954. During the Seventies, just like Peppers producer Michael Beinhorn, he'd worked both with Herbie Hancock (on his 1976 LP, *Man-Child*) and Bill Laswell, for whom he'd played guitar and co-produced some tracks. McKnight had first hooked up with Clinton and Funkadelic for their 1979 Anti-Tour, so named because the nearly broke band had been required to scale down their once elaborate stage set. That same year his guitar work – he was described by one reporter as a "six-string samurai", which was just what the Chili Peppers needed – was a feature of the Funkadelic album *Uncle Jam Wants You*. He stayed with the band, touring constantly and working on the band's final album, 1981's *Electric Spanking Of War Babies*. McKnight has also worked alongside Flea on Warren Zevon's 1987 record, *Sentimental Hygiene*.

Although it was acknowledged that his recruitment was only a stop-gap measure, designed to remind the public that The Red Hot Chili Peppers had survived the death of a brother, McKnight's background seemed perfect for the Peppers. Being African-American also added to the band's visual appeal and all-round freakiness.

The pedigree of drummer Darren (aka DH, aka Dirty) Peligro was very different to that of McKnight. A player in the San Fran punk scene since 1978 – and a good pal of Flea's, who referred to him as "his beloved friend" – he'd joined the iconoclastic Dead Kennedys as drummer in 1980. Fronted by one of punk's most vocal vocalists, Jello Biafra, The Dead Kennedys were possibly the most dangerous band in hardcore music, especially in the eyes of right-wing politicians and Christian conservatives, whom they pilloried in such amp-burning anthems as 'Holiday In Cambodia', 'Nazi Punks Fuck Off' and 'California Über Alles' (which was directly aimed at the then California governor, Jerry Brown). Biafra even ran in the San Franciscan mayoral election race of 1979, one of his policies being that downtown businessmen should dress in clown suits. He finished a respectable fourth. Biafra, along with Frank Zappa and Twisted Sister's Dee Snider, was also one of the most articulate and outspoken opponents of the PMRC, the entertainment-censoring vigilante squad headed by Tipper Gore.

Just like the Chili Peppers, The Dead Kennedys often felt misrepresented. As their guitarist, East Bay Ray, would state, "A lot of people don't realise how important the musicians were to The Dead Kennedys." To most, the band's stridently political viewpoint was far more attention-grabbing than their raw, furious take on punk rock. Although the band were eventually torn apart by a court case instigated by the artwork of their *Frankenchrist* album, the Kennedys lasted longer than most three-chord wonders. Peligro drummed (and sometimes thrashed a guitar and wailed) on the albums *Plastic Surgery Disasters* (1982), *Frankenchrist*, which came out in 1985, 1986's *Bedtime For Democracy* and 1987's *Give Me Convenience Or Give Me Death*.

Peligro had no real plans to continue to play music when he and McKnight were asked to join the Chili Peppers. He was burned out by the 12-month court case that had debated whether the graphic image on the cover of the *Frankenchrist* LP was a valid case of "distributing harmful material to minors". But a call from Kiedis changed his mind.

The punk-funk pedigree brought to the Peppers by McKnight and Peligro seemed perfectly valid and right for the rebuilding of the band. And the Peppers knew both these guys; at this point in their musical lives they were looking for friends as much as like-minded players. It turned out to be another bad decision.

In the midst of this Pepper resurrection, Flea had become a father, the first Chili Pepper parent. His daughter Clara was born a few weeks prematurely but perfectly healthy, on September 16, 1988. Hillel Slovak's prediction that Flea and Loesha were going to have a girl proved to be correct, as Flea would remind himself for weeks after Clara's birth. To celebrate, Flea had her name inked permanently into his left arm, between the face of Jimi Hendrix and an elephant and not too far from a tattoo of her mother's name. Flea was jubilant, but quietly wished that his friend Slovak had been alive to witness this huge, life-changing event.

"I wish he could see my daughter," Flea said in 1989. "When my wife was pregnant, he was really into it – more than anything, he was so into that. I'll never have the chance to share anything with him again – that's the worst thing."

In the same month, the new, hopefully improved Chili Peppers line-up made its debut on MTV's weekly alternative music show, *120 Minutes*. They aired footage of the four-piece playing at the LA venue Alcohol Salad.

Backstage at a show at the University Memorial Center in Boulder, Colorado, Flea was asked about the development of this latest version of the Chili Peppers. "At this point I'd say we're rawer and funnier and a little sloppier than before," he shot back with a gap-toothed smile.

These were prophetic words, because the Chili Peppers Mk IV

would only play four shows, along with some jams recorded at Flea's home, that were quickly scrapped.

The rapid exit of Peligro and McKnight was amicable enough, according to statements made by the band at the time. The former Funkadelic guitarist was the first of the two new recruits to leave. McKnight's style of playing just didn't fit with the Peppers; maybe he was a little too funky. Flea would only say that the chemistry between McKnight and the band "was awkward and not working out". As Kiedis would announce, "I think the best thing for him was not to be in The Red Hot Chili Peppers, but writing his own music and choreographing his own dance steps.

"When you get a guy in the band you've got to be prepared to embrace him emotionally for years and years – very much like being in love and being married. And you have to be willing to accept and tolerate and compromise sometimes, and with Blackbyrd that didn't work out."

Lindy Goetz agrees. "Blackbyrd was wrong for the Peppers, but he was right for P-Funk."

While Kiedis would declare that McKnight was "an incredible guitar player", he had no such praise for Peligro, whose skills with the sticks had clearly faded since the demise of The Dead Kennedys.

"With DH, it was tough," Kiedis said of the drummer's sacking, "because we love him as a person and he's a lovable guy, and like everyone else he's got his problems, but I think we hired him on the basis of wanting to work with him. He's great to hang out with, he's a wonderful human being, and we wanted a guy that was a friend. That's why we hired him. I think his drumming skills had deteriorated from the time he was at his peak with The Dead Kennedys [although] we really tried to work out the situation."

Flea wasn't so ready to denigrate his friend's skills, but admitted that "what he did with The Dead Kennedys was wild, thrashing drumming, and it wasn't tight precision funk drumming, which is what we're all about."

Goetz recalls that the best times they had with Peligro were off-stage. "He was a lot of fun, but he was the wrong drummer."

The McKnight/Peligro/Kiedis/Flea version of the Chili Peppers was a short-lived, flawed experiment. Flea and Kiedis had now learned that it wasn't absolutely essential to recruit buddies to the band, or players whose work they loved. What they needed was a drummer and an axeman who understood where the band came from musically – and if they looked hot with their shirts off, well, better still. Flea and Kiedis set to work auditioning players; they needed a new line-up to be in place by Christmas 1988.

However, it was while sitting in on another band's auditions that they would find the next Chili Pepper.

Just like Flea and Kiedis, John Frusciante endured both an itinerant upbringing and a family pulled apart by marital discord. He was born on March 5, 1970, in New York. His father, John Sr, was a Juilliard trained pianist who became a lawyer and later a judge. His mother, Gail, was a promising singer who, according to her son, gave up her musical career to be a homemaker.* The Frusciantes lived in Queens, New York, before moving to Tuscon, Arizona and then Florida for a year. At this time, his parents separated and John relocated to Santa Monica, California, with Gail. In his pre-teen years, John Frusciante's three key obsessions were Aerosmith, Kiss and skateboarding.

Frusciante's rootless youth made him the perennial outsider; music was a natural outlet for him. He had played some sport at school, but spent most of his time standing in the outfield, thinking up derogatory songs directed at the more popular members of the team. He eventually gave up sport because he felt he lacked the necessary competitive edge. Frusciante found his true calling when his parents gave him his first guitar. He would lock himself away in his room for up to 15 hours a day (which didn't help his outsider status in any way), playing along to records from Jimi Hendrix, The Germs, Captain Beefheart's legendary *Trout Mask Replica*, and anything from Frank Zappa. Frusciante once even declared that he had set out to audition for Zappa's band, but left before plugging in, because, as he would state, "I realised that I wanted to be a rock star, do drugs and get girls, and that I wouldn't be able to do that in Zappa's band." Zappa was renowned as one of the toughest rock'n'roll taskmasters.

But Frusciante was making light of his eclectic musical tastes and upbringing. When he and his mother moved on to Mar Vista, in

---

* Much later on, Frusciante would allude to there being domestic drama in his early years, though he would never clarify exactly what that drama was.

California, his stepfather was a major influence on the budding guitarist. He was an avid reader of philosophy and a fan of both Beethoven and Fifties R&B, and he encouraged his stepson to learn about music; he told him to keep playing the guitar. Frusciante was soon mixing his punk and classic rock favourites with the austere prog rumblings of Yes, King Crimson and early Genesis, as well as guitar heroes Jimmy Page and Jeff Beck. As his future bandmates would reveal, Frusciante was a musical sponge. He didn't just spin records, he learned every guitar note and would be able to replicate some of the most complex playing heard in rock'n'roll. He would also devote hours to transcribing the music that he was absorbing. Frusciante would describe himself as "formally self-taught", boasting that he knew how to "write for orchestra . . . for horns; I can write for any instrument you want me to write for."

Frusciante also had one ear glued to the radio. Writing in the liner notes for the Chili Peppers' *Greatest Hits* collection from 2003, he would declare that "radio has been very important for me at various times in my life". While driving with his mother in the family car, he would hear such hits as Elton John's 'Tiny Dancer' and wonder "how such beautiful sounds were made". Then he fell for Donna Summer's 'I Feel Love', embracing "the stereophonic godliness" of the song. He was soon tuning into Rodney Bingenheimer's "Rodney On The ROQ" show, where he was turned onto The Ramones, The Clash, Black Flag, The Weirdos and The Circle Jerks. Frusciante would reminisce how he would lie "in the dark with my radio/cassette recording, listening as soft as possible because I'm supposed to be sleeping, recording all my favourite music off Rodney's show, often taping the whole thing." He had never heard music like this before. To him, punk was truly liberating. "It was your war against those fucking average white suburban bland idiots who were destroying the world. That rage connected so well with me."

By the age of 16, Frusciante had moved into his own apartment in LA, just as Flea, Kiedis and Keith Barry had done after graduating from Fairfax High. It was then that he had another life-changing musical experience: he checked out The Red Hot Chili Peppers at the Variety Arts Center in LA. He quickly became a diehard devotee, whose bedroom walls were decked out in Chili Pepper colours. He was particularly enthralled by the guitar playing of Hillel Slovak. Sometimes Frusciante would even pay for his friends to attend Peppers shows with him, just so they could experience the body-rocking thrill of their live sets.

"I just thought that everybody should see them," Frusciante would tell Steve Roeser, "because I thought they were the most fantastic thing to ever hit the earth.

"Their music meant everything to me," he gushed. "I thought it was the most perfect, beautiful music that I had heard in my life. The wide variety of emotions in the music inspired me. Just the whole attitude of the band and the way they thought, and the way they looked and – just everything. I felt it was a direct extension of my own personality.

"There was this real kind of historical vibe at their shows," Frusciante would add. "I didn't even watch the shows. I'd get so excited that I'd flip around the slam pit the whole time. I really felt like part of the band."

When not following the Peppers, Frusciante had met and jammed with DH Peligro. One day, Peligro called his friend Flea, still deep in mourning over the loss of Slovak, and invited him to come over and jam with this "new kid".

"It was a fun time," Flea recalled, but he thought nothing more of it.

At that stage, Frusciante wasn't hunting for work, he was simply hoping to connect with his favourite bassist in his favourite band. He and Flea jammed again soon after, and Flea asked him back to his house where they threw some ideas onto a four-track. (Two *Mother's Milk* tracks, 'Nobody Weird Like Me' and 'Pretty Little Ditty', emerged from these jams.) Flea was duly impressed with Frusciante's playing. "John laid into it real nice and sweet like," he would state. "I thought, 'Yeah, this kid's got it, I think he's onto something.'"

But it's unclear whether the idea of Frusciante becoming a Chili Pepper really entered Flea's mind, even though in the *Mother's Milk* liner notes he would state how, upon playing with Frusciante, he had said to himself, "He's gotta be our new guy." The 19-year-old guitarist was a sizeable risk: he was incredibly raw (his nickname would soon become "Greenie", Michael Beinhorn describing him as the "fresh new guy") and he'd never actually played in a band. To Flea, Frusciante was a typical bedroom prodigy, the kind of outsider most likely to spend his life undiscovered and unfulfilled, like a thousand other skilled but unlucky hopefuls.

Flea thought that he was simply "a good kid". "He's really talented and knowledgeable musically. He knows all the shit I don't know. I basically know nothing about music theory and he's studied it to death, inside out. He's a very disciplined musician – all he cares about is his guitar and his cigarettes."*

Over time, Flea got to know Frusciante reasonably well, in part because the guitarist lived nearby, sharing a house with a friend named Bill. "John's dad was a judge," Flea recalled, "and Bill's dad was a senator and they were two wild-ass, John Waters-watching, Frank Zappa-listening, over-sexed intellectual freaks." Former Pepper Jack Sherman also spotted Frusciante's manic side. "When I met John he was this 19-year-old chain-smoking maniac with a Mohawk. He was literally bouncing off the walls when I met him."

Their fast lives were in sharp contrast to Flea's domestic domicile, a time in his life that he would describe as "wife and baby and Laker-watching, pot smoking". Flea was becoming restless; he missed his life as a good time boy, a pivotal member of the Fax City Four.

Thelonious Monster were another LA band that meant the world to the teenage John Frusciante. They were very tight with the Chili Peppers, often sharing bills in Hollywood or touring with them outside California. Lindy Goetz was also their manager. The Monster were a loose-knit, heavy-drinking, hard-drugging outfit, with a revolving door policy when it came to band members. But they were just as committed to making quality music as their more successful Chili Peppers brothers. When they were in need of a guitarist, the band's driving force, Bob Forrest, called his pal Kiedis and asked for a recommendation. Kiedis then spoke with Flea and Frusciante's name entered into the conversation. "Greenie" seemed perfect for the Monster; he was young, keen, good-looking in a skinny-assed, raw-boned kind of way, and very obviously gifted. An audition was organised and Kiedis acted as chaperone, accompanying Frusciante to the rehearsal space.

Frusciante's admission that he hadn't played in a band beforehand worried Forrest; the Thelonious Monster frontman suggested that it might be best for him to go and do that first. But as soon as Frusciante plugged in and started playing, Forrest changed his mind. Forrest was standing alongside Dix Denney, the erstwhile Weirdo, who was the Monster's other guitarist, and the pair were stunned by Frusciante's

---

* Frusciante was a chain smoker at the time.

dexterity with the guitar. But out of the corner of his eye, Forrest could see Kiedis taking in his dazzling playing; he knew something was up. When Forrest offered Frusciante the Thelonious Monster gig on the spot, he had a feeling that Kiedis had bigger, more lucrative plans for the teenager.

According to Frusciante, "When I got the job he [Kiedis] ran home to tell Flea. That night he told me he had tears in his eyes because he felt I should be a Pepper, not a Monster. I agreed and that was it, I was officially a Red Hot. It was a dream come true."

It was a musical wet dream for Frusciante – he'd just been offered spots in his two favourite bands. And he idolised Kiedis like a big brother (only to later "hate him for a while", according to Lindy Goetz).

Poaching Frusciante didn't endear the Peppers to the LA punk brotherhood. Rob Graves, who was in the highly touted outfit the Gun Club, told Flea that he wasn't impressed with their deceit. "That's not cool, man," he said to Flea. "He plays great, he looks cool – that's fucked." Flea took it all in and signed Frusciante regardless.

As far as Chili Pepper legend is concerned, there was one further qualification required for Frusciante to become a Pepper: he had to strip for Flea and Kiedis and convince them that he was "man" enough for the band. "They insisted they see my erect penis," according to Frusciante. As it turned out, this was not a big problem for a guy who had confessed that his main concern in life was "playing like I've got a huge cock". So it was official: John Frusciante was a Chili Pepper.

Frusciante seemed perfect. He was young enough to take direction from the senior members of the band, but had the right type of musical imagination to help the Peppers keep developing their punk-funk sound. And although it would be unfair to call him a mimic, Frusciante had Slovak's moves and sound down perfectly; Peppers insider Alain Johannes felt that he was almost a clone of the late guitarist. To Goetz, "He felt right, he looked right and he moved right, just like Hillel had." Frusciante freely admitted that Slovak was a major influence on his playing – after all, he'd spent so much time spellbound at their shows.

Frusciante realised his limitations. "I wasn't really a funk player before I joined the band," he admitted, but he had studied Slovak's playing closely enough to adapt quickly. "I learned everything I needed to know about how to sound good with Flea by studying Hillel's playing, and I just took it sideways from there."

As for Kiedis and Flea, they were thrilled with their new recruit. "John has been living, eating and breathing The Red Hot Chili Peppers from the age of 13," Kiedis announced to the press. "It's kind of weird, that he was that big a fan, but for him to join the band is a miracle and a dream come true."

Kiedis would reiterate the band's mission statement to the new recruit: they were going to be the "utter perpetrators of hardcore, bone-crunching, mayhem sex things from heaven". And he insisted that Frusciante was totally in sync with that. "John understood immediately," Kiedis crowed. "He fit in perfectly."

John Frusciante's Chili Peppers' debut was also DH Peligro's final act. They undertook what would become known as the "Turd Town Tour of '88", a brief jaunt designed mainly to break in their new guitarist. Once the Peppers returned to LA, Peligro was shown the door and Kiedis and Flea organised an open audition for a new drummer, as sessions for their fourth album inched ever closer. They checked out what seemed like an endless procession of tub-thumpers ("about 50,000," according to Flea's sketchy memory, although it was probably closer to 30), before a bandanna-clad Midwestern man mountain going by the name of Chad Smith settled himself at the kit. Smith had been steered in the direction of the Peppers by Denise Zoom, the wife of X guitarist Billy Zoom. "There's this guy from Detroit," she then told Flea, "[who] eats drums for breakfast." The six foot three inch tall 26-year-old from Saint Paul, Minnesota, did just that, laying into the drums like they'd bad-mouthed his mother. Kiedis and Flea were knocked out by his physical, powerful style. They were, however, confused by his habit of screaming expletives as he flailed away.

"Chad sat down and lit a fire under our asses," said Flea. "It was an intense jam."

Kiedis, who felt that the try-outs had been a "painful process", recognised that Smith was "a human power plant behind the drums".

"This monster walks in from Detroit," he told a reporter not long after Smith's audition. "Sits down behind the drums. Explodes on contact. It left us in a state of frenzied laughter that we couldn't shake ourselves out of for half an hour. We hired the guy."

Smith was a drummer for life who'd been playing since he was in single figures. His first drum kit was a pile of giant, round ice-cream cartons that his father stole from behind the local Baskin Robbins outlet. His second kit, which Smith remembers as "real cheesy", had been acquired legally; his folks bought it from K-Mart. His mother moved his drums into the family garage and as he began to learn the basics, she struck up a deal with her son – he'd only play whenever she went shopping. She already had to contend with Smith's guitar-playing brother Brad and pianist sister.

Kiedis once spoke of the Peppers' "blue-collar mentality", and Smith epitomised that to the letter. He was from the Midwest, a keen basket-baller and fervent supporter of the Detroit Pistons. He would be variously described as an "unadulterated rock dude and Detroit native" and a "beer drinking steak eater", who was raised on a fibre-rich diet of the classics: Led Zeppelin, The Who, Black Sabbath, Jimi Hendrix, Sly Stone and John Coltrane.

"I'm from the Midwest," Smith would explain in his cut-the-crap style. "I have good morals. I was a fuckin' peanut-butter-and-jelly guy, really involved in sports. More on the normal side."

He spoke proudly of appearing in the front cover shot of the *Kiss Alive* album. ("I was there. In the twelfth row.") Unlike Kiedis or Flea, he came from a solid family and he wasn't a fringe dweller at school; during his time at Bloomfield Hill's Lasher High School, he even dated a cheerleader. Smith would remember her fondly, especially the times when she used to "don her cheerleader outfit without any underwear and jump around on the bed".

Smith had lost his virginity early on, but it wasn't the unpleasant experience that Flea had endured, or the weird partner-sharing scenario that Blackie Dammett had manufactured for his son Anthony. Instead, Smith's first sexual encounter occurred in his early teens. "I was in 8th grade, so I think I was 13 or 14. She was my girlfriend. It wasn't like one night in the back seat of the car type of thing."

Upon graduating ("barely", according to Smith) in 1980, the future Pepper – who would namecheck drummers Mitch Mitchell, John Bonham and Keith Moon as heroes – moved through a variety of bill-paying jobs. In rapid succession, he was fired by a paint company, when he screwed up a large order; a Gap store (his sweater-folding skills were questionable) and a pancake house, where he upended a big vat of maple syrup. All the time he would be thumping the tubs at night, seemingly for every Detroit-area band whose name started with the letter "T" – Tilt, Tyrant, Terence. The most successful were Toby Redd, whom Smith had joined in 1984. The band once opened for prog-rockers Kansas, where Smith discovered the joy of the backstage "rider", an assortment of free food and drink laid on for the performing bands and crew. The quartet were signed to Nemperor, an imprint of the Epic label, and cut two albums. Smith drummed on their second and last, 1986's *In The Light*, before leaving the band. One of the last things Smith did before heading west was audition for Grand Funk Railroad vet Mark Farner. He accepted that Smith was a shit-hot drummer, but was concerned by the guy's insistence on polishing off a six-pack of beer – during the audition. Once in California, Smith signed on at the LA Musician's Institute (as had John Frusciante). Within six months of unpacking his kit he was fronting at the Chili Peppers rehearsal.

Even though his brawny, muscular style seemed perfectly suited for The Red Hot Chili Peppers, Flea and Kiedis, especially, were actually reluctant to hire Smith. Flea thought he might even be too rock for the band; he was put off by his bandanna "and leather jacket mainstream rock'n'roll look". According to Goetz, "Anthony thought he was wrong." Michael Beinhorn, who was about to move into pre-production with the resurrected Peppers for their fourth album, was surprised by their dithering.

"It was so obvious he was the man for the job," he told me, "yet the guys baulked at hiring him on the spot because they were afraid that he was too goofy and too rock. I never understood that."

Keith Barry remembers the audition. "The first time they laid eyes on him, they went, 'No way, next!' But as soon as they heard him play they sent everybody else home. In [both] John and Chad's case, as soon as they met them it was pretty obvious that these were going to be the guys."

Eventually, Kiedis and Flea came to the logical realisation that Smith was their man; that was especially true in light of the "weako-potamuses" (Kiedis' description) that had auditioned before him. It was Lindy Goetz who talked the band around – he'd even called Smith and told him to be patient, the band would eventually hire him.

"Big old Chad," he laughs, looking back. "He should have been playing in Lynyrd Skynyrd. But the rhythm section was now better than it ever was; and it became one of the most powerful rhythm sections in the world."

"I remember thinking, 'I don't know if this guy understands the funk, but that could come in time'," said Kiedis. "[But] he is amazing. His drumming just hits that part of my brain."

Unlike some of their predecessors, the recruitment of both Frusciante and Smith was very carefully considered, as Keith Barry explained. "Flea is a very wilful, determined conceptualist and anybody who wants to play with him really has to follow him. Anthony needs a conceptual partner, he needs support from whoever the guitar player is. That's always been the chemistry thing with the band. Chad was that kind of drummer and John was that kind of collaborator for Anthony."

Lindy Goetz also recognises that. "John helped Anthony to find his confidence to sing. Before that it was all yelling and rapping. John gave him melody – no one had done that before."

In December, Flea broke his thumb while skiing, which forced the band to cancel a year-closing show in Seattle. But by February 1989, eight months after Slovak's death and the assumed demise of the band, The Red Hot Chili Peppers began pre-production on their fourth album, at Silverlake's Hully Gully rehearsal studio, a location also favoured by fellow Angelenos Jane's Addiction. They were finally moving in the right direction.

In comparison to the stop-start sessions for *The Uplift Mofo Party Plan*, where Kiedis frequently opted for smack over music, pre-production for what would become the *Mother's Milk* LP progressed smoothly enough, even though Beinhorn remembers the time as "long and dull". Such tracks as 'Knock Me Down', one of the many songs very clearly inspired by the death of Slovak, came out of these early jams during March and April at Hully Gully. Unlike most of his experiences with the Peppers – "being prepared," their two-times producer would tell me, "was never a strong suit for the band" – Beinhorn remembers that 'Knock Me Down' was one song that didn't require tweaking in pre-production. The band brought it into Hully Gully fully formed, thanks mainly to the work of Kiedis and Frusciante. It would prove to be a significant tune for the Peppers, a poignant, honest statement

about their fallibility as human beings and the potentially fatal conse-
quences of over-indulgence. They'd clearly learned something from
the loss of their brother.

"I never expected that it would be as successful as it was," the producer said of 'Knock Me Down', "but I loved it the moment I heard it
– and it's still a great song."

The Kiedis/Frusciante collaboration on the track was significant, as far
as Flea – and the creative future of the band – was concerned. Flea would
refer to "a new, melodic, chord-change-based style of songwriting to
our band that wasn't there before" which was epitomised by 'Knock Me
Down', the most immediately tuneful track the band had yet composed.
The bulk of their past music had been built from rhythm upwards,
whereas 'Knock Me Down' took a more traditional path.

"Most of the [previous] songs were groove based and had started
with basslines," Flea stated. "It was an immense new element to the
sound of our band and a big opening up for us."

Flea remembers their stint at Hully Gully as "a time of a lot of very
physical playing. We played hard and fast more than [at] any other time
in our career, I think. A lot of chops were going down . . . we played
constantly, got to know each other, and came up with the record."

What became clear during these early sessions was the musical prowess
of "Greenie" Frusciante. Even at this nascent stage in his career as a Chili
Pepper, Frusciante was proving that his claim that "I can write for any
instrument" was more than the idle boasting of a feisty 19-year-old. He
was rapidly developing into an able replacement for Hillel Slovak.

According to Beinhorn, "It was apparent early on that John was the
perfect guitarist for the band – he brought the elements of songwriting
and composition to the band which they'd never truly had prior to his
involvement. I believe that John is a pivotal figure in the Chili Peppers,
being that he is such a distinctive songwriter."*

Taking a break from pre-production, the revitalised Chili Peppers
hit the bitumen for a short tour, where they could road test both new
members and new songs. Beinhorn remained in LA, where he began
preparations for tracking at the legendary Ocean Way Studios (this

---

* Frusciante would receive co-songwriting credits on all original tracks on *Mother's
Milk*, while DH Peligro was giving co-songwriting credits on 'Stone Cold Bush' and
'Sexy Mexican Maid', tracks that were worked up prior to his dismissal.

album would cost $178,000 to record, another relatively cheap production).

The band may have dismissed EMI as being unhelpful to their careers, but they certainly weren't miserly when it came to placing the Peppers in the best studios – first United Sound in Detroit, then Capitol Studios, now Ocean Way, the point of origin for such immortal records as The Beach Boys' 'Good Vibrations', The Mamas & The Papas' 'California Dreamin'' – a particular favourite of Kiedis – and albums from Bob Dylan, The Rolling Stones and many others.

But as with so much of their career, a backstage incident on April 21 at George Mason University Patriot Center, in Fairfax, Virginia, put a serious crimp in what seemed an uncharacteristically positive time for the band. Maybe they should have seen it coming. In March, after a show at the Respectable Street Cafe in West Palm Beach, Frusciante – fast warming to his place in the spotlight as guitarist for LA's studliest band – was asked by two middle-aged female fans, with a toddler in tow, for an autograph. Frusciante smiled, grabbed a piece of paper and wrote: "I'm so painfully huge I want to destroy your hymens. Love, John."

The ever-vigilant Flea spotted Frusciante's change in personality – the perennial outsider was now coming on like a rock star. Insisting that he was still a "good kid", the bassman understated how his guitarist's ego "got a little swollen" when he joined the Peppers. "He was running around being rude to girls and getting them pissed off. But that's to be expected, I mean, shit, you're 18 years old [19, actually] and you want to get laid really bad and all of a sudden you're in a band, the girls want to fuck. You're bound to go crazy."

But events took a turn from stupid to deadly serious after the George Mason University show on April 21. The band had finished their set and were backstage, changing clothes, preparing to leave. As they collected their gear, a female student named Joan A. Crown, who had offered to drive them to their hotel, knocked on the dressing room door.

A smiling, sweaty, naked Kiedis answered the door and then made some casual innuendos towards the woman. Ms Crown, who was both a student at George Mason University and a member of the university's programme board, was completely unprepared for Kiedis' callow stunt. She was so shocked, in fact, that she filed a complaint with the police, accusing him of the misdemeanour charges of sexual battery and indecent exposure. Kiedis was arrested and released on bail; the case was due to be heard in a Virginia court at a later date.

Kiedis was bewildered by the charge, insisting that the incident was harmless. "[It was] a playful thing that happened backstage – there was never any harmful intention. Speaking for my band and myself, we're all very friendly people who would never want to hurt anyone or make people uncomfortable."

Kiedis denied the accusation that he'd waved his penis in the woman's face – and was stunned with a later accusation that he'd actually brushed her face with his "swan". "I'm not that type of person," he insisted.

Regardless of the exact levels of backstage depravity to which Kiedis had exposed the student, the band's mood darkened as they returned to Ocean Way. Not only did Kiedis have a court appearance hanging over his head like a noose, but the band were beginning to realise the inherent problems of becoming popular. While not yet huge stars, they were now public property and their every (mis)step would be closely monitored by the media. A few years before, when the band were nothing more than an LA sensation, they might have gotten away with waving their dicks in people's faces – most of the punters at their shows were friends, they expected these types of antics from the Fax City Four. But to the unprepared, the Peppers' dopey backstage (and onstage) stunts were hard to handle.

Kiedis nailed the change in the band's life when he was asked about their devotees. "Our fans have always been very intense, loyal and emotionally moved by us. It's just that the numbers are increasing."

He couldn't count Joan Crown amongst those fans, that's for sure.

Once the band were safely cocooned in Ocean Way, sealed off from the court case for a few months, their fourth album began to come together, though not without the expected conflict that comes with any creative act. Producer Beinhorn, who was this time around teamed with engineer Garth "GGGGarthatron" Richardson (so named because of a stutter), who would go on to work with Rage Against The Machine, L7 and The Melvins, pushed the band as hard as he could in order to get the best takes. Beinhorn, Goetz and the band knew that if this album stiffed, they might as well give it away. Their incremental career rise over the course of three albums was satisfactory at best; what they now needed was a hit record.

Behaving more like a coach with a dream of winning the pennant than a journeyman producer, Beinhorn wouldn't give up until the band had laid down what he considered to be the absolute best take for each of *Mother's Milk* 13 tracks. Recording continued into the northern summer of 1989, mainly at Ocean Way, but also at Hollywood's Image Studios and Track Record, where the track 'Taste The Pain' was cut. Several other LA studios were used but as none of these sessions made the album, they weren't listed in the record's credits.

"The Peppers are great players," Beinhorn freely stated, "but as with all people, some of their takes were better than others and occasionally it was necessary to keep trying something until it was right."

In the Peppers' past, most in-studio stress had been generated by band members' overindulgence or the sheer recklessness of youth. This time around any studio drama was generated by a desire to get the songs down. Kiedis and Beinhorn did clash, more than once, but both insist that their intentions were honourable. Contrary to previous reports, however, the producer says he didn't have any problems with the new Peppers' guitarist.

"I don't recall any disagreements with John when we were making *Mother's Milk*," said Beinhorn. "Rather, it was Anthony who I seemed to be at odds with. Suffice it to say that I had very intense personal relationships with both Flea and Anthony and somewhere along the line I fell out with both of them [after the release of the album].

"I think the only time there was a disagreement [with Frusciante] was when we all told him he couldn't use his precious Ibanez guitar and instead was only permitted to play a Les Paul or a Strat[ocaster]."

The band did direct some anger towards engineer Richardson, who had a tendency to be chatting on the phone when he was most needed. Richardson worked on the tracking of the record but was fired when they began recording overdubs, mainly because the album's budget was pretty well exhausted. No doubt his phone bill didn't help.

Beinhorn admits to the occasional "communication problem" with his engineer, but he still regards Richardson's work on *Mother's Milk* and elsewhere as "exceptional". "He did a wonderful job on the record and I picked up a lot from watching him work."

Dave Jerden, who had worked alongside Andy Gill during the disastrous *Red Hot Chili Peppers* album, was brought in to mix the record at Royal Recorders in Lake Geneva, Wisconsin. He barely recognised the band; they'd grown musically since the 1984 sessions that Jerden recalled as "God-awful" and it was clear that the death of Slovak was the cause of Kiedis' and Flea's more adult-like behaviour. Jerden also recognised that John Frusciante was the perfect guitarist for the Peppers. "He brought a whole new dimension to the band," he said.

Jerden's work was crucial to the album's success. Along with their new A&R manager Rob Gordon, and (mainly) with the band's approval, he performed seven key edits to the finished tracks. Crucially, he trimmed almost an entire minute from 'Knock Me Down', which not only made for a far stronger track, but reduced it to a very consumer-friendly three minutes and forty seconds.

Of the rest of *Mother's Milk*, such tracks as 'Good Time Boys' and 'Stone Cold Bush' were way more representative of the band's hot-wired energy than anything they'd recorded before, while wisely chosen covers (Jimi Hendrix's 'Fire', which also appeared on the *Abbey Road* EP, and Stevie Wonder's 'Higher Ground') helped both to fill out the album and pay dues to their musical heroes.

"It had its good points and bad points," an ambivalent Kiedis stated once the record was completed, "although the good points won out. We were so hungry, so fresh. These people [Frusciante and Smith] knew what the intention of the Red Hot Chili Peppers was, but it was their own interpretation that helped us define it."

One of Flea's favourite moments on the album was the recording of 'Higher Ground', when a swarm of Pepper-friends were summoned to the studio to belt out a giant crowd vocal. Amongst the mob were some close buddies of the Peppers: Keith "Tree" Barry, plus Gretchen Seager and Julie Ritter, of Mary's Danish, who'd toured with the Peppers. Also in the house were Vicki Calhoun, the cousin of Living Colour's drummer Will Calhoun, and Kristen Vigard, an LA singer/songwriter who'd fallen in with the Fishbone/Peppers crowd. She'd recently duetted with Kiedis on her solo debut, covering Leon Russell's 'Out In The Woods'.

There was a real sense of occasion in the studio. In the wake of Slovak's death and the subsequent soul-searching that the band had endured, the Stevie Wonder track spoke eloquently of their need to keep "sailing on, sailing on", as Kiedis half-sang, half-rapped during the song's outro.

Former Pepper Jack Sherman was also there, shouting along. He was so awestruck by the development in the band that he buttonholed producer Beinhorn after the session, seeking answers. "I went in and I said 'explain'. He said that after Hillel died and they were ready to quit, they had the guts and the balls to hire some really good musicians, Chad and John. And he said that John is a million times the musician that he is on this record."

Director Drew Carolan, who'd shot videos for Living Colour, The B-52s and Ziggy Marley, was hired to direct clips for both 'Higher Ground' and the cautionary tale 'Knock Me Down'. The New Yorker loved the band on first meeting. They may have been holed up in an EMI conference room, with the obligatory football-field-sized table, plush leather seats and so on, but the band reclined in typical, clothing-optional Chili Peppers style. "Anthony was just wearing shorts," Carolan laughed. "No shirt. Flea was pretty much undressed as well – and Chad and John wore just a tad more than that. It was certainly the antithesis of corporate. They were just funny and passionate."

Carolan had heard an advance release tape of 'Higher Ground' and loved the song so much he knew he had to work on the video, even though the band insisted he collaborate with Bill Stobaugh, a friend of theirs who did "freaky styley animation".

" 'Higher Ground' kicked my ass," Carolan gasped. "Flea's bassline is ill!"

'Higher Ground' was the perfect cover for the band, a high-energy, carb-burning take on the Wonderman's pointed consideration of a world gone terribly wrong, originally a number four hit in 1973. Teaming an impossibly funky bassline from Flea with some heavy power-riffing from new boy Frusciante, it was easily the best non-original that the band had ever cut, simply because they made it their own. From the now famous bassline intro onwards, it was signature Chili Peppers.

Kiedis was convinced of that. "I think 'Higher Ground' is perfect for us," he said, "because of the way it translates to our sound. Obviously, the version we do has our own personality interjected into a song that he [Wonder] had already written, but it seemed like the perfect song to us. A definite challenge, but I think we tackled it."

As Carolan and the band got down to work on the video, they sent out feelers to the song's famous composer, asking if he'd be involved. Their original plan was to have Wonder seated sagely in the lotus position as the band and their friends danced wildly around him. Sadly, Wonder declined, so Kiedis reverted to their back-up plan, which he relayed to Carolan. "I don't care what we do," he declared, "as long as you make us look like the Gods of Funk."

To do just that, Carolan used plenty of low-angle shots of the singer. And they also brought in some band buddies: Angelo Moore and Fish from Fishbone, Ione Skye, Kiedis' girlfriend, plus Vicki Calhoun, Flea's infant daughter Clara and members of Thelonious Monster. This same gang of Peppers insiders would also appear in the video for 'Knock Me Down'.

The idea to turn the video of 'Higher Ground' into a party was inspired, because the band – who were in no way advocates of lip-syncing – charged through the shoot as if they were playing for their lives (not just their careers). Flea and Kiedis repeatedly "chest butted" each other at the opening of the clip, an act which was shot repeatedly to ensure that music and brute force were correctly synced. Another friend of the band's, a gorgeous woman named Cindy, who would go on to star in the clip for Young MC's 'Bust A Move' (a tune on which Flea would play) was brought in to bump and grind with Kiedis. In the process she helped him reinforce his rep as funk-punk's number one ladies' man.

"Of course the Peps were a stylist's dream," said Carolan, "because they hardly wore anything."

While the video for 'Higher Ground' was a bring-your-friends party, 'Knock Me Down' had a deeper intent: the song was an elegy for their dead guitarist. As Carolan would tell me, it "was a very special track for the band and it needed to be treated with utmost care and respect. Anthony and Flea just wanted it to be real soulful with a sense of urgency." Kiedis' concern was that it would simply be viewed as "an anti-drug song".

"That's a limiting analysis," he would say at the time. "It's really [about] being free to relate with your friends. Being free to relate in an honest and sometimes needy fashion. It's about letting your friends know that you need help and then being willing to accept the help of others when you need it, whether it's from drugs, or from a number of other personal problems."

'Knock Me Down' was clearly the most important track that the band had ever laid down; it proved that these Peppers were more than knuckleheads with socks hanging off their cocks. It was a heavy-hearted, admittedly radio-friendly farewell to Slovak, made even more poignant by Vicki Calhoun's soulful backing vocals, which exploded into a full-throated wail as Kiedis implored that "it's so lonely when you don't even know yourself". It was powerful, passionate stuff.

Curiously, though, the song had actually started to take shape even before the *Uplift Mofo* sessions. But it took Slovak's death to remind Kiedis of the song-under-development; he then brushed it off and finished the lyric. "I hadn't really thought about completing it until then," he admitted.

The 'Knock Me Down' video was planned to be part performance clip, part tribute to their fallen buddy. Actor Alex Winter, who'd appeared in the hit teen flick *Bill & Ted's Excellent Adventure*, was hired to play the tramp who drifts through much of the video, while Carolan and crew managed to source an old mansion in the Hancock Park area of LA, on the agreement that band and friends would only wreck the rooms of the mansion that were currently awaiting renovation. (New drummer Smith, however, did accidentally bring down some interior walls when his playing got a little too physical.) The Peppers behaved in the manner to which they were accustomed – they threw a day-long bash.

"Needless to say," Carolan chuckled, "the Peps and their friends – Fishbone, Thelonious Monster, lots of cuties and what not – took over the place. Since it was summer and it was hot and the Peppers never liked clothes all that much, everybody was running around the pool area naked and crazy – and the location manager was starting to come unglued. When he came to me flabbergasted, I just laughed."

The more serious intent of the video was represented by a "dead rocker's gallery", which featured portraits of Jimi Hendrix, Jim Morrison, The Germs' Darby Crash and jazzman Charlie Parker. Winter drifts through the gallery, with the camera following him like a shadow, as the band plays on. According to Carolan, the message was simple. "They were all [visual] reminders that drugs were not the answer."

Even though the frantic two-day shoot (one day for each clip) left Carolan, band and crew in a near-exhausted state, the videos became key elements of *Mother's Milk*'s success.

"That was a magic time," Carolan surmised, "in the sense that the band had a simple vision of what they wanted to be. Their management let them do their thing and they were fiercely proud of where they came from. Both Flea and Anthony knew that they had something special going on and took it seriously – but they never took it all too seriously. If they couldn't have fun at what they were doing then they weren't going to do it.

"The energy of the band was like having endorphins injected into your veins," Carolan enthused. "They just did not stop – and obviously the soul of Hillel was in that room, rocking."

At the end of two wild, totally draining days of work, Carolan edited the clips in Hollywood's Magic Hotel. Downstairs, the desk clerk was a hopeful called Jeff Buckley.

The band may have received some "spot play" for such past videos as 'True Men Don't Kill Coyotes' and 'Jungleland', but MTV's response to 'Knock Me Down' was emphatic. College radio reacted in much the same way. Within a week of its release, the single was perched at number 24 in the Postmodern chart of industry journal *Hits*, a chart compiled from both sales and airplay in select North American regions. By August 21, *Hits* reported the track was "sweeping the airwaves". MTV quickly put 'Knock Me Down' into "breakout" rotation, while radio and MTV reacted to 'Higher Ground' with just as much zeal. Finally, the Chili Peppers were making some real noise, even though they'd lost a soulmate getting there.

Released on August 28, 1989, *Mother's Milk* was a well-balanced album with little filler. It was a far more representative document of the band than any of their three earlier long-players. It screamed into life with 'Good Time Boys', which was as valid a signature song as the band had yet written. Kiedis' part-rapping/part-yelping vocal style was greatly improved; he was much sharper, much more coherent, as were his lyrics, as he proudly declared "One day the good time boys might just be president." The band, meanwhile, have never sounded so huge, especially during the shoutalong chorus. (This "wall of voices" would become a *Mother's Milk* trademark, also found on such tracks as 'Taste The Pain' and 'Higher Ground'.) Kiedis took time out during the opening track to namecheck some of his LA buddies and heroes, including Fishbone, Thelonious Monster, John Doe (of the band X, whose track 'White Girl' is sampled during the song) and fIREHOSE. As it turned out, the band would soon be outstripping all of their contemporaries, thanks to the surprise success of this, their fourth album.

Elsewhere on the record, the band were in any number of different moods. 'Pretty Little Ditty', the track that Frusciante and Flea had worked up during their introductory jam, lived up to its title: it was a dreamy, sweetly stoned instrumental featuring deft picking and strumming from Frusciante, intertwined with blasts of trumpet from Flea. Unfortunately, the song wouldn't be heard in its complete, three-minute-long, Peppers-approved version until the 2003 reissue of the record. Regardless, it was a new sensation for the band – and the song took on a second life when, years later, it was heavily sampled by one-hit-wonders Crazy Town for their hit 'Butterfly'. In a twist that would no doubt give the Peppers some joy, 'Butterfly' became a strip club and pole-dancing standard through much of 1999.

'Taste The Pain' reflected the more soulful side of the band and the album. It was one of several meditations on love and loss that dotted the landscape of *Mother's Milk* – although it should be said that the band resisted the temptation to lay on the sentimentality too heavily; this was still a party record at heart.

'Magic Johnson' was an indulgence piece, a mile-a-minute tribute to Flea and Kiedis' favourite basketballer, LA Laker star Magic Johnson. Kiedis came on like a punked-up cheerleader, chanting about watching the Lakers on telly because they had more moves than a bowlful of jelly, as Frusciante laid down more tasty rhythm guitar at his back. The track's marching-band-on-speed style is no accident: the song's working title was 'Fairfax High'. It was written with their old high school's band in mind.

"Magic is a hero to us," Kiedis explained. "Not only is there such a beautiful relationship between the sport of basketball and music, but [Johnson] is probably one of the biggest influences on the band. Just the style of basketball that he plays, where it's a style of assisting and supporting the other guys on your team, so that the team can do well. That's the same approach the Red Hot Chili Peppers take to making music."

When asked how he felt to be honoured in song, Johnson was suitably humbled. "Since I can't sing," he figured, "it's an honour having someone write a song about me that I can at least hum to."

Yet even such throwaway tracks as this and 'Subway To Venus' were

improved by the band's ever-expanding musical vocabulary. Behind Kiedis' headtrip of a lyric on 'Subway' (shades of 'Green Heaven'), Flea and Patrick English blast away on horns, while Keith "Tree" Barry wails on the tenor sax. During 'Stone Cold Bush', an ode to a streetwalker whose talents are vividly portrayed, teen porn star Traci Lords moans and writhes and groans, laying on all the tricks of her trade.*
Frusciante was so impressed that he thanked Lords in the album credits, along with fellow porn star Harry Reems. The only letdown with 'Bush' is that Kiedis went soft lyrically, modifying the original line about fellatio to something altogether benign.

'Punk Rock Classic' was another breakneck, turbocharged rampage, where the band cheekily sampled the now famous power riff from Guns N' Roses 'Sweet Child O' Mine', in between – in a case of biting the hand that makes you famous – taking a swipe or two at bands who would happily bend over for MTV airtime. In 'Sexy Mexican Maid', Kiedis couldn't resist his inner frat boy, crooning how the object of his affection enjoys plenty of orgasms, as he transformed a sweet, sultry valentine into a raunchy ode to a one-night stand, helped out by a positively filthy sax solo from Barry.

But *Mother's Milk* sometimes displayed a more serious side to the band than its three predecessors. That was driven home in the barnstorming, head-banging closer, 'Johnny, Kick A Hole In The Sky', which was Kiedis' chance to prove that his empathy for Native Americans ran deeper than some inkwork on his gym-toned shoulders, or an on-stage headdress. That he no longer believes what he reads in history books is beyond question. A distant musical relation of the first track from their first album, 'True Men Don't Kill Coyotes', the song was delivered with such steely conviction that it was hard to question exactly what this LA party boy had in common with suffering Native Americans. Strangely, the song's working title was 'The Power Of Equality', which would become the name of a totally different track on their next album. Just like Frusciante, Kiedis used the album credits to express his own agenda, thanking "Sitting Bull for killing Custer".

---

* During downtime while making *Mother's Milk*, Lords' infamous screen work became mandatory Peppers' viewing.

The Chili Peppers were not the kind of band to bring too many extra tracks into the studio – not until their next album, anyway – so there wasn't a lot of *Mother's Milk* left on the studio floor. A planned cover of Jimmy Cliff's 'The Harder They Come' was scrapped, mainly because the song was way outside Kiedis' limited vocal range. (The rarely heard demo is excruciatingly bad.) An instrumental simply titled 'The Dub Song' was also shelved. The only true "bonus track" added to the 2003 LP reissue was 'Song That Made Us What We Are Today', a rambling, 13-minute-long jam that gave John Frusciante the opportunity to play at being Jimi Hendrix. The instrumental would have been a clumsy fit on the original album, needlessly breaking up its momentum, but its appearance on the reissue showed how the band had sharpened its playing. Also included on the reissue was the original, unedited 'Knock Me Down'.

The Peppers were justifiably proud of their fourth album. Their playing was stronger, the songs were, in general, better written and Beinhorn's production shone a bright light on their numerous strengths. When asked about the album's title, Kiedis lapsed into a typically prolix reply. "Mother's milk is a life-giving, nurturing, intoxicating, good-natured, health-building, loving, comforting, warm, soothing substance," he stated. "When you drink it, it makes you feel good and makes you grow up strong and healthy. It wards off infection and disease. And it's honest. It's pure and wholesome and that's what we like to think our music represents."

Flea, as ever, chimed in. "I've been drinking a lot of it from my wife's tit," he said with a smirk.

Yet no Chili Pepper release came controversy-free: this time there was trouble with the album's cover art. A striking image, it shows the shirtless four nestled in the loving embrace of a topless, giant beauty (Kiedis' girlfriend, Ione Skye, was one of two models who posed for the cover, but her shot wasn't used). Kiedis, who came up with the concept, obscures one of her nipples with his torso; a strategically located rose hides the other. Not only did the model, Alaine Dawn, complain that the Peppers hadn't asked for permission to use her image, but a major US chain store – who had pre-ordered 50,000 albums – baulked at the cover. It was too racy for middle America. So it was agreed to enlarge the band members so that even less breast was visible. This backdown was nothing new for a band whose track 'Party On

Your Pussy' had been watered down to 'Special Secret Song Inside' at their label's request. Right now, the Chili Peppers just wanted to sell some records and were willing to do whatever was required to accomplish that. "We never change our music as a compromise for anybody's desires or tastes," Kiedis figured. "That we should have to enlarge ourselves on the record is really not that big a deal."

The album also came plastered with an "Explicit Language" warning sticker. "That doesn't bother me," said Kiedis. "Our lyrics are very explicit, whether it's about sex or friendship or love for life in general. If they wanna inform the buying public that it's explicit, I have no problems."

As for the album's back cover, the band chose one of Slovak's vivid paintings, a reclining nude, with an understated dedication to its creator underneath. (In the 2003 CD reissue, it was adorned with Flea's additional tribute. "I have beautiful images of him in my head all the time. He showed me what rock music was.") Slovak's musical legacy was maintained by the inclusion of a 1987 concert version of Hendrix's 'Fire', where just like Frusciante he got the chance to lose himself in a Hendrix fantasy.

These tributes to Slovak gave writers plenty of angles when analysing the band's new-found success ("Drug Death A Catalyst For Chili Peppers" yelled one headline), but the majority of critics focused on the band's new-found tunefulness and musical dexterity, not just its recently deceased member.

Playboy praised the album as "the most dynamic punk funk connection you're likely to hear for a long time". In their review, The *Toronto Star* were struck by the band's newly discovered eclecticism, labelling them "a Mothers Of Invention for the 1990s". *The Boston Globe* also noted their diversity, tagging *Mother's Milk* "sort of Prince meets Jimi Hendrix in the *Twilight Zone*". The *Orange County Register* commented, reasonably enough, that in light of Slovak's death and the fact that everyone "from Living Colour to The Beastie Boys whizzed by them like they were standing still," it was a shock that the band had even survived to a fourth album. But their music critic, Cary Darling, was impressed, if a tad cautious in lavishing too much praise on the record. "*Mother's Milk* is an energetic and fun restatement of the RHCP whiplash-funk attitude, but with the exception of the dreamy instrumental, 'Pretty Little Ditty', it doesn't break any new ground."

Although his review was just as ambivalent, highly regarded critic JD Considine, writing in *Tulsa World*, noted the significance of the album's more deeply felt tracks. "It's only when the Chilis sink their teeth into a real song, like the moving 'Knock Me Down', that this album seems red hot." *The Washington Post* praised Frusciante's "solid metal chops", while *Guitar Player* wrote how the guitarist known as "Greenie" "plays as if he grew up with one ear glued to a boombox and the other to a Marshall stack. [He's] a living archive of Seventies metal and funk riffs."

Many reviews were also spotting the Peppers' influence on other bands breaking through at the time, including Living Colour, plus 24-7 Spyz and Faith No More. Finally, the band were starting to receive kudos for being bold enough to slam together musical styles that seemed too divergent, too unlikely a mix. The Peppers found themselves repeatedly playing down both their impact on these bands and any hint of rivalry.

According to Kiedis, "Living Colour to me sounds nothing like the Red Hot Chili Peppers. But I have to deal with [this] on a daily basis: 'Wow, Living Colour's really biting your style, Swan. Y'ever see the guy onstage? He moves just like you.' "

As for the short-lived and little remembered 24-7 Spyz, Flea was equally dismissive. "It would be a bummer if that record became huge and they were hailed as innovators. Then, obviously, there would be some anger going around. Power to them, though – they're playing organic music and they are happening."

The band was less tactful when it came to discussions about San Fran rap-metal hybridists, Faith No More, who were now fronted by a Kiedis clone called Mike Patton. They were not a favourite band of the Red Hot Chili Peppers. Speaking with UK mag *Kerrang!*, Kiedis admitted that Chad Smith had plans for the wild-maned, move-busting Patton.

"My drummer says he's gonna kidnap him, shave his hair off and saw off one of his feet, just so he'll be forced to find a style of his own."*

---

* Their feud continued for years. As late as March 2000, Patton's band Mr Bungle were bumped from three European festival dates that also featured the Peppers. According to Mr Bungle's Trey Spruance, Kiedis requested they be thrown off the shows. "Our manager called their manager to find out what the hell was going on. He was very apologetic and said, 'We're really sorry, it's Anthony Kiedis who wants this.' "

Kiedis needn't have concerned himself too much with soundalikes in 1989, because *Mother's Milk* had started to gather both positive press and some genuine momentum, thanks to heavy radio airplay and the back-to-back high rotation videos of 'Higher Ground' and 'Knock Me Down'. By September 9, the album was sticking tight to the *Billboard* Top 200 chart. And 'Higher Ground' had reached a *Billboard* singles chart high for the band, peaking at number 26 in the Mainstream Rock Tracks chart and number 11 in the Modern Rock Tracks (only to be eclipsed by 'Knock Me Down', which hit number 6 in the Modern Rock Tracks list). The band were in Seattle and the Mother's Milk roadshow was ready to roll. It was the biggest North American tour of their careers. After five hard years, several departures, sackings and one tragic death, the Peppers were now much more than a hometown sensation.

CHAPTER SEVEN

"You can't go around taking your dick out, some people don't like it."

THE Chili Peppers had finally gotten it right with *Mother's Milk*. The songs were strong, the playing was sometimes dazzling and the band chemistry was perfect, thanks to the recruitment of new guns Chad Smith and, especially, John Frusciante, whose songwriting had given the band's rap-rock blend a much-needed transfusion of melody. There was also a poignancy and a sense of emotional truth to some of the songs that had never been heard before from the Four Stooges of rock.

Up to this point, EMI had considered the band a middling priority; to the suits, they were the kind of act who would sell enough albums to justify their relatively low recording budgets, but superstardom wasn't a word found in their marketing reports (not that this was an unusual attitude; most bands were viewed this way). But things changed with *Mother's Milk*. Their new A&R manager, the New York-based Rob Gordon, was young, ambitious and music-savvy. He'd studied engineering, had played in a band with Trey Anastasio, later of Phish, and had also tried to sign R.E.M. to EMI, just prior to their breakthrough hit *Green*. Gordon had just struck gold, literally, with Seattle art-metallists Queensryche and their 1988 LP *Operation: Mindcrime*. He'd achieved this by going outside the typical company guidelines, tapping into the band's black T-shirted fanbase and spreading the word via the use of street teams. When Gordon approached his boss and asked for the Peppers job, the response from his manager typified EMI's attitude. "Really?" he was asked. As expected, the band treated Gordon with disdain – when he first met Kiedis, the singer asked him: "What are you going to do for us?" It typified the band's dislike of EMI.

For the Peppers, Gordon and his equally driven team – marketing

'Mommy, Where's Daddy?': Flea sends out a greeting to his daughter Clara, backstage at the MTV Music Awards, 1995. "Look, Papa, it's going to be OK," she told him when he suffered a breakdown. "You're such a good person." *(LFI)*

Pepper Don't Preach: Kiedis and long-time pal Madonna, backstage at the MTV Awards, 1995. Kiedis' father revealed "they've known each other since the mid- Eighties". *(LFI)*

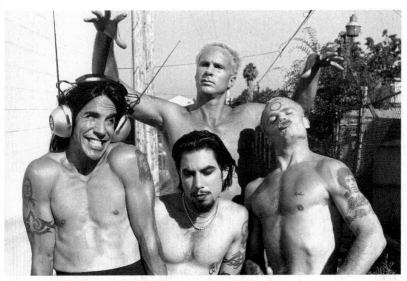

Hired For Sound: Dave Navarro (second from left) with Kiedis, Smith and Flea. The band knew he was a perfect Pepper. "He was a real cool guy, very Hollywood, very hip." *(Steve Double/Retna)*

Life's A Drag: Navarro, Smith, Kiedis and Flea (from left). When Navarro and Kiedis snogged during the 'Dosed' video, a rumour circulated that they were a couple. *(Richard Faulks)*

manager Tommy Manzi, video specialist Matt Murray, Kim White, who looked after alternative/college radio, publicist Cathy Watson and a second Rob Gordon, who kept an eye on west coast sales – targeted the areas of video and touring, because they knew the band wouldn't get a look in at pop radio, despite being embraced by college radio. Gordon and his crew were excited by the band on every level. "They were revolutionary musically, phenomenal live, could play their instruments as well as anybody else, they worked really hard, gave great interviews, great photo shoots – there's almost everything you can do right contained in this band," he asserted.

Rather than disappear from the live circuit while they were making *Mother's Milk*, the band played at least three shows a week, airing new songs, getting their fans excited about the upcoming record. The cash generated by these shows also helped the band eat, because they weren't yet making any money from record sales.

The California four had also finally got their timing just about right. Though 1989 and 1990 wasn't quite the golden age for alternative music, *Mother's Milk* did emerge in the midst of some first-rate records. And these albums weren't just critics' favourites; they also made some commercial impact in the US and the UK, amidst the usual fluff from such perennial hitmakers as Paula Abdul, Kylie Minogue, Bon Jovi, Janet Jackson and Tears For Fears.

Living Colour, four African/Americans playing heavy rock, and one of several acts accused of being Chili Peppers clones, had followed up 1989's *Vivid* with the equally powerful *Time's Up*, which packed hit singles in 'Elvis Is Dead' and 'Love Rears Its Ugly Head'. The album sold two million copies. Faith No More reached a commercial high with *The Real Thing*, which sat just outside the *Billboard* Top 10 while the roaring single 'Epic' peaked at number nine. Fellow fusionists Primus, fronted by an eccentric musical madman called Les Claypool, and Sublime, who were destined for a similarly tragic twist of fate as the Chili Peppers, had started to make some noise in the rock'n'roll underground. 24-7 Spyz were about to sign with a major label after their second independent release, *Gumbo Millennium*.

As Peppers buddy Bob Forrest would admit, when asked about the Peppers' influence: "They're my friends, and I love them, but I never realised how great they were until I heard every other band trying to rip them off."

Even more cultish rock acts, including Midwestern dipsomaniacs The Replacements, and Arizona punks The Meat Puppets (soon to be key players in the grunge revolution), received plenty of column inches and reasonable sales for their albums *All Shook Down* (The Replacements' swansong, as it turned out) and *Monsters*. Grunge godfather Neil Young was in the midst of a two-album strong comeback, first with 1989's *Freedom* and then in 1990 with the riff-sodden *Ragged Glory*, which was cut with his ageless backing combo, Crazy Horse. Both sets, unlike so much of Young's later-career work, snuck into the Top 40 of the *Billboard* Top 200 Albums chart.

The real noise, however, was being heard in the land of hip-hop. Public Enemy were fast rewriting the rules of the game with their seminal long-players *It Takes A Nation Of Millions To Hold Us Back* and *Fear Of A Black Planet*, albums which blended frenzied beats with the fearless polemics of frontman Chuck D. Not only were these albums unstoppable hits in the R&B/Hip-Hop charts, but they made serious inroads into the pop lists. The New York outfit also found the time to pay some dues, turning up on George Clinton's *The Cinderella Theory* (a comeback that was only recorded after Prince paid off Clinton's debts, allowing him to return to the studio). LL Cool J reached a career high with *Mama Said Knock You Out*, Digital Underground moved on up with the excellent *Sex Packets* and Salt-N-Pepa delivered a powerful feminist statement with *Black Magic*. Meanwhile, The Beastie Boys' most recent pair of albums, 1987's *Licensed To Ill* and 1989's *Paul's Boutique*, powered by the hit singles '(You Gotta) Fight For Your Right (To Party)' and 'Hey Ladies', continued to sell by the warehouse-load. It was a great time to be making music and *Mother's Milk* sat quite comfortably with music being made on both sides of the hip-hop/rock'n'roll divide.

As with their previous trio of albums, the Chili Peppers knew that the best way to spread the word was to tour hard. But now, for the first time, they had some real excitement building with *Mother's Milk* and its pair of much-spun singles, 'Higher Ground' and 'Knock Me Down'.

The album's official east coast launch was held in early August 1989, at the downtown Manhattan venue Tramps, as part of the influential New Music Seminar. After the set, guests were invited across the street to Manhattan's only indoor miniature golf course, which was about as un-Chili Peppers a location as could be found in New York (even though Flea and Chad Smith would soon become keen golfers). From there, the Peppers hopped the Atlantic for a short European tour; its highlight was a free show in Amsterdam's Dam Square. The band also found time to check in with Henky Penky, who continued working on the massive sprawl of ink that was taking residency on Kiedis' back.

Back in the USA, the trade journal *Hits* spread the untrue rumour that Kim White, the EMI staffer in charge of college radio airplay, was *Mother's Milk*'s cover star. It might not have been true, but interest in the record intensified.

And the band kept touring. The official US tour to push *Mother's Milk* kicked off in Seattle on September 8. Band buddy Keith "Tree" Barry and two female vocalists fleshed out the Peppers' line-up, while LA pals Mary's Danish, who were also making some impact on the alternative charts with their album, *There Goes The Wonderland*, were hired as openers. The Peppers had built up a 30-song set, throwing in covers of Hendrix's 'Fire', 'Crosstown Traffic' and 'Castles Made Of Sand', which gave Frusciante plenty of opportunities to unleash his inner voodoo chile.

The band were also flexing their sex god muscles. Women were spotted fighting with each other to gain the shirtless four's attention at their Seattle show at the Moore Theater. From there the tour travelled south to Portland, Oregon, for a sold-out gig before 1,100 slamming punters at the Starry Night.

As soon as the band exploded onto the stage at Portland, the moshpit burst into life, and didn't let up throughout their lengthy set. Stage-divers had a field day, sometimes even clambering from the upstairs balcony to the stage, using the PA speakers as an unsteady bridge. It was pure rock'n'roll anarchy, a vivid snapshot of the Peppers' increasingly high profile.

The *Portland Oregonian* reporter, John Foyston, was taken by the band's "genuinely dangerous rock'n'roll". But it was the crowd response that really grabbed his attention. "The Hollywood-based quartet," he wrote, "fomented an audience reaction that had to be seen to be believed.

"The stage-divers started rushing the stage from the moment the band walked on. Once on stage, it was an issue of luck and chutzpah; the meek would make the briefest of pirouettes before one of the security guys honed in like a missile. The most inspired would dodge their way to a clear spot – eluding the four or five bouncers stationed onstage – and dance for whole seconds before gracefully swan-diving into the audience."

The response from the band's growing fanbase was equally fervent at subsequent shows, as the tour moved onto the Fillmore in San Francisco, then the Venture Theater, returning for a hometown show at the Hollywood Palladium. After the show, EMI hosted a far more lavish album launch party on the rooftop of the Sunset Hyatt; they were wising up to the fact that the band were finally fulfilling some of their seemingly still-born promise. After a multiple sclerosis fundraiser in Arizona, band and crew headed west for well-received sets at the Ensemble Warehouse in Houston, the Austin Opera House and the Bronco Bowl in Dallas. Then they put in a two-night stand at the Vic in Chicago, followed by shows in Minneapolis and Omaha.

By the time the Peppers reached Boston in mid-October, *Mother's Milk* was gaining some serious chart heat, with sales moving quickly into six figures, which far outstripped their three previous long-players. But the band were still dealing with the aftershock of losing their brother, Slovak, as Flea would tell *The Boston Globe*. "We miss Hillel and there's been a lot of crying and bumming out since [his death]," he explained, "but we think it's made us a tighter band. And his energy will always be with us."

Despite the band's climb up the rock'n'roll ladder, Flea still found himself defending the Peppers from accusations that they were better known as a novelty act. Although polite as ever, his weariness with this line of questioning was starting to show. "We're known as 'those Eighties guys that like to get naked'," Flea shrugged, "but we don't want that to take away from the innovativeness [sic] of the music. That's what we want people to remember the most."

The band, however, had temporarily retired their tube socks. It wasn't until a show in Green Bay, Wisconsin, that they returned to their crowd-pleasing, set-closing stunt. When Keith Barry's sock went flying into the crowd, he didn't bother replacing it. As for Flea, he'd spent most of the show in either his Y-fronts or a disposable nappy, so "socks on cocks" seemed like the natural next step.

The Peppers' reluctance to revive the stunt may have been well founded, because after the Green Bay show they were busted by the local security for indecent exposure. This was not the type of exposure Kiedis needed, especially with the George Mason University incident still going through the courts. Fortunately, the band were let off the hook when the real police arrived. It helped that the constabulary recognised the Peppers from MTV.

Flea may have preferred the band's fans to choose music over mayhem, but they kept winning new converts, as they headed north to Toronto before returning to the Big Apple for a set at the CMJ Music Marathon Conference Award Ceremony, and their own headlining show at The Ritz (where Joey Ramone had hung out backstage with them five years earlier).

By mid-November they were in Washington, for an appearance at the Lisner Auditorium. The show received a lacklustre review – "much of the Peppers' [material] didn't rise above a low smoulder," wrote *The Washington Post*'s Kathi Whalen – but John Frusciante was starting to receive the same kind of attention as his more senior, stage-hogging bandmates. "The Peppers' latest guitarist, John Frusciante, is a new Hendrix, or at least a . . . copy of the old one," wrote Whalen. "His licks . . . were a sweet and supple diversion."

And Frusciante was fast developing a taste for life in the spotlight. The perennial loner was now getting more loving than he'd ever dreamed of.* By the time the LA four had returned to Chicago for a show at the Riviera, Flea was boasting that the band were "the hottest studs in Hollywood".

He may have been playing with the journalist, but Flea wasn't telling the full story. The band's non-stop touring, and the occasional liberty that they would take with the very willing women lurking backstage at their shows, was starting to take its toll on their offstage lives. Kiedis had broken up with Ione Skye, who – and this must have hurt badly – had moved on to Beastie Boy Adam Horowitz, whom she would marry in 1992 (and later divorce). Flea, meanwhile, was caught in a very typical new parent dilemma: in order to provide for Loesha and Clara, he needed to work. But in order to work, he needed to spend

---

* Years later, Frusciante would look back at his early days with the band and admit, "I was totally abusing the situation . . . partying and screwing a bunch of girls. At 19, I might have looked like a stud, but I was a weakling inside. I wasn't proud of who I was then."

long stretches of time away from his infant daughter and his wife and the strain was starting to show in their relationship. Their problems were exacerbated by bizarre on-tour incidents, as reported in the media after an Atlanta show:

> Local rock gossips are still trying to identify the young Atlanta female who tried to crawl out of a 4th floor hotel room window in search of fun after being rejected by Flea, after the band's show at the Fox Theater last month. According to *Spin* magazine, the fan met Flea at the Masquerade and accompanied him to the band's hotel, only to have the musician lock himself in the bathroom. Flea told *Spin* that thinking of his wife and daughter dampened his ardour.

At the start of December, Kiedis took the time out to assess the last few months. "We've taken a big step up," admitted an obviously pleased "Swan". "[It's] something we've been trying to do. And we're averaging between 1,000 and 3,000 fans a night at our shows."

But the unhealthy mix of break-ups, fractures in existing relationships and Kiedis' looming court case had soured what should have been the band's finest year.

Still the Peppers kept moving. They understood that rock'n'roll was a fickle world where only the loudest and most visible survive. In order to hang onto their new-found popularity, they had to keep playing and stay in people's faces. "When we go to New Orleans or Seattle or London or wherever we go," Kiedis said during a seemingly endless string of interviews to push *Mother's Milk*, "there are hundreds of kids who want to escape from all the weirdness of the outside world and engulf themselves in this music and this performance.

"[We] might not always be so lucky. There may come a time when no one cares about you."

They closed the decade with urgent sets at St Petersburg's Jannus Landing – "it was adolescent catharsis," wrote the *St Petersburg Times'* Eric Snider, "it was primal release" – and San Francisco, where Kiedis tore ligaments in his ankle, one of many injuries from the tour. At Long Beach they filled a 6,000-seat arena before moving onto the 1,500-seat Colorado Indoor Sports Center.

"The whole picture was one of total sensory overload," noted local reporter Todd Caudle of the Colorado show. "People in the audience, steeped in sweat and pressing against the barricade in front of the stage, threw their arms up in unison and barked out approval of one fast, furiously played song after another."

As they dragged their weary bones back to Hollywood for the new year, the band were coming off a crazy few months. But their lethargy lifted when Lindy Goetz advised them that *Mother's Milk* was perched just outside the Top 50 of the *Billboard* album chart. The second part of the band's three-step mission statement – to make a great album – was firmly in place.

The Peppers were in better spirits by the time they touched down in London in February of the new year. They were coming off a hit-and-run tour of Japan that the band themselves described as "a much heavier frenzy" than even their healthy egos could have envisioned. Speaking with staunch Peppers supporters, the *Melody Maker*, Kiedis joked how Stevie Wonder pressured the band into covering 'Higher Ground'.

"Stevie begged me to do it," he laughed. "He persisted until it got to the point where I'd wake up in the morning and go to get my paper and he'd be waiting on my porch.

"And he went on a hunger strike," Kiedis continued, dragging the joke out a little too long, as usual. "He got into this serious thing that we either cover the song or he'd commit hari-kari. I said, 'You can dust yourself Stevie, we're still not gonna do your tune.' It finally came down to a financial settlement whereby he bought everyone in the band a Rolls-Royce."

This was the new, improved Anthony Kiedis, now very openly discussing his drug-free life. He claimed to have been clean for two years, which was not quite accurate, considering that he had his final bender just after Slovak died in June 1988.*

"My life is a much more wonderful occasion without them [drugs]," he boasted. "For a time, growing up as a kid, I think it was kind of an enlightening experience to go through. But when it got to the point of death and destruction, it was time to either die, be miserable or get off. So I got off. I feel very lucky and grateful and blessed to have been able to start a new style – a fresh, clean style that I like."

---

* He claimed 21 months of drug-free living in another interview from that tour.

Kiedis' only complaint, as the band readied themselves for another series of shows and product-pushing, was that the Peppers weren't making any inroads in the UK. "We just headlined at Long Beach Sports Arena in front of 6,000 people," he moaned. "We're huge in the States and it's sort of frustrating and confusing that no one knows who we are here."

Kiedis continued this theme in another interview, admitting that "England is not our favourite place to go." He went on to compare the band's plans for world domination to "the long-term process of making love to somebody". "You start off with the foreplay," he explained. "You kiss them and you suck their neck and you titillate their sensory areas with your fingertips. That's the first couple of records. Maybe you start giving them head with your third record, then you finally slip it in [after] the fourth. *Mother's Milk* was incredibly well received in the States; we're still involved in the foreplay section with the rest of the world."

It seemed as though the Peppers were out to correct the situation while in the UK, by using their loud mouths as much as their music. First they instructed the local music press that punk rock's origins were in Hollywood rather than London (or New York); they then decided to exhibit "the evidence" during a London show. Even their best friends the *Melody Maker* weren't impressed, describing the band's take on 'Anarchy In The UK' as something "that could have dropped out of a Yes box set".

Their next step was to insist that they appear naked when performing 'Higher Ground' on the popular *Jonathan Ross Show*. Threatened with being dropped from the programme, the band made a compromise: could they hang Flea upside down by his feet for the broadcast? That was acceptable. Kiedis had to be content with bounding over Ross' desk during the performance and running amok in the crowd.

With the blood still returning to their bassist's feet, the band returned to the USA, where *Mother's Milk*'s third single, 'Taste The Pain', had begun to chart. And the album's sales had ticked over the 500,000 mark. It was the Peppers' first gold record.

But as with so much of the band's early career, 1990 was another stop-start year. It seemed that for every great leap forward, there were even more backward steps. Flea and Loesha, who had started to drift apart, agreed to separate. The bassman was very reluctant to speak about the split, but insists that it was amicable.* They agreed that Clara would be allowed to visit Flea three nights a week.

When I asked Flea's father, Mick Balzary, about the split, he felt that it was a typical case of "two young people who met and decided it [marriage] wasn't for them." But he insisted that Flea and Loesha did then, and still do today, maintain amicable relations.

It was as though no one in the Peppers could hang on to a relationship, something which would haunt all of the band for much of their lives. But given that so much of a musician's time is spent away from home, it's not surprising that successful long-term relationships are rare in the rock'n'roll world. Add the ever-available sexual temptations on the road and it becomes clear why many musicians end up either single or with other players: they're the only people who can truly understand the compartmentalised, spoilt-brat life of a rock star.

By March 14, the band's fortunes appeared to be improving. They were understandably pumped to learn that they'd be taping a performance for MTV's *Spring Break* programme, which would be shot at the Texan Motel, on Florida's Daytona Beach. The network had been incredibly supportive of the band's previous two videos, and this was another chance to spread the Peppers gospel to several million viewers. And the Peppers seemed to be the ideal band for the gig, given that *Spring Break* was an annual opportunity for America's youth to go very, very wild. There simply wasn't a better outfit to provide the soundtrack.

The only problem was that the band, who were scheduled to perform 'Knock Me Down', were asked to lip-sync, a necessity of live broadcasting which they'd very publicly denounced. Still, the tape rolled and they pretended to rock like Californian madmen. But as the performance continued, Kiedis, Frusciante, Flea and Smith started to shoot looks at each other. If they had to mime, they all silently agreed, they could at least have some fun. So they downed their instruments and heaved each other on their shoulders – Flea on Kiedis', Frusciante on Smith's – and then ran into the audience. What began as a dumb lark turned very ugly when Flea fell from Kiedis' grip. His first reaction was to grab whoever was nearest to him. "It just happened to be a girl," Flea recalled afterwards.

---

* He would admit to dealing with the break-up in what was then typical Peppers fashion: "I just got high and got laid and forgot about it."

Flea tossed the 20-year-old student from Virginia over his shoulders. Chad Smith, not realising that the situation was getting out of hand, joined his bandmate and reluctant fan on the beach, partially removing the bottom half of her bikini and slapping her backside. When his passenger started to yell at the bassist, insisting that he put her down, they fell onto the sand in a clumsy tumble. Foolishly, Flea then climbed on top of the woman and started to both dry hump and swear at her. The cameras were quickly shut down.

After their hugely flawed attempt at audience participation, Flea was understandably contrite. "I didn't know that Chad had spanked her, which was *faux pas* number one," he admitted. As for yelling obscenities at the woman, he realised that was a major mistake. "I did verbally abuse her and it was wrong. It was a really stupid thing to do. I was out of control. But I did not assault anybody, and it was not sexual," he insisted. "It had nothing to do with sex."

The Florida constabulary were not so easily convinced. Two nights later, backstage at a show at Daytona Beach, Flea and Smith were arrested. Flea was charged with "battery, disorderly conduct and solicitation to commit an unnatural and lascivious act". He was released on $2,000 bail. Smith was charged with battery and released on $1,000 bail. The MTV gig may have appeared lucrative, but the band hadn't won any friends in high places in Florida.

"We're not putting up with this garbage," stated Volusia County beach police chief, John Kirvan. "If it was my daughter, I'd be pounding on someone's chest to get some action."

The band's timing couldn't have been worse. After the George Mason University incident, and the drug death of Slovak, there was already some wariness about the band's antics, both on and off stage. Now Kiedis had to face his verdict with this latest controversy fresh in the judge's mind. The accidental publicity may have helped get the Red Hot Chili Peppers attention in mainstream media, but the backlash was pretty damned swift. Authorities at the State University of New York in New Paltz pulled the pin on a planned free show, despite the band's offer to send them a video which would illustrate how audience-friendly they were.

"We were becoming a target," figured Lindy Goetz.

On April 4, almost a year after the event at George Mason University, Kiedis was convicted of sexual battery and indecent exposure. During the case, Ms Crown had also stated that she suffered "shock, loss of standing in the community and irreparable injury to her reputation" as a result of Kiedis' flashing. Fairfax Circuit Court jurors recommended that Kiedis be fined $1,000 on each charge, rather than the possibility of 60 days' jail time. Kiedis appealed his sentence with the assistance of heavy-hitting Washington, DC, attorney William Moffitt, but the verdict remained unchanged.

What emerged from the two days of testimony, watched by a courtroom packed with Chili Peppers fans, was that Kiedis seemed to be suffering from selective memory. Despite statements from various witnesses that suggested that Kiedis had touched Ms Crown, Kiedis denied that. The jury wasn't convinced.*

When Kiedis sat down to discuss the events with US *Rolling Stone*, he would admit to being "guilty of indecent exposure", but nothing more. "I didn't do it with the intention of hurting anybody – it was just a stupid prank," he told writer Kim Neely. "Maybe I learned something from that, which is, you can't go around taking your dick out, because some people don't like it.

"But once you get into court, anything can happen," Kiedis ruminated. "It's her word against my word, with a bunch of very conservative jurors who are more likely to believe a girl who's going to college than a rock'n'roll boy who has a reputation for lewd activities."

Kiedis' case wasn't anything new. Ever since British police first busted Keith Richards and Mick Jagger for drugs, or Jim Morrison unzipped during a Doors performance in New Haven, Connecticut, the law has suspected rock'n'rollers of upsetting the natural order of things. Kiedis understood this, and from then onwards would become increasingly conscious of his behaviour.

Flea and Smith came next. On August 6, they were called into court to face Judge Freddie Worthen and hear the verdict on the Daytona Beach disaster. Both Peppers were directed to pay a $1,000 fine and

---

* A little less than two years down the line, in February 1993, the band settled a civil suit with Ms Crown, only hours before it was due to be heard in the same court. Although the amount of the pay-out was never officially revealed, Crown had filed for $2.35 million.

make a $5,000 donation to the Volusia County Rape Crisis Center in Daytona. They were also ordered to pay $3,000 each in costs and write a letter of apology to their victim, which was the maximum sentence for the first-degree misdemeanour. Reputedly, the woman involved in the incident approved of the sentence.

In his letter of apology, Smith wrote: "I clearly got carried away in the theatrics of the moment and I now realise how inappropriate and wrong my actions were."

"They totally tried to make an example of us," Smith stated after his trial. "I'm not trying to blame anybody else, but the way it came out was that it was a real malicious thing, that we tried to beat this girl up."

As for Flea, just like his bandmate Kiedis, he decided a new approach was needed. From now onwards, he would be far more circumspect in his behaviour (even though he could never completely retire the concept of playing nude). He also understood that the higher the band's profile, the more attractive a target they would become.

"Being this popular now," said Flea, "it upsets me to be perceived in a way that I don't want to be perceived – as misogynistic or homo-phobic or unsympathetic to other people. I have to be more careful not to say things that are misunderstood."

However, Flea refused to downplay the significance of sex in the band's music – this was funk'n'roll, after all. "The relationship between sex and music is there to begin with," he stressed. "And the relationship between sex and funk music is even more [pronounced]. To deny that is preposterous."

Upon the announcement of the verdict in the Florida case, reporter Steve Dougherty perfectly summed up the shift in the band's fortunes. "Until very recently," he wrote, "the group couldn't get arrested." Things had changed.

When not in court, or defending their sometimes lewd and lascivious acts, the Peppers continued to tour on the back of *Mother's Milk*. They revisited New York's The Ritz, headlining the Punky Funky Lovefest. Their set was forceful enough to inspire writer Peter Watrous to declare the band an Eighties version of The Beach Boys.

"But it is modern California," he explained, "where everybody walks around in shorts, doesn't wear a shirt and has big tattoos and a great physique. And their music, hyperactive and loud, is meant for a party."

Billboard's Evelyn McDonnell wasn't so thrilled by the Peppers. She noted the "mostly white, mostly male" make-up of the crowd – though she didn't mention their reaction to the band's cover of Sly Stone's 'Don't Call Me Nigger, Whitey' – and slammed the band's puerile mannerisms. "On stage," she wrote, "the Chili Peppers looked like adolescents drunk on ego and hormones – running, tumbling, spitting, screaming, drinking, cursing, and, of course, grabbing their crotches. The band seems to get paid to act out its audience's ids. Or is that idiocy?"

Keith Barry, however, remembers the *Mother's Milk* tour as "beautiful". "I think it was a healing thing; we had a nice personal thing going on."

During one break in the tour, Barry's father, who'd played in Fifties' revivalists Sha Na Na, arrived at the airport to collect his son. He was astounded to see the Peppers and crew almost in tears as they said their goodbyes. "Those [Sha Na Na] guys hated each other," Barry explained, "and when they would get back to the airport from a gig they'd stand as far apart as they could from each other, not saying a word. So my dad came to pick me up and he was so surprised to see us all hugging. It sure wasn't like Sha Na Na."

The tour might have been winding down, but the band were red hot. While in Baltimore, the Peppers were guests of honour for a post-show party at the home of director John Waters, a particular favourite of Frusciante. Back, briefly, in the studio, they ripped through three different versions of the Bachman Turner Overdrive classic rock staple, 'Takin' Care Of Business', the title track of a buddy flick starring James Belushi and Charles Grodin. This one-off created even more trouble with their label EMI, who wanted to release the cover as a single. The band justifiably felt there were stronger songs on *Mother's Milk*.

The track 'Show Me Your Soul' also turned up on the *Pretty Woman* soundtrack – and the piss-taking *Freaky Styley* outtake, 'Millionaires Against Hunger', finally found a home, on a benefit album for an LA charity called LIFE (Love Is Feeding Everyone).

The momentum continued when the Dick Rude-directed clip for 'Catholic School Girls Rule' was given new life, courtesy of *Playboy*'s

Hot Rocks programme. And Kiedis made a brief return to acting in the surf-crime thriller, *Point Break*, playing – oh the irony – one of a gang of drug-dealing surfers. Various band members also broke out in one-off outfits, just for kicks. Flea and Frusciante put together the outfit Hate, while Flea also helped out a combo by the name of Trulio Disgracias, whose members included Fishbone's Norwood Fisher and Angelo Moore plus future Pepper Arik Marshall.

EMI, meanwhile, capitalised on the heat that the band was generating by pumping out two video compilations. The first was an eight-track-long collection of clips entitled *Positive Mental Octopus*, segments of which prompted one reviewer to accuse the band of "gay baiting", evidence of the politically correct mindset that had crept into mainstream media. The other video was a live set named *Psychedelic Sex Funk Live From Heaven*, taken from their wild headlining set at Long Beach, just prior to their last UK tour.

The year 1990 had seen a flurry of activity and interest in the band that they'd never experienced before. But once the buzz started to wear off *Mother's Milk*, the band and management knew that it was time to free themselves of the grip of EMI.

Just as the Peppers' legend had gradually developed, so had the reputation of manager Lindy Goetz and his LGM Company. By the time the band began talking about extricating themselves from their EMI contract, he had management interests outside the Chili Peppers, including Thelonious Monster, who had split in a drug-addled mess in 1989, looked on as guitarist Rob Graves died in 1990, and then re-formed in 1991. He was involved with former Monkee (and erstwhile child star) Davy Jones; he would also look after Seattle rockers Candlebox and LA punks The Dickies. But right now, Goetz, along with Peppers attorney Eric Greenspan, knew they had to buy the band out of their contract with EMI, three albums short of the seven-record/seven-year deal that they'd signed in 1984.

They'd made their dissatisfaction with EMI very public – there was the dispute over the title of their first album, the lack of pop radio airplay for the bulk of their first three albums and the fatal mistake when it came to not releasing 'Behind The Sun' as a single. Neither of their first two albums had been released outside of North America. Also impeding the band/label relationship was the corporate culture: due to

214

various mergers and takeovers, the band's US label changed from EMI America to EMI Manhattan, EMI USA and EMI Records Group, all within the course of four albums. They'd also had four different A&R managers during their time with the label.

But to EMI's credit, they had tried to connect them with the most appropriate producers, especially George Clinton and Andy Gill, and had secured time for the band in the best studios. They'd also gradually developed a fanbase for the Peppers in Europe, the UK, Australia and parts of Asia.

Yet in spite of the unprecedented success of *Mother's Milk*, which had now sold more than 600,000 copies in the USA, charted much higher than any of their earlier three records and established the type of following that meant they could now headline profitable tours through-out any number of US states, the band felt the record simply could have sold more. And that meant the label weren't doing their job.

As Kiedis crowed, "We knew the record [*Mother's Milk*] was the greatest piece of music we had ever compiled, and EMI simply wasn't deserving of us. They had always sucked in the past, they were always dropping the ball, coming up short on a regular basis."

Kiedis wasn't finished yet. "There was no way we wanted to pour our lives into a record," he added, "and give it to this inept company, so we decided to look for a company that was more competent, more musically connected."

Looking on from the sidelines, Jack Irons agreed that the album could have gone even larger than it did. "*Mother's Milk* could have done more," he said. "EMI just didn't have the vision to make it go further than it did."

But the band and management didn't want to be dragged into a lengthy court case with the label. That was the type of potentially career-stalling trouble that could ruin the band's forward momentum. They'd already spent enough time in court over the past year, anyway. According to Kiedis, "No one knows who would win in court. It would only be a waste of time and money."

So Greenspan and Goetz struck a deal with EMI; for a to-this-day undisclosed settlement amount, EMI were given the option to lift a single track from the band's next album for inclusion on any Red Hot Chili Peppers compilation in the future. In exchange, the band were now free agents. EMI made a last-ditch attempt to keep the band –

even offering to hire Prince to produce their next album – but the band knew they had to move on.

And the Peppers weren't shy about advertising their availability. Working a room came naturally to the extroverted Kiedis. He freely admitted that once released by EMI, he and the band went on a "schmoozefest".

"Everybody was talking to us," Lindy Goetz recalled. "Richard Branson [CEO of Virgin] wanted to fly us to the Bahamas."

Twelve months earlier they would have struggled to get a meeting, but now with a hit record and a certain level of notoriety, every major label wanted a piece of them – and any A&R guy worth his corporate credit card could see that the band hadn't reached their creative (or commercial) peak. And with a ready-made fanbase, the publicity department of their new home wouldn't have to work the Peppers like a new band, because the groundwork was already in place. Despite their legendary wildness, they were a pretty safe bet – maybe even a hugely profitable investment for the near future – given that Generation Lollapalooza and the alternative music revolution were just a fuzzy riff into the future.

One of several record companies negotiating with the band was Rick Rubin's Def American label. The last time the Peppers had crossed paths with Rubin, he was riding high on his success with The Beastie Boys. But now things had changed. The Peppers were a successful act (finally), while Rubin, as well as working on such albums as Public Enemy's *It Takes A Nation Of Millions To Hold Us Back* and LL Cool J's *Walking With A Panther* (he'd even directed the Run-DMC movie, *Tougher Than Leather*), had set up his own label and signed a roster of artists that included Scotland's answer to The Velvet Underground, The Jesus And Mary Chain, and had established a distribution deal with the Time Warner empire. But Rubin could use the association of a hit record, because his decision to work with misanthropic comic Andrew Dice Clay hadn't won him any new fans. The time was right to connect with the Chili Peppers.

Rubin had met with the band, briefly, backstage during the *Mother's Milk* tour, telling Flea that he felt their show was "phenomenal". On the spot, Flea floated the idea of Rubin working with the band.

The notion of recording with Rubin – maybe even signing to his label – seemed every bit as attractive to the band now as it did in 1985.

But when Epic Records, a subsidiary of Sony Music, offered an estimated $5.7 million for three albums, the band were caught between
Rick and a hard place.

"It was more money," gushed Kiedis, "than we thought humanly
possible."

Goetz agreed. "Sony wined us and dined us pretty good," he told
me.

Kiedis was fully aware that even if they didn't sign with Def American, Rubin was still the right producer for the band, especially if they
were to build on the success of *Mother's Milk*. "If Baron von
Munchausen had ejaculated the four of us onto a chess board," he
explained in his roundabout way, "I'm sure that Rick Rubin would be
the perfect chess player for that particular board."

Then, briefly turning more lucid, Kiedis stated why Rubin could do
the job. "Our sound has so many diverse elements to it," he figured. "I
just realised he could probably comprehend and put all of these elements into a cohesive format."

Flea said much more with fewer words. "He manages to keep his
emotional distance from the music, which is what he has to do."

As Greenspan quietly gave the Epic contract the once-over, the band
grinned for photos with Tommy Mottola, the president of Sony Music.
It seemed as though the deal was locked in, and the band were to be
labelmates of Seattle up-and-comers Pearl Jam. But displaying his
incredibly astute business sense, Warner Brothers chairman, Mo Ostin,
had a few eleventh-hour calls to make.

Ostin was a music biz legend. A former accountant who'd then
become one of Frank Sinatra's personal bodyguards, he had been promoted to the president's post at Sinatra's Reprise records by the chairman of the board himself. When Warners swallowed up Reprise in
1967, Ostin proved just what an astute judge he was, signing rising stars
Jimi Hendrix, Neil Young and Emmylou Harris. He understood "real"
music and he also knew how to sell it.

Ostin had been desperately keen to sway the Chili Peppers in
Warners' direction, but he knew of the Epic offer, so he decided to call
the band members individually and wish them well for the future, with
or without Warners. His first call was to Chad Smith, who was gobsmacked by the geniality of the man. "Hadn't all these record company

suits made their legend by being hard-assed, unbreakable bastards," Smith thought? Ostin didn't come on like that at all.

"Fuck me," Smith said to himself, hanging up the phone after Ostin had called. "Who'd have thought the boss of Warner Brothers would call and admit that he'd lucked out? What a guy."

Not long after Smith's call, Kiedis, Flea and Frusciante had similar conversations with Ostin, and a band meeting was hastily called. Flea told his bandmates about his call from Ostin, how the chairman of the board had rung to tell him, " 'Congratulations and good luck with your career, and we're sad you didn't go with us, but I wish you the best.' That was a real sign of a class act," Flea figured, "a gentleman, just a good guy." The others agreed. Ostin even invited the band and manager Goetz for dinner. "It felt like hanging out with your uncle," Goetz remembered.

As far as the band was concerned, Warners seemed a better option. Ostin's call "really made me feel that Warner Brothers was the place we could feel more at home," Kiedis said. And according to Lindy Goetz, Warner's offer was pretty much identical to Epic's $5.7 million, "more or less".

"At the very last minute," Kiedis told music trade mag *Billboard*, "it just dawned on us that it might be worth taking a little less money to go with a West Coast company that we really believed in."

It certainly didn't sour the deal that their new labelmates would be LA brothers Jane's Addiction, whose *Ritual De Lo Habitual* album was one of 1990's biggest crossover hits, and R.E.M., who were about to drop the quadruple-platinum, number one album *Out Of Time*. Hell, Warners had even signed the band often accused of being Peppers clones, Faith No More. The label seemed to understand music that was both well-crafted and commercially viable; this was exactly what the Chili Peppers needed. And not only were they LA-based, but Warners also owned MTV, a ready-made, must-watch vehicle for breaking bands, whose high rotation of the Chili Peppers' clips for 'Higher Ground' and 'Knock Me Down' had helped make *Mother's Milk* such a breakout hit.

Greenspan called Epic to break the bad news, while the Peppers inked a three-album deal with Warners. *Billboard* magazine got the call to drop the photo of the Peppers posing with Sony's Tommy Mottola, and replace it with a hastily arranged shot of the band, Greenspan and

Goetz with various Warners execs, plus a cardboard cut-out of Ostin, who was elsewhere at the time.

Warner Brothers President Larry Waronker was justifiably proud of the coup. They'd grabbed one of the potentially hottest bands of the Nineties from under the nose of another multi-national. "I think the reason we signed them," he said, "outside of your normal record-company greed, really has to do with the future – the future in terms of a band that really has a musical point of view and a tremendous amount of strength, that has reached a certain level. You can just tell they have all the intangibles.

"Musically," he added, "they're messing around in a neat area, [but] if there's a trend, it wasn't about that. We all want the success factor, in terms of commerciality, but the other thing with long-term careers has to do with credibility and the aesthetic of what a band is up to. When you have both these things going for you, I think those are the best bets you can have."

As for Rick Rubin, he couldn't match the money being thrown around by both Epic and Warners, but he was offered a solid-gold consolation prize: the chance to produce the Chili Peppers' first album for their new label. It was the beginning of a beautiful – and hugely profitable – friendship.

CHAPTER EIGHT

"I see that erection as being my enemy."

THE Chili Peppers' early days with Warner Brothers couldn't have been any further removed from their stretch at EMI. These were high times. Lindy Goetz and label president Lenny Waronker fully appreciated the commercial viability of the band – and the fickle nature of music buyers – and set out to ensure the public wouldn't forget about their heroes, even as they disappeared into six months of pre-production for their fifth album. The band, meanwhile, quickly adapted to the extra dollars being thrown in their direction.

As 1990 turned slowly into 1991, the Peppers turned up in the most unlikely place, a television commercial for Nike, where they featured alongside tennis ace Andre Agassi. The ad's slogan, "You wanna play rock'n'roll tennis?" hinted that the band ranked almost as highly as the master of the topspin lob.

By March, Anthony Kiedis found himself in an equally unlikely situation, seated on the Warner corporate jet, alongside Mo Ostin and Lenny Waronker, en route to Paisley Park Studios in Minneapolis. The trio were to be received by the Prince of pop, and given a sneak preview of his album-under-development, *Diamonds And Pearls*. When it came to labelmates, the Chili Peppers couldn't ask for a more eccentric or dazzling partner than the man in purple.

Upon arrival at what Kiedis described as "the wizard's castle", Waronker and Ostin were ushered into Prince's quarters, "an apartment straight out of Baron [von] Munchausen", according to a bewildered Kiedis. The singer was left alone for several hours, taking in the bizarre surroundings.

"It was this huge studio and sound stage with little munchkins running around and women designing psychedelic clothing," Kiedis would report. As the hours ticked by, he began to get the feeling that it would be easier to meet the Pope, when finally Waronker emerged and invited him inside. "Prince wants you to hear his new record," he was told.

Kiedis was floored by the sight of Prince, in a dimly lit studio, behind a control panel that could have been lifted from the Starship *Enterprise*. "Prince [looked] so impeccably cool I couldn't stand it. He had on a pinstriped jacket with matching pants and shoes. He looked bad and beautiful.

"I say, 'Hello', he says, 'Hello'. [He] isn't completely vivacious, but he's extremely friendly and not at all abrasive. He seems peaceful, direct and very considerate."

Prince then proceeded to play the entire album, very loudly, for the trio, announcing each tune's title and then playing either air guitar or bass throughout the song.

Kiedis looked on, amazed by the scene. And he was also blown away by the fragrance of the man, who, Kiedis revealed, smelled "like a greenhouse of flowers – and there's not a speck of dirt on him."

It was another day in paradise for Anthony Kiedis, who on the flight back to LA quietly pondered how much things had changed since the days when he and Flea used to organise band meetings with Goetz just so they could hustle a free meal.

Much of their new album's pre-production took place in Alleyway, the band's rehearsal space, which was run by a strange biker/hippie couple who'd decorated the place in quirky Seventies artefacts. Rick Rubin would occasionally drop by, curl up on the sofa and appear to take a nap. But what he was actually doing was mapping out their next album in his head. It was during these periods of meditation that Rubin decided, wisely, that the band could use a change of scenery for their new album. The Peppers had worked in some impressive studios, but the bearded, shade-wearing producer-cum-mogul had a far more radical plan in mind. He didn't want to use a studio at all. Hawaii was suggested, but Rubin preferred to stay close to LA. He was a busy man.

The plan really fell into place while he was driving in Laurel Canyon, in the Hollywood Hills, during pre-production. He spotted a TO LET sign on a four-storey, 13-bedroom, dilapidated stone mansion. It was a brilliant brainwave on Rubin's part: why hide the band away in a dark, chilly studio when you can relocate them to a mansion and bring the studio to them?

Rubin pitched the idea to both the band and Warners, and they were thrilled – especially when Warners' bean-counters did the sums and realised that hiring the mansion for the duration of the album would roughly equal time spent in a studio. But it was still a sizeable financial risk for a band with exactly one gold record in their trophy cabinet and a history of drugs, death and debauchery. Lenny Waronker, however, saw the benefits of the deal. "In the big picture, it may be less expensive than staying in the studio for months. This was a way they could work at any time and control the environment. I don't think it was all that costly."

As soon as Flea checked out the mansion, he was a convert. "There's no one here except who we want here," he said, "just the people who are working on the record and the people we love [including his daughter Clara, who would visit three times a week]. That's it. It makes for a creatively fertile situation."

Kiedis wasn't quite ready to give Rubin total credit for the idea, but he was completely down with the concept. "Somebody said maybe we should make a record in a huge house," he recalled, "and we said that'd be great because we wouldn't have to deal with the anal retentiveness of the studio. We could be focused on what we wanted to do, which was make the most beautiful record in the world."

Rubin looked on and smiled. "It was my idea to get the house," he admitted, "[but] the guys decided they didn't want to leave."

The mansion's sprawl made Lindy Goetz smile, as he started to think about their low-budget past. "It was a lot different to recording in Detroit," he figured, justifiably.

The house, if publicity spin at the time was to be swallowed whole, offered the kind of blood, sugar, sex and magic that would appeal to a band such as The Red Hot Chili Peppers. Built in 1917, it had, allegedly, belonged to Twenties screen idol Rudolph Valentino; Harry Houdini reputedly lived next door. Jimi Hendrix may have been a one-time tenant. Kiedis was convinced that it was the house where two of The Beatles had first tried acid (even though Harrison and Lennon had gone on record saying that it happened in London, with their dentist, no less). The *Chicago Sun-Times* gave their own interesting spin when they announced, probably wrongly, that the band was working in a "big Hollywood mansion where Jimi Hendrix allegedly turned The Beatles onto LSD for the first time."

Regardless of its shadowy past, the mansion was the ideal environment for the band. As far as Rubin was concerned, the "in-house" idea may not have worked for all acts, but it was right for the Chili Peppers. "I thought being in a house, in an environment different than they'd ever been in before, would give the whole project a different flavour. It just changed the feel of the whole project.

"What I thought was fun about the idea," he said in a rare interview, "was this was a band that had made a fair number of albums prior. And just to kind of clean the slate of everything they had done before and start with a fresh approach."

Rubin and crew, including engineer Brendan O'Brien, who would go on to major acclaim when he worked with Pearl Jam, started to build a studio as spring gradually bloomed into summer. The production team spotted the sonic potential in many of the mansion's rooms: they transformed the library into the main control room, shifting Neve and Soundcraft consoles into the room. The amplifiers for bass and guitars were miked in the basement and two different rooms were used for drums. The main recording area was the former dining room, which was soon packed with amps, a baby grand Yamaha piano and John Frusciante's collection of instruments, which included an electric sitar, a lap steel and mandolin, amidst the usual selection of electric and acoustic six strings.

O'Brien and Rubin also decided that the foyer was the perfect area for recording percussion, so they dispatched their crew on a mission to locate hubcaps and crumpled pieces of sheet metal. They had a percussion "hoedown" in mind for the track 'Breaking The Girl', and needed every piece of metal that could be found on the Laurel Canyon streets.

"If it's not here," the hirsute Rubin announced, as the band took in the final set-up, "then you can't have it, because you don't need it. And don't be thinking that if you make any mistakes, you can just go back and erase them later. We're recording the basic tracks live and we're not going to stop the tapes for anything." Rubin would eventually relax his old-school recording approach, allowing each band member the chance to record whatever overdubs they deemed necessary. But his organic outlook clearly helped the band come even closer to nailing their live sound in this mansion-cum-studio.

Now it was the band's turn to make themselves at home. When they learned that Flea and Kiedis' favourite hoop-shooter, Magic Johnson, was among their neighbours, they located a huge cardboard cut-out of the man and installed it immediately. An *Abbey Road* poster was tacked up on the wall, alongside various raunchy centrespreads, ripped from the many porno mags that were littered throughout the mansion. A selection of Frusciante's paintings dotted the walls, strangely echoing the artwork of his predecessor, Hillel Slovak.

Kiedis, meanwhile, decided to do more than sleep in the space he claimed as his bedroom. He recorded most of his vocals there.

But while Kiedis maintained his drug-free lifestyle, Frusciante and Flea – who broke his ankle as soon as he moved into the house – were smoking up a storm. "John and I were stoned out of our brains all day long," Flea said in a VH-1 interview.

Their carefree attitude to drugs angered Kiedis. "We would fight and hurt each other's feelings and hold grudges and all of that stuff," Flea recalled of the time.

Flea's other outlet during recording downtime was sex. The recently divorced bassman found the boy's club atmosphere perfect for cutting loose. "At that time in my life I was into fucking anyone that I could," he would confess. "Any girl that wanted to have sex with me I was into having sex with. I had split up with my wife and was like, 'Bring it on!' I was living more in my cock as opposed to my heart and my head. None of us had a girlfriend or were in long-term relationships, but sex was on our minds all the time."

British-born, LA-based videographer Gavin Bowden, who was married to Flea's sister Karen, also moved into the mansion. He was given a $60,000 budget by Warners to shoot a video of the creation of the album, which would be a handy marketing tool for the label when the time came to sell the record. It was originally planned to be used only as a video press kit, but was ultimately packaged and sold as *Funky Monks*, a handy snapshot of the band at work in their Laurel Canyon playground-cum-studio. It would also unintentionally chart the growing alienation and meltdown of John Frusciante. The film opens with him seated on a rooftop, contemplating suicide and the "fourth dimension". His bedroom in the mansion was monastic; there was very little apart from a limp mattress and some guitars, while odd scrawls could be seen on the wall. "He was starting to use drugs, to get high," said Goetz.

"He was getting a little stranger – and it got harder after the record."

The band hired a live-in cook – a former *Playboy* model – for the eight weeks of recording sessions. They also hired a video-game-obsessed security guard, who would be fired because he spent too much time absorbed in Nintendo.

Peppers, staff and crew, however, faced a strange and unexpected dilemma once they were settled in the house: it turned out that the mansion was haunted.

Chad Smith decided he wasn't equipped to deal with the strange noises that rattled through the house. He collected his stuff, grabbed his Harley and drove the 20 minutes back to his home in the Hollywood Hills. He'd report for duty with the rest of the band every afternoon, but he would ride home as soon as his tub-thumping work was done (or he and Rubin had finished air-drumming to Led Zeppelin, which fast became a popular pastime for the two rock dudes). There was no way he was going to stay there after dark, even if it did, at first, annoy his bandmates-cum-frat-brothers.

"Chad feared the wrath of the ghost," Kiedis reported. "He's got a Midwestern fear of spirits."

It appeared to be the band's cook who unknowingly awoke their unwelcome guest. As soon as she brought a book on the supernatural into the mansion, the mood turned decidedly spooky.

Flea, for one, could sense the difference. "The second she walked into the house, the equipment started squealing," he said. "Everything had been working fine and suddenly the tape machines started acting up."

The only option was for the cook to conduct a seance, which revealed that a male ghost had occupied the house for years.

Photographer and film-maker Gus Van Sant, hired by Warner Bros to take publicity shots, had a nasty shock when he closely examined the film he had shot. He could detect a "ghostly image" in at least four of the frames.

"There are definitely ghosts in the house," confirmed Frusciante, a man who was closer to the spirit world than most. He swore blind that he could hear the sounds of a woman making love in his room. "But they are very friendly. We have nothing but warm vibes and happiness everywhere we go in this house. Flea's daughter Clara loves it, and she knows better than anyone else."

A pair of psychics and a medium were brought in to investigate whatever was going bump in the night. No one could agree on whether it was a good or bad spirit, but it definitely had a sexual presence, as Frusciante would relate during the *Funky Monks* rockumentary. He spent almost all of the eight weeks of recording with a permanent hard-on.

"A lot of the time I'll get an erection when I'm working on something, playing the guitar, and I'll just go masturbate," he confessed. "Other times I'll hold back because I'll try to see the orgasm as something that might be detrimental to my strength creatively. So sometimes I see that erection as being my enemy."

Amongst the 24 tracks recorded at the haunted Laurel Canyon mansion was 'Under The Bridge', the song that was set to turn these up-and-comers into solid-gold, million-dollar stars. But the track, a reflection on the darkest days of Kiedis' heroin addiction – and a companion piece to 'Knock Me Down' – almost didn't make the album at all. Kiedis thought the lyric was simply too personal, too deeply felt, to connect with a larger audience. Rubin found the song by accident, when he was flicking through one of Kiedis' "word books", where he collected his potential lyrics.

"What is this?" the producer asked Kiedis, pointing to the scrawled words for 'Under The Bridge'.

"Aw, that's not really a Chili Peppers song," Kiedis replied.

But Rubin was a man with an ear for a hit, so he persevered, asking Kiedis to sing the melody to him. He was awestruck by what he heard.

"I thought it was beautiful," said Rubin. "I said, 'We've got to do this.' He said, 'Well, if you think so, I don't mind, but . . .'

"He never intended it for the band," Rubin revealed. "I think that the Chili Peppers, up until their last album [*Mother's Milk*], had put certain limitations mentally on what they thought they should be doing."

Clearly the song's lyric – "Sometimes I feel like I don't have a partner" – was equally inspired by the desperation of his former addiction (Kiedis had now been clean for almost three years) and the loss of his main man, Hillel Slovak. The sad lyric had come to Kiedis as he left a rehearsal prior to the *BloodSugarSexMagik* sessions.

As he would relate to *Rolling Stone*'s David Fricke, "I was driving away from the rehearsal studio and thinking how I just wasn't making any connection with my friends or family. I didn't have a girlfriend, and Hillel wasn't there.

"The only thing I could grasp was this city," Kiedis added, taking in the City Of Angels with a sweep of his bronzed, toned arm. "I grew up here for the last 20 years and it was LA – the hills, the buildings, the people in it as a whole – that seemed to be looking out for me more than any human being. I just started singing this little song to myself: 'Sometimes I feel like I don't have a partner.'"

As Kiedis drove home, he began to try to comprehend the sadness that had overwhelmed him. Sure, his best friend was dead and he'd opted for a heroin bender rather than attend his funeral, but Kiedis was on the mend. He wasn't using any more and the band were making some serious inroads. They'd signed a multi-million dollar deal and Kiedis had spent his advance on a stunning home in the Hollywood Hills. His new neighbours were film stars and members of Guns N' Roses. There might only be a few miles' difference, but this was a long way from their days shoplifting and mainlining coke in the Formosa Pad.

"I was reminding myself, 'OK, things may feel fucked up right now, but I don't ever want to feel like I did two years ago.'"

Kiedis found a pen and some paper and started jotting down the lyrics that were swimming around his head. At this nascent stage it was purely words, the music could come later – if he ever decided to show this to his bandmates, that is. "It wasn't like I was writing in any sort of pop-song format," he said. "I just started writing about the bridge – and the things that occurred under the bridge."

The bridge in question was in downtown LA. It was on street-gang turf, drug land, where Kiedis would go to score from what he referred to as "miniature Mafioso drug rings". It was a no-go zone for strung-out civilians such as Kiedis, so he needed to create a story to gain access to the off-limits spot where he could score.

Kiedis filled in the blanks when he spoke candidly during the *Funky Monks* video. "All I had was this connection of mine called Mario, who was this Mexican Mafia ex-convict," he said. "He and I would stroll the streets downtown looking for our next score. On one hot afternoon in the middle of summer we found what we were looking for and we went to this bridge downtown in this ghetto – it was this freeway bridge. Only certain members of this Mexican gang could go in there.

"The reason they let me in was because this guy Mario said that I was going out with his sister, which was a lie. That always sticks in my brain as the lowpoint in my life – about as low as I could get."

"I was a hardcore junkie for many years," he admitted, "and during that point my life was a very sad time and everything that was beautiful and sacred and precious to me took a back seat as my need for this chemical just got more disgusting and insane. Fortunately my life took some massive changes."

Kiedis would then tell *Rolling Stone* that this was one of hundreds of predicaments that he found himself in during his addiction. "That's just one day that sticks very vividly in my memory. Like, how could I let myself get to that point?"

When Kiedis finally finished the lyric and premiered the song to the band, they still couldn't see the commercial potential in a heavy-hearted song about scoring smack.

"It doesn't really have a hook," Chad Smith stated. "And not to take away from Anthony, but he's not the greatest singer in the world. [His voice is] just cool and soulful. It's not like the guy who wins all the awards, Michael Bolton."

As the band began recording the track, Rubin had a brainwave. What the song needed was a choir, a natural progression from the wall of voices that Beinhorn had used so effectively on such tracks as 'Higher Ground' and 'Knock Me Down'. Frusciante mentioned that his mother, Gail, sang in her church choir. Flea was particularly keen on the idea of using her to sing on the track. She would go on to add the key harmony vocal to the song, which was then multi-tracked by Rubin.

'Knock Me Down' might have been a change in mood for these shirtless punks from Cali, but 'Under The Bridge' would be their first legitimate, lighters-in-the-air ballad. And the band recognised the potential commercial power of a hit ballad. One hit track, regardless of whether it was representative of an entire album, could entice specula-tive record-shoppers, not just Chili Peppers diehards.

"Take a group of Kansas housewives," Kiedis said with a smirk, "who turn on the radio and say, 'Oh, I like that sweet, sentimental song. Honey, would you go out and get me this record?'

"They get the record and there's 'Sir Psycho Sexy' and 'The Power

Of Equality'. They are going to have their little world turned upside down.

"I have this wonderful image of this lady washing the dishes in her little home in Kansas, with her little tape deck," he added, "popping this in and taking off her clothing, running into the back yard and getting loosened up a bit."

Alongside the atypically downbeat 'Under The Bridge', there were tracks cut during the sessions where Kiedis got the chance to flex his favourite muscle. 'Sir Psycho Sexy' pulls few punches about the singer's one-eyed trouser snake while 'Suck My Kiss' says it all in the title. As for the album's first single, 'Give It Away' – featuring some propulsive basswork from Flea, teamed with a tongue-twister of a rap from Kiedis – it positively dripped sexual innuendo. It's hard to misinterpret Kiedis' intent when he bellows a concluding line about the moment of penetration.

The idea for 'Give It Away' had come to the band during a summer day in the rehearsal studio, when Flea conjured up an impossibly fat bassline. Somehow this led Kiedis to start thinking about German punk performance artist Nina Hagen, who was his girlfriend, briefly, when he was 20. "I had been thinking about this concept Nina planted in my mind," said Kiedis. "She believed that the more she gave, the more she received. When I got sober, I realised that sobriety revolved around giving something away in order to maintain it. So this idea of 'give it away' was tornado-ing in my head for a while. When Flea started hitting that bassline, that tornado just came out of my mouth."

(But interpretation is everything, as Kiedis would later discover. While 'Give It Away' was receiving saturation airplay, he was shopping in New York, when a new Peppers convert – a young girl – spotted him. "Her mom came running over," he told *Rolling Stone*, "and said, 'Oh, I've got to thank you, you've made my life so much easier.'" As a surprised Kiedis would learn, it turns out that the only way she could dress her child in the morning was to sing: "Gimme an arm, gimme an arm, gimme an arm now," to the addictive melody of 'Give It Away'. "This happens a lot," the singer shrugged, "with kids literally from the age of one." Talk about crossover appeal.)

As the sessions continued into July, the Peppers and Rubin started to stretch out, wheeling in the mellotron to add a haunting melody to the gently eerie 'Breaking The Girl' and flesh out the raucous epic 'Sir Psycho Sexy'. Band buddy and Thelonious Monster drummer Pete Weiss contributed some Jew's harp, another Peppers' first, to 'Give It Away'. And Kiedis had now developed the confidence to experiment vocally, lowering his tone to an almost Tom Waits-like rumble on the album's title track and daring to stand alone during 'My Lovely Man' and 'Under The Bridge', the two strongest meditations on the loss of their fallen comrade, Hillel Slovak. Elsewhere, 'The Greeting Song' packed a Led Zeppelin-like crunch.

Also for the first time in the band's recording career, there was simply too much material recorded to squeeze onto one album, despite the generosity afforded by the relatively new revolution of CD technology. Rick Rubin had actually planned *BloodSugar* as a double CD. "It would have been much more digestible in that format," he figured.

But Warners were adamant that it should be a single disc. The way they read the situation, at this stage in the band's evolution from the cocks in socks dudes to fully fledged stars, their fans weren't quite ready to dig deep enough for a double CD set. Several songs were left on the Laurel Canyon mansion floor, including the instrumental 'Fela's Cock' and 'Sikamikanico', as well as 'Soul To Squeeze', which would appear on the soundtrack to the 1993 film *Coneheads* (and become yet another Peppers chart hit). Warners' thinking was sound. Rather than fleece a few extra dollars for a double album, they were giving fans serious bang for their buck. The album clocked in at three seconds under the maximum 74 minutes and came complete with a dedication to former Minuteman and fIREHOSE bassist, Mike Watt, plus handwritten lyrics from Kiedis and some lascivious cover artwork from their Amsterdam inkman, Henk Schiffmacher.

Rubin was still disappointed by the deletion of those few songs. To his mind, a single CD running this length was "harder to digest . . . being 18 songs in a row [17, but who's counting?]. I thought that volume of material would have been OK, as long as you stop and take a breath and then change CDs. Or maybe live with one CD for a few weeks, and then move onto the next CD. It would have been more digestible."

Regardless of their producer's concerns, *BloodSugarSexMagik* was a career-making album, a great leap forward from *Mother's Milk*. It was a record that was clearly destined to turn this band into a brand. Anthony

Kiedis would also admit that the record's success had an enormous impact on him as a human being, turning him into "an asshole and paranoid reclusive". As for Flea, the record's breakthrough would lead to a complete breakdown, likewise John Frusciante. Chad Smith, meanwhile, sat back and enjoyed the good life, as he admitted a few years later. "We're rich, pompous rock stars who stay in fancy hotels and smoke cigars and drink wine. You sell more records and that's changed things, obviously."

After eight weeks of recording, as the band began bumping their gear out of the mansion, they finally had the chance to reflect on their efforts. The quartet knew that this was the most diverse set of songs that they'd ever recorded – this record had something for everyone. Even though they hadn't toned down their raw, horny sexuality, you could actually call 'Under The Bridge' and 'My Lovely Man' soulful – sensitive even. That was a Chili Pepper first. While 'Under The Bridge' had a melody seductive enough to win over pop fans, there were other cuts, such as the title track, 'Give It Away' and 'The Power Of Equality', that could maintain their alternative fanbase and score heavy college radio airplay. Frusciante and Smith had proved to be a comfortable fit for the band; Frusciante, in particular, thanks to his sponge-like musical brain, had pulled the Peppers in some startlingly new and original directions.

But before they could post-mortem their new record, Rubin reminded them that the album lacked one Chili Pepper essential: a cover. Jimi Hendrix's 'Fire' had been given a Peppers makeover on *Mother's Milk*; Sly & The Family Stone and The Meters received similar treatment during *Freaky Styley*, likewise Bob Dylan on *Uplift Mofo*. For *BloodSugarSexMagik* the Peppers chose 'They're Red Hot', from legendary bluesman Robert Johnson.

Tired of flailing away indoors, the band found a cosy spot on a hill behind the mansion and quickly set up. When Rubin hit the record button, they grinned their way through a good-hearted take on the song, with the brawny Chad Smith dwarfing a scaled-down drum kit. Headphone examination reveals 2 am Laurel Canyon traffic noise lingering in the background of the track.

The spooky, mythical past of bluesmaster Johnson had intersected with the Peppers' thoroughly modern take on rock'n'roll, while LA thundered past them. The album was now officially completed.

Early in the process, John Frusciante had boasted that they were making "an amazing ground-breaking revolutionary beautifully artistically heightened incredible record". Two months later, with his erection finally subsiding, he felt pretty much the same. "I've never been so proud of anything I've ever done because I've always felt like I was a failure," he said. "Now we've done something as a band of friends that I'm a 100 per cent proud of."

To his admittedly skewed perspective, Frusciante compared his time in Laurel Canyon to a sexual partner. "Fucking somebody may be the most beautiful experience in the world but you can only fuck her for so long. It's not like I'm going to miss anything," he said, as he packed away his few possessions.

But there was still a touch of the FNG (Fresh New Guy) about John Frusciante. "When we were making *BloodSugar*, the thought never even crossed my mind that this was something that people were going to buy all around the world.

"I said to Flea, 'People are going to buy this and take it home and listen to our music that we recorded over at the house?' And he goes, 'Yeah.' And I go, 'All over the country?' And he goes, 'All over the world.'"

The machinations of the music industry stunned Frusciante. "I was just closing my eyes and swirling around, like 10 thoughts at once, and going places with no conscious thoughts at all."

Once they'd collected the last of their gear, all the Peppers had left to do was name this set of songs. *BloodSugarSexMagik* was perfect. As one writer would observe, it captured their "hazy philosophy in which lusty hedonism and New Age spirituality are conflated". Kiedis managed to say roughly the same in far more words. "The album title is an eloquent but abstract description of how we feel. We live in a world packed with desensitising forces," he continued, "that strip the world of magic. And music can help restore a sense of magic."

The response to *Mother's Milk* had been upbeat, but the early reviews for *BloodSugarSexMagik* were absolutely euphoric when the album was released in late September 1991. *Billboard* was the first major publication to detect the shift in the band, who were now as adept at handling stadium-filling ballads as they were rocking with their cocks out. "LA homeboys jam it down solid on label debut. Audition with care and then roll with it," the hugely influential trade mag declared. "This should be the Peppers' platinum breakthrough."

In their four-star review, *Rolling Stone* gave producer Rubin due credit for the album's added shine. "Insisting on airborne melodies, filtering the rhythmic rumble down to a brutal essence, the acclaimed Beastie Boys producer changed the Chilis' dynamic," wrote long-time Pepper advocate Tom Moon. He also spotted that it was the more downbeat material, the lashing, triple-metre 'Breaking The Girl' and Kiedis' drug-confessional 'Under The Bridge', "that reveal new dimensions".

Rubin was also on the receiving end of some heavy praise. The *Los Angeles Daily News* crowned him "pop music's greatest living rock'n' roll producer". "He makes the enigmatic Red Hot Chili Peppers sound accessible while leaving their mystique intact."

USA Today observed how Rubin guided the band through the album "with a minimum of technology and an abundance of energy." *The Globe And Mail* continued the trend. "Credit goes mainly to producer Rick Rubin, who must have diverted Santa Monica Boulevard right through the recording studio, because this furious combination of funk, rock, pop and rap is virtually the perfect mix of streetwise savvy and studio gloss."

Not surprisingly, *Guitar Player* magazine singled out Frusciante for lofty praise. James Rotondi wrote that Frusciante had stumbled on a thrilling alchemy. "Blending acid-rock, soul-funk, early art-rock, and blues style with a raw, unprocessed Strat-and-Marshall tone, he hit on an explosive formula that has yet to be duplicated."

Mainstream media also noticed how this once marginalised act were now team leaders. Writing in *The St Petersburg Times*, Eric Snider stated how "as the funk-punk-metal-rap sub-genre continues to proliferate, it's increasingly obvious that the Red Hot Chili Peppers are the best of the bunch. Earlier albums were fuelled by raw funk'n'roll," he added, "and the nearly unintelligible raps of frontman Anthony Kiedis. The band now incorporates the occasional melodic hook, some serviceable singing and a variety of different feels – even stuff that leans to the mellow side." *The Milwaukee Journal* said it straight: "*BloodSugarSexMagik* puts the Peps back on top of the hill they built."

There were more measured reviews, such as that of the *Chicago Sun-Times*, whose Michael Corcoran felt that the band was "all meat and hair". "This LP throws more musical twists and tempo changes into the Peppers' bag," he wrote. "Sometimes it's great and sometimes it's not, which is the most you can hope for from the Chili Peppers." Corcoran also noted the album's excessive length, which he didn't think was necessarily a great thing. "74 minutes with the Chili Peppers? That's like having Thanksgiving dinner with GWAR: this is wonderful, but will we ever get out of here alive?" The *Richmond Times-Dispatch* didn't actually feel that too much had changed in Pepperland. "The Chili Peppers stick with the subject they know best: sex. [And] Kiedis gives Axl Rose a run for the money in the foul language category, which won't endear him with right-wingers or feminists, but that shouldn't hurt sales a bit."

The album would go on to feature in *Rolling Stone*'s year-end wrap-up, "The Year In Records", alongside such pivotal long-players as Pearl Jam's *Ten* and Soundgarden's *Badmotorfinger*. It also made *Spin*'s 90 Greatest Albums Of The '90s list, where Marc Spitz shrewdly noted that the band had finally got the underground and mainstream blend just right. "Punk-funk and radio-ready pop songcraft need not be mutually exclusive," he wrote.

The band, especially straightshooter Chad Smith, were equally thrilled and amused by the reviews of *BloodSugar*. Smith chuckled at the suggestion that the band had turned mellow, sarcastically replying that when the Peppers tour the record that "maybe we'll just sit there, play some Grateful Dead covers and hopefully everyone will enjoy it."

By late 1991, mainstream radio was very ready for the Chili Peppers. *BloodSugar*'s first single, 'Give It Away' was a tasty entrée, quickly reaching the pole position on *Billboard*'s Modern Rock Tracks. Its eye-popping video, shot by Frenchman Stephane Sednaoui, featured the band in the middle of nowhere, coated from head to toe in what seemed like glow-in-the-dark paint. Its funky brew of goofy looks, a subtly invasive hook, Flea's spindly fingered bassline and Kiedis' crotch-hugging shorts made the clip essential viewing across MTV throughout the last few months of 1991. It would eventually receive several MTV video award nominations.

The majestic 'Under The Bridge', however, was the bona fide, across-all-formats radio hit that the band had been working towards for seven years. Early in the new year, the single peaked at number two in the *Billboard* Hot 100 chart, only held back by Eric Clapton's blubbery

'Tears In Heaven'. *BloodSugar*, meanwhile, busted through the platinum barrier – a first for the band – and took up a long-term residency in the Hot 100, where it peaked at number three, having debuted at number 14.

Kiedis was playing basketball at home when Chad Smith rolled up and broke the news about the album's chart placing. Kiedis smiled a winner's grin and then "proceeded to win all my basketball games".

Writing in *Rolling Stone* after the song became a massive hit, David Fricke freely stated that 'Under The Bridge' was an impressive fluke. "Gently anchored by a lilting, skeletal guitar riff that faintly echoes Jimi Hendrix's 'Little Wing', the song is light on radio-friendly pomp and direct in its confessional detail."

Its success proved that the long-hinted-at overhaul of the mainstream had finally kicked in. As the band well knew, timing is everything in the record-buying world. Whereas their previous four albums had seemed like forlorn cries from the rock'n'roll underground, *BloodSugarSexMagik* was actually part of the mainstream.* But the left-field rumblings that had been set in place by such erstwhile college radio darlings as R.E.M. were now in their fully blown, big-shorted glory. While the usual fluff from Mariah Carey, Michael Jackson and the reborn Genesis could still be found in the charts, *BloodSugarSexMagik* was also sharing record store racks with such crucial "grunge" albums as Nirvana's *Nevermind*, Pearl Jam's *Ten* and Soundgarden's *Badmotorfinger*. This trio of lank-haired, Black Sabbath-fancying monster riffers had transformed the logging centre of Washington State into the new rock'n'roll heartland, with Seattle as its very own Los Angeles. What constituted "rock" in the Eighties – typified by the airbrushed, large-haired, skirt-chasing antics of bands such as Mötley Crüe and Bon Jovi – had been rendered obsolete by a harder, heavier, darker sound. Whereas the Crüe celebrated the simple joys of 'Girls Girls Girls' and Warrant yelled for 'Cherry Pie', Eddie Vedder of Pearl Jam sang solemnly of his turgid family secrets, while Kurt Cobain adopted a kidnapper's point of view in the perverse 'Polly' and sneered at the "music

---

* Of course the band still had its naysayers, 'American Pie' creator Don McLean among them. "If the Red Hot Chili Peppers have a hit record," he stated, "what does that say about people and their taste? This is a trashy group, they do trashy things, they don't make decent music."

biz" during 'Smells Like Teen Spirit'. Heroin not only fuelled some members of Alice In Chains, but references to the drug littered the soundscape of their gloomy hard rock anthems.

With the recently concluded Gulf War still fresh in memories, where the US military destruction of Iraq was beamed non-stop into millions of households, and with ex-CIA chief George Bush in the White House, young America felt alienated and lost. The "greed is good" attitude of the Eighties had been kissed well and truly goodbye. Grunge provided the perfect soundtrack to their lives.

The Chili Peppers might have emerged from a very different musical bloodline, where LA punk, dirty funk and New York hip-hop collided, and good times ruled, but these bands were now all part of the "alternative" community – and they were now gate-crashing the mainstream. Major labels quickly steered their A&R staff in the direction of Seattle, where six- or even seven-digit record deals became more common than smack and espresso. Generation Lollapalooza was born and Perry Farrell, the astute frontman of Jane's Addiction, was a man with a plan: a travelling festival that would not only celebrate the music of this new generation, but embrace its out-there ideologies. But Lollapalooza was in the Peppers' future; right now they had their own tour to headline.

By October 16, 1991, their album tour was set to roll. With the Chili Peppers in the headlining slot, their opening act for the early part of the tour was Chicago's Smashing Pumpkins, led by the almost unbearably intense Billy Corgan. They would soon be joined by Pearl Jam, whose debut album *Ten* – with its radio staples 'Jeremy' and 'Alive' – was inching its way up the *Billboard* chart. Flannel-clad grungesters Nirvana, whose second album, *Nevermind*, was already in the top position on *Billboard*'s Heatseekers chart, having dethroned Michael Jackson and his *Dangerous* album, would hook up when the tour reached the west coast in December. It was the hottest rock ticket of the northern winter, the indoor, scaled-down alternative to Perry Farrell's Lollapalooza. Ticket prices were kept within an affordable range of $16 to $20 – although by tour's end they would be scalped for up to $35 – and the venues were a mixture of halls, university auditoriums and beer barns, with crowds ranging from 2,500 to almost 10,000.

With *BloodSugarSexMagik* hogging the number one spot on *Billboard*'s

College/Alternative Albums list, the tour warmed up in front of 2,500 punters at Milwaukee's Central Park Ballroom. According to *The Milwaukee Journal*, the crowd put on almost as good a show as the Chili Peppers.

"From the first thump of music," wrote Thor Christensen, "the audience was a swirling mass of airborne cups, ice cubes, shoes, shirts, pogo dancers, body-passers and stage divers." And it wasn't purely a boy's club in the moshpit – many female punters bought into the mayhem, stripping down to their bras and flinging themselves about madly as the band tore through 'Higher Ground', 'Suck My Kiss' and 'Give It Away', which was Goth-ed up by Frusciante when he added a riff from Black Sabbath's 'Sweet Leaf'.

Kiedis was 'Sir Psycho Sexy' personified. Bare-chested as always, he was wearing metallic silver shorts with a hefty handprint on the crotch, a black Chili Peppers cap and elbow-length gloves. And he did his best to let the good times fucking well rock'n'roll, pulling off impressive handstands and throwing himself around the Ballroom's stage like some punk gymnast. In fact, he looked more like a crazed aerobics instructor than a recovering junkie.

Christensen astutely noted the band's shift in musical mood, writing how their "updated approach wasn't as provocative as the Peppers' original concept. But as far as free-for-alls go, the show was hard to beat."

The *Milwaukee Sentinel* noted the key difference between the Peppers of *BloodSugar* and the band that had rocked the city several times before. "Nobody expects maturity from a young funk band. Strangely enough, you get it anyway with this group."

With Pearl Jam now on board, the tour moved through Pittsburgh and then on to Cleveland, where their show at the Music Hall was a sell-out. Even though ushers did their best to restrain frenzied fans at this rather elegant venue, it was a losing battle. But the band weren't at their best; Flea was wrestling with a new bass, on loan to him from Kevin Scheuring of local band Sosumi. The bassist had smashed his during the previous show in Pittsburgh. Kiedis, meanwhile, wasn't pleased with the venue, preferring halls that supported a no-seats policy.

"To be honest," he gasped backstage, "our Pittsburgh concert on Friday was better. That's because there were no seats in the venue. People could dance all they wanted to."

Jane Scott, the reporter from Cleveland's *Plain Dealer*, didn't share the singer's pain. "The show was terrific," she wrote. "Completely engulfing."

As the tour headed north for a Toronto show on October 29, the Peppers' on-stage bravado was clearly growing. But to the dismay of the *Toronto Star* reporter, the band had, at least temporarily, left their athletic socks back on the bus. The band truly believed that, given the strength of their new songs, it wasn't necessary to pull off their standard X-rated encore. Instead, Flea dyed his Mohawk to a greyish hue and got down to hard-funkin' business, pulling off an especially turbo-charged take on 'Higher Ground'. Pearl Jam's Eddie Vedder, mean-while, was starting to make an impression of his own, with his permanently furrowed brow and the band's brooding set of grunge rock. He even inspired one journalist to state that "Vedder should audi-tion as stunt double for Killer Bob in the movie version of *Twin Peaks*." However the Smashing Pumpkins, whose set was mainly made up of tracks from their debut album, *Gish*, weren't exactly slaying them in the aisles. The same reporter, Peter Howell, was unimpressed. "The Smashing Pumpkins couldn't catch the wave early on. [They] left the stage in an oath-cursing snit after the crowd failed to fall down dead for its sound, a sort of lo-cal Jane's Addiction."

The tour was big business, although the Peppers would experience one of the few let-downs of their exceptionally hot stretch when they were bumped from the hugely influential *Letterman* show. Though the late-night programme was hardly at the cutting edge of humour, any act that was granted the nightly live spot could be guaranteed hefty sales and across-the-board exposure.

Regardless, *BloodSugar* continued to sell, and Warners geared up for the early 1992 launch of 'Under The Bridge', a track that they knew had massive hit potential and the ability to push *BloodSugar* sales well over the million mark.

Another wild show followed, this time at Boston University's 4,200-capacity Walter Brown Arena on November 1. The sheer physi-cality of the shows was now perfectly clear: a six-foot pit, policed by security, separated band from sweaty, adoring public. That didn't deter the volley of crowd surfers, many of whom ended up crash-landing in the pit and being thrown back into the fray by security. At the Boston show, Kiedis' 29th birthday was marked by Flea's on-stage rendition of 'Happy Birthday'. The singer then baited the Boston crowd about the recent misfortunes of their basketball team, the Celtics, before driving home his point with a red-hot version of 'Suck My Kiss'. But Kiedis' birthday bash wasn't quite over yet: as the Peppers bounced back on stage for what was fast becoming their regular encore, a rip'n'tear take on the Stooges' 'Search And Destroy', several male dancers in drag joined them, dancing around Kiedis like he was some kind of totem pole, and happily groping Sir Psycho Sexy. "This was funk-rock at the boiling point," wrote *The Boston Globe*'s Jim Sullivan, "heavily spiced and not played for the timid."

The tour inched closer to Kiedis' heartland, swinging through Michigan State University at East Lansing, where Kiedis' mother, Peggy Idema, looked on. Idema spoke quietly with her son after the Michigan U show, before telling a reporter how she thought the band had changed. "I think they've all matured greatly," she said. "And a lot has to do with Hillel's death.

"For years," the usually publicity-shy Idema added, "I never wanted him to come back here because of all the hassles and controversy it would cause. Now I think they've grown up so much, and I don't think they're any worse than some of the other groups I've seen."

But there were some hassles at that show, especially now that the stage-diving craze had reached a frenzied, highly competitive peak. As the band poured itself into the soulful 'I Could Have Lied' – an incongruous choice for crowd athletics – another in the seemingly endless procession of shirtless, big-shorted loons leapt on stage. A bouncer swiftly moved in, grabbing him by the throat. Kiedis and Flea moved in to defuse the potentially ugly situation.

"No choke holds," Flea shouted to security.

"Yeah, we use a special control hold," chimed in Kiedis. "It's called a hug."

Earlier in the night, Eddie Vedder proved himself to be a man of the people, climbing the PA and then clambering upstairs in the theatre, as the band jammed on. "The audience went crazy," reported the ever-faithful *Grand Rapids Press*.

By November 26 they were tearing paint off the walls of Illinois State University's Braden Auditorium. But the Peppers were still without a Grand Rapids date: the memories of Flea's cock-out display at their 1984 show at the Top Of The Rock still flashed a warning sign in the minds of local promoters.

Kiedis' father, Blackie Dammett, tried to explain Flea's lewd move in an interview at the time with *Grand Rapids Press*. "In the beginning," he figured, "things were so competitive that you had to do something spectacular to get your foot in the door."*

Having now relocated to Grand Rapids from Hollywood, Dammett even tried to set up a hometown show himself. But he couldn't find a venue, and Lindy Goetz was concerned that despite his best intentions for this homecoming of sorts, Dammett had no experience promoting a rock show.

A disappointed Kiedis spoke with *Grand Rapids Press*, as the tour marched on elsewhere. "He wants to show Grand Rapids a good time," Kiedis said of his debonair father, "and bring something culturally exciting to a town hungry for something like that. [And] we've matured since then," he added.

Grand Rapids Press, however, had plans of their own, encouraging readers to speak up as to whether these almost hometown heroes – well, both Kiedis and Smith were midwesterners – should perform there. The majority of responses were positive; even local radio "personality" Robert Chase, of WLAV, said loudly and proudly that "I want to get a petition or something started . . . and give Anthony the credit he deserves." The owner of local 200-seat venue, the Reptile House, offered to book the Peppers for a week of shows. Several callers suggested the city council build a venue large enough to house one of 1991's breakout bands. But the memories of 1984 hadn't totally been erased, as one call to the newspaper proved. "Keep a band like the Red Hot Chili Peppers as far away from Grand Rapids as possible," the caller yelled, before hanging up.

By mid-November the band were in New York, for a pair of sold-out shows at the Roseland Ballroom. This was followed by full houses at Chicago, Houston and then Denver, and another trip north to Canada, where they appeared on MuchMusic, Canada's answer to MTV, where fans were squeezed like sardines against the station's glass booth, which was located on Toronto's Queen Street, to get as close to the Peppers as they could. The band's influence on their north-of-the-border fans was clear, too, because one Chili Pepper diehard waved

---

* Whether or not the sight of Flea's dick was "spectacular" escaped further exploration.

"a pink rubber dildo the size of a Thermos". The band looked on, bemused.

In spite of the frantic crisscrossing of North America and the dozens of shows and promo work for radio, TV and print, the Peppers refused to tire. At one show, Flea invited the entire crowd on stage, which resulted in an orgy of goodwill that held up their set for at least 10 minutes. In Chicago, the band brought their crew of roadies on stage to help them with the shoutalong chorus of 'Higher Ground'. Now dwarfed by a glowing, 50-foot high, blazing red logo on stage, the Peppers were virtually bulletproof.

"The Peppers were crash-free pilots touring behind the strongest songs that they have written in their careers," gushed an excitable reporter from the *Austin American-Statesman*. "Flea laid down groove after groove, playing lead chops on his bass, not just relegating it to background rhythm fodder." Flea sometimes even took the mic for his own twist on Thelonious Monster's already twisted 'Sammy Hagar Weekend'.

On December 14, 6,000 punters filled Denver Coliseum, a venue typically used for stock shows and professional wrestling. "The stomping grooves turned the Coliseum into a sweatbox," *The Denver Post* reported the next day. Stage diving and crowd surfing reached a furious peak at the show. "With arms raised as though they were on a ride at Disneyland, they [crowd surfers] were passed overhead until a gap in the audience dropped them to the concrete floor," said the *Post*. Three fans at a Seattle show were injured in stage-diving accidents.

The Peppers rounded off the biggest year of their rock'n'roll lives with a two-night stand at the LA Sports Arena and a New Year's Eve bash at San Francisco's Cow Palace. With Fishbone and the increasingly hot Nirvana now on the bill, these shows sold out in just a few hours.

A wildly received 95-minute set at LA Sports Arena was just a warm-up for their huge Cow Palace 1991 finale. While tie-dyed, terminally wasted Deadheads drifted along San Fran's Haight Street, in preparation for the Grateful Dead's traditional Oakland Coliseum space jam, they were almost outnumbered by skate punks in combat boots and flannel. A generational change was clearly happening – the Deadheads' domain was being taken over by their Gen X offspring. Inside the house-full Cow Palace, Eddie Vedder greeted the 16,000-strong crowd by asking: "Want to hear some songs by the Dead?" As one, the crowd booed, so instead he sang an a cappella version of Fugazi's 'Suggestion'.

The Chili Peppers, however, had to sweat just that little bit harder for this year-ending show. Nirvana, who followed Pearl Jam on stage, had commandeered the *Billboard* number one spot the week before with the epochal *Nevermind*; its sales were outstripping *BloodSugar* by four to one. Though only on stage for 45 minutes, with no encore, Nirvana's set was incendiary, one reporter watching on in amazement as "members of the moshpit, which stretched from the stage to the back of the arena, were being thrown in the air like clods of dirt caught up in a live minefield."

When the house lights went down just before midnight, 16,000 pairs of eyes turned upwards as Flea was lowered to the stage by ropes tied to his ankles. It was quite an entrance. Even though the Peppers took some time to find their trademark groove, they still managed to upstage the young, wild Seattle punks with old-school showmanship. They knew they couldn't match them for sheer noise thrills, because Nirvana's sonic assault could have stopped a tank. So the Peppers didn't hold back, bringing on a pair of fire eaters and several dancers wearing only Day-Glo paint, as 1991 ticked over into 1992. When Eddie Vedder joined the stage-diving masses during the encore of 'Yertle The Turtle', alt-rock's golden year was officially over.

Yet backstage during the tour, which recommenced in the new year with a run of shows through the Pacific North West, it was clear that John Frusciante was a changed man. The music geek and bedroom virtuoso, whose first band was his favourite band of all time, was being observed with some concern by his older, more battle-scarred band-mates. "They didn't want him turning into another Hillel," I was told by someone who worked on the tour, who prefers not to be named. Frusciante and his girlfriend at the time, nicknamed "Yoko" by the band and crew, kept their distance. On the tour bus, they'd be holed up in the back, while the party would be happening elsewhere. For most shows Frusciante wouldn't be seen until the band were due on stage.

"She was controlling him," Lindy Goetz said. "He was drinking a lot, guzzling really good wine from the bottle, he was using drugs – and he was not getting along with anyone in the band."

Frusciante, a self-confessed "pothead", had begun to use heroin. It was a very clear snub at Kiedis' abstinence, which was now at three years and counting. Though they didn't realise it at the time, the Chili Peppers were in the process of losing another guitarist, just as the band's star was reaching its apogee.

Frusciante would eventually admit that he wanted to leave the band after the recording of *BloodSugarSexMagik*. It was only the bond of playing alongside his friend Flea that kept him touring throughout 1991 and the early months of 1992. "I spent a long time in the Peppers not liking anything about it except for playing with Flea," he admitted. "Staring in his eyes and staring at my amp – those were the only good times."

Frusciante had begun to hate the band's fans openly. He despised the way "they like singing along with the slow songs, because it's the only fucking thing they can be part of. They're all stuck in seats, watching these guys jump around like wild maniacs." He hadn't joined the band to become a rock star – he simply loved their music and their energy.

A clearly confused Frusciante stated that he didn't have a problem with being a rock star, "because of people like Bowie or Hendrix".

"But I do have a problem with the shitty sort of rock star, like people treating Bowie like he's [Mötley Crüe's] Nikki Sixx or people expecting of Bowie what you do of Nikki Sixx. That's the aspect of rock stars that I think is bad. I was like, 'I'm not a rock star! I'm nothing! I hate the whole audience!'"

Frusciante's problems ran deeper than his perception of the band's audience and their needs. He and Anthony Kiedis – whom he idolised when he first became a Pepper – had drifted to the point where an icy silence separated them. As Frusciante would confess, it was becoming impossible for the two of them to coexist in the band. It was virtually a repeat of Kiedis' treatment of one of Frusciante's predecessors, Jack Sherman. "We couldn't look at each other on stage or talk to each other without being angry. He was a real jerk for periods, so arrogant," said Frusciante. "We had gotten to a point where any sort of communication between us that was positive would have been forced, because there had been so many bad vibes accumulated over the course of the tour."

It took several years before the guitarist realised that he too was at fault. "I was a jerk the first couple of years I was in the band," he would state in 1999. "I tried to be Mr Hotshot guy, get laid as much as possible, get drunk, wear flashy clothes."

But Frusciante wasn't the only Chili Pepper having a tough time dealing with their endless touring and the band's new status as superstars. Flea, normally the Peppers' driving force and the one man with the willpower to keep this wayward group together and focused, was also slowly unravelling.

"That was a really crappy tour," he'd reflect in 1996. "I wanted to go home. I like playing live, but I wasn't happy then. I had just gotten divorced and I missed my daughter and we weren't getting along well in the band. The whole emotional state of the band at the time just wasn't happy."

But still they kept playing, wrapping up four solid months of North American dates with a show at Vancouver's PNE Forum on February 3. Now they would turn their gaze overseas; throughout April and May the Peppers had tours scheduled for Europe and the Far East, with Australia locked in for May. With this relentless workload, it was no wonder that John Frusciante had started to utter strange observations to journalists. He was coming apart in public. "It's a wordless state I'm in, as if outer space were walking through a room outlined like a person," he told one reporter. When your life becomes a blur of hotel rooms, sound-bite interviews, grungy backstages, drugs, booze, "Yoko" and screaming fans, not much really makes sense any more.

With 'Under The Bridge' now a massive hit, the band were in huge demand. Penelope Spheeris, who had directed Flea in the "punk" film *Suburbia*, asked them to contribute a track to the soundtrack of her film *Wayne's World*. They also appeared on the huge-rating *Saturday Night Live* programme, performing 'Under The Bridge'. During the show's final curtain call, Kiedis stood arm-in-arm with Madonna – Queen Of Pop meets the new Lord Of Rock.*

As the band toured the UK and Europe, the saturation airplay that radio and MTV had given 'Under The Bridge' ensured that their North American sales momentum didn't abate, even if Nirvana continued to outsell them. The only flat spot was their refusal to mime their hit on the BBC's *Top Of The Pops*, which resulted in the band being dropped from

---

* In 1993, the couple warbled 'The Lady Is A Tramp' on talk-show host Arsenio Hall's 100th programme, fuelling rumours that they were a couple. Blackie Dammett did little to play that down, telling one journalist that "they've known each other since the mid-Eighties."

the venerable pop institution, just like their erstwhile heroes The Gang Of Four. But after the disaster of their Florida *Spring Break* appearance, when they were forced to mime and ended up in court on assault charges, the band's reluctance to lip-sync was understandable. As they flew into LA to headline Magic Johnson's ACT UP AIDS benefit night – which raised $150,000 – Lindy Goetz had some big news for the band: *BloodSugarSexMagik* had just sold a million copies. It was the band's first platinum album. Warners were now scheduling 'Breaking The Girl' as the album's third single. To their new label, one million sales was only the starting point – this album had legs.

Flea hadn't been to Australia since 1967, when he, his mother and sister Karen left Melbourne for New York and a new life. Understandably, the bassman was excited about touring there for the first time. Much of the Balzary clan still lived in Melbourne, and the sunnier, mellower Australian lifestyle might help calm the tension within the band.

The anticipation for the Peppers' first Oz tour was huge. While their first three albums had been available only as imports, and mentioned mainly by music critics and collectors, *Mother's Milk* had been a minor hit; as had 'Higher Ground'. But most significantly, *BloodSugar-SexMagik* had transformed their cult following into serious chart action. By the first week of November 1991, the album was number one in Australia. Four months later, 'Under The Bridge' did likewise in the singles chart. As 'Suck My Kiss' stormed into the Australian Top Five, the timing was absolutely ripe for their first Oz shows.

The Peppers had six Japanese dates lined up before they headed south; the fourth of these was in Tokyo on May 7. Kiedis was on the phone with a reporter from New Zealand, discussing their upcoming tour, when Flea walked into his room. Kiedis ended his conversation quickly; he could tell that something was seriously wrong. Flea looked as though he was in shock.

"Flea looked at me with this completely puzzled and surreal, sad face," Kiedis would tell *Rolling Stone*. "He said, 'John wants to quit the band and go home right now.' It stunned me and it shattered me because things had been going so well."

When a band meeting was hastily arranged, it was clear the spaced-out stringman wasn't blowing smoke. He wanted out of the band. Right now.

"I could tell by the look in his eyes that he was deadly serious," Kiedis continued. "He said, 'I can't stay in the band any more. I've reached a point where I can't do justice to what we've created, because of stress and fatigue. I can't give what it takes to be in this band any more.'"

Frusciante, of course, was downplaying his real concern with life as a Chili Pepper. The band had grown too large, too soon, for the 22-year-old guitarist. They were no longer the free spirits that used to rock Hollywood's Club Lingerie. They were big stars, public property, who, in exchange for crazy sums of money, were expected to smile in photo shoots, laugh during interviews and rock like madmen for massive crowds that were invisible to him beyond the first few rows. For a true rock'n'roll believer such as Frusciante, this just wasn't the reason why he joined the band. His hefty consumption of smack, booze and pot only added to his confusion.

Band manager Goetz was on his way to Japan when Frusciante started to melt down. As soon as he checked into his hotel, he received a call from tour manager Tony Salinger. "You gotta get down here," he yelled down the line, "John's freaking out."

Goetz ordered Frusciante to play the gig – "a terrible show" – but knew that it was over. "He snapped like a cookie," Goetz said, and "Greenie" was allowed to fly home.

In one of the many post-mortems that Frusciante would conduct after he left the band, he would admit that the Peppers had outgrown their original plan, to be "utter perpetrators of hardcore, bone-crunching, mayhem sex things from heaven".

"At the last Chili Peppers show with Hillel Slovak that I saw," he told *Guitar Player*'s James Rotondi, "my girlfriend at the time asked me, 'Would you still like the Chili Peppers if they were so popular they played the [20,000 seat Inglewood] Forum?' I said, 'No, but they would never play the Forum, because that would go against the whole reason that I come to every show and jump all over the place and feel like one with the band. I can't imagine that being gone.'"

But the Chili Peppers had made it to the Forum and beyond and Frusciante now dismissed their audience – of whom he used to be a key member – as "fucking idiots". There was no way he could stay in this band any longer.

Frusciante admitted that the relationship between him and Kiedis hadn't been strong for some time, despite Kiedis' previous assertion that "things had been going so well".

"I had this feeling that the road was really gonna fuck with me," Frusciante said in 1994. "The road had been fucking with Flea for so many years. I felt like a guy with 400 ghosts telling him what to do all the time. I just wanted to lay back on the couch and think about nothing. The unity hadn't been good with the band for ages. Anthony and I hadn't talked for a couple of tours and we didn't look at each other much onstage."

Flea was, as ever, the only person in the band to confront Frusciante and ask his friend whether he had a problem playing with the Peppers. This was a full year before Frusciante had his Tokyo meltdown. They went to a park, sat down, and Flea asked him straight-up: "Is there anything you like about being in the band?"

Frusciante replied in the negative. "No, I'm just in the band 'cause I love you. I love playing with you and I don't want to just leave you. But there's nothing I like about being in the band."

If the band's shock about Frusciante's split is an accurate gauge, Flea had either not related Frusciante's concerns to the others, or he'd simply forgotten the conversation.

It took Kiedis several years to fully come to grips with the problems that Frusciante was trying to deal with. "I was too self-centred and self-absorbed to even begin to experience what he was going through," Kiedis would finally admit in 1999. (Ex-Pepper Jack Sherman claims he was "mindfucked" by ego-monsters.) "All I knew was that John and I were becoming more and more distant. I didn't see our success as a sell-out. I saw it as something really powerful and beautiful that we had created together. Getting through to the masses was something we had been aiming for and now that it was here why not embrace it?"

"We'd paid a lot of dues," Goetz figured, "and we'd tasted a bit of fame. We were ready. For John, it happened too fast. He didn't play the 50-seat clubs, he didn't get to climb that ladder. When the guys were becoming pop stars, he wanted to become a punk rock star. He was turning away from Anthony, especially, because he was becoming famous."

As Frusciante returned to LA and proceeded to disappear into a deep, almost life-ending drug bender, the other three Peppers travelled to

Australia. They'd put in an SOS call to Thelonious Monster guitarist Zander Schloss, who would meet them in Sydney for emergency rehearsals. Warner Brothers and the Peppers' management, meanwhile, engaged damage control.

Frusciante helpfully suggested that the band's label issue a press release stating that he'd gone insane. Instead, publicist Bill Bentley admitted that Frusciante's problems may have stemmed from his inexperience in matters of touring and promotion. "John has had . . . I don't want to say problems . . . he's from a different mode," he announced. "This came out of the blue."

The Australian press quickly jumped all over the Frusciante story, as Flea, Kiedis and Smith tried to find some higher ground in a Sydney rehearsal studio with Schloss. "Mystery still surrounds the sudden departure of Red Hot Chili Peppers' guitarist John Frusciante," reported Melbourne's *Sun-Herald*, "who up and quit the band in Japan . . . forcing the postponement of the group's Australian shows. Rumours doing the rounds say the departure was less than amicable, with some suggesting Frusciante may have actually taken a beating from his volatile former bandmates."

As the Frontier Touring Company, the local promoter behind the band's Australian tour, fielded calls from guitar hopefuls angling for a shot at the vacant guitarist's spot, the band and Schloss came to the realisation that a few days' rushed rehearsals simply weren't enough to nail the Peppers' signature guitar sound. Musical relationships were built over years, not days, so this just wasn't going to work. With Kiedis announcing that "Australia deserves better than the ordinary," the tour was cancelled.

Looking back, Lindy Goetz remarked, "It's amazing what you try to do to keep the ship floating."

Once again the Chili Peppers were in disarray. The only immediate solution was time-out: Kiedis headed to Bangkok, Flea flew to Europe, while Smith returned to LA, where he married Maria, his "Greek goddess", on June 13. Even with a platinum album still riding high in the charts, the band were in as much turmoil as they were at the time of Slovak's death in 1988. Frusciante had seemed like such a natural fit for the Peppers and now he had told them that they simply weren't the same band that he fell in love with when he was a wild Hollywood teenager.

When the Chili Peppers became part of the rock'n'roll elite, appearing naked on the front cover of US *Rolling Stone* on June 25, 1992, there was one face (and torso) missing: John Frusciante. He'd been digitally removed from the shot. It was almost as if he'd never existed in the first place.

CHAPTER NINE

"We're just like Spinal Tap, although it isn't our drummers who keep exploding."

ORIGINALLY conceived in 1990 as a farewell tour for Perry Farrell's fast-living, highly strung band, Jane's Addiction, Lollapalooza – its name taken from a word Farrell heard in a Three Stooges film – was planned as the Nineties answer to Woodstock. It was to be a celebration of the alternative music that was steamrolling such mainstream staples as Michael Jackson and Mariah Carey. The plan of Farrell – along with fellow organisers Ted Gardiner and Marc Geiger – was to bring together both east coast and west coast musical styles and attitudes.

They welcomed various non-profit political and environmental organisations, as well as human freak show the Jim Rose Circus, and the Shaolin Monks. In an all-embracing gesture, Farrell had even invited the very right-leaning National Rifle Association and the US military. "It is important to have both sides [represented], otherwise you are preaching to an already converted crowd," he figured. (Both passed.) Lollapalooza's charter wasn't just a super-star rock jam, it was a cultural festival, albeit for the newly formed Nineties counterculture; the so-called Generation X. But unlike Woodstock, Lollapalooza was a travelling musical sideshow, stopping to party in much of the USA and parts of Canada. "To be compared to Woodstock is an incredibly nice thing to say," Farrell admitted, "but time marches on and things are a little different."

The 1991 Lollapalooza line-up featured Jane's Addiction, Siouxsie & The Banshees, Nine Inch Nails, Living Colour and Henry Rollins, although many thought that the stars of the show were politicised hip-hoppers Body Count. They were led by the fierce, confrontational Ice-T, the kind of frontman who could win over a crowd with one menacing stare.

Described as both "the underdog tour that could" and "like getting hit over the head with a sledgehammer, and loving it," Lollapalooza 1991 was a critical and commercial smash, the surprise hit tour of the year. Farrell stressed that it was the show's diversity that appealed to the predominantly white male audience. He recognised that, just like himself, many punters had become bored by the huge, bloated rock'n' roll extravaganzas of the Eighties; now they simply wanted more bang for their buck.

"If you just keep giving kids the same thing and keep working on the same old formulas, it's going to get boring," he explained. "How many times have you felt like you have already had it by the third or fourth song? So if you do already feel like you've had it by the third or fourth song [at Lollapalooza], go and check out the short film festival."

When it was announced that there would definitely be a Lollapalooza '92, the line-up featured the usual selection of cutting-edge acts spread over two stages: Pearl Jam, Ministry, Ice Cube, Soundgarden, Farrell's new outfit, Porno For Pyros, The Jesus And Mary Chain, plus hip-hoppers Cypress Hill, the Boo-Ya TRIBE and House Of Pain – with The Red Hot Chili Peppers as headliners. (They'd been confirmed as the festival's closer in mid-March.) The bill was rounded out by the usual freaks, such as the Amazing Mr Lifto, who could hang various heavy objects from parts of his body not necessarily designed for the purpose, the glass-eating Torture King and Paul The Sword Swallower, who kicked off his act with the ingestion of an entree of live worms, crickets, slugs and maggots. Farrell truly was offering something for everyone.

The tour, scheduled to kick off in San Francisco on July 18, would hit 29 cities in an eight-week run, winding up at Irvine Meadows Amphitheater in Laguna Hills, California, on September 13.

Although they weren't invited along for Lollapalooza 1991, the Chili Peppers were big fans of the festival; Kiedis insisted that this was the main reason that they'd agreed to be headliners. But the money couldn't have hurt, either – Lollapalooza '91 had grossed $9,625,924 from 430,888 paying customers at 27 dates in 20 cities. And with 'Under The Bridge' having spent five of the past six weeks at the number three spot in the *Billboard* singles chart, the Peppers couldn't be any hotter, even without a guitar player.

Admittedly, Kiedis was concerned about the lack of femme rockers on the bill: the only women featured were in British band Lush, who would open each day's festivities before a few hundred curious onlookers. Kiedis even tried to call Farrell to discuss his reservations about the bill, but found Mr Lollapalooza impossible to reach. He eventually resorted to faxing Farrell via the event's booking agency, asking if all-female act L7 could be added to the bill.

"Everybody in the agency just scoffed," he told *Rolling Stone*. "They said, 'They don't mean anything.' What do you mean? They rock and they're girls. [But] if I didn't get off on it [the festival] so heavily last year, I wouldn't have been so inclined to be part of it this year.

"The world at large is just completely bored with mainstream bullshit," Kiedis figured, trying to explain the "alternative" boom that peaked with the Lollapalooza roadshow. "They want something that not only has a hardcore edge but that is real music, written by real people who wake up and have the unignorable need to create music."

But before they could address that "unignorable need", the Chili Peppers required a new guitarist. There were also two European festival dates prior to Lollapalooza II, which speeded up the recruitment process even further.

The first name on the band's wishlist was Dave Navarro, the leather-trousers-clad axeman for the now defunct Jane's Addiction. Navarro, whose volatile on- and off-stage relationship with Farrell was a key part of the Addiction's wild dynamic, had plenty in common with the Peppers. As the "Los Angeles" tattoo on the back of his neck testified, he was a product of Hollywood. He'd lived through a wild youth – like Kiedis and Flea, he came from a broken home – and he'd also endured a serious heroin addiction; so serious, in fact, that he admitted to a failed OD attempt after the first Lollapalooza show in 1991. The recently divorced guitarist also believed that a shirt wasn't essential, pretty much at any time. Lindy Goetz felt he was right for the band. "He was a real cool guy, very Hollywood, very hip."

Since the split of Jane's Addiction, Navarro had received and rejected one offer: Axl Rose had invited him to play with Guns N' Roses. Nor was he ready to join a band as volatile as The Red Hot Chili Peppers – just yet, anyway – so he refused their offer, too.

Chili Pepper wannabes started to bombard their management's office with calls about the vacancy. One hopeful, Brent Paschke, even unearthed Flea's home address and set up camp outside his house, hoping for a sighting of the diminutive bassman. When Flea arrived home, Paschke approached him and Flea politely invited him back the next day for an audition in his garage, the spot where much of the Peppers' later music would be created. Obviously the kid deserved some kind of respect for his commitment. Flea did, however, mention that the band already had a few guitarists in mind.

"I knew my chances were pretty well shot right then," Paschke told *The Associated Press*. "But I figured anything could come out of this, so I said, 'OK, just let me play. That's all I'm asking.'"

He didn't get the job, though he did get to jam with his heroes.

Another name on the Peppers' shortlist was Arik Marshall. Along with his brother Lonnie, Marshall had been a music fan for life. Marshall had been born in LA, and according to the occasionally unreliable Anthony Kiedis, was a member of the Bootsy Collins fanclub at the age of 12. What is true is that while still at school, the Marshalls befriended a schoolmate whose father worked with P-Funk. The Marshall brothers (Arik, Lonnie and Mario) would be the youngest fans standing backstage at P-Funk shows, soaking up the madness. Several years later, Arik had played alongside Lonnie in the band Weapon Of Choice, which had morphed into Marshall Law, who had been offered a record company development deal (which eventually fell through). The brothers had scored some studio work, playing together on LA rapper Tone Loc's 1989 album, *Loc-ed After Dark*. Arik had worked on Etta James' *Stickin' To My Guns*, which was released in 1990, and Sting's 1993 reworking of the Police single, 'Demolition Man'. He had also been a member of the short-lived band Alpha Jerk.

But it was Marshall's work with Trulio Disgracias that caught the Peppers' attention. One of the many casual, all-star Hollywood outfits that would jam whenever and wherever they could, Trulio Disgracias was a funk collective pieced together by Fishbone's Norwood Fisher, who'd not only worked with the Peppers but was a trusted LA insider. Blackbyrd McKnight, a former Peppers guitarist, had played in the outfit, as had Fishbone's Angelo Moore.

Flea, who had seen Marshall play several years earlier and "wasn't that impressed", changed his mind when he caught the Trulio's act. As he would recall, "I said, 'Whoa!' Then I heard him play . . . in Marshall

Law and it was phenomenal! Amazing! Incredible! Like this psychedelic, funky, liquid trip. I thought, 'This guy is the greatest fucking guitar player.'"

Marshall, nicknamed "Freak", also jammed with Alain Johannes, Norwood Fisher and a recovered Jack Irons in a one-shot outfit called Floppy Sidecrack, playing funk covers at a well-heeled Beverly Hills graduation party. That was enough proof for the Peppers. If they couldn't poach Dave Navarro, then Marshall was their man.

No musical novice, Marshall knew what was required to succeed in the Chili Peppers, as he would reveal in an interview he gave much later, when he became a regular in Macy Gray's band. "With the Chili Peppers," he explained, "all you've got is the bassline and the drums and Anthony going 'ta-ka-ta-ka-ta-ka-ta-ka' – you gotta come up with a lot of shit to make him sound good.

"[Now] I get to use more colours on the canvas; with the Chili Peppers it was more sticking to what had already been done by Hillel and John. My strong point is not what I play, it's how I play it. There are so many guitar players who play circles around me technically and who have more musical knowledge, but what I have is feel. I have a good sense of how to groove."

Band and guitarist entered a three-and-a-half-week-long crash course in Pepperdom; at its conclusion, Marshall would step out in front of 60,000 Belgian festivalgoers. It was easily the biggest gig of his life. But Lollapalooza was the band's main priority and the real test of Marshall's Pepperness – the European shows were merely extremely well-attended, well-reimbursed warm-ups. Early reviews of Lollapalooza '92 were promising, as the band worked through what was almost a legitimate greatest-hits set, comprising cuts from *BloodSugar, Uplift Mofo* and *Mother's Milk*.

Rolling Stone reported that they'd made a good choice with their new recruit. "Marshall, from the sound of things," wrote Kim Neely, "won't have any trouble picking up the ball dropped by Frusciante. With only two Belgian shows under his belt as a warm-up, he's slipped right into the Peppers' groove."

Billboard's Robin Tolleson, who reviewed the Mountain View, California show, was impressed straightaway with the Peppers' fifth stringman, describing his solo in the set opener 'Give It Away' as "tasty, slightly bent". The *Seattle Times* declared that the Peppers were the "undisputed stars of the festival . . . with a fired-up, athletic romp fuelled by shotgun drumming and intense songs".

Backstage, Kiedis was more than ready to praise their new recruit, as much for his grace under pressure as his musical pedigree.

"We were incredibly lucky to find Arik Marshall," he said. "He's into the funk, the real, heartfelt, honest expression of life through music. [And now] he's thrust into the biggest tour of the summer, and he's got to deal with the whole craziness of it – the bus life, the plane life, the hotel life, the backstage life, the mayhem – which is a beautiful thing if you keep it in perspective. He's been a chilled cucumber from the beginning. He hasn't let anything wig him out."

Marshall even kept his head, literally, when he was shown the band's latest on-stage fashion statement, which they'd don during their encore of Hendrix's 'Crosstown Traffic' and 'Manic Depression' – a hard hat that spewed flames a metre into the air. He'd come a long way, in a very short time, from Trulio Disgracias.

As the rock'n'roll circus rolled on through the North American summer, the male bonding rituals increased. On one night, Ice-T, Ice Cube and the Boo-Ya TRIBE joined the Peppers for a jam. On most nights, Flea – whose on-stage costume of choice in 1992 consisted mainly of Y-fronts – could be spotted sidestage at Ice Cube's incendiary sets, bobbing his head. The hip-hopper was a festival favourite, whose idea of audience involvement consisted of asking the huge crowds to chant "Fuck you, Ice Cube" at the top of their lungs.

"Ice Cube's the greatest, we love Ice Cube," said Flea, acting as the Chili Peppers' spokesman. "But I wish there was another black band playing."

Despite the occasional disappointment, such as the washout of the Long Island show, Lollapalooza 1992 made an even bigger splash than its predecessor. When it wound down on September 13, the Peppers had played to almost three-quarters of a million punters. The tour grossed $18,797,689 from 36 dates in 29 cities, almost double the gate of Lollapalooza 1991. Don Muller, from Triad Artists, who organised the 1992 tour with Farrell and Gardiner, stated that by the tour's end the Peppers "were more popular than when we made the [original] offer". And while Perry Farrell may have talked up Lollapalooza as a genera-tional change, he, Muller and Gardiner were fully aware of the tour's huge financial pay-off, with merchandise sales averaging $10 per punter; food and beverage sales $15. Recession be damned – there was some serious cash to be made from the alternative boom. As the *Seattle Times* reported, "There's a counterculture thrust to the music and merchandising, and a politically correct tone to the information booths, but essentially [Lollapalooza] is a slick operation that skilfully exploits all the profit angles."

The Red Hot Chili Peppers' transformation from band to brand was now complete; they were huge stars. Not only had they headlined the summer's biggest tour, but they picked up three MTV Awards in September (Viewer's Choice, Art Director and Breakthrough Video), where fresh Pepper Arik Marshall had once again demonstrated commendable grace under pressure.

As the band powered through 'Give It Away', several of their friends danced around them onstage, bouncing madly. One of them accidentally knocked Marshall's plectrum from his grasp. Instead of freaking out, which would have been a perfectly understandable reaction, he stopped, smiled, nudged the over-zealous dancer and pointed to the pick. It was returned and the song – and the broadcast – continued. No problem.

The Peppers had been nominated for two Grammys. Sales of *BloodSugar* were now at the three million mark; the single sales for 'Under The Bridge' were at 500,000 and rising, while the video for 'Breaking The Girl', their second with Frenchman Stephane Sednaoui, was on high MTV rotation. Three years earlier, the band had played St Petersburg, pulling 3,000 fans. In 1992 they rocked hard for 30,000.

The flipside was this: for long-time fans, such as erstwhile guitarist John Frusciante, they'd simply grown too large. The drama of Frusciante's departure – and the subsequent initiation of Arik Marshall – had been played out very openly, proving that the Peppers were as much a public commodity as Madonna or Michael Jackson. The band could do their best to keep their music real, but their every step would now be closely monitored by a story-hungry media.

Kiedis tried to play this down in an interview with MTV (an irony in itself). "You might get off on the music," he said, "but there's no reason to fawn over a human being. It's a media creation. People see so much of your face on television that they have this connection with you that is semi-false."

256

Chad Smith was equally defensive. "The price you pay for MTV loving you is all those little preppies out in the midwest watching 'Under The Bridge' and all of a sudden thinking they know exactly what this band's about. When in fact that song is no more or less representative of this band than 'Higher Ground' was or 'Give It Away', or any other single track."

They could talk as much as they liked, but the Peppers couldn't deny the truth – they were now about as punk as Right Said Fred.

Seizing the moment had become the band's specialty – by October they were touring Australia, making up for the dates blown-out by Frusciante's breakdown. It was during this tour that Flea met Marisa Pouw, an aspiring actress, who would become his partner for several years.

Post-tour, Kiedis hooked up with his tattooist Henk Schiffmacher for a trip into the more remote parts of Borneo. Schiffmacher's quest was to find the last remaining tattooed members of the primitive Dayak tribes, who had once practised tattooing as a religious art. Kiedis' quest was more indulgent; he'd had enough spotlight for now and this was the perfect escape. Or so it seemed in theory, anyway.

In a boys–own type of adventure that would eventually inspire the track 'Californication', Kiedis and Schiffmacher excitedly headed into the jungle. But within a few days, the not-quite-jungle-hardy Kiedis noticed three small spots on his leg and began to panic – surely he had malaria, right? He tracked down a local priest and asked him flat out: "Am I going to die?"

Reassured that his life wasn't in any immediate danger, Kiedis resumed his journey. But a few nights later he awoke with the strange sensation that some jungle creepy-crawly had wriggled inside his ear. Now seriously freaked out, Kiedis woke Schiffmacher and announced that something was "making its way towards my brain".* This time he was partly right: he'd been invaded by a large Bornean cockroach, which eventually tired of the inside of Kiedis' ear and crawled out of its own volition. Schiffmacher and Kiedis persevered for a week,

---

* Or, as Kiedis would recall in a slightly different version of the incident, he declared: "I woke up Henk and said, 'Please look in my ear, my head is vibrating and I'm going insane.' "

but when they were stricken with diarrhoea and various other jungle afflictions, the intrepid pair decided to turn tail and head home. At this point, the Californian deep inside Anthony Kiedis came to the rescue.

"Kiedis decides it's time to start waving around his American Express card," Schiffmacher wrote of their adventure. The Chili Pepper frontman grabbed the radio and announced: "This is Anthony Kiedis of the United States of America! I want a helicopter! Now! This is an emergency." He did get the helicopter and, diagnosed with dengue fever, ended up spending two weeks recuperating in an LA hospital. So much for the great escape.

As Kiedis recalled, "I had these great images of myself swinging from vines and finding orang-utans and playing amongst exotic flowers. But it turned into more of a Vietnam experience. When you're a white guy from California, and you've run out of food, and you can't fluently communicate with your guides, it becomes a source of concern."

When he recovered, in a move that finely juggled bravery and fool-hardiness, Kiedis hooked up with Flea and took a trip to Costa Rica. South America must have seemed pretty tame in comparison to the jungles of Borneo.

The Red Hot Chili Peppers may have thought that EMI were in their past, but they knew that their back catalogue was EMI's and the label could do with it as it damn well pleased. In November 1992, the label released *What Hits!?*, a retrospective that included the one track recorded for Warners – 'Under The Bridge' – that EMI were granted permission to use as part of their severance deal. The album was a mix of the familiar – 'Higher Ground', 'Knock Me Down', 'Fire' – and earlier tracks such as 'True Men Don't Kill Coyotes', 'Jungle Man' and 'Fight Like A Brave', which showed a band and a sound strictly under development. The companion video also gave newer fans the chance to check out the rarely screened Dick Rude-directed masterwork, 'Catholic School Girls Rule', plus live footage and other early, hard-to-find clips.

Lindy Goetz looked on and shrugged his shoulders. "There's not much we can do about it," he told *Billboard*. "EMI owns the catalogue, and I'm sure they'll do the best they can."

But EMI's timing couldn't have been better, with the band off the road and the heat just starting to cool on *BloodSugar*. They had reached a gentlemen's agreement with Warners, the band's new label, assuring them that the best-of wouldn't be released until the label had finished working 'Breaking The Girl', the third single from *BloodSugar*. But what caused distress for both the Peppers and their management was the success of 'Behind The Sun', which was lifted as a single to promote *What Hits!?* Five years earlier the band had pushed for the track to be the lead single for *Uplift Mofo*, but EMI had turned them down cold. Now it was riding high at number 13 on the *Billboard* Modern Rock Tracks chart, while the album galloped into the Top 50. A video was also pieced together for the track, featuring animation and outtake footage from the Drew Carolan-directed 'Higher Ground' clip. It copped several weeks of "stress rotation" from MTV. The song was a hit.

"The band and I felt this could have been our first radio track back [in 1987]," Goetz snarled, adding that EMI's "old regime" disagreed. He did, however, accept that the success of the single and album kept the band "visible". It also kept the royalties rolling in.

As part of the "new regime" at EMI, Mike Mena, who was VP of alternative promotion and marketing, recognised the potential of 'Behind The Sun'.

"It's got that typical Chili Peppers funk aspect," he admitted, "and is a nice hybrid of styles that a brand-new Chili Peppers fan would like, as well as the diehard fan."

The band could do very little but sit back and watch the single and album blitz the charts. *What Hits!?* would eventually peak at number 22 in the *Billboard* album chart, going on to shift more than a million copies.

The next step in the Peppers' seemingly unstoppable rise came at the Grammy Awards, held in late February 1993. The band had been nominated for Best Hard Rock Performance (for 'Give It Away') and Best Rock Vocals, Duo Or Group (for 'Under The Bridge'). Flea was uncomfortable with the Hard Rock nomination, believing that 'Give It Away' was a "funk song".

"The only reason it was nominated for hard rock is because of the colour of our skin," he snapped.

But the band agreed to perform, deciding that if you've got somewhere near a billion people looking on, it's best to leave an impression. Kiedis opted to wear what one onlooker described as a "mutated geisha gown", topped off by an Indian headdress, while the rest of the band were decked out in "faux-sackcloth". Inside the venerable Shrine Auditorium, Michael Jackson held hands with Brooke Shields, and Whitney Houston and Billy Ray Cyrus looked on, as the Peppers segued 'Give It Away' into George Clinton's 1978 anthem, 'One Nation Under A Groove'. At this point, Clinton (and fellow P-Funksters) shimmied onto the stage, sporting an amazing technicolour funkcoat and shaking his blue-and-yellow dreadlocks furiously. The band were fulfilling a promise made to Clinton when they were recording *Freaky Styley*. It was a big moment, a sincere gesture of payback from funk apprentices to the master.

Backstage, Clinton revealed that playing 'One Nation' was Kiedis' idea. "That's a lot of good-time vibe," Clinton said of the funky jam. "It choked people up. The vibe was so thorough, the music was so hard, everyone froze in their chairs until it was over, but then everybody went crazy. Damn, that was neat."

The Peppers' night was made complete when they won Flea's cursed Hard Rock Grammy. The bassman had softened his line, just a little, when they spoke with the media backstage. Holding up his Grammy, Flea announced: "Music is a beautiful, spiritual thing, and we got this thing here, which is plastic or ceramic or wood or whatever the deal is. So let's be real."

But Flea also understood the gravity of the situation, because he quickly added: "We'll take it. They probably just felt sorry for us."

The band then gave an a cappella rendition of 'Tears In Heaven', the hit track from the night's big winner Eric Clapton, along with snippets of X's 'Los Angeles' and Glen Campbell's 'Wichita Lineman', strictly for laughs.

It was a huge night for the band, further confirmation of their place in the rock'n'roll hierarchy. This band of former "latchkey kids" were now rich rock superstuds. Kiedis, who was now living in what one writer would describe as "shoeless, shirtless luxury high in the Hollywood Hills", was even locked in to co-present an MTV Movie award with bewitching actress Marisa Tomei. The Chili Pepper was a man in demand and the band were raking in the cash.

All they really needed for their final induction into entertainment's big league was a *Simpsons'* cameo. Since the Matt Groening-created cartoon had been sprung on an unsuspecting American public in 1989, stars had been willing to crawl over each other in the desire to get animated for the small screen. Music, especially rock'n'roll, had always been a major feature of the programme, and to be granted a cameo was a serious coup. Not only might you sell a few more units, but there were serious credibility points attached to featuring in this shrewdly observed take on Anywhere, America. The programme had featured a Lollapalooza episode (sorry, make that Homerpalooza), while mock rockers Spinal Tap had even agreed to appear on the show.

The Chili Peppers made the grade on May 13, 1993, during the episode 'Krusty Gets Kanceled', along with fellow guest stars Barry White, Bette Midler, Johnny Carson, Hugh Hefner and Elizabeth Taylor. It was the last appearance that Arik Marshall would make with the band – as an animated figure in Y-fronts, tearing through 'Give It Away' in Moe's Bar. His swansong with the Peppers was almost as peculiar as John Frusciante's airbrushing from the cover of *Rolling Stone*.

Marshall's funk-fuelled style of string-bending might have meshed well with the Peppers' sound, but they also required a guitarist who was personally compatible with the rest of the band. To Lindy Goetz, "Arik was a great guitar player, but just not a Chili Pepper." They needed a man who could balance Smith's earthiness, Kiedis' ever-increasing superstar/superstud status and Flea's hippie-dippie nature. A journalist on the set for their 'Breaking The Girl' clip, which was shot in LA, observed that Marshall "was quiet, reserved, shy, even a bit of a loner", qualities that were very un-Chili Pepper-like. Blackie Dammett, as ever, had a comment. "Arik never meshed with the rest of the band . . . as a cohesive unit," he said. "He's quite an introspective guy, which never fit into that Chili Pepper crazy, funky personality."

The band were tight-lipped on yet another guitarist's departure; Arik Marshall made no official comment about his leaving. All Kiedis would say was that Marshall and the Peppers were lacking "the emotional connection you need with a new person in your band". Chad Smith insisted that "it's not a personal thing at all. We toured with Arik and it was really cool. We love him – he's a great guy and an amazing guitar player." However, Smith noted that the core problem was songwriting.

The band were now planning their sixth album – they needed to capitalise quickly on *BloodSugar*'s massive success – and creative sparks simply didn't fly with Marshall. "We never tested those [songwriting] waters with Arik," Smith added. "So when we went into the studio to write more songs, the chemistry just didn't feel right and we decided to go our separate ways."

Almost a year to the day that he was hired, Arik Marshall was out of the band.

Dave Navarro remained the guitarist that the Peppers truly craved. He looked right, he played brilliantly, he was available – but despite various pleading calls from the band, he turned them down for the second time, opting to work on Deconstruction, a low-key project with Eric Avery, his bass-playing bandmate from Jane's Addiction. Sitting in his Gothic lair of a Hollywood Hills mansion – described by one visitor as "the Addams Family's vacation home" – surrounded by his skeletons and prints of Francis Bacon's 'Screaming Pope' and Warhol's 'Electric Chair', with his Ouija board laid out on his coffin–cum–coffee table, Navarro watched the Peppers drama unfold.

Even though the now guitarist-less band had pulled out of several lucrative European festival dates, they still needed a new axeman. The band opted for a radical new plan: they'd run a help wanted ad in the free alternative newspaper, *LA Weekly*. The ad, which was written in a child's scrawl and decorated with illustrations from Clara Balzary, appeared in mid-June 1993, and read: "Boys AND girls! The Red Hot Chili Peppers need a guitar player. If you truly believe you are it call (213) 726-1325. No wheedlers."*

On the first few days that the ad ran, the band realised two things: they'd made a big mistake, and there was no way that one phone line could handle the volume of calls. Amidst the 5,000 hopefuls were the obligatory joke applicants, such as Jim "Crash'n'Burn" Florio, who was better known as the Governor of New Jersey. His name was volunteered by a morning talk-show host, Eddie Davis. When an assistant

---

* A few weeks earlier, speaking with *Rolling Stone* about the vacancy in the band, Chad Smith had stated: "What are you gonna do, put an ad in the paper? 'Chili Peppers looking for guitarist?' We'll get every bozo." Then they did just that, calculating that "by sheer numbers" they would find a new guitarist.

was asked whether the Governor was much of a guitarist, she replied: "No, but he has been seen with a saxophone." Another applicant was well-regarded former Canned Heat guitarist Harvey Mandel, who was 44 at the time and almost famous for having failed a try-out for The Rolling Stones many years earlier. There were even calls from Icelandic hopefuls.

"It turned out to be the hugest, most preposterous fiasco to which we've ever voluntarily subjected ourselves," conceded Kiedis. "It was hordes of hundreds coming from around the globe, and we weren't feeling it with anybody."

An increasingly forlorn Kiedis then checked out an LA band called Mother Tongue, led by guitarist and songwriter Jesse Tobias. Kiedis wasn't very taken by the band, but he spotted Chili Pepper potential in Tobias. Then serendipity took over – Kiedis was at a friend's house at the same party as Tobias. They struck up a conversation and Kiedis was impressed by his musical taste. He also thought that Tobias was "a cool guy".

"That's half the equation," Kiedis reasoned. "[He's] someone you'd like to hang out with." Blackbyrd McKnight had been a cool guy, too, as had DH Peligro and Cliff Martinez – and look what happened to them. But Kiedis persevered.

By July, an informal jam had been arranged with Tobias. "It just turned out to be a highly magical experience for everyone," Kiedis explained, and Tobias was hired.

Mother Tongue had released one self-titled album in 1994, but the response was lukewarm (one reviewer described the album as "mostly average funk-tinged retro-rock"). Clearly Tobias recognised the endless financial, if not creative, possibilities of becoming a Chili Pepper.

As ever, Kiedis and the band were more than willing to talk up the talents of their new recruit. To the Peppers' frontman, Tobias was "definitely the rawest, most unbridled-style horse we've ever had in the band. He's got this incredible raw power."

Kiedis was also quite willing to state that Tobias would have creative input towards their next album, which was a brave, probably short-sighted comment to make, given the ongoing court case with Jack Sherman about the worth of his songwriting input to the band's earliest work.

Regardless, during their early jams, Tobias brought in a piece that, according to Kiedis, was "as soulful as shit, long and strong. So I think it's going to pan out."

But of all the Chili Pepper guitarists – Jack Sherman, Hillel Slovak, John Frusciante, Arik Marshall, DeWayne "Blackbyrd" McKnight – the recruitment of Jesse Tobias was the most ill-conceived, and his departure the most clumsily handled, of the band's long history. It was a far more public disaster than the kids-stuff antics of Kiedis and Flea when they sacked Jack Sherman back in 1984. Tobias lasted exactly a month before being shown the door.

Kiedis would go on record stating that it was Tobias' musical incompatibility with Flea that led to his going. But it seemed a strange coincidence that Dave Navarro suddenly made himself available to join the band just as Tobias was fired. Kiedis, naturally enough, defended the Peppers.

"Though it may seem like a case of Dave uprooting Jesse, it wasn't exactly like that," he would state during an interview for yet another *Rolling Stone* cover. "The discontent had already planted itself. We really liked Jesse's playing, but it just didn't develop into the musical camaraderie that we were used to. Flea didn't feel right about it and the fate of this band relies on Flea having a sense of musical contentment with the guitar player."

Flea tried – and failed – to make light of the unfortunate scenario. "Jesse made his own bed," he said, "but we bought him the sheets and the mattress." When pushed for more details, he explained how things weren't working out as well as they should have with Tobias. "There were a lot of places we needed to go musically that just weren't happening, both in terms of what we've done before and what we want to do now. We just weren't getting multi-dimensional enough."*

Lindy Goetz felt the hiring and firing of Tobias "was a terrible thing", especially in light of the fact that his former band, Mother Tongue, refused to re-hire him.

As for Tobias, he left the band quietly and quickly, rebounding from his misfortune to play with Alanis Morissette, before forming an outfit

---

* This statement contradicted the explanation given to me by band insider Keith Barry, who felt that it was Kiedis, not Flea, who needed an empathetic guitarist to write his best music.

called Splendid with his wife, Australian Angie Hart, who once fronted the band Frente. One journalist who had interviewed Tobias after leaving the Peppers told me that, if anything, Tobias seemed embarrassed discussing his time as a Chili Pepper. Just like Marshall, and McKnight before him, Tobias said very little about his brief tenure, or his hasty leaving. Chad Smith, however, did have a comment. He jokingly compared the band to Spinal Tap, with one key difference. "It isn't our drummers who keep exploding."

But like a shark, the Peppers needed to keep moving for fear of drowning – or being laughed out of Hollywood as an employer with questionable business practices. On September 5, 1993, it was announced that Dave Navarro had finally agreed to become a Chili Pepper. Flea went public about Navarro's appointment when he wrote a press release for *Guitar Player* magazine.

"Hey, I want to tell you about our new guitarist," he announced. "I mean, our *new* new guitarist. Yeah, the rumours are true – it's Dave Navarro. I'm so happy about it! I had been really worried about how things were going with the band, now I feel so good.

"Dave totally knows where we're coming from, has the capabilities to do everything we need and brings a whole new dimension to the sound. Dave plays like himself only, which is great. It felt like a real band from the first second we started jamming."

Flea also revealed that the revitalised band celebrated by treating themselves to Harleys. The Hog-riding rockers called themselves the Sensitives. Navarro's nickname was "Angel", Kiedis' was "Sweetheart", Smith was called "Tender" and Flea now preferred to be known as "Mr Softy".

"We're the gnarliest fucking gang," he explained, "but we don't want to hurt anyone's feelings."

Flea pushed hard for Navarro's inclusion in the band. He boasted about being a strong Jane's Addiction fan, admitting that they had a huge influence on his own music and naming them "the greatest rock band of the last 10 years". But Navarro was more circumspect when it came to returning the compliment. As much a straight-shooter as Chad Smith, Navarro didn't own a Chili Peppers album when he was approached to join the band – hell, he didn't even like basketball, which was one of the Peppers' main reasons for breathing.

The band may have conducted a group hug and then splurged on Harleys, but the truth was that the early work with Navarro was difficult. As Navarro stated, he had problems with the band both on a personal and creative level. "I had a stereotypical notion of this band. I expected them to be funky, wacky, funny, cute – all of the things that I generally don't have in my personal existence.

"[And] they aren't a band like Mötley Crüe, where you could just stick in any guitar player and it would work OK. I felt strange for a long time because the band played a style of music I didn't."

That was a fair call, too. Funk – or anything vaguely resembling groove – didn't play a huge role in the sound of Jane's Addiction, who formed in LA in 1986. Their bastard rock'n'roll sound was dark and turbulent, fuelled by heroin, sex, death and Hollywood, as they meshed myriad rock styles and sounds. Wild-eyed frontman Perry Farrell (aka Perry Bernstein) had a tragic past; his mother committed suicide when he was still a child, a subject he explored in their song 'Then She Did . . .' The 26-year-old Santa Monica native Navarro – who'd started playing guitar at 11 and was an early fan of Hendrix and Jimmy Page – had endured an even more disturbing upbringing. His mother Constance Colleen Hopkins and her sister were killed by Constance's ex-boyfriend when Navarro was 15. Revelations about this double murder would actually intrude on his work with the Chili Peppers. "Tragedy brought me where I am," Navarro would state after becoming a Chili Pepper. "If my Mom hadn't died, I wouldn't have turned to music as intensely as I did."

As for his playing, Navarro's style was radically different to any of the previous Peppers' guitarists. He was more interested in texture than form, piling on wave upon wave of effects and improvisations, building a monumental wall of sound. Most Peppers guitarists simply plugged in, prayed to their God Jimi Hendrix and let rip (often brilliantly).

"In Jane's," Navarro said, "I literally didn't know what the hell I was going to play when I went into the studio. In rehearsals and gigs prior to recording, I would make everything up every time."

Such Jane's Addiction epics as 'Mountain Song' were dazzling works of sonic construction; it seemed as if the band were recording from the top of a canyon, wailing into the valley below. Just like the Peppers, Jane's loved to shock. Many retailers refused to stock their multi-platinum *Ritual De Lo Habitual* album because they considered the cover image of Farrell's nude sculptures way too confrontational. What the band also shared with the Chili Peppers was a love of the sleaze and glitter of LA: to many, Jane's Addiction were the definitive Hollywood band of the late 20th century. And both Kiedis and Navarro were recovering junkies, whose new addictions were health food and bench presses.

Kiedis believed that he and Navarro were "telepathically connected". "We both came out of a very near fatal junkiedom," the singer explained, "and we both made it to the other side of that without frying our spirit or our mind or our body. If you strip away all of his cynicism, he's just pure love that guy – and he's interesting as hell."

During those early "getting to know you" sessions, Navarro and the band realised that some musical compromises needed to be made in order for him to become a reasonable fit. As Navarro admitted, "I tried to take a step towards the band, and they took a step towards what I did, but neither of us did each other's thing comfortably. We were coming up with unnatural, forced things.

"Jane's Addiction created its art through a self-destructive process," he added, "whereas the Chili Peppers create their art through the healing process. That's something I needed to learn about."

Flea agreed that Navarro wasn't an immediate fit. "When Dave first joined," he said, "we did have a really awkward time for a few months. We made the mistake of trying to meet each other at a halfway point, as opposed to just creating something totally new." Navarro realised that he and the remaining Peppers had rushed the process, attempting to write songs "within 20 minutes" of him signing up.

"To me," he said, "that was overwhelming. It's like meeting a girl at a club and the very next morning going to brunch with her parents, grandparents, brothers and sisters."

The rest of the Peppers knew that the band would become a joke if their newest recruit didn't fit – Chad Smith's Spinal Tap gag wasn't actually that far from reality. But during those uncomfortable early sessions with Navarro, Flea had his own problems to deal with; in mid-July 1993 he had been diagnosed with chronic fatigue syndrome. The combination of the band's stop-start progress, too much touring, too many drugs and the pressure of making another hit record had run the most effervescent Chili Pepper into the ground. Flea had also learned that fame and its trappings didn't necessarily amount to spiritual wealth. "We had achieved all this success we had been working for for years," he said. "[And] I was just miserable." Flea's drug consumption and his admission that he was "being wild all the time thinking I was Superman and could stand anything" truly took their toll. He would spend some time in therapy dealing with his accumulated problems.

"He just pushed it too much and he got real run down," according to Chad Smith. "His body just kind of gave up on him. Then it screwed up his head."

Flea had actually been sick for some time. He would backdate his malady to a brief South American tour that the band undertook with Nirvana at the end of the *BloodSugarSexMagik* period, in 1992.

"I was extraordinarily run down from being on tour. I had gotten divorced not too long before, I missed my daughter, and I didn't feel close to anyone. I couldn't sleep. I'd sit in my room, crying and shit – I was bumming out."

The bassman wasn't convinced that his ailment could simply be dismissed by the medical term chronic fatigue. As he explained: "It was emotional and spiritual imbalances that needed to be corrected."

With Flea out of action and Navarro struggling to adapt, the obvious solution was to slow down. Individual Peppers did make sporadic appearances in the latter months of 1993, but there wasn't a whole lot of Peppers' music-making going on.

Kiedis and a recovering Flea cameoed on the video for George Clinton's 'Paint The White House Black', taken from their mentor's comeback record, *Hey Man . . . Smell My Finger*. They also added parts to the album track 'Martial Law'. Then in September the pair put in a memorable appearance at the MTV Video Music Awards, where they shared a stage with the most dapper man in music, balladeer Tony Bennett. With Kiedis and Flea dressed in what was called "Bennett-esque dinner finery" and the man himself outfitted like a mature-age Pepper, decked out in black knee-length shorts, black T-shirt, top hat and white-rimmed shades, they joked their way through a co-presenting spot. While Flea croaked a few bars of Bennett's signature song, 'I Left My Heart In San Francisco', Bennett responded with a very familiar rap: "Give it away/ give it away/ give it away now". Bennett was so taken by the pair – Flea in particular – that he compared the diminutive bassist to vaudeville star Jimmy Durante.

"Far away from the cool school, he and the band just want to entertain people," declared the elder statesman of croon.

But what was seen on stage was in no way spontaneous. Many of those close to the Chili Peppers have said that much of their success is due to their willingness to work and rehearse parts endlessly. As Bennett revealed, this attitude even carried on into comedy routines.

"They rehearsed it over and over again before we went onstage – more so than a lot of my contemporaries would have. Then they made it look completely spontaneous."

But little more than a month later, on Halloween night, Flea's recuperation from chronic fatigue was rocked by a personal disaster. He was at the Viper Room, the Hollywood rock club operated by his sometimes jamming partner, *très* cool actor Johnny Depp. Butthole Surfer Gibby Haynes was playing with Depp that night, along with erstwhile Pepper John Frusciante, in his last public performance before becoming a full-time junkie. Also in the club was actor River Phoenix, who'd become a young star thanks to his roles in a pair of films from 1986, *The Mosquito Coast* and *Stand By Me*. Phoenix was very tight with the Peppers. He had quietly appeared in their 'Under The Bridge' clip, standing alongside director Gus Van Sant. More recently, he and Frusciante had recorded an eccentric pair of songs for the former Pepper's solo album, *Niandra LaDes And Usually Just A T-Shirt*. Frusciante had given Phoenix – who loved rock'n'roll possibly even more than acting, playing in a band called Aleka's Attic with his sister Rain – typically cryptic directions for a song called 'Bought Her Soul'. As Frusciante would remember, "I said to River, 'Make sounds with your voice and I'll record you backwards but you're not allowed to hear the song.' It went perfectly with the song. We were cosmic together."

Frusciante may have described Phoenix as his "closest friend, champion and protector", but the actor was equally close to Flea. Phoenix had helped Flea score a small part as Budd in Van Sant's film *My Own Private Idaho*, where Flea relied on memories of Slovak's death to help generate waterworks during one particularly intense close-up. After the art-house hit was released in 1991, the pair had developed a strong bond away from making music or cinema. They were often spotted amongst groups hanging out along Sunset Strip.

Flea's favourite Phoenix story emerged from a time when the actor told him that he should be playing rhythm guitar in the Peppers, in order to "fill out the sound". "He seemed really serious. I was just stammering, not knowing what to say, and then he just started laughing. He just wanted to see me sweat."

On Halloween night, just before 1 am, in the bathroom at the Viper Room, Phoenix had accepted a snort of high-grade Persian Brown heroin from a drug dealer. Immediately he started to tremble; he then vomited. Someone handed him a Valium and Phoenix then stumbled back out to the bar, where he found his sister Rain and actress Samantha Mathis. He told them he couldn't breathe and briefly passed out. Mathis and River's brother, Joaquin, who was also in the club, took him outside where he collapsed on the footpath. He then lapsed into the first of several seizures.

According to photographer Ron Davis, who called an ambulance from the scene, Phoenix "looked like a fish out of water; [he was] thrashing spasmodically, his head flopping from side to side, arms flailing wildly."

When the paramedics arrived at 1.14 am, Phoenix was in cardiac arrest. Twenty minutes later they arrived at Cedars Sinai Memorial Center, where the actor was pronounced dead at 1.51 am. Flea had ridden in the ambulance with his dying buddy.

The autopsy performed on Phoenix revealed that he had ingested a potent drug cocktail: it showed lethal levels of cocaine and morphine (heroin shows up as morphine as it is metabolised), Valium, marijuana and ephedrine, which is the main ingredient found in crystal meth. The official cause of death was acute multiple drug ingestion. He was 23 years old.

Flea was devastated. "He was one of the most beautiful and loving guys I ever met," he stated. Equally distressed were the many fans of the actor, who had nurtured a reputation as a strict vegetarian and animal rights activist – he once purchased acres of Costa Rica land to save it from development. What confused most people was that Phoenix had very openly spoken out against drugs. "I don't see any point or any good in drugs that are as disruptive as cocaine," he once declared. "I never tried heroin. I tried alcohol and most of the others when I was 15, and got it out of the way. [I'm] finished with the stuff."

The bassist would try to deal with his loss in the song 'Transcending', which appeared on the *One Hot Minute* album, and 'I've Been Down' – which would appear on the soundtrack of the *Basketball Diaries* film in March 1995 – a song that one critic described as "a strange acoustic song about the darker side of being a rock star". For Flea, the loss was almost as deeply felt as that of Hillel Slovak – so deeply felt and publicly expressed, in fact, that the Hollywood rumour mill even suggested that he and Phoenix may have been lovers, although there is absolutely no evidence of this.

Kiedis was in New York when Phoenix died; it was the day before the singer's 31st birthday. He'd been taking in various events at New York Fashion Week, usually in the company of his soon-to-be girlfriend, model Jamie Rishar. The singer put his birthday celebrations on ice when he got the call about his friend's overdose death.

"I fell into a state of shock," he said. "I could not talk, I just cried for 24 hours." Kiedis' New York pals persevered, insisting he try to enjoy his birthday. But a stunned Kiedis sat in a nightclub, "wondering why it had happened".

By now, Flea and Kiedis were becoming very accustomed to death. From the Germs' Derby Crash to Hillel Slovak and Phoenix, it was as if they were surrounded by peers and friends who died far too young. Several months later, on March 30, their former touring partner Kurt Cobain, from grunge supernovas Nirvana, also joined the death list when he blew his head off with a shotgun.

The unfortunate combination of sacked guitarists, dead friends and chronic fatigue syndrome would contribute to the overwhelmingly dark mood of their next LP, *One Hot Minute*. But that was still some way off in the future – what the band felt they now needed was a spot of R&R, ideally away from Hollywood and its tragedies.

It was agreed that they would spend three months in Hawaii, early in 1994, where Kiedis, Smith and Flea would get to know their new guitarist and work out some music. Or, as Kiedis would later fondly describe the male-bonding experience, "We ate a lot of food together, drank some coffee, smelled each other's farts."

Before they departed, the band had volunteered to appear in a Public Service Announcement for AIDS awareness. What seemed like a well-intentioned gesture regarding sexuality – a field in which they were acknowledged experts – turned out to be another case of the Peppers' reckless past coming back to haunt them.

The radio spot itself was good-natured fun. While Smith, Flea and Navarro laid down a mellow, funky groove, Kiedis announced: "I'm Anthony Kiedis of The Red Hot Chili Peppers. I've been naked on stage. I've been naked on magazine covers. In fact, I was born naked and of course I'm naked whenever I have sex. So I might as well get naked again. (Clothes can be heard hitting the floor.)

"There, I'm naked, see?" Kiedis continues. "And what I have here is a condom. A latex condom. I wear one whenever I have sex. Not whenever it's convenient. Or whenever my partner thinks about it. Every time. Look, they're very easy to open. (The next sound heard is that of a package opening.)

"A breeze to put on," Kiedis then says. "And best of all, they stop the spread of HIV.

"Now I'm naked. With a condom. But I'm not saying you should have sex, and I'm not saying you shouldn't have sex. But I'm saying wear a latex condom if you're going to have sex.

"Just think of this helpful demonstration," he said in conclusion, "and remember: you can be naked without being exposed."

The 60-second ad was one of four radio spots and nine TV ads designed to raise AIDS awareness; the US government had sunk $850,000 into the project. But hours before the Kiedis spot was due to run, the US Federal Government's Health and Human Services Secretary, Donna E Shalala, stepped in and had the ad pulled, citing Kiedis' 1990 sexual battery and indecent assault conviction as the reason. Focus groups, who had been played the ad, were also wary of Kiedis' past crimes and misdemeanours.

"We do not feel he is an appropriate spokesperson," announced Dr David Satcher, director of the Centers For Disease Control And Prevention, who launched the advertising campaign.

Kiedis was dismayed. The band had offered their services pro bono and genuinely believed that they were performing a worthy community service. It was a great chance for the band to get on the right side of the mainstream.

Lindy Goetz was every bit as upset as his star band. "It seems ridiculous," he stated. "It seems like a good thing he did."

Kiedis lashed out. Speaking with *Rolling Stone*, he stated: "That's one of those stories where, from my point of view, everybody loses out. This ad agency commissioned by the government came to me and said, 'Will you do a radio ad for the use of condoms?' And I said to myself, 'Well, that sounds like a productive and very positive thing to do.' And the ad agency was pleased and the government was very pleased.

"But then this woman who was in charge of the whole thing finds out that it's me and says, 'This guy did something to a girl' and she was very rigid about getting me kicked off the programme."

Feeling both wronged and disappointed, the Peppers flew to Hawaii in early 1994, for several slow, sunny weeks of bonding and tune-smithery. About three-quarters of their new record was created during these beachside sessions. By June of that year, they were ready to start work with Rick Rubin on the album that would become *One Hot Minute*.

But while Flea, Navarro and Smith had locked into some juicy grooves while in Hawaii, Kiedis was in the midst of a major writer's block. This was enhanced by his mysterious, never-fully-explained personal problems. On his return to LA, he claimed to have become "heavily surrounded, wrapped up and engulfed in a personal unsolved tragedy", but he failed to fill in the blanks. Rubin explained away his absence – after the band completed much of the tracking for the album in June 1994 – as simply this: "Anthony got sick." Flea was equally vague, telling a reporter, "I think Anthony [is] coming out of definitely a rough time."

There was no evidence that he and covergirlfriend Rishar were having problems. They were seen together very publicly as late as April 1995, when Kiedis flew from LA to New York to join in her 19th birthday bash. She'd even had the name ANTHONY tattooed between her thumb and forefinger.

And while there's nothing on public record to suggest that Kiedis' return to heroin occurred in 1994, there was something powerful preventing him from crafting words to accompany the band's new tunes. Much later, in 1999, he would admit to "spurts where I would go out and use [heroin]," adding that "over the last four years, the lion's share of my time has been clean," which wasn't quite an avowal of abstinence from hard drugs. There is the real possibility that he could have slipped back into heroin use during 1994.

Again in 1999, Flea would tell a reporter of Kiedis' drug troubles. "Anthony is still fighting [his addiction]. We can never be sure that he is going to be clean; the only thing we can do is to be there for him as much as possible." And when *One Hot Minute* did finally appear – 15 months after the original tracking was done – there would be more than enough lyrical references to drugs and death to imply that Kiedis had been through some very dark days.

Arik Marshall's baptism as a fully fledged Chili Pepper had come during the massive, ground-breaking, money-spinning Lollapalooza tour of 1992. Continuing the trend, it was announced in late April 1994 that Dave Navarro would finally step out as a Chili Pepper at no less an event than the 25th anniversary of the Woodstock Festival.

The original Woodstock had been held on the muddy slopes of farmland belonging to Max Yasgur in Bethel in upstate New York. The first chords had been struck a little after five o'clock on Friday August 15 and the music continued for almost three days. Stragglers were still getting their heads – and their possessions – together by midday on the Monday, after Jimi Hendrix had closed the festival with a mid-morning set. Although it was virtually impossible to calculate exactly how many attended, the count was somewhere near 500,000 fans – enough people to start a revolution, or at least create their own state. The positive, people-together mood of the event had inspired career-making sets from Santana, Joe Cocker & The Grease Band, Ten Years After and Crosby, Stills & Nash.

To some, this headline-grabbing event – which, amongst plenty of sex, drugs, births, deaths and rock'n'roll, also led to the worst traffic jams in American history – was the pinnacle of the hippie era, an affectionate valentine to the late Sixties. To the more sceptical (and less wasted), it was a lawless mudfest populated by wild-eyed stoners and horny teenagers. "For three days," reflected one newspaper when the line-up for the 25th anniversary festival was announced, "people danced, ate, frolicked in gargantuan mud puddles, skinny dipped and took lots and lots of drugs." If there was one band who could pump out the perfect soundtrack for a late 20th-century version of such pure hedonism, it had to be the Chili Peppers.

Scheduled for three days, starting on August 12, 1994, the line-up featured the Peppers, Metallica, Bob Dylan, Aerosmith, Alice In

274

Chains, Joe Cocker, Crosby, Stills & Nash, Nine Inch Nails, the Rollins Band and Santana – a solid balance of so-called "heritage" artists (many who had played at the original bash) and alternative acts that would lure punters to an event that they'd overheard their parents rhapsodising about. The huge commercial success of Lollapalooza was also reflected in Woodstock ticket sales: it may have cost hippies the princely sum of $6 a head at Woodstock '69, but in 1994, Generation X would have to shell out $95.

By the time they took the stage on the Sunday evening, the Peppers realised they needed to work extra hard to impress. The night before, Nine Inch Nails, fronted by the fierce Trent Reznor, had put in a performance that left the crowd – and the scores of media reporting from the site – in raptures. In a repeat of the original Woodstock, the rain had pelted down during the day, leaving much of the crowd caked in mud. Prior to plugging in, Reznor and band coated themselves from head to Doc-Marten-clad toe in mud as a sign of respect to the "Mud People" who populated Woodstock '94. Their ensuing set was described as "potent and memorable".

On the following day, the Peppers were the victims of some unfortunate scheduling; they were sandwiched between the voice of a generation, Bob Dylan, and righteous pop activist Peter Gabriel. When they finally reached the stage – flanked on either side by Mounties – the Peppers proved that they still knew how to dress for success. In a tradition that began with socks on cocks and had been revisited with Lollapalooza's flaming headgear, the band appeared before 250,000 fans wearing astronaut suits topped off with giant, illuminated, lightbulb-shaped helmets. The quartet's heads emerged from holes cut in the bases of the bulbs.

Dave Navarro, every inch the Hollywood rock stud, wasn't impressed. "Being a lightbulb [stinks]," he groaned afterwards. "You can't hear, you can't see, and it's heavy. It looks good, but . . ." (He would describe the outfit as "the second worst thing I've ever had on my body.") Kiedis shrugged and stated, "The things we do for showbiz," before stripping down to cut-offs and sneakers for the rest of the set. But the Peppers weren't finished yet. For their encore, they returned in Afro wigs and outfits that matched Jimi Hendrix's famed fringed ensemble of 25 years earlier. A child, also dressed *à la* Hendrix, sang 'The Star-Spangled Banner', and then the band roared into a cover of

'Fire'. To bring it on home, Flea asked the crowd to remove their shirts and "swing them over your head like a helicopter", as they shifted gears into another cover, Stevie Wonder's 'Higher Ground'.

Dave Navarro mightn't have been a fan of the bulky outfits and costume changes, but the band's live return was well received. As for his fellow Peppers, they were more than satisfied with their comeback.

Speaking not long after the festival, Kiedis agreed that there had been a huge ideological shift in the 25 years that had passed between the two Woodstocks. "The promotion of music has become much more corporate," he admitted.

"[But] personally, Woodstock was a true pinnacle of exhilaration for me," he continued. "I was totally nervous and excited and I had about 20 gallons of adrenalin running through my body, because . . . I was going to be playing with my friends onstage. And we were getting ready to party with over a quarter-million people."

Flea was equally turned on, despite his initial wariness. "I think we went there really questioning the whole thing, that they were advertising peace and love and at the same time it seemed to be about corporate structures and merchandising. But when we got to play, the energy of the whole thing took over. It was our first show with Dave . . . and we had a fun time."

As with the first Woodstock, there was no ensuing revolution – just a mammoth traffic jam snaking its way back in the direction of New York City. Once Kiedis' adrenalin rush had subsided, he knew that he needed to begin composing lyrics for the band's new record. The Peppers' sixth album was now scheduled for a March 1995 release. At least, that was the plan.

CHAPTER TEN

"It's still about pelvis thrust."

WHEN the Peppers emerged from their Laurel Canyon hideaway after cutting *BloodSugar*, they swore they'd never record in a regular studio again. Working in the converted house had truly liberated them – apart from the property's ghostly presence, the experience had made for the most memorable recording sessions of their lives. There were none of the hassles of fighting traffic to get a day's recording started, or dealing with the aftermath of the night before. All they had to do was walk downstairs (or feel the wind in his hair during a 20-minute ride, in Smith's case), light up and get to work. By 1995, however, their attitude had changed. The latest incarnation of the Red Hot Chili Peppers spent much of the early months of the year holed up in a variety of studios, adding to the basic tracks that were laid down with Rubin during June 1994. These sessions took them to San Rafael, then Indiana's Grand Master Studio, plus Ocean Way, LA's Sound City and Hollywood Sound. *One Hot Minute* was turning out to be one slow grind.

There were also other setbacks. In November 1994, the band suffered yet another public image disappointment. Their AIDS PSA had been an attempt at performing a community service that backfired; now they tried to polish their profile by appearing on the peerless kids programme *Sesame Street*. In a *Rolling Stone* cover story that ran in May 1994, Kiedis had expressed his enthusiasm for appearing on the show. After all, it was Kiedis who once admitted that tots were some of the band's biggest fans.

"I've seen Dizzy Gillespie on *Sesame Street*," he told writer Kim Neely, "and a number of musicians have appeared in sketches. They play music, and the kids gather around, and it's a really cool thing." The singer went on to state that the Peppers had been pursuing this goal for some time, even though the show's producers had been unsure about green-lighting the idea. "But they finally said yes," he revealed. "So as soon as we finish this record, we're gonna do a spot. That could be the pinnacle of our careers."

Several months later, however, and *Sesame Street* publicist Carolyn Miller had some bad news for junior Peppers fans. "It's a hot band," she agreed, "but we just don't feel they'd be suited to our audience." This was in spite of Kiedis' assertion to *Rolling Stone* that the show's producers "took . . . a while to realise that we have an understanding with kids and that kids dig what we do."

Selling millions of records and filling stadiums was one thing, but it seemed that complete mainstream acceptance for the Chili Peppers, not just big record sales and sold-out shows, might remain more of a dream than a reality.

On November 8, not long after their *Sesame Street* rejection, another ghost from the band's past returned to haunt them. Erstwhile guitarist John Frusciante, who'd jumped the rocky ship Chili Pepper in Tokyo during 1992, reappeared with his debut solo album, *Niandra LaDes And Usually Just A T-Shirt*. It was a record that proved, disturbingly, that the rumours of Frusciante's descent into drug hell had some pretty strong basis in fact.

Very much a one-man band, Frusciante had locked himself away with an arsenal of guitars and a home four-track machine to make what started out as an album and ended up as an exploration of his gentle madness. The only other person to appear on the album, apart from some uncredited female vocalists, was the Peppers' recently deceased pal, River Phoenix, whose voice – in one instance, on a reversed tape – can be heard on two tracks. Half of the album's 28 spooky, truly out-there songs – which were written while the guitarist was touring in support of *BloodSugarSexMagik* – remained untitled when Rick Rubin's American Recordings quietly released the record. (Warners, the Peppers' label, could have exercised a leaving-artist clause in Frusciante's contract and released the LP, but happily handed it over to Rubin when they realised how difficult an album this would be to promote.) American Recordings decided against producing the mandatory video to promote the record; it's possible that Frusciante was simply in too poor shape to fulfil that marketing essential.

Previewing the record in October, *Billboard* magazine admitted –

euphemistically – that Chili Peppers fans might "be daunted by the album's elusive experimentalism". Danny Ornelas, a rep from the retail-marketing wing of American Recordings, was closer to the mark when he described the reaction of retailers who'd been exposed to the slow-motion meltdown that was *T-Shirt*.

"They freak out about it," he stated. "[They say] 'Oh my God, this is insane.'" In-store or radio play was also out of the question, given the salty language used in such highlights as 'Your Pussy's Glued To A Building'. "[That's] kinda pushing it for a Musicland," Ornelas said.

Frusciante did some low-key promotion for the record, where the guitarist's fragile state of mind was painfully exposed. When asked about Phoenix's death, the guitarist quietly mumbled, "I don't have anyone to play with any more." Upon being asked what a listener would need to savour his album fully, he stressed "imagination".

"If their heads are capable of tripping out, they'll get it," insisted Frusciante.

Reviewers compared the record to such eccentric burn-outs as Moby Grape guitarist Alexander Spence and acid-fried ex-Pink Floyd songwriter Syd Barrett. Frusciante was moving in some seriously disturbed company.

In a lengthy yet fragmented discussion with *Guitar Player* magazine, Frusciante appeared to drift in and out of lucidity. At one point he mentioned, casually, coughing up "like $20,000", so that the album could be transcribed for a string quartet. Problems arose when the guitarist insisted that everything on the album was in 4/4 time. According to Frusciante, "It's really trippy-looking on paper."

When asked if the piece would – or could – ever be performed, Frusciante figured that was unlikely. "Not unless I find a string quartet that understands why Ringo Starr is such a great drummer, can play Stravinsky, and also smokes pot." His plans for the Kronos Quartet to play the piece were scrapped because their drug of choice didn't mesh with Frusciante. "They play 'Purple Haze' like a fucking marching band on speed," he said.

Frusciante readily stated that *T-Shirt* was essentially an album inspired by dope. It was recorded "partly just to have fun, smoke pot and trip my head out". But its eerie, darker-than-night soundscape made it clear that heroin – which Frusciante had begun to use immediately after the *BloodSugar* sessions – was part of its muse. Anyone connected with the troubled, talented guitarist feared that he was heading into the same type of insularity that killed Hillel Slovak.

When the public meltdown of their ex-guitarist was combined with the on-going court battle with Jack Sherman, plus Kiedis' mysterious personal problems, it was really no shock that the Chili Peppers were having big trouble completing the follow-up to the multi-platinum *BloodSugar*. There seemed to be distractions everywhere.

When EMI released *What Hits!?* in September 1992, it was done with the tacit approval of Warner Bros. Yet the Peppers' former label were on their own when they dug deeper into the band's archives in November 1994, releasing *Out In LA*. It was a 19-track barrel-scraping of remixes, live cuts, demos and unreleased tracks dating as far back as the band's first recordings with Spit Stix. Apart from raw takes of tracks from their self-titled debut – which suggested the unrealised funky potential of these songs – *Out In LA* wasn't much more than a historical artefact with, admittedly, some revealing liner notes scribbled by Kiedis and Flea.

It had been a year since the band's last charting single, 'Soul To Squeeze' and a full three years since they exploded with *BloodSugar-SexMagik*. EMI may have been doing their former band a favour by returning them to the charts – *Out In LA* reached number 82 in the *Billboard* album chart, a fair result for such a diehards-only set – but the band's huge following were becoming restless. They were hungry for new material. As for 'I've Been Down', the new track that appeared on the *Basketball Diaries* soundtrack in March 1995, that was little more than an outtake, a studio cast-off. And the use of 'Higher Ground' in a parachuting sequence in the kids movie *Mighty Morphin Power Rangers* was agreed to mainly because Flea's daughter was a fan.

What they needed to do was finish the album. The Peppers' sixth LP, originally slated for a release towards the end of 1994, was now a rescheduling joke: the album's release had been put back to March 1995, then May, then "summer".

Smith, Navarro and Flea were becoming just as restless as the band's fans with the inability of their frontman to produce lyrics. Navarro had even publicly questioned whether Kiedis was actually suffering from writer's block. "You can't rush a man to do his artwork [and] Anthony writes about personal things," he told *Guitar World*. But then he added, intriguingly, "I've heard a lot of talk about writer's block, but I wouldn't call it that."

Flea hinted that Kiedis was dealing with his writer's block from the confines of detox. There were even rumours that Kiedis had been in detox and had busted out, much like Kurt Cobain before his unfortunate demise.

The gregarious Chad Smith decided it was time to step out. He was spotted in some unusual places, including Bondage a Go-Go, a weekly S&M themed hard-rock night at San Francisco club Trocadero Transfer. According to one report, Smith, along with Primus drummer Tim Alexander, "weren't beating the [drum] skins; they were watching the skin-beating in the club's upstairs playpen." Flea and Navarro, meanwhile, were developing a musical camaraderie that was similar to that shared by Flea and Frusciante, and Flea and Slovak before that. They figured that if the Chili Peppers couldn't get it together in the studio, they might as well take on some freelance work. Navarro quest starred on records from Nine Inch Nails and Porno For Pyros (Perry Farrell's new band). Although he turned down an offer to play with Tom Jones at the *Billboard* Music Awards, Navarro did remix Janet Jackson's 'What'll I Do', with a little help from Flea and Chad Smith. Flea was even busier: in the period of almost 40 months that elapsed between Chili Pepper albums, the bassman put in more guest appearances than a Hollywood hopeful. He turned up on *Ball Hog Or Tug Boat?*, an album from Mike Watt, bassist of the Minutemen and fIREHOSE. He contributed to records from hip-hopper Bam, sometimes Stone Mick Jagger (*Wandering Spirit*), plus Jon Hassell, Pigface, Cheikha Remitti, Sir Mix-A-Lot, The Weirdos and Street Military. Together, Flea and Navarro cameoed on Alanis Morissette's smash *Jagged Little Pill* album, playing on the biting 'You Oughtta Know'. They also worked with Tori Amos and Michael Stipe on a track for the soundtrack of the Johnny Depp vehicle, *Don Juan DeMarco*. This was definitely a case of kindred musical spirits. When Navarro asked Amos what type of guitar sound she was after, Amos replied: "An unshaven Moroccan spice." Navarro replied, "OK, that's just what I was planning on doing."

It was an incredibly active time for the pair, but not quite the creative thrill they were seeking. They needed the band to finish *One Hot Minute* and then get back on the road, or else the Chili Peppers risked becoming yesterday's heroes. They faced the possibility of becoming lost in the wake of the R&B/hip-hop renaissance, which had made the Notorious B.I.G., Tupac Shakur, TLC, R Kelly and Coolio big stars of the mid-Nineties. Kurt Cobain was dead, Jane's Addiction had imploded, Pearl Jam had been embroiled in a career-stalling altercation with Ticketmaster, while Soundgarden were heading towards a split. It appeared that all the big American rock acts of the Lollapalooza age were opting to burn out rather than fade away.

There was no shortage of working titles for the album that would become *One Hot Minute* – and not all of them were entirely facetious. There was *The Sensitives* (or, as Smith suggested, *Ritual De Sensitivos*, a nod to both their motorcycle gang and Navarro's former band Jane's Addiction). Then there was *Turtlehead*, *Black Fish Ferris Wheel*, *The Blight Album* and *The Good And Bad Moods Of The Red Hot Chili Peppers*. All reflected the severe moodswings that went into the creation of the record. *BloodSugar* had only taken a few weeks to commit to tape – the follow-up took more than a year. For the Peppers, it felt like forever.

What the band realised – just like all those who tuned in to the album when it finally appeared mid-September, 1995 – was that this was a very different sounding Red Hot Chili Peppers.

"I don't know if hardcore Pepper fans are going to get into it or not," Navarro asked out loud, "though it's certainly not wimped out."

Navarro's epic guitarscapes, of course, provided the key difference between *One Hot Minute* and anything the band had recorded before. "The Dave Navarro sound, which is very orchestrated and built up in layers, changed the whole Chili Peppers sound," said Rick Rubin. "Nothing about what a Chili Pepper guitarist historically has been fits Dave."

Navarro, along with the other Peppers, readily accepted that the album was a meeting point between the two bands – or, as *Spin* magazine shrewdly noted, "an unholy alliance" between two of LA's wildest acts. It was a brave attempt to merge the more turgid psychodramas of Jane's Addiction with the Peppers' spicier spin on rock'n'roll. Navarro had stated that, although he was a huge admirer of the style of previous Peppers' guitarists, he found their sound "too dry and percussive". On this album, the guitar sound was more about "Led Zeppelin meets The

Cure". It was a massive sonic shift for the band – and also a totally different recording process. Whereas Frusciante or Slovak would lay down their guitar parts and move on, Navarro, a self-confessed obsessive/compulsive, would labour for hours, overdubbing endlessly.

"Our other guitarists were atmospheric in different ways," Flea reasoned. "But this sort of echoey, atmospheric playing over a funk groove is where we've hit a whole new sound. It's brand new, but it's still about pelvic thrust."

The result was the richest-sounding record of their lives, although not necessarily their most satisfying songs.

Kiedis, too, had moved into different territory as a lyricist. In order to unplug his writer's block, he turned inwards, pondering the death of Kurt Cobain in 'Tearjerker', as well as the loss of such close friends as Phoenix during the heavy-hearted 'My Friends', a very radio-friendly cut in the 'Under The Bridge' vein. (Flea half-jokingly referred to it as a "money maker" of a song, but it did become the LP's biggest hit.) The album's sprawling closer, 'Transcending', examined Phoenix's death in even greater detail, confirming Flea's analysis that this was "a darker record . . . a pretty sad record".

To Flea's way of thinking, 'Transcending' was more than just a downcast closer. As ever, the bassist was searching for some upbeat vibes amidst the emotional debris of the record. "The overall sadness of this album is positive because it's all about transcending that and getting through it," he told *Rolling Stone*.

Elsewhere, Kiedis also exorcised his own personal demons. When he sang of his "tendency for dependency" during the cut 'Warped', it hinted that the singer's relationship with narcotics was ongoing. When asked to explain his lyrics, Kiedis confessed, simply, that it had been a rough few years. "A lot of people that we loved were dying . . . all that went in."

These were deep, dark lyrics, which hardly made *One Hot Minute* the party-hearty record that the band's fans were aching for.

Kiedis – with, for the first time, Flea's help as a co-lyricist – also tapped into personal history, especially in the track 'Deep Kick', which was accurately described as "an autobiography of the band's first decade in 16 bars". Kiedis sang about how he and Flea had emerged from broken homes, how they'd dealt with Slovak's death, their own addictions, road-tripping escapades with a transvestite, life in LA, The Butthole

Surfers – even Kiedis' teenage fondness for leaping off rooftops into swimming pools. Anyone who knew even a little of the pair's shared history recognised the song's many characters and episodes.

There were other sizeable shifts in the way the band crafted their music. Flea wrote on acoustic guitar for the first time; he even contributed 'Pea', a warped acoustic ditty about "homophobic redneck dicks" that he wrote while trekking in South America. The song – described by one writer as a "curse-filled nursery rhyme" – was immediately banned in the more conservative parts of Asia (as had been *BloodSugar*'s 'Sir Psycho Sexy'). Keith Barry thought this was the most "Flea song" that the band had ever recorded. "My all-time favourite is certainly 'Pea'. It's just a great tune. It's a very Flea tune."

The Peppers were also taking their inspiration from new and unusual sources. 'Walkabout' – a jazz-tinged, slow-motion groove of a song that Navarro disliked so much he referred to it as 'Crapabout' – was inspired by the soundtrack of the Spike Lee film *Crooklyn*, a tribute to the director's hometown. Many, however, thought it was a nod to Flea's purported aboriginal roots.

"That music [from *Crooklyn*] has a great party atmosphere," said Flea. "It's from that time when everybody was doing coke and not worrying about getting AIDS. This place [America] has been turning to shit in every possible way since then."

And as with so many of their records, the band welcomed their friends into the studio to help out. Keith Barry added viola to 'Tearjerker'; John Lurie wailed on harmonica during the title track; Stephen Perkins, formerly of Jane's Addiction, laid on the percussion during the frantic 'One Big Mob', a guaranteed hit with the moshpit. And Flea, who'd recently become a yoga convert, brought his instructor, Gurmukh Kaur Khalsa, into the sessions. You can hear him chanting during 'Falling Into Grace', alongside his new acolyte and producer Rick Rubin. And Navarro's baby brother, James Gabriel, can be heard crying during 'One Big Mob'.

This bit-part was an act of pure serendipity. Recording strange sounds on a Dictaphone had become a habit of Navarro's and he had just happened to have his brother's sobs on tape. While working on the song, he wanted to steer clear of an obligatory guitar solo, fearing it "would be really retro Seventies". "I was banging my head against the wall, trying to come up with something to put there. Then I realised,

'Wow, I have the perfect thing!' I ran home and got the tape of my brother. It seemed to fit the mood perfectly."*

There were other youthful cameos on *One Hot Minute*'s 'Aeroplane' (which was the only track on the album to feature Flea's signature bass-slapping). The 'Aeroplane Kids' included the voices of Flea's daughter Clara, as well as Phillip and Perry Greenspan, the offspring of the band's lawyer, Eric Greenspan. It was one of the few moves on the album that could be called "typical Peppers", fusing the sweetness of a kid's choir with a profanity-laced pop song. 'Aeroplane''s lyric examined Kiedis' relationship with Hope Sandoval, the sultry, doe-eyed singer of the band Mazzy Star. She is "the star of Mazzy" that he refers to, the writer of a song that "could fuck me where I lay".

Ultimately, it was a varied, often surprising record, even if its overall tone was darker than night. But, as with most Peppers recordings, there was some drama during its making. New guy Dave Navarro suffered what he referred to as a nervous breakdown during sessions at Hollywood Sound, one of the five studios the band visited while making the album. It was set off when his past came back to scare the hell out of him.

In 1982, when Navarro's mother Constance Hopkins and her sister had been murdered by her ex-boyfriend, not only did the 15-year-old Navarro witness the crime, but he looked on as the murderer escaped. Immediately afterwards he moved in with his father, where drugs, the guitar and Jimi Hendrix quickly became the three key ingredients in Navarro's retreat from a tough puberty.

"After my mother was killed, everything was about escape," said Navarro.

Hopkins' murder went unsolved until it was featured on *America's Most Wanted*, almost 10 years afterwards, and the fugitive murderer was recognised and captured. As the *One Hot Minute* sessions crawled along, the trial of his mother's killer began. It had an understandably huge impact on the 27-year-old Navarro.

"I had to see him in court," Navarro said, "and let me tell you, it was fucking heavy. There was no concrete evidence, but I could testify to a

* Navarro was a self-confessed fan of Lou Reed's smacked-out rock opera, *Berlin*. One of the album's most tumultuous tracks, 'Kids', features the wailing of producer Bob Ezrin's children. It's possible Navarro picked up the idea from there.

lot of stuff that had happened earlier, so I was the only witness. I hadn't seen him for, like, 12 years, but he'd lived with us for five years before the murder.

"It was rough when my Mom was killed, and her death was a major contributing factor to my drug problems. I went to therapy for a long, long time and then to anonymous group meetings."

When the case closed and his mother's killer was given the death penalty, Navarro also had to contend with his feelings about capital punishment. "It's weird," he said afterwards, "I spent all these years wanting him to die. Now I question how I feel about it."

Amongst the many personal demons it unearthed for Navarro, the trial's timing couldn't have been worse. Its impact on Navarro was channelled into his playing, making a sombre record even more tragic in tone.

For a newly hired guitarslinger, Dave Navarro didn't appear too keen to toe the company line. While apparently promoting *One Hot Minute*, Navarro couldn't hold back. He was willing to admit that parts of the album "could have been done better". He recommended that if he were a listener, he might keep the remote nearby.

"Let's just say that if I were listening to the CD," he very frankly admitted, "there are some songs I would skip, such as 'Tearjerker', 'Walkabout' and perhaps 'One Hot Minute'. They don't really speak to me. There have been times when I've laughed out loud at the stuff that I was playing."

Asked if he now truly felt part of the Chili Peppers, Navarro's reply was equally uncertain. "Sometimes I do," he said, "other days, I don't feel that way. Sometimes I wake up and wish I never was [a Chili Pepper]. But I think that's part of being me."

Navarro's ambivalence was shared by most reviewers of the band's sixth album, although long-time supporters *Rolling Stone* gave the album the full four-star treatment, giving due credit to the more austere tones of these older, battle-scarred Peppers. The band may have explored dope and death with 'Under The Bridge' or 'Knock Me Down', but their new album was virtually one long meditation on loss. It was heavy going.

"*One Hot Minute* dives into the emotionally deep end of drug addiction and loss," wrote *Rolling Stone*'s Daina Darzin. "For these guys, seriousness turns out to be a lot more liberating than any misadventure. After a 10-plus-year career, they're realising their potential at last."

Spin magazine also noted the LP's downbeat tones, describing *One Hot Minute* as "an album that charts the band's passage through a melancholic landscape nearly devoid of the sox-on-cox punk-funk that once characterised the Peppers."

Although it was reassuring for the band that the two key American music magazines understood the album, and recognised the band's need to transcend their usual obsessions (sex, drugs, even more sex), the mainstream media weren't quite as ready to buy into this *One Hot Minute*.

The *San Francisco Chronicle* responded to the album with the great review of indifference. "Although it has a couple of interesting moments," observed Gina Arnold, "it breaks no real new ground for the harsh, fast, funk-happy band . . . *One Hot Minute* is a valiant effort at retaining their musical validity, but the fact remains that theirs is simply not a medium that ages well."

Other newspapers responded likewise, unsure if the band's new direction amounted to any kind of natural progression. "Yeah, this is just what I've been waiting for," Bill Eichenberger of the *Columbus Dispatch* noted, dripping sarcasm, "a 13-song philosophical treatise on religions of the world penned by four guys who used to appear in concert wearing socks on their private parts." He even went on to compare Kiedis' New Age-y use of language in 'Transcending' to the lyrics of prog-rock plodders, Kansas. Another critic was insistent that the chorus for 'My Friends' belonged in a Tears For Fears song. That had to hurt.

The band may have moved a long way from their origins as funked-up miscreants, yet no one was going to let them forget their past. One writer was still sizing them up against their former east coast rivals, stating that "when it comes to brash, witty craziness, The Beastie Boys have Kiedis beat by a mile", conveniently overlooking the fact that the rivalry died out in the early Nineties, along with the Beasties' stardom.

While giving the Peppers due credit for capturing precisely Hollywood at the end of the 20th century – "mythologising a California that still involves babes and sunshine but with a Nineties update: drugs, decadence and soul-searching" – the *Austin American-Statesman*, like many other reviewers of the album, simply found it hard to get excited by *One Hot Minute*.

Nonetheless, most reviewers had no trouble spotting the radio-ready quality of much of the album. The band's commercial appeal had continued to sharpen as they moved further and further away from anything resembling the cutting edge. *Grand Rapids Press* said it out loud: "The Peppers continue to funkify its righteous blend of alternative rock and soul with 13 new songs that seem destined to get heavy radio airplay for years to come." And the *Dayton Daily News* made a prediction: "Watch for the album to debut at number one," before countering with this closer: "Just don't expect us to be so anxious for the next one."

That was another ongoing theme of much of the press that appeared on the album's release – sure, the album was a hit, but there was something hard to swallow in the band's exploration of more melancholic themes. The Peppers were no longer the dicks-out, wild-rockin' dudes of such early albums as *The Uplift Mofo Party Plan* and *Freaky Styley*. The pants were definitely on with *One Hot Minute*.

With such a ready-made fanbase, especially now that *BloodSugar*'s sales had surpassed six million, the album was a hit straight out of the box, charting at number four in the *Billboard* Album Chart. The band weren't now so much reacting to such huge names as Michael Jackson and Bryan Adams, but were competing with them for chart positions and sales. Flea and Navarro celebrated with a man-on-man snog for the cover of *Guitar Player* magazine (which was duly banned in America's more conservative backwaters). Flea kept the good times rolling when, during a video hook-up with the south-east Asian press, he dropped his pants and flashed his big boy to journalists. When a band reaches the multi-platinum status of the Chili Peppers, any puerile act or tantrum is tolerated by their money-hungry label – sometimes it seems as though the mollycoddling of stars is encouraged in rock'n'roll – so Warner's ever-obliging staff stepped in to clean up the cultural faux pas. Johnson Soh, the promotions executive of Warner's Singapore office, stammered out an apology. "We apologise to any member of the press," he cringed, "who had to witness his flashing his instrument for seven seconds.

"It might have been an offensive action if he did it to spite people.

We wish that it had never happened, but I don't think he was intentionally trying to embarrass anybody from our culture."

The Peppers had looked into their hearts of darkness for their new album, but their bassist just couldn't resist showing off other parts of his anatomy. Yet again the band were caught in the ongoing tug of war between maturity and behaving according to expectations. Unlike Flea's pants, some things were hard to shrug off.

Just as with every album up to this point in their careers, the band knew that touring – and plenty of it – would give an additional boost to whatever chart momentum was happening for them. And given that the volume of new album releases had increased in the early and mid-Nineties, in a desperate attempt to corner a youth market that now had such new diversions as video games and the Internet, touring was an even more essential sales tool. Only a band as successful and influential as R.E.M. had disproved the theory, going off the road in 1990 and still shifting millions of units – but even Georgia's finest had returned to the grind of touring by the time of 1995's *Monster* album.

Yet the plans to tour *One Hot Minute* echoed the album's stop–start creation: it was as though the entire project was cursed. The schedule looked perfectly familiar to these seasoned road warriors – after a quick promotional junket through Asia and Europe, the band would tour for the last three months of 1995. The tour would kick off in Europe during September, swing through Australia in November and then travel to New York, returning to the west coast by Christmas. Easy.

And September did begin as planned, with the expected manic display at the MTV Awards, where legendary ear-biter and sometimes boxer, Mike Tyson, introduced them as "the band who put the f-u into 'funk'." And Flea's dress code for the night consisted of Y-fronts and boots. So far, so Peppers. They then breezed through promo duties in Europe, where Flea expressed his dislike of the Germans – "I always feel as if I'm being looked at and disapproved of" – before reaching London. Their set at the Brixton Academy was as notable for the band's dress sense as it was for a setlist that mixed such anticipated fare as 'Suck My Kiss', 'Give It Away' and 'Higher Ground' with a verse of Bowie's 'Sound And Vision' and a brave stab at *One Hot Minute*'s 'Walkabout'. Chad Smith turned up in a dressing gown, which was peeled off, boxer-style, by his drum tech when the band plugged in. Flea wore a pair of Bermuda shorts (and nothing else), Navarro went for black tights and nipple rings, while Kiedis wore a black waitress dress and a white apron. It was another day in the office for these cross-dressing Californians, proving that just because their audience was heavy with sweaty, rock-hungry Cro-Magnons, didn't necessarily mean that they were a reflection of the guys in their beloved band. "Macho guys have always been my least favourite brand of people," Flea readily confessed.

As Caroline Sullivan, *The Guardian*'s music critic, observed: "The cackling, jiving Peppers prove it's possible to be 30, act 16 and get paid handsomely for it."

The rest of their better-laid touring plans fell apart, however, when Chad Smith broke his wrist almost as soon as the band had stepped off the plane at LAX. The burly drummer's accident was incredibly untimely – after its healthy *Billboard* chart debut, *One Hot Minute* was in freefall, mainly because the band needed to be on tour, promoting the hell out of the record. The lead-off single, 'My Friends', had raced to the top position in *Billboard*'s Mainstream Rock Tracks chart, but the follow-up, 'Warped' – the wrong single choice, according to Lindy Goetz – crept to number 13, where it stalled. *One Hot Minute* lacked an 'Under The Bridge' or a 'Higher Ground', so the only reliable method of shifting units was to work their fans into a state of concert-hall delirium.

That plan was now indefinitely on hold. Smith broke his wrist during a weekly softball game with a crew of friends that he referred to as "a bunch of Hollywood knuckleheads". Those close to the band were probably thinking that Smith fitted pretty well with his team of "knuckleheads", given the disastrous timing of his accident. There was simply no way that his fellow Peppers could work with a replacement drummer – breaking in one new guy (Navarro) was plenty. And Smith's on-stage physicality was an integral part of their live sound. He was the band's tower of power, the backbone of their sound; the Peppers needed to have him on stage with them at all times.

The tour was reluctantly postponed and the Peppers wouldn't hit the road until February 1996, by which time *One Hot Minute* was in serious chart decline (despite having shifted over a million copies by the end of 1995). Back in LA, Flea returned to his yoga mat, Navarro to the free-lance life and Kiedis to his supermodel partner, as they waited for their drummer's wrist to heal. It was a frustrating end to a disappointing year.

Smith was all apologies by the time the band finally played their rescheduled dates. "I feel bad about it," he said, as the Peppers reached Seattle in April, "because it really [screwed] up a lot of people when the tour had to be cancelled. I'd like to apologise to all those people who bought tickets or waited a long time to see us. I'm really sorry."

Although the very large-scale tour – where they played "basketball arenas named for banks", according to one caustic onlooker – would be a sell-out, it seemed as though their fans didn't quite have the patience that Smith had hoped for. *One Hot Minute* simply lacked the commercial staying power of *BloodSugar*, while the critical reaction had been lukewarm, at best. Even the video for 'Warped', which featured yet another homoerotic snog, this time between Kiedis and Navarro, failed to shock their fans into action at the cash register. All it did was enhance rumours that there was some atypical sexual behaviour going on amongst the seemingly very male, very straight Red Hot Chili Peppers. Navarro, naturally, laughed off any suggestion that he and certain band members had "gone to the other side", reminding whoever was willing to listen that he was no stranger to "making out" with men. "Perry [Farrell] and I used to do it all the time," he stated. "I'm pretty open with sexuality."

Kiedis hosed down any talk of a romance between him and Navarro. "When we kissed in the 'Warped' video," he said, "it was totally unplanned – and it wasn't [evidence] of a homosexual affair. To me, it's more important to express a feeling of love and not be at all concerned about what people are going to think about you."

The video for 'Warped', however, did draw some negative feedback from the band's label. Flea was given an ultimatum by at least one staff member at Warner. "[They] told us to stop making pretentious, faggy videos." This left Flea confused. He thought he looked "really suave and handsome" in the clip.

Manager Goetz was equally turned off by the clip. "I thought it was a stupid thing to do." He felt that the band had needed to strip things back and cut a "rocking performance video", but instead they opted for something artier.

One video that was unlikely ever to receive airtime was a rockumentary that Navarro had started to compile of himself and his fellow Peppers, in the vein of Led Zeppelin's mighty *The Song Remains The Same*. A writer from *Spin* magazine, who was given a private screening by Navarro, was suitably shocked. "It features Smith," she wrote, "in some sort of medieval metal-head executioner drag sporting a papier-mâché strap-on [dildo] the size of a Scud. As for Navarro, who best resembles a Mexican dominatrix, he spends his camera time being prodded from behind with the aforementioned phallus."

In the end, 1996 was another downbeat year for the band in commercial terms, as their chart worth started to slide – if you can call almost two million domestic sales of *One Hot Minute* a "slide". Yet despite the sell-out tour through America, Europe and Australia, despite the heavily suggestive – sometimes even pornographic – videos and their penchant for bringing strippers on stage (much to the shock of Oz teen rockers Silverchair, who shared several US bills with the Peppers during '96), *One Hot Minute* wasn't inspiring Kansas housewives to get "loosened up a bit", as Kiedis wished during the *BloodSugar* days. And Dave Navarro was looking less like a permanent member of the band.

But it wasn't as though the tour was completely without highs. Long-time hero Iggy Pop joined them on stage at New York's Madison Square Garden for a wild take on the Stooges' 'Search And Destroy'. River Phoenix's sister Rain joined the band, singing back-up vocals, helping Flea and Kiedis deal with the loss of another comrade. And the band's reach was now so wide that as conservative a publication as the *Christian Science Monitor* covered – and enjoyed – their Madison Square Garden show.

But the album simply refused to sell at the same rate as *BloodSugar*. And it wasn't as though there was some major generational change happening in music, as the band had witnessed (and benefited from) during Generation Lollapalooza. Apart from yet another Beatles resurrection, with the massive *Anthology* set, and more rumours of the second British invasion, this time headed by Oasis, the charts in 1996 still reflected the usual mix of R&B, some less threatening hip-hop and mainstream pop.

On the alt-rock front, the Peppers' former touring partners, The Smashing Pumpkins, had finally broken through the indie barrier with their *Mellon Collie And The Infinite Sadness* album. This was a familiar scenario for the Peppers: first Nirvana, then Pearl Jam and now the Pumpkins – all who had opened for the band in the Lollapalooza era – had crashed their way into the mainstream consciousness. Yet the Pumpkins still had to share airtime with such easy-listening rockers as the Goo Goo Dolls or Hootie & The Blowfish – there was no underground riot going on in 1996, as there had been in 1991.

In the past, the band would have responded to their low year with either a return to the studio, where they'd be hell-bent on making a better album, or another all-points tour. But the Chili Peppers decided to do neither. Instead, they decided to go into an extended recess. Apart from a few one-offs – a take of John Lennon's 'I Found Out' for a tribute album, compiled by Goetz, who was also tiring of the band's inertia, a cover of the Ohio Players' 'Love Rollercoaster' for the *Beavis And Butthead Do America* soundtrack – the Chili Peppers wound down towards the end of 1996 to the point that the following 12 months would be described by Flea as "a year of nothing". For a band that played and talked so loudly, their silence had many fans and pundits wondering if the Chili Peppers would ever work together again.

CHAPTER ELEVEN

"I don't care whether I live or die."

"HIS upper teeth are nearly gone now; they have been replaced by tiny slivers of off-white that peek through rotten gums. His lower teeth, thin and brown, appear ready to fall out if he so much as coughs too hard. His lips are pale and dry, coated with spit so thick it looks like paste. His hair is shorn to the skull; his fingernails, or the spaces where they used to be, are blackened by blood. His feet and ankles and legs are pocked with burns from unfiltered Camel cigarette ashes that have fallen unnoticed; his flesh also bears bruises, scabs, and scars. He wears an old flannel shirt, only partially buttoned, and khaki pants. Drops of dried blood dot the pants."

When Robert Wilonsky, who was the Arts Editor of the *New Times LA*, eventually tracked down John Frusciante at Hollywood's Chateau Marmont Hotel in late 1996, this was his harrowing description of the once lean, mean riff machine. Via a connection at American Recordings, Wilonsky had organised an interview with the reclusive guitarist, who reluctantly agreed after months of negotiation. When Wilonsky finally met Frusciante, he understood why.

"I don't know what I expected to find," Wilonsky told me, "but I walked into that hotel room and found this mess. My most vivid memory was that I thought, 'That's not how a guy who played on those records should be living.' I was saddened. He just looked a mess; this sickly shadow.

"And given what had happened to Hillel Slovak, this was just too much. I mean, another Chili Peppers death? I remember thinking that he just didn't deserve that kind of fate."

Since leaving the band mid-tour in 1992, Frusciante had gradually fallen apart. When he returned from Japan, he retreated to his Hollywood Hills home, hit the couch and sank into a bottomless depression, punctuated only by the recording and low-key release of his 1994 solo album, infrequent jams at the Viper Room and occasional trips to his easel. Tales of Frusciante's meltdown drifted around LA, in much the same way that the legend had spread about Hillel Slovak's wayward-ness. "All I'd ever hear about for years and years," Jack Sherman told me, "were stories about him and Brian Wilson in Tower Records and who was in the worst state." Frusciante was racked with doubt, unsure if he should have quit the Peppers. He was unsure if he should have joined them in the first place. He was also becoming a stone junkie.

"Can you imagine what it's like?" Wilonsky said. "You're in the band you love – it must have been as thrilling as it was horrifying."

But, perversely, Frusciante was convinced that his life improved when he turned to smack. "I became a junkie and came to life again and became happy and started playing music again," he insisted. "But I couldn't exist at first [after leaving the band]. I was so depressed.

"I just decided without [heroin], I have no control over what thoughts take over my brain. See, with this, I have control over what I want to think about. With heroin, I was able to all of a sudden have the power to get rid of those things that would pop up into my head and think about something else. Like, all of a sudden I wasn't the boss of my head any more."

When Wilonsky spoke with the former Pepper, Frusciante didn't eat regular food; instead he gulped cans of a high calorie formula normally fed to invalids. And his hotel room not only reeked of faeces and urine, but radiated "the smell of death", according to the journalist. Frusciante's only possessions were a few guitars, some CDs and his junkie paraphernalia. (He disappeared once during his interview, Wilonsky presumed, to get high.) Before moving to the Marmont – often called the "Hotel California" – Frusciante had left behind a nearly unlivable house in the Hollywood Hills whose walls were scrawled with such bizarre (and unintentionally comic) messages as: "Stabbing pain with discipline's knife" and "my eye hurts". The scene was so downright creepy that Johnny Depp and Butthole Surfer Gibby Haynes had made a private film about both the house and the state of Frusciante's mind. After he missed payments – and an accidental fire – Frusciante was evicted.

Frusciante recalled the chaos in a later interview. "It [his house] burned down, then it was rebuilt, and then I moved into it, but I stopped paying for it. And eventually it was taken away from me. I almost saved it – my lawyer got me the money to get it back. But it was sold the day I got the money. That was fine with me, because that was 50,000 extra bucks I could spend on heroin."

When Frusciante was thrown out of the Chateau Marmont (where, according to Wilonsky, "bigger names than he have checked in to check out", including comic John Belushi, who OD'd there in 1982), he then picked up his guitars, CDs and syringes and shifted to the Mondrian, on Sunset Boulevard, another infamous Hollywood hangout. But he was again evicted. When Wilonsky tried to track him down after the interview, Frusciante had simply disappeared, leaving him with this chilling farewell: "I'm not [afraid of death]. I don't care whether I live or die."

Flea was the only Chili Pepper to keep in regular contact with their former guitarist, jamming with him and former Jane's Addiction drummer Stephen Perkins, in an outfit called the Three Amoebas. Wilonsky is sure that Frusciante's former bandmates knew of his slide, but were frustrated by their inability to connect with him on any level. But even Flea would have been stunned when he read in the *New Times* of Frusciante's deterioration, which was reflected in his second solo album, *Smile From The Streets That You Hold*, which emerged in August 1997. If *Niandra LaDes* had been a tough listen, this was downright harrowing. "It's a dark ode to the demons and spirits that inhabit Frusciante's head," wrote *Guitar Player*'s James Rotondi, when he heard this set of fractured four-track recordings, rife with cryptic lyrics, strange guitar noises and an overwhelming sense of despair. To Wilonsky, the record accurately reflected Frusciante's decrepit state at the time. "It was interesting, far out, frightening, weird, cool, scary – it seemed like the kind of record a man with demons would make."

Yet by the time of *Smile*'s release – on the Burbank-based Birdman Records label, home to such avant-gardists as Thee Headcoats and Omoide Hatoba – Frusciante was insisting that he was on the mend. Wilonsky had heard that the guitarist was so embarrassed by his sorry state when he read the story, it may have inspired him to seek help. He'd definitely bottomed out at the end of 1996, checking himself into a drug-treatment facility when he was told that if his rotting teeth weren't replaced by dentures, the infection could kill him. He'd lost his

Smell My Finger: Flea, Frusciante, Smith and Kiedis (from left) collect yet more silverware at the 1999 *Billboard* Music Awards. *(Frank Trapper/Corbis)*

Firestarter: As Flea stripped down for Woodstock 1999, riots and looting erupted in the crowd and the place went up in flames. "I had no idea what was going on; nobody on stage did," Chad Smith insisted. *(Reuters/Corbis)*

Me And My Bodyguard: Flea and muscle, leaving the taping of TFI Friday, London June 1999. *(LFI)*

Two Peppers in a pod: "My best friend is Flea." *(Steve Wood/Rex Features)*

Chili Jam: Kiedis, Flea and Frusciante (from left) dig deep, Reading Festival 1999. *(Brian Rasic/Rex Features)*

They're Red Hot: Smith, Flea and Frusciante collect more silverware at the 2000 MTV Video Music Awards, New York. *(LFI)*

Can't Stop: Kiedis and girlfriend Yohanna Logan, Flea and daughter Clara at a film premiere, LA, November 2000. *(Pacha/Corbis)*

Michael Balzary, aka Flea: "I'm just a
sensitive little fuck."
(Anthony Saint James/Retna)

John Frusciante: "I was this close to
killing myself."
(Anthony Saint James/Retna)

Chad Smith: "Big old Chad should have
been playing in Lynyrd Skynyrd."
(Clay Patrick McBride/Retna)

Anthony Kiedis: "I have no regrets or
shame or guilt."
(Anthony Saint James/Retna)

Mainstream Acceptance: Kiedis and Logan at the Academy Awards, March 2001. "I had a huge 'love at first sight' kind of a wallop," Kiedis would reveal. *(LFI)*

The Chili Peppers 2004: "Professional craftsmen, with or without their shirts." *(Anthony Saint James/Retna)*

"This guy from Detroit eats drums for breakfast": Chad Smith and his Harley; during 1997 he dislocated his shoulder in a spill. *(James Cumpsty/Redferns)*

Sergeant Peppers Funky Hearts Club Band: Kiedis, Smith, Flea and Frusciante (from left).
(Clay Patrick McBride/Retna)

John Frusciante returns to the Peppers: "It got into my head that stardom was something evil." *(LFI)*

My Friends Are So Distressed: Dave Navarro and Chad Smith reunite backstage at the filming of 2001's *MTV 20: Live And Almost Legal. (Kevin Mazur/WireImage)*

The Californicators: Flea, Smith, Kiedis and Frusciante (from left).
(Clay Patrick McBride/Retna)

home, his health, most of his friends – now even his damned teeth. Frusciante was also stone-cold broke, accidentally giving away his last $2,000 to a lucky cabbie. Frusciante couldn't sink any lower.

Flea visited him in rehab – as, unexpectedly, did Kiedis – and by March 1997, the slowly recovering guitarist plugged in for a set at The Whisky A Go-Go with Thelonious Monster. Flea got up and jammed with him, grinning broadly. It appeared as though, in Wilonsky's words, John Frusciante was "no longer a rumour".

Back in camp Chili Peppers, their "year of nothing" plodded along. Chad Smith became a father again in March, when his daughter Manon St John was born (sadly, Smith and his "Greek goddess" wife, Maria, would eventually divorce). There were some vague Pepper plans in the works – July shows in Alaska and Hawaii, the possibility of a set at the now annual Tibetan Freedom Concert. But two more accidents – Kiedis broke some ribs after coming off his bike, Smith dislocated his shoulder when he fell from his Harley – meant any gigs were either canned or indefinitely placed on hold. Maybe The Sensitives weren't born to be wild, after all.

If Kiedis hadn't been dabbling with heroin beforehand, he definitely was now, as he tried to wean himself off the painkillers that he swallowed as his ribs were mending. ("When I use drugs," he told MTV, as he slowly recovered from his injury, "my life sucks.") His relapse was distancing himself from his bandmates and frustrating manager Goetz, who was starting to think about retirement.

Flea and Navarro were not the kind of guys to stand still, waiting for something to happen. *Kettle Whistle*, an assortment of Jane's Addiction unreleased tracks, demos, live recordings and one new track (the title cut), was released in November. When Navarro was asked to join the reunion tour to promote the album, he readily agreed, inviting Flea to fill the spot left vacant by former bassist Eric Avery (who opted to keep working with his new band, Polar Bear). When Flea signed on, the rumour mill kicked in: were the Chili Peppers about to be cannibalised by their LA brothers Jane's Addiction? The rumour grew even stronger when Navarro and Chad Smith hung out and started jamming ideas for a project called Spread. As for Kiedis, he was long gone: he'd disappeared to Mexico, "to get high", according to Lindy Goetz.

In early interviews talking up the album and tour, Flea and Navarro were adamant that the Peppers were alive and well and currently on an extended vacation. Or so it seemed.

"I want to clarify that the Chili Peppers are not breaking up," Navarro announced. "Flea and I are more than happy to do both projects, time permitting. The way I look at it is, I'm in the Chili Peppers and I'm doing this thing with Jane's Addiction."

Flea was even rhapsodising about the next Chili Peppers album, although the band had absolutely no new music in the works – or even any plans – to record a follow-up to *One Hot Minute*. "I look for the next Chili Pepper record to be the greatest Chili Pepper record," he crowed.

But he wasn't telling the full story. At the time, Flea had started planning a solo album and he'd approached Goetz not only to help him promote the record, but manage his solo career.

Flea's frustrations intensified when the Jane's Addiction tour began. Once on stage, he could see a significant change in Navarro. He saw something in his playing that he'd not witnessed when he was a Chili Pepper.

"The first night I went out with Jane's Addiction," he said, "I felt this incredible unleashing from Dave. He was just going for it and I realised he could never do that in the Red Hot Chili Peppers."

Dave Navarro's days as a Pepper were fast running out.

Kiedis knew that in order to get clean, he needed to leave LA. Nine years earlier, when Slovak died, he'd holed up in Mexico, but this time around he'd gone there to get high, so he needed to drift even further. The now-recovering singer ended up in India, travelling through much of the country by himself (obviously his survival skills had improved since his aborted jungle journey with Henk Schiffmacher a few years earlier). He led a charmed existence. One night, hanging between two rail carriages and taking in the evening sky, his train derailed, yet he walked away with only a few bruises. He visited an ashram and then hiked into the foothills of the Himalayas, where he made it to the source of the Ganges. There he boldly swam in the wild waters. "The local guys told me this river is like a mother," he said upon his return. "'It will love you' [he was told], so I kinda believed them and I went swimming for days on end. The currents would hurl you around these giant boulders and nothing bad would ever happen."*

Though Kiedis would never admit to it, it is likely that he also underwent drug rehab while on the subcontinent.

The only chance that The Red Hot Chili Peppers had to set foot on stage during 1997 was at Japan's massive Mount Fuji Festival, during August. But any notion that the band's fortunes were changing were swept away by the devastating hurricane that blew in, not only terminating their set, but blowing the entire festival out to sea. No one realised it as they ran for their lives, but this was to be Dave Navarro's last stand as a Chili Pepper.

Navarro had never been a comfortable fit, both as a guitarist and a bandmate. He seemed diametrically opposed to everything the band was about: they loved to play goofy, he was as serious as death; they dressed in day-glo colours, he wore basic black; they loved Funkadelic, he leaned towards Joy Division and *Berlin*. Not only did the band's flaming helmets and spaceman outfits not gel with Navarro, he also needed a broader musical palette to work with. The Peppers didn't truly offer that, because there was a certain expectation on the part of millions of listeners as to what they should hear from a Peppers record. The difficult *One Hot Minute* proved that they weren't mad about experimentation.

"Personality-wise, they are really at odds, really different kind of people," Rick Rubin said of Kiedis and Navarro. "Dave is dark-humoured, dark-souled, and Anthony doesn't appreciate that." Navarro's occasional dabbling with drugs only distanced him further from the band; by April 3, 1998, he had officially left the Chili Peppers. Again, the rumour mill kicked into overdrive, one even falsely suggesting that Navarro had left the band after a break-up with Kiedis (an observation based solely on their snog in the 'Warped' video).

As with so many of their former members, the band had nothing but warm feelings for their latest departure – at least publicly.

"I love Dave and I miss him," said Kiedis, who did admit that the "chemistry" wasn't right between the band and their latest axeman. "I

---

* Kiedis' powers of survival are remarkable. During the early Eighties he once drove a car into a tree, allegedly at somewhere near 90 miles an hour. Despite a body cast, he was back onstage within weeks. In 1996 he fractured a leg while skiing after attending the Sundance Film Festival, but kept touring *One Hot Minute* regardless.

hope we had fun and go on to be friends at a later time."

"I was honoured to play with Dave for the time that I did," Flea said in his typically lofty manner. "He is an epic and beautiful musician and human being, and I'm sure that we will do something again in the future."

When asked why Navarro was leaving, Flea's reply was ambiguous. "Not his fault, not our fault; it just wasn't working chemically."

The level-headed Navarro reciprocated accordingly – and he also had some sound advice for the band. He knew who would help the Peppers survive their latest crisis.

"I will miss the band very much. I have and always will have a tremendous amount of respect for all of them," he stated not long after jumping ship. "And I'll also say that my favourite [ex] member is John Frusciante."

This was all too much for Lindy Goetz, a true believer since signing on as Chili Pepper manager in 1984. He'd experienced the band's lofty highs and bottomless lows, but by 1998 he'd simply had enough. Kiedis was back struggling with junk; Flea was threatening to go solo; while Dave Navarro, who'd recently been on the outer with most of the band, had now jumped ship. "I was frazzled," Goetz admitted to me, "and everything was falling apart again. Plus there'd been a bunch of mistakes made with that album [*One Hot Minute*] – the wrong single release, the problem with the video. But I had accomplished everything with the band that I'd wanted to."

But before they made any kind of overtures to their slowly rehabilitating ex-guitarist, the band had to decide whether they actually wanted to keep rolling. Even long-time producer and band buddy Rubin was unsure. "Anthony was dealing with his own insurmountable problems, [the others] thought the band would not continue, there was too much anti-momentum," he said at the time.

And statements from Kiedis – "I embrace the bad, and bad or good" or "beauty can be found in darkness as well" – didn't exactly radiate positivity on his part. He admitted that even he was unsure what was going on with the Chili Peppers. "We'd never actually broken up," he insisted, "but I'm sure there were times when everybody thought to themselves, 'How can this carry on? It seems like it's not happening any more.'

"There were times in my most despondent periods when I couldn't see it getting better."

But it was Flea, as ever, who was the driving force behind this third coming of The Red Hot Chili Peppers. Having given up on the idea of a solo career, he knew that he needed the band as much as anything else in his life – and he also knew that the recovering Kiedis did as well. Despite all the tragedy that the pair had endured, as well as their recent fall from the top of the rock'n'roll ladder, it was the Chili Peppers, this band of brothers, that helped the two guys from Fairfax High hang onto their sanity. As rocky as the ride sometimes was, the band offered more stability than anything else in their lives.

Kiedis would eventually recognise that Flea – and also Smith – were the glue that held the band together during 1997 and into 1998, which proved to be two of their toughest years. "Flea was beyond patient and beyond compassionate," he admitted. "There was me going back and forth [and] things not panning out with Dave. I can't believe he was willing to hang in there as long as he did. Chad too."

But yet again they needed a guitarist. Flea sensed that Navarro was right – maybe John Frusciante was ready to return to the band. Of course, that would also depend on whether the band would welcome him back, or whether Frusciante was even interested in his old job. Flea's relationship with the guitarist was fine; he'd attempted to remain friendly with the guy, even when he was going through pure junkie hell. "I'd visit him," he recalled, "and he was always intense and into something, but I didn't think his brain and body could stand up to the amount of drugs he was doing."

But the relationship between Kiedis and Frusciante was different. Towards the end of Frusciante's first stretch with the band, the singer had turned very cold, not bothering to look Frusciante's way on stage. Nor did he speak with him during their long hours of downtime.

"When John quit the band, we weren't so friendly with one another," Kiedis understated, "and we had stopped enjoying what we were doing together. I was too self-centred and self-absorbed to even begin to experience what he was going through."

Frusciante would also recall the playground politics that went on between band members. "Before, it was always that Flea and Anthony were at odds with each other and I was always friends with one of them. It couldn't just be the three of us all being friends equally." Flea flatly refused to be interviewed alongside Kiedis, because, according to Lindy Goetz, "He was becoming too much of a rock star." Frusciante had his moments, too: when he and Kiedis were sent to Europe to promote *BloodSugar*, the guitarist was so out of control that Warners sent him home without completing a single interview.

But Kiedis' visit to the rehab hospital had been a minor break-through in his relationship with Frusciante, who'd openly admitted beforehand that, "I couldn't continue being in a band with him [Kiedis]."*

"Whatever happened before," Kiedis insisted, "it was all over with."

Flea then went to work: he invited Kiedis and Smith to his house, purportedly to watch a Lakers basketball game. It was there that he floated the idea of Frusciante returning to the Peppers.

"I knew something was up," Smith said about the bassman's call. When asked about the possible return of Frusciante, Smith's immediate response was very positive. "If it works and he's into it, sure."

But the singer was unsure. Would Frusciante even consider the idea, given his rejection of everything the band had embraced during the success of *BloodSugar*?

As Kiedis would recall, "He [Flea] said, 'What do you think about playing with John?' I said, 'That would be a dream come true, but it seems very unlikely.'

"And he said, 'Well, I don't know, I have a funny feeling about this,' and he called John up.

"Flea had more contact with him than anybody else," Kiedis contin-ued. "I ran into him a total of three times during that period [once, pre-sumably in the hospital] and it was always kind of strained and difficult for us to communicate. It was just a case of praying for him all the time – when I was well enough to be praying for anybody else."

Although no one would say it out loud, Frusciante was a far better guitarist for the Peppers, in part because he was more malleable than Navarro, a man who was very accustomed to playing exactly what he wanted. A lot had happened since he first joined the band, but there was still a little of the "Greenie" in John Frusciante. The now retired

* Chad Smith backed this up, stating that the relationship between Frusciante and Kiedis was "bad, really bad".

Lindy Goetz also knew it was a smart move to bring him back. "It was great they were doing this."

When Flea spoke with Frusciante and floated the idea of him rejoining the band, there was one key problem from his past – excluding smack – that he had to confront. When he left the band, Frusciante had no interest in playing the rock star. The band had simply become too big for him to handle, and he was repulsed by the way that Kiedis had embraced the spotlight. Now, despite the indifferent reaction to *One Hot Minute*, they were still a big business, whose every movement was documented by a Peppers-hungry press and a fanbase that covered much of the planet. Did Frusciante have the mettle to deal with this? How different was the 1997 version to the run-down, overwrought, drug-fucked John Frusciante of 1992?

It appears that one thing he did address during his season in hell was the concept of fame. Frusciante now had a better understanding of stardom – and how to cope with it. "I was very confused when I left the band," the mild-mannered Frusciante told *Rolling Stone*. "It got into my head that stardom was something evil. If you were a rock star, you were trying to put people on. I don't see it that way any more."

In a subsequent meditation on stardom, Frusciante proved how much his outlook had changed. "I think the rock star, his role in society, is a very beautiful thing," he told *Spin*. "Nothing more important to me was communicated at the age of seven than thinking about Zeppelin and Aerosmith and Kiss. There's something magical about it that transcends intelligence.

"That's the cool thing about being a rock star," he figured. "People don't really judge you. If they do, they can shove it up their ass, because you're a person who can do whatever you want."

John Frusciante had finally made peace with the past, which freed him up for the next stage in his life as a Chili Pepper. He was also able to find some meaning in the time that he'd spent slowly killing himself. "I spent six years going inside myself in a way that people who are stuck with the idea that they have to accomplish something with their lives never get a chance to do," he said of his time in junkie wasteland. "I was able to do what I was dreaming about, which was just sit there and do nothing – to feel no obligation to do anything for anybody. Or for myself."

He realised that he needed the Peppers in order to continue being a useful, productive musician. That was entirely logical; after all, the man had based his entire playing style and on-stage manner around the Hillel Slovak template – and the freewheeling days when he'd follow the band from one Hollywood club to the next were the best time of his life. "I realised that while I wasn't in the band," he would confess, "that I had this whole style of guitar playing that was now dead. Without these people to play with I had no place to play this style I had worked so hard to develop."

When Frusciante OK'd the idea of returning, Flea now had his beloved band together yet again. It was a Herculean accomplishment on the bassist's part, a challenge that required UN-worthy negotiating skills. But just as the band started to convene in his garage for some lengthy jam sessions in the spring of 1998 the 35-year-old Flea had another problem to deal with. He and Australian Marisa Pouw, with whom he had been living for some time, had broken up after several years together. He was distraught.

"It just didn't work out," recalled Flea's father, Mick.*

And whereas when he'd split with his wife Loesha in 1990 he'd been able to cope by getting laid constantly and smoking ounce upon ounce of pot, he now knew that those were ephemeral solutions, at best. This time he simply broke down and cried. A lot. It was a struggle for him to make it to his own garage and jam; all he really wanted to do was curl up on his couch, ideally in the foetal position.

"This time," he revealed many months after his second breakdown, "I didn't go with other girls – I dealt with it. I dealt with the most cold, empty feelings I could ever imagine. I walked through the pain."

He also had some assistance this time around: his daughter Clara was mature enough to help him cope. Clara assured her old man that she'd be there for him. One day, when she found Flea crying, she had some rock-solid advice for him. "Look, Papa, I don't know why you're so sad," she said, "but no matter what, it's going to be OK. You're such a good person."

"It was an amazingly touching thing," according to Flea.

In his typically cockeyed manner, Flea decided that one way to cope with his problems was to ditch all the superstitions he once held sacred, such as never leaving a book open on his bed in case the ideas leaked

---

* Pouw married after her break-up with Flea.

from the pages into his psyche, or refusing to wear black underwear.

"I was trying to do all these little things to prevent myself from being hurt," he said. "It's basically losing trust in the universe. I'm just a sensitive little fuck, you know?"

While the self-confessed "sensitive little fuck" gradually got his head together, the band had to start mapping out their next record. Flea, despite his pain, was the man with a plan. He wanted to make an electronica album. It was a bizarre notion – *One Hot Minute* might have confused their fans with its prog-rock stylings and lack of simple pleasures, but a virtually guitar-less Chili Peppers would have been a major shock to his fellow band members, fans, their record company, and the world at large. Even a group as universally loved as U2 had received a mixed reaction when they dabbled with electronics on their 1993 LP, *Zooropa*.

In the capable hands of such headliners as the Chemical Brothers or Prodigy, electronica – an urgent, rave-ready fusion of rock's volume and dance music's chemically enhanced energy – had the potential to change the musical landscape. It's unlikely a band with such a clear-cut range as the Chili Peppers could dare to be too different for fear of losing everything: fans, commercial worth, respect; the lot.

But still Flea persevered. "Personally," he confided in a *Spin* interview, "I feel the most exciting music happening is electronica, without a doubt." But when the band was turned down by producers William Orbit (who'd worked with Madonna on *Ray Of Light*) and Flood (U2's *Pop*), they knew it was time to get back to what they knew best. *One Hot Minute* had been a bold failure; they realised their next album should be simpler. More signature Chili Peppers funk'n'roll was needed.

"You know, we rock like a motherfucker," Flea acknowledged, once his electronica idea had been shelved. "I know that we can dig deeper and harder than anyone and people are always going to want that."

The first song that the band attempted to write in Flea's garage, as the summer of 1998 rolled around, would become the title track of their next album. The notion of 'Californication' had come to Kiedis during his disastrous Borneo adventure with Schiffmacher in 1992. Despite the title's suggestion, the song wasn't a trademark Chili Peppers' celebration of sexuality. It was more a consideration of the pervasive influence

Western culture has had on the rest of the world. As part of the band's return to familiar territory, Kiedis was back examining a place he understood better than most – California.

"I'd visit all these markets in remote and bizarre places," he explained, "and they were full of Guns N' Roses and Chili Peppers T-shirts and videos of all the Hollywood movies. These were locations that even Marlboro and Coca-Cola had a hard time with commercial infiltration. But California had found a way to seep into these tiny nooks and crannies of the globe and affect people."

But it wasn't until Kiedis was on the recovery trail, during 1997, on a boat crossing the Andaman Sea between Thailand and India, that he got around to coming up with the lyric that neatly pinpointed California's position at the westernmost point of America and therefore civilisation. It was one of Kiedis' most shrewdly observed pieces of writing.

'Californication' might have been the first song that he and Frusciante would attempt to write together, but it would be seven more months before Frusciante found the right notes, as he explained, in his pseudo-spiritual manner. "I didn't have the skill to figure out what chords God wanted until right before we went into the studio."

Songwriting was second on Frusciante's list of priorities during these early sessions. He was readjusting to playing with his former bandmates – and he was also working in a set of dentures, which replaced the rotting stumps he once called his teeth. He grew a straggly beard to hide the facial swelling. Combined with his stringbean-lean frame and shaggy hair, he resembled a kind of beatnik Jesus. Having sworn off drugs, alcohol and cigarettes, Frusciante would frankly state how he was simply coming to grips with once again being a human being. He was coming out of what seemed like a bottomless spiral, a time in his life when he felt "like an impostor who didn't deserve to even be called John Frusciante.

"I was trying to record songs, but never finishing any. And I was smoking crack all day long, shooting heroin, shooting cocaine, drinking wine, taking Valium. I was this close to killing myself."

Remarkably, Frusciante had still managed to be sufficiently lucid to know just when to pull back. "When I was . . . feeling I was about to die, I would get these warnings from the spirits saying, 'You don't want to die now.' I [could] see them, it was like they were there in my room."

The guitarist's talk of the fourth dimension and the spirit world might have been downright creepy, but somehow his invisible friends had kept him alive.

By the end of summer 1998 the band – except for Kiedis, who was once again struggling to generate lyrics to keep up with the output of new songs – were ready to head into Ocean Way Studios, where they'd tracked parts of *One Hot Minute*, to begin recording what would become *Californication*.

The only interruption to their garage sessions was a chance to re-introduce the band – and the newly revitalised John Frusciante – to the public, in early June. When the Chili Peppers were invited (again) to perform at the now annual, two-day-long Tibetan Freedom Concert at Washington's RFK Stadium, this time around they agreed (they had played the event in 1996, when Navarro was in the band, but had withdrawn at the eleventh hour in 1997). However, a huge storm washed out most of the first day's acts, which meant that the Peppers' slot was pulled. But still the band emerged after headliners Pearl Jam to deliver a surprise set. Just as the funky four were about to take the stage, photographer Tony Wooliscroft snapped them in a group hug. The image showed a band truly reunited; the photo was so evocative that it was used in the album sleeve of *Californication*.

Yet it was the night before, at a "secret" show at Washington's 9.30 Club, that Frusciante remembered what it was like to be a Chili Pepper again. In fact, it reminded him more of his days as the band's number one fan, when the Hillel Slovak-era Peppers would rock Hollywood clubs and, at least to John Frusciante, play like the greatest band on the planet. Once the Peppers completed a few more warm-up shows in Las Vegas during September, they knew they were ready to get back to serious work.

One Hot Minute was a musical marathon, a five-studio epic that took a year to cobble together. *Californication* may as well have been the work of an entirely different band, taking a little over three weeks to complete. Basic tracks took just five days.* It was a return to the *BloodSugar* period, when the idea of labouring over a track meant that it had

---

* It may have taken even less, but a replacement engineer, Jim Scott, was brought in a week into the recording.

actually taken more than a couple of days to complete. And this time around there was simply too much material, the band having mapped out somewhere between 30 and 40 new songs. ('Phfat Dance', Kiedis' own spin on Sir Mix A Lot's tribute to a big bottom end, 'Baby Got Back', was left on Ocean Way's floor, amongst several other discarded tracks.)

Rick Rubin was back producing, even though the band had dithered, briefly, after he first accepted their offer. Rubin had generously recommended other producers to the band, when they told him that they were thinking of going elsewhere. Naturally enough, they came back to the ZZ Top-lookalike who'd helped them strike gold with *BloodSugar* and then soldiered on during the tough, seemingly endless *One Hot Minute* period. That was especially the case when occasional producer – and another Peppers hero – David Bowie, who was top of their wishlist, rejected the idea of producing *Californication*.

"They had been writing a lot," Rubin told one reporter invited into the *Californication* sessions. "They hadn't made a record in a while, which was a positive thing. There was a lot of energy there; they were ready." Rubin even compared the 1998 version of the Peppers to the band with whom he'd shared a house back in 1991, during the *BloodSugar* sessions, although he did recognise that "they're more grown-up now than they were then." This time around there'd be no day-long pot sessions or sexual indulgences. They really had to work.

As for Anthony Kiedis, he felt stronger, having recovered from his slip off the wagon. He'd also fallen in love with a fashion designer named Yohanna Logan, whom he'd met while she was working at New York's über-trendy Balthazar restaurant.

Kiedis admitted to being smitten by Logan as soon as he cast eyes on her. "I walked in and had a huge 'love at first sight' kind of a wallop," he said. Her involvement with the lead singer had inspired him to start writing lyrics again. Kiedis would examine love from any number of angles during the *Californication* tracks 'Porcelain', a beautifully fragile ballad unlike anything the band had attempted before, and 'This Velvet Glove'.

And in the album's opening cut, 'Around The World', over one of Flea's signature slap-bass funk-ups, Kiedis makes what virtually amounts to a marriage proposal to Logan when he shouts, "You say hello and I say I do."

"Listen to that first track," Kiedis said at the time. "It's a straight-up love song. It's a marriage reference! There's three or four of them on the record. "I was so deeply in love when I wrote it," Kiedis added.

Another inspiration for Kiedis the lyricist was a male-bonding trip he'd taken with Frusciante and Flea, just prior to the sessions. The three of them had packed Flea's truck with food and music (The Germs, The Cure, David Bowie) and driven to Big Sur to catch some waves. The acoustic-guitar-driven album closer, 'Road Trippin'', documents the adventure. "Road trippin' with my two favourite allies," Kiedis wrote on the first night, as the trio lit a fire and strummed acoustic guitars like funk-rock hikers. Then he added a line about Big Sur, and closed by referring to themselves as three hunky dorys.

"By the end of the day," Kiedis said, "I had this song about our trip – that we were together after all this time and doing something as pure as surfing and writing music."

But recording *Californication* wasn't easy for them on a personal level – Frusciante was working his way back into the band, Kiedis and drugs were a day-to-day proposition, and Flea was still trying to cope with his break-up, what he described as "a breakdown, a psychological melt-down . . . I was falling apart at the seams".

Even Kiedis was unsure how long this creative surge would last, euphemistically admitting that the band did suffer from "an instability factor".

"We all know not to project how many years this thing is going to work," he said during a brief period of recording downtime. "[But] right now, it's working like crazy."

The songs were virtually pouring out of the band – John Frusciante had even located the missing chords for 'Californication'. When asked about the track, Kiedis continued to defend its misleading title; this was no celebration of macho posturing. "It's a natural reaction to be inspired by your environment," Kiedis said, referring to what he would describe as California's "competing energies".

"It's got the lowest-of-the-lowlife-superficial-liposuction-mania-wanna-be-famous-for-a-minute weirdos," he added. "And then it's got the most beautiful mountains, deserts, oceans and history of creativity of almost any place on earth."

Kiedis wouldn't say it out loud, but if there was one superstar who encompassed the inherent contradictions of his adopted hometown –

physical perfection contrasted with deep personal flaws, the simultaneous search for real meaning and the desire for an escape from reality – it was Kiedis himself. The album's title track was as much about him as his adopted hometown.

As ego-driven as he was, Kiedis wasn't above a little self-deprecation. The track 'Around The World', a raucous slice of rockin' funka-motion, came complete with a lyric that ran along the lines of "ding dang dong dong ding dang dong dong ding dang". Kiedis defended it as "scat singing", but it seemed more like the desperate act of a man short of worthy lyrics. It was quite a backwards step for someone who prided himself on the sometimes spiritually searching tone of his words.

"I always intended for it to be that," he insisted. "When it came time for the recording, I did that during the session and they said, 'OK, so you need to get the rest of those lyrics written.' I said, 'No, that is the song.'"

Fortunately for Kiedis, Clara Balzary, as good a sounding board as anyone else for the merits of a pop song, liked what she heard. "She thought it was the best part of the song," Kiedis boasted. "So it stayed."

Californication's centrepiece was 'Scar Tissue', which would also become its lead-off single. A downbeat ballad from the 'Under The Bridge' school, it was flavoured by a genuinely aching solo from Frusciante – described as the sound of "California sliding into the Pacific" – and loose-limbed, supple backing from the band. It was another of Kiedis' Hollywood stories, a sad tale of wannabes and drifters, of a "young Kentucky girl in a push-up bra" and a "southern girl with a scarlet drawl" who are used and abused by the City of Angels.

The song's evocative signature line – "with the birds I'll share this lonely view" – came to Kiedis as he and the band jammed the song in Flea's garage, well before shifting base to the studio.

"I heard something resonating in the room," he recalled, "a particular sound that wasn't necessarily exactly what they were playing, but a sympathetic sound." Without warning, Kiedis ran out of the band room, so "my brain could isolate it from what they were playing. And it was both that melody and that lyric. And . . . there were these giant hawks circling around. Maybe for a minute I connected with them, being a solo flier, and the idea of looking down on the world like that.

"That's the type of lyric I like best," Kiedis said, "because I didn't have to come home, sit at my desk and look out the window and search for it. It was like an arrow shooting into my head."

Whatever the source, it was one of the band's finest moments, a few minutes of soulful pop that would stand alongside 'Under The Bridge', 'My Lovely Man' and 'Breaking The Girl' as one of their most sadly beautiful ballads.

The band knew that in order to return to the rock'n'roll winner's circle, it was necessary to revisit some of those elements that made the band so big in the first place: Flea's urgent basslines, the white boy funk of Frusciante's tasty fretwork, the muscular crack of Chad Smith's drumming. They needed to recapture the manic energy of *BloodSugar*, the type of sweaty surge that could light up a moshpit. And amidst Kiedis' scat singing and the high, lonely wail of John Frusciante's haunting harmonies, *Californication* had plenty of these explosions, such as the gurgling bassline of 'Around The World', the dumbed-down, sweaty jam that was 'Get On Top' and the plain old-fashioned juiciness of the title track. The band had settled on a reasonable middle ground, embracing a lyrical and musical maturity on the more restrained 'Otherside' and 'Porcelain' and yet delivering exactly what was expected for a good chunk of the album. Flea stated, "If you eliminated *One Hot Minute* and made another record after *BloodSugarSexMagik*, it would be this record. This record picked up right where we left off with *BloodSugar*."

But even as the record was being prepared for release – complete with a deceptively unsettling cover image, visual proof of their complicated relationship with California – no one in the band, or elsewhere, was willing to bet on this being any kind of comeback success. When 'Scar Tissue' was released as a single, it was battling for airtime with such acts as TLC, Destiny's Child, Eminem and Puff Daddy, while Limp Bizkit, Korn and Marilyn Manson were the newly crowned spokesmen for hormonally confused, shirtless moshpit loons. What *Spin* described as the "Great Alt-Rock Gold Rush of the early Nineties" was history. The advent of on-line downloading, led by the controversial Napster operation, gave music consumers even more freedom of choice.

Other albums scheduled for release at and around the time of *Californication* – which hit the shelves on June 8, 1999 – included long-players from Nine Inch Nails, Stone Temple Pilots and Chris Cornell, the erstwhile Soundgarden belter. In 1995 all of these records would have been guaranteed hits; now it wasn't so clear-cut.

"A couple of years ago, I would've predicted a rush of people for these albums," said Joe Kvidera, a manager at one of Tower Records' Chicago outlets. "But I don't think any band has a built-in following any more." When he was asked of the chances for the Peppers to score a comeback hit, he replied: "No one cares."

"Generation X is ageing and Generation Y is coming up," stated Jim Kerr, who was then alternative radio editor at *Radio & Records*, a music industry trade journal. "If you're 18 years old, you've lived your life exposed to hip-hop."

The cold fact was that an 18-year-old in 1999 would have been exactly three years of age when *The Red Hot Chili Peppers* was released. The band and their new management, Q Prime (who were also Metallica's minders) knew this. So to reintroduce the Chili Peppers to a newer, younger audience they set out for a swift five-city tour of all-ages clubs, taking in Portland, Seattle, Minneapolis, Pontiac (in Michigan) and Philadelphia. The theme of the shows was Stop The Hate, in the wake of the recent horrific Columbine killings. This mini-tour was to be called 'High School Spirit', where the prize for the band's biggest fans was a private show at their school. But that was quickly revised after Columbine. Price of admission to the shows was a written suggestion on how to end hatred among high school students.

But apart from the community service, the unspoken intent was this: the band were searching for new converts. Most of their original fans now had the more pressing concerns of families and mortgages occupying their time and cash; what the Peppers needed was a following with expendable incomes and a willingness to embrace hard-bodied men in their mid-thirties as new rock heroes. The band also developed its Internet presence, opening themselves up to a whole new type of listener – the cyber geek. "Fleamail", an open letter from the band's bassist, came into existence just as the band went on the road towards the end of 1999 to tour *Californication*. Since then it's become an essential part of the band's web presence, plotting both their touring and recording activities and the strange thoughts that sometimes pass through the mind of their diminutive bassman. And from June 4 to

June 8, three new *Californication* tracks were "streamed" every day on the band's official website.

If it was true that "no one cares" about the Chili Peppers in 1999, someone forget to tell both the media and the record-buying public. *Rolling Stone*'s Greg Tate summed up both the evolutionary vibe of the record, and the band's recovery from the depths of *One Hot Minute*, when he reviewed the album.

"While all previous Chili Peppers projects have been highly spirited, *Californication* dares to be spiritual and epiphanal, proposing that [they] are now moving towards funk's real Holy Grail: that salty marriage of esoteric mythology and insatiable musicality that salvages souls, binds communities and heals the sick. Not exactly your average white band."

Many reviewers sagely noted that the band's return to form coincided with the re-hiring of Frusciante (although the guitarist would later admit that he wasn't operating at 100 per cent during the *Californication* sessions). "An obvious reason for their rebirth," wrote Greg Prato in *AllMusic Guide*, "is the reappearance of guitarist John Frusciante. Many figured that the Chili Peppers' days as undisputed alternative kings were numbered after their lacklustre *One Hot Minute*," he continued, "but like the great phoenix rising from the ashes, this legendary and influential outfit [has] returned to greatness with *Californication*."

Radio agreed. 'Scar Tissue' – complete with an appropriately downbeat video, where bruised and battered Peppers drove through the desert in a beat-up convertible – was an immediate hit across any number of radio formats. It spent an outrageous 16 weeks at the top of *Billboard*'s Modern Rock chart, which monitored radio airplay. The track was added to playlists by all 91 US radio stations with a modern rock format – the last track to receive the same kind of response was U2's 'Discotheque' in 1996. 'Scar Tissue' was also added by 168 mainstream and so-called "heritage" rock stations. It eventually peaked at number nine on the *Billboard* Hot 100 chart, while the album streaked to number three, pipped by only The Backstreet Boys and Ricky Martin. It was an amazing turnaround for a band that seemed ready to give it away only 18 months earlier.

With a huge global tour now planned for much of 2000, the Peppers shrewdly chose high-profile shows to celebrate their turnaround. On

July 25 they returned to Woodstock for the latest revival of that legendary festival. Woodstock 1999, however, was not the good-natured mudfest of five years earlier, when Dave Navarro made his first large-scale appearance as a Chili Pepper (very large scale, considering the massive lightbulb that was perched on top of his head).

Pre-Woodstock, the Peppers warmed up with a set outside the HMV store in Toronto on July 22, where the response was so over-whelming that local police were forced to close downtown Yonge Street to traffic during the 45-minute show.

By the time they reached Woodstock, however, the good vibes were definitely gone. The band didn't just look out on a sea of bodies; a wall of fire had also erupted in the huge crowd. But the Peppers didn't believe that the fires that began to blaze during their set were any cause for concern; they'd seen similar outbreaks at Lollapalooza. Kiedis simply thought, "Oh, must be about time for those fires." What the band didn't realise was that the fires were the result of a growing anger amongst the hundreds of thousands of parched, sunburnt punters at Woodstock 1999. Left without any kind of shade, and being forced to pay upwards of $4 for warm bottles of water, the crowd turned ugly as the Peppers' gig progressed.

Immediately before their set, the Peppers had been introduced to Janie Hendrix-Wright, Jimi Hendrix's half-sister who now controlled his estate and who was a surprise backstage guest. She was at Woodstock to try to organise a grand finale, in which upwards of a dozen guitarslingers would come together to perform one of her father's songs; they would then segue into what Smith described as "this big holographic Hendrix tribute". It didn't happen, but her presence did give the Peppers serious pre-show jitters. Flea dealt with the problem in a characteristic way – he asked Kiedis if he felt that playing nude would be appropriate. Singer turned to bassist and replied, "Well, nothing could be better for Woodstock." But their nerves turned to serious concern once on stage, when the fire chief began to indicate that he needed the Peppers' help.

According to Kiedis, "Some guy with a radio attached to his head said, 'We need your help, there are fires out there. We need to get the fire engines in.' So I expressed the need for a fire engine path."

Just as the band launched into Hendrix's 'Fire', Woodstock '99 quite literally went up in flames, even though the band were checking into their Manhattan hotel by the time the serious looting – and rapes, according to some reports – began. Tractor-trailers were torched, a sound tower was knocked down, souvenir stands were looted – even the "Peace Wall" that surrounded the site was torn apart before police arrived. Five people were injured and seven arrests made at what event co-producer John Scher described as "a frat party". For several hundred thousand, that is.

From the stage, as Chad Smith later recalled, there were no obvious signs of unrest. "I could kind of see these fires way, way away," he recalled, "it was like a mile away or something, the place was so huge. But I had no idea what was going on; nobody on stage did."

Kiedis was understandably concerned about the aftermath of the riots, although he wasn't ready to turn against the fans that were racing out to buy *Californication*. "As I understand it," he said after some kind of order was restored, "the kids had been treated unfairly for days. Why not make it so there's water for everybody and reasonably priced food and just the essentials of living for three days?"

By August 15, the Peppers bandwagon had moved on to a free show in Red Square in Moscow, where they were invited to help launch MTV Russia.* While the gathering was better behaved than Woodstock's one big mob, no one had quite predicted the band's popularity behind the former Iron Curtain. A crowd of 90,000 was expected; 300,000 Muscovites turned up. And they truly let it all hang out, as the *Moscow Times* reported, especially as the band moved into 'Under The Bridge'. "The slower ballad gave some fanatics an excuse to still their head-banging, take a swig of Baltika, urinate on someone and dash the bottle on the pavement."

Although Kiedis felt the city was still haunted by the "ghost of Stalin", he was dazzled by the response. "The people are beautiful and very soulful," he gasped as band and crew pulled away from Red Square, which he noted contrasted sharply with the American idea of Moscow being full of "gangsters and prostitutes". "They deal with adversity all the time and they make us look like spoiled brats." Flea, meanwhile, swore that he would marry a particularly attractive woman he had spotted on a Moscow street.

---

* An excited Kiedis agreed to the gig halfway through reading the contract's opening paragraph.

Next stop was Paris, where the venue was considerably smaller – they played at the 7,000-capacity Le Zenith – but the band were just as charged, seguing from 'Right On Time' into The Clash's 'London Calling' and 'Guns Of Brixton', then encoring with a rusty ramble through AC/DC's 'Back In Black', before bidding au revoir with Hendrix's 'Fire'. Three days later, with Clara Balzary, Rick Rubin and Sporty Spice (aka Mel C) sidestage, the band rocked the annual Reading Festival.*

The next day Flea got naked, yet again, at the Leeds Festival, while Kiedis reminded the huge crowd how things had changed since their first UK trip, when the band "played Dingwalls in London to 47 people".

As for John Frusciante, he was gradually playing himself back into the band, indulging in a solo spot most nights. Although he'd usually settle for a favourite cover, it did give him the chance to perform the rarely heard 'Your Pussy's Glued To A Building'. Punters scratched their heads, went and bought drinks and waited for the next hit.

'Scar Tissue' had been followed by another single, 'Around The World', which was the standard opener during the *Californication* tour, whose set lists were notable for the almost complete absence of *One Hot Minute* tunes. Though not quite the runaway hit that 'Scar Tissue' was, 'Around The World' – which was launched on October 26 with a set on the 107th floor of New York's World Trade Center – rode high in both *Billboard*'s Modern Rock Tracks and Mainstream Rock Tracks charts, as the band prepared for a headlining slot at the Australian Big Day Out during January 2000.

Despite a worrying crowd crush at the Sydney show, where their set was interrupted for 10 minutes while some kind of order was restored, their return to Oz was another huge success. There were, however, backstage rumbles that recalled the band's frequently frosty past. But this time around the arguments were about performance, not drug abuse or disinterest.

Ken West was one of the Big Day Out's two event producers. West was a festival veteran who understood that his role was almost as diverse as the bills that he presented to half-a-million Australian punters each

---

* Kiedis would document his brief fling with the Spice Girl in the song 'Emit Remmus'.

summer. During Big Day Out 2000, he found himself in the unfamiliar role of boxing referee.

"I broke up a backstage fight between the Chili Peppers," he admitted. "They totally had their fingers in each others' faces about someone being out of time or out of tune. I've seen bands get into full-on punch-ups over this stuff [before]. I just barged in and pointed out how bloody lucky they were. Their tour manager cringed but they took it OK."

Yet Kiedis was spreading the word of band unity when he returned home from the Big Day Out. "Our Australian experience will go down as probably our favourite touring jaunt of all time," he announced. Somehow he'd forgotten about the backstage flare-up.

Once the band had each returned to their neutral corners, *Californication* sales figures started to trickle in. By early 2000, their comeback LP had sold three million copies worldwide, with almost 2.2 million of those in the USA alone. It was in the top 25 selling albums of 1999, right alongside *The Backstreet Boys*, Lou Bega's *A Little Bit Of Mambo* and Mariah Carey's *Rainbow*. And their gigs raked in the cash – when they wound down their big year with a show at San Francisco's Cow Palace, the gross was almost $500,000.

When 'Scar Tissue' was awarded the Best Rock Song Grammy in February 2000, their reinvention was complete. The Chili Peppers were the band that simply refused to die.

CHAPTER TWELVE

"The results are considerably better than they were during my junkie time."

THE *Californication* album was the sound of a band of brothers reunited. And its success proved to Kiedis, Flea, Smith and, most crucially, Frusciante, that – commercially speaking – this was the definitive Chili Peppers line-up, the perfect intermingling of brawn, brain, sweat, tattoos and musical empathy. The fact that the album eventually sold 12 million-plus copies, and spawned a two-year-long tour of full arenas, sweetened the deal considerably. It also gave the band the luxury of taking a year to prepare their eighth long-player, which would eventually become *By The Way*.

But while they might have been a band reunified, when the four reconvened in Flea's LA garage in early 2001 to start jamming song ideas, working during the week and recharging at weekends, it became clear that Frusciante was taking the songwriting lead. He was hell-bent on atoning for his years out of creative commission, as well as making up for the time – and brain cells – he'd burned during his half a decade away from the band (along with his house in the Hollywood Hills, of course).

He admitted that the *Californication* period was a struggle, a period of readjustment. "As good and as happy a time as it was for me, I felt barely adequate as a member of the band," Frusciante said. "I was really practising a lot and trying to make up for all the lost time when I hadn't been playing guitar for a few years."

By the time they moved into rehearsals for their new album, Frusciante had straightened out, giving up every conceivable vice – coffee, alcohol, cigarettes, pot – along with smack. His new drug of choice was Ashtanga yoga. He made a point of finding 45 minutes every day to work through his bending and stretching routines.

Frusciante was also in love with music again. In the midst of his smack addiction he'd totally given up on music – not just playing it, but listening to it. Now his stereo was thumping 24 hours a day, as he spun everything from New Order and Depeche Mode to Abba and Queen. On the few nights he left his home, he'd go to drum'n'bass clubs and "freak out" to the music, just like he'd done years earlier at Chili Peppers shows. He found a sonic soulmate in producer Rick Rubin (who'd already turned much of the band onto transcendental meditation); together they would get lost in such chestnuts as The Association's 'Cherish' and The Seekers' squeaky-clean 'Georgy Girl', not exactly the type of pop cheese you'd expect to be faves of the producer of records from The Beastie Boys and Slayer, let alone the Chili Peppers. But so it came to pass – and in a strange subliminal way these songs would have an influence on their next record. "He's got these CDs of AM radio hits from the Sixties," Frusciante said of the burly, bearded producer. "Those songs were all about harmonies."[*]

A regular visitor to Frusciante's home during this time of writing and listening was his pal Josh Klinghoffer, a member of LA band The Bicycle Thieves, who'd supported the Peppers on some *Californication* dates. He and Frusciante had become harmony freaks. They'd sit cross-legged, singing along to any song they knew that was powered by harmonies. Their playlist included dozens of Beatles songs, as well as such tunes as The Velvet Underground's 'Jesus'.

Instead of hearing the voices of spirits in his head, Frusciante was now hearing rich harmonies. Every bit the musical student, he was a regular at LA's huge Amoeba Records warehouse, snapping up every doo-wop record he could find. He would take them home and study them closely, in order to get his harmonies as note perfect as humanly possible. He was also soaking up such pop masters as The Beatles, Burt Bacharach and The Bee Gees, as well as the music of jazzman Charlie Mingus. The Mamas & The Papas were another Frusciante favourite at the time.

When Radiohead's Thom Yorke wrote the lines, "Fitter, healthier, happier" on the band's breakout 1997 album, *OK Computer*, it was as

---

[*] *By The Way*'s harmonies would so impress Fugazi's Ian MacKaye – a man whose opinion Frusciante respected greatly – that he told him they were the best thing on the record.

though he was foreseeing the improvements in this gently freaky 32-year-old guitarist/songwriter.

But before the Peppers could begin work on *By The Way*, Frusciante had another solo record, his third, to get out of his system. Though not a perfect album by any stretch, *To Record Only Water For Ten Days* was Frusciante's most lucid solo release. For starters, it was the only album he had recorded while straight – he admitted that his previous solo records, 1995's *Niandra LaDes And Usually Just A T-Shirt* and 1997's *Smile From The Streets That You Hold* were made mainly to raise money for drugs. The album was entirely Frusciante's baby. He wrote and played every note, as well as recording and producing the record himself. All the music was crafted at his Hollywood home, using mainly acoustic guitars, an Akai sampler, a 1980 Korg analogue synthesiser and a drum machine. It was all recorded onto the most bargain-basement eight-track equipment. Frusciante's use of the ancient synth and a drum machine was very much a nod towards the music that meant so much to him when he was a teenager: the first couple of (rarely heard) Human League albums, and especially the bleak Goth-pop stylings of Depeche Mode. These records had now become the soundtrack to his daily exercise regime.

"I usually think about [Depeche Mode's] David Gahan and Martin Gore when I do yoga," he admitted. "That's the best meditation for me, just to start thinking about a rock star that I really love."

To take his love just that one step further, Frusciante had played a one-off show as part of a Joy Division covers band during Chili Peppers downtime with Flea and Josh Klinghoffer at Spaceland in LA. They played a fund-raiser for a local school that Flea would go on to describe as one of the best shows of his life.

Naturally, Frusciante's obsession with dark Britpop extended to his own playing. It got to the point where he taught himself how to play most of the period's better-known synth lines on guitar.*

"That was very much the way I wanted my guitar playing to be," he explained, when asked what influence this time in music had on his playing. He spent much of his time learning parts from Kraftwerk and Depeche Mode, Human League and Orchestral Manoeuvres In The

---

* Proof of that influence can be heard on *By The Way*'s chilly sounding 'Warm Tape'.

Dark. "I was finding that people who were programming synthesisers in this early electronic music were playing in a very minimal way, where every note means something new."

To Record Only Water For Ten Days was a world away from the Rick Rubin-produced albums of the Chili Peppers; this had all the intimacy of a home recording – which, given the way the LP was created, made perfect sense.

"It's probably inspired by the songwriters who I like, like Lou Reed and David Bowie and Syd Barrett," Frusciante said. He would name-check *The Madcap Laughs*, by Pink Floyd founder Syd Barrett – who eventually pickled his brain with LSD and was tossed out of the band, something Frusciante could easily relate to – as one of his favourite albums.

The songs started to come to Frusciante between November 1999 and April 2000, while the Chili Peppers were touring *Californication*. Still adapting to the wider world after his five years locked away bingeing on drugs and communing with spirits, Frusciante spent most of his downtime on the *Californication* tour locked away in a succession of hotel rooms, avoiding the many temptations that can be found on the road. Writing songs was a logical thing for him to do to fill in the empty hours between shows, the period that many acts have called "long stretches of nothing in between two hours of bliss".

As he recalled when the album was released on February 13, 2001, "When the Chilis were first touring for *Californication*, I was carrying around a Fender Mustang electric for a while. I started writing so many songs that I decided, halfway through the tour, that I might as well bring an acoustic with me. Having an acoustic with me made it twice as much fun to be in my hotel room and be on the road and stuff."

Though occasionally as sweetly muddled as the guy who wrote them, Frusciante's lyrics on *To Record* offer handy insights into the man and his thoughts. The vivid opener, 'Going Inside', says plenty about his idiosyncratic inner world, suggesting that retreating into yourself is an enlightening experience, as many a meditating rock star has discovered before him. Obviously he hadn't quite finished with the spirit world.

When promoting the album, which included a low-key promo tour of Europe, Frusciante spoke at some length about these inner voices and how they had started to possess and torment him. "I always heard voices in my head as a little kid, but now I had an excessive amount of voices in my head all the time," he confessed. "So by the time I quit the Chili Peppers in 1992, I was devoting myself to nothing but magical process. I got to the point [at the peak of his heroin addiction] where I could sit in a room with a ghost or an astral body for half an hour at a time, which takes a tremendous amount of concentration. [But] now," he continued, "I have a very rich inward life functioning as part of the world."

As for the album's title, while it was a clear reference to fasting, Frusciante meant it to indicate a much less literal form of cleansing. *To Record Only Water For Ten Days* was a reference to what he needed to do to purify himself after his addiction. "It's like imagining one's body as a tape recorder," Frusciante explained, "and what it would mean to record only water for 10 days. I was so infested with all kinds of spirits eight years ago that it was really necessary for me to have a certain amount of fights and battles to cleanse myself."

Such frankness when discussing his album would lead to the occasionally cutting headline – "Freak Patrol Reporting for Duty", wrote *Guitar World* magazine – but *To Record Only Water For Ten Days* was a pivotal album, not just for Frusciante, but for the band. It mapped out the musical direction for the Chili Peppers' next long-player, as Frusciante started to channel deep harmonies and synth-pop melodies, not just abstract beings from the spirit world. He was becoming increasingly prolific as a songwriter, too, an obvious step to reclaiming the years he'd wasted getting wasted.

Despite their patronising tone, *Guitar World* praised the record, noting the influence of kindred spirits Lou Reed, David Bowie and Syd Barrett, Depeche Mode and New Order.

"The whole is still quite simple – stellar guitar work, impressive vocal range, drum machine, and minimal effects," stated *AllMusic Guide*'s Melissa Giannini, in her four-star review of the record, "but it's a much healthier and 'together' sound [than his previous solo albums]. Still a departure from the Peppers, *To Record* has an overall almost Goth-like singer/songwriter vibe, at times colliding into rock catharsis."

"*To Record Only Water For Ten Days* lacks the flashes of experimental brilliance found on Frusciante's earlier albums," wrote *Rolling Stone*'s

Neva Chonin, "but it quietly reaffirms the promise of a songwriter who can be simultaneously impenetrable, strange and oddly magnificent."

While Frusciante was busy making his third solo album and conjuring up ideas for *By The Way*, Anthony Kiedis was in the midst of rare domestic harmony with girlfriend Logan. Kiedis and Logan were spending plenty of time in his home in the Hollywood Hills, where every morning the most recognisable of all the Chili Peppers would be found exercising with his dog, Buster. Man and ridgeback would speedwalk two miles downhill – Kiedis was living at the highest point of the Hollywood Hills, north between the Hyatt Hotel and the Hollywood Palladium – and then run back up to his house together. Occasionally his father, Blackie Dammett, would visit and they'd hang out at Venice Beach or double-date at LA's seemingly endless assortment of chic eateries.

When he was alone, Kiedis would either be checking in on his favourite team, the LA Lakers – Kiedis once admitted that "we use the Lakers as a guideline for our own team" – or riding his scooter around Hollywood, shopping for art to sit alongside the Warhols that lined the walls of his home. Life was so good that the once-restless playboy was now starting to consider the once seemingly impossible path of marriage and children. Kiedis might still hang out with his father, but he was finally shaking off the bedpost-notching influence of Dammett.

Chad Smith had already started a family, but he was occupied during band downtime coughing up maintenance and sharing custody of his three children. His eldest, Justin, was now four. "I have more grey hair," he said at the time, when asked about the contrast between life as a Pepper now and in 1989, when he first joined the band. "[I have] more money in the bank, though I've been divorced once and in California they take half of everything."

Smith had also started taking his drum clinics on the road. This was a pastime that was now soaking up more and more of his energy when the Peppers weren't touring (although he sometimes held clinics while on tour). But he had no problems putting something back into music; after all, it had saved him from a life of Midwest dullness, even if California was working him over when it came to the matter of alimony.

Smith had started to appear in drum clinics when he attended the Percussion Summit '94 at the Memphis Drum Shop. He'd since become a key player in such events as the Guitar Center Drum Off, the world's largest and most well respected drum comp, where as many as 4,000 wannabe time-keepers would compete. Smith had performed at these events, alongside Mötley Crüe's Tommy Lee, former Prince drummer Sheila E, Jane's Addiction's Stephen Perkins, Travis Barker from Blink 182 and A Perfect Circle's Josh Freese. For his clinics, Smith would begin by giving a tutorial and he'd then drum his way through both Chili Peppers songs and such hard-rockin' standards as Led Zeppelin's 'Good Times Bad Times'. During 2000, alongside former Style Council drummer Steve White, Smith took the Smith 'N' White With Attitude tour to the people.

Flea, meanwhile, was bouncing between his daughter Clara in Los Angeles – she was now 12 – and his beachside retreat in Congo, on the Australian east coast, which he built in 1996.* A good half hour from the sleepy rural centre of Bateman's Bay, the even sleepier Congo existed in an entirely different universe to LA. The village, which can only be reached by a single dirt road, was so remote that it had no supermarkets, pubs or clubs. Locals would stock up on groceries and supplies in nearby Moruya and then retreat to Congo. There were no more than 100 houses in the hamlet, although it wasn't hard to spot Flea's $1 million plus spread, which overlooked the ocean and came with its own recording studio, should inspiration strike.

When in Congo, apart from his usual pursuits of meditation, yoga and surfing – which he took up during an Australian holiday in 2000 – Flea started mentoring a raw teenage garage band, Quirk, who would eventually open for the Peppers on their late 2002 Australian and New Zealand tour. Whenever Flea was back in LA, the core of the band, brothers Rory and Dane Quirk, would house-sit for the Chili Pepper. The brothers, who had met Flea by chance when surfing, were so in awe of the Chili Pepper that their first band was named Leaf, an anagram of Flea. Flea would sometimes spend months in Congo, surfing, lying on the beach and checking out the dazzling show put on most nights by the southern skies. Flea's birth father, Mick, with whom he'd become quite close, lived in nearby Tuross Head.

According to Jo Rugg, music writer for the local paper *The Narooma*

---

* He'd purchased the land in 1994; Kiedis bought a New Zealand property not long after.

News, "The locals are definitely protective of him. They don't make a big thing out of his celebrity and he enjoys the anonymity. It's good he can come here and unwind and not get hassled."

It was an unusual time for the Chili Peppers as 2000 wound down and the band recovered from the lengthy *Californication* tour. Not only were they all madly busy outside of Pepperland, they were also clean. They finally had no major concerns about drugs, relapses or off-stage friction. No wonder it all felt so unfamiliar.

Back in California in early 2001, Flea had his own non-Chili Peppers musical goal in mind. Ever since he blew the trumpet with his step-father and his jazz-playing pals, and especially once the Chili Peppers became a hugely successful act, he'd dreamed of opening a music school. Just like Smith's drum clinics, it was a valid act of payback. Music, after all, had helped get the drugged-up teenage drifter off the streets. A guest-conducting spot with the Junior Philharmonic Orchestra of California (in which he once played) was a big motivator, as was a very recent visit to his alma mater, Fairfax High, where he played for students and offered some career guidance. He declared that "being a musician is a very valuable thing and as worth studying for as any other profession". But what he learned was that the school's music pro-gramme was non-existent, killed off by California's Proposition 13 "tax revolt", which effectively put an end to all arts programmes. (The school's music programme has since been reinstated.) Flea was fired up. Music class at school had been the one discipline that he actually enjoyed – now they'd gone and shut it down.

The Junior Philharmonic guest spot was pulled off in typical Flea fashion. He stood on his hands at the venerable Dorothy Chandler Pavilion and led the orchestra, with his feet, no less, through a rousing rendition of '76 Trombones'. When he won the much-prized Golden Baton award that night, he made an acceptance speech that was clearly inspired by his recent experience at Fairfax High. He talked up "how public education needed to have music programmes". While driving home Flea realised that this was even more reason to start what would become known as the Silverlake Conservatory Of Music.

The third big motivator was a book that Flea had recently read, called *Songs Of The Unsung*. It was the autobiography of Horace Tapscott, which told the story of how the late jazz pianist had, in Flea's words, "formed an organisation in South-Central Los Angeles, sort of a cross between a music school and a community centre for art and poetry – he wanted to do something for his community that he came up in." In typical Flea fashion, he put down the book and got to work. "Fuck it!" he declared. "I'm doing it, no matter what!"

By early 2001, Flea was sufficiently wealthy – and idle – to start looking for the right venue for his house of music. He recruited two others – Keith "Tree" Barry, his long-time friend, as well as Pete Weiss, another Thelonious Monster alumnus (he was their drummer for a time) and Peppers pal. Flea approached Weiss with the idea in early 2001. Even though running a music school wasn't something that appeared on Weiss' CV, he was put in charge of the practical work required to make a reality out of Flea's dream.

Flea wanted him to help establish the school, to be built around and run by Barry, someone Flea considered "an amazing music teacher" with "a gift for kids and making people listen". Though mainly a viola player, Barry could play and teach virtually every instrument in the orchestra; he'd spent much of the past 20 years teaching music to children in the suburbs of LA. He'd recorded a solo album, entitled *Blew Year's Proposition* and had performed with Ray Charles. He was also an occasional Chili Pepper, having played on various Peppers tracks, arranged music for the band and toured with them. Even before then, Barry had played with Flea in the school band and orchestra during the Seventies, first at Bancroft Junior High and then at Fairfax. They'd also shared drugs and wasted days in a variety of Hollywood crash pads during their wild teenage years.

Flea's role, meanwhile – as described by the *LA Weekly* – would be "the genial house spirit". Or, as he put it: "Overseer and financial . . . guy." He would pick up the bills for renovation and equipment, as well as paying wages and rent. His Chili Peppers commitments would mean he wasn't frequently spotted at the conservatory, but his name and status were a sure-fire attraction for students. He gave the school serious street cred.

The trio knew there was really only one location for this kind of utopian notion: Sunset Junction, a Moroccan-style complex situated in a funky, slightly motley block of LA's famous Sunset Boulevard. Weiss felt that this section of Los Angeles was "a small town in a big metropolis". Weiss, who lived in the neighbourhood, noticed a For Lease sign one afternoon while he was doing his laundry. Weiss, Barry and Flea approached the landlord the next day and without a moment's thought Flea decided to sign up on the spot. (Weiss: "I was going, 'Dude, I think you're like supposed to, like, negotiate about rents.'") The site, located between the Carniceria San Antonio and an anonymous store front, had once been a thrift store. Right across the street was the Rough Trade Emporium, promoting "Sex, Leather & Spurs". The spot must have reminded Flea of the band's debauched early days of socks on cocks and The Kit Kat Club. The lease was signed in June 2001, at a time when the Chili Peppers were deep in preparations for *By The Way*. Weiss then hooked up with a designer, Wade Robinson; together they toured other music schools and music departments to work out Silverlake's exact needs (apart from three bohemians with a dream).

By the time of their first recital, in December 2001, the Silverlake Conservatory of Music looked pretty much like Flea had imagined. The large front room was decked out with photos of Bob Dylan, Jimi Hendrix, Joni Mitchell, The Beatles and John Coltrane; Flea supplied the Oriental carpet in the main foyer. Half a dozen tuition rooms-cum-cubicles ran off a corridor behind the reception area. About 25 teachers contributed their time to the school, teaching approximately 400 students, a reasonable balance of both children and adults. Clara Balzary even took some bass lessons there, although her blue-haired dad admitted that it possibly wasn't right for her. "She just kind of got out of the seriousness of it; and I'm not sure whether to force her to continue doing it or not." Such well-known local players as Barry Matos, a Latin percussionist and bandleader, were offering their services to the non-profit music school. Flea's fanciful musical dream had become a community service reality.

While Flea was doing his bit for music-loving Los Angelenos, John Frusciante was bursting with musical ideas. During the little downtime he would permit himself, he'd either be checking out his much-loved *Star Trek* or be kicking back with his girlfriend Stella Schnabel, the daughter of renowned artist and film director Julian Schnabel, who would design *By The Way*'s very impressionistic cover art. "She is a beautiful woman who makes me feel very good about myself; she is one of those girls who can spot an asshole a mile off," he said of her.

"Greenie" Frusciante, the wild man who would size women up as sexual trophies, was long gone.

But most of his time was devoted to songwriting benders, often for incredibly lengthy stretches of time. With his concentration sharpened by hours on the yoga mat, Frusciante was searching for the perfect riff. "Sometimes I will sit in my home, looking for new riffs for 24 hours in a row," he confessed, "and the results are considerably better than they were during my junkie time."

Frusciante's Zen-like levels of commitment impressed his bandmates. Kiedis was moved to remark on the insatiable nature of Frusciante's musical appetite: "Eventually he will have been influenced by every form of music ever invented." Smith, typically, when asked about Frusciante, cut through the hyperbole: "Having John back really made a big difference," he said. "He's an incredible musician who is inspiring to be around." Smith was sure that Frusciante could have written the band's next record "in about half an hour". Even Rick Rubin chipped in, stating that the string-bean thin guitar man "lives and breathes music more than anyone I've ever seen in my life."

Flea would also buy into the Frusciante lovefest. "He's so focused and dedicated, he's inspiring to me. He just plays all the time. He gets up, gets out of bed, grabs the guitar and starts playing." But this was not uncommon behaviour for Frusciante. While the four were recording *Californication*, at the end of each day's session, three quarters of the band would go home and crash. Not Frusciante. Flea recalls calling the guitarist one morning and asking him about his evening. "What did you do last night? I slept." Frusciante replied, "Well, I wrote three songs."

Strangely, it was a very different *By The Way* that started to take shape in Frusciante's now yoga-supple mind. In the same way that *Californication* was originally planned as an electronica record, the album that he first dreamed up bore little resemblance to the record that eventually emerged in July 2002. He'd envisaged a tough, gnarly punkish set of songs, inspired by The Germs and other hugely influential but short-lived outfits he'd seen when he was a kid wandering up and down Sunset, dreaming about playing guitar in the Chili Peppers. The Germs, of course, were also big faves of the teenage Flea and Kiedis.

And Frusciante had also recently been tuning into The Damned, a

British band of punks with a sharp pop sensibility, who'd lived in The Sex Pistols' large shadow for years, even though they were the first UK punk band to record, tour and chart in the USA. They'd reached LA in May 1977, the same year that the seven-year-old Frusciante and his family had moved there from New York. They eventually hit the UK Top 10 in 1986 with a soaring cover of 'Eloise', a Europop monster from the Sixties, before splitting in 1989 (and then re-forming in the 21st century when punk nostalgia became a big-earner).

"We came up with all these punky, rough songs," Frusciante recalled of the first batch of demos for *By The Way*. "I was listening to The Damned a lot and got influenced by their rock'n'roll-like punk style. Originally I was thinking of having this be a more authentic punk-rock album."

But when Rick Rubin heard some of the songs in development, he felt this new, punky outlook was a step in the wrong musical direction. His observation would turn out to be incredibly canny. Rubin had also heard some of the warmer, more gentle melodies that the band were mapping out – songs not unlike those on Frusciante's *To Record Only Water For Ten Days* – and he thought that the contrast between that kind of pop and the punk demos Frusciante was talking up was simply too great, too abrasive. He convinced the rest of the band into sticking with the sweeter songs. Frusciante, who was now generating musical ideas at a freakish rate, also acquiesced, albeit reluctantly.

"At first I didn't agree with him," Frusciante admitted, "but in the end we agreed that the melodic songs sounded more innovative. And that is the important thing for me; to be able to develop yourself on a musical level as well as on a personal level."

Frusciante did, however, find some value in writing the punkish songs that were discarded. "In retrospect, that was a way of getting our energies flowing in a certain direction. I don't think that these songs [that ended on *By The Way*] would ever have been written if it wasn't for the small collection of Damned-style songs."

Along with The Damned and doo-wop, this musical mix of classic pop and sun-kissed harmonies would go some way towards explaining the rich mosaic of musical styles that drifted through the finished album's 16 tracks.

Not the kind of guy to do things in a half-assed way, Frusciante even took lessons from Kiedis' singing coach, in order to get his harmonies note perfect. His drug addiction had been superseded by a musical obsession.

Kiedis, Flea and Smith were knocked out by the sheer number, and the quality, of musical ideas Frusciante was bringing into Flea's garage as their rehearsals continued. But just as they started to bang the songs into shape, the horror that was 9/11 occurred. Two US commercial airliners, hijacked by members of the Al Qaeda terrorist group, crashed into New York's Twin Towers, killing upwards of 2,000 people. Another hijacked airliner crashed into the Pentagon, killing more than 200, while a fourth was brought down in a field outside Pennsylvania. Everyone on board that plane was also killed. It was America's worst peacetime disaster, an act of terrorism that ranked only with Pearl Harbor in sheer ferocity, surprise and body count. While the entire nation shut down and tried to understand what had happened, most Los Angelenos started looking at the skies; surely, they justifiably figured, they would be the next to be attacked after New York and Washington?

As for the Chili Peppers, they had to decide whether to continue with these pre-production sessions for *By The Way*, which were well advanced. Flea's first thought was to retreat to his hideaway in Congo; that had to be a safer option than staying in the USA. "I don't know if it consciously changed what we were doing or not," Flea would comment later on. "I can't really speak for anyone else, but I was really affected by it. It was a pretty incredible blow for the psyche of America and the psyche of the world. It was very sad."

Kiedis was equally bewildered, although he eventually found something positive to take away from the disaster. "For a couple of days, we stopped rehearsing," he told *Billboard* magazine. "Then John started feeling antsy. He was like, 'We have to make music. This is what we do and this is how we make the world a beautiful place.'"

Frusciante, now clearly the driving force behind *By The Way*, wanted to carry on and use the music they were making, in Kiedis' words, "to fill the air with something beautiful".

"I can't say that [the band] had a collective reaction to the terrorist attack on America," Kiedis added. "Will it affect what we do? At our core level of working to make music, the answer is no. We get together and give opportunity to our creative spirit to thrive like we always do.

As to how our music circulates through the population at large, there may be changes. Corporations seem to be psychologically impaired as a result of the attack. That won't stop us from rocking the fuck out, and we will play live wherever we feel like it when the time is right."*

Having decided to return to the garage, the band now had to work out just who would produce the songs that would become *By The Way*. Rubin – who'd helped them break out with *BloodSugarSexMagik*, had hung with them through the torturous sessions for *One Hot Minute* and had brought them back to life with *Californication* – had already checked in on the sessions (when not playing retro DJ with Frusciante). It seemed logical that the band should stick with the guy, now widely regarded as the fifth Chili Pepper. He was becoming as essential to the band's record-making process as George Martin was to The Beatles' evolution from goofy moptops to studio masters. There was the type of unspoken understanding between the Peppers and Rubin that would take years to develop with another producer. And he'd also helped resurrect their career (and livelihoods) with *Californication*, so there was some serious payback due here.

Unlike their uncertainty at the time of *Californication*, the band didn't even opt for a show of hands when it came to choosing to work with Rubin again. As Kiedis explained, they were comfortable with the producer; why mess with a multi-platinum formula? "It's a non-choice at this point," he said. "There have been times in the past when we've thought about working with a new producer – and discussed it – and it might be interesting to create a new chemistry by hiring another person. But in the end we were thinking that it didn't amount to anything. There is something really powerful about sticking with the camaraderie, the fifth member being Rick. It was just kind of a given."

To Frusciante, Rubin brought unity to the band's songs. "As long as we have Rick to give us a sense of balance," he figured, "[the band is] always going to wind up creating a perfectly balanced album. I don't know anybody else that I would trust in that way."

---

* Curiously, though, the band had cancelled a one-off show in Israel during August 2001, citing security reasons. When asked about this, Flea turned decidedly testy. "We were scared of getting bombed in Israel. That's not funny – and don't you dare fucking laugh."

The band rented Room 78 of LA's notorious Chateau Marmont to fine-tune the new songs, and Kiedis and Frusciante virtually moved in. It was familiar turf for Frusciante, who had actually lived there for a stretch during his darkest days, not long after he accidentally burned down his house. Being elegantly wasted at the Chateau Marmont was a given, so it was a peculiar choice for a band whose members included a recovering addict in Frusciante and a twice reformed heroin dabbler (possibly more) in Kiedis. Maybe they were challenging themselves – it says something about the pair's recovery that the serious temptations of the Chateau Marmont didn't interfere with their creation of new music.

The room they rented was on the top floor of the hotel, facing Sunset Boulevard. Frusciante surrounded himself with guitars and a ProTools recording rig, while a microphone was set up in the bedroom. Kiedis assigned himself the job of interior decorator, lining the walls with movie posters from the Forties and Fifties: *Creature From The Black Lagoon*, *This Gun For Hire*, *Sullivan's Travels*. He also installed an Andy Warhol poster of Jean Cocteau. Frusciante loved Room 78 so much that he stayed there during most of the pre-production for the album. The band also recorded parts of the album there. The location that was very nearly Frusciante's final resting place had now become a cosy, creative second home.

After almost a year of rehearsals, pre-production and recording, at Flea's garage, the Chateau Marmont and LA's Cello Studios, the basic tracks for their eighth album were finished by Christmas 2001. All that remained was for Kiedis to record his vocals. A tired but satisfied Flea spoke with the British press briefly at the end of the year.

"I've more or less done all my contributions to the record," he said. "And since I'm a terrible singer there's not much for me to do at this point."

But even before their end-of-year departures – Flea was disappearing to his Congo retreat, where he would end up spending a month coping with life- and property-threatening bushfires, former rivals Frusciante and Kiedis were planning to kick back together in the Caribbean – there had been some gentle rumblings of activity in camp Chili Pepper.

In November, the band were acknowledged at the annual Musicians Assistance Program (MAP) awards. MAP's purpose in life was to aid musicians suffering from drug and alcohol addiction; its coordinator was the ubiquitous Bob Forrest. As Kiedis acknowledged on the night, he and his band had plenty of reasons to thank the organisation.

"Without MAP being there for my band," he said, "we may not have been able to make music for the past few years."

It didn't hurt that Kiedis, along with other formerly drug-troubled performers Dr John, David Crosby and Hugh Masekala, had helped MAP raise $250,000 at a $500 a plate dinner held in LA during October 2000.

The band gave something more back in December, when they put in a surprise set at the annual Silver Lining Silver Lake concert, a fund-raiser to support the Hollywood Sunset Free Clinic, which had been offering free health care for hard-done-by Los Angelenos for over 30 years. Introduced by host Robert Downey Jr, the Chili Peppers put in a set that premiered new tracks 'Don't Forget Me' (which would turn up on *By The Way*) and 'Fortune Faded', which was held aside until 2003's *Greatest Hits* set.

"Thank you Silver Lining Silver Lake for giving my band a chance to be of service to my community," Kiedis said from the stage with no small amount of humility. "Let the good health flow freely to the people who need it."

It may have been a charity gig, but the band's label, Warner Bros, weren't going to miss the chance to start spreading the word about the band's new music. By January 16 the label began streaming video footage of the Silver Lake show at the Online Live Concert Series section of their website, a useful reminder that 2002 was going to be another banner Chili Peppers year. Four days later, more than 20,000 tickets were grabbed by eager Irish fans for their late June Dublin show. All signs were positive on the Peppers front.

In April the band were given an Artist Contribution award at the second annual ESPN Action Sports and Music Awards, in recognition, as one reporter cheekily noted, "of the skaters and surfers who've had the band's songs blaring out of their headphones for years". Later that month it was announced that the Peppers would be the star attraction "at the bash of the [Canadian] summer", the Molson Canadian House Party, to be held in August. Kiedis wasn't too enthralled – the gig probably reminded him of their MTV Spring Break debacle in Florida back in 1990. He admitted that he "loved small arrangements [but] not necessarily this variety of small arrangement.

"Any time when it's a contest or there's some sort of commercial involvement," he added, "it becomes a little bit humiliating. [But] it's nice to play with people right up in your grill."

This wasn't the first time the band had found themselves involved in a strange promotion. They'd once been the "gift" during an Internet-based competition that resulted in them playing at a student girl's apartment complex. But right now they were happy to be back spreading the word.

Kiedis continued working on his vocals throughout the first quarter of 2002, stopping only briefly for a speaking engagement at UCLA, the same school where he had bailed out of being a Political Science Major some 20 years back.

Sitting in front of 15 keen students who were interviewing him about his life and career, Kiedis twitched and shifted in his chair. He was as nervous – possibly more so – than standing in front of 20,000 fans screaming their lungs raw. "Coming back here gave me some creepy feelings," he admitted. "I hated it here. I really did. My personal experience at that time didn't meld with any kind of conformity or structured environment. But . . . I love certain ideas about school. I love what it does to your head to be forced to read and write. I had a couple of cool teachers, but the rest just terrified me."

When asked about their record under development, Kiedis described some tracks as "the Bee Gees meet The Beach Boys" and also came clean about his heavy-hearted lyrics. After an autograph session, he was back in the studio, alongside Frusciante, who was still sprinkling his sonic fairy dust on the 20 tracks that had been recorded. During rehearsals in Flea's garage, the band had erected a blackboard, which filled up very quickly, according to Kiedis, as their jams morphed into something resembling songs. "It was covered with about 50 different working titles of . . . pieces of songs and ideas and grooves."

"There's a lot going on," Frusciante reported from the studio in April. "There's a lot of overdubs and a lot of work has gone into the production."

By this stage, an exhausted Kiedis admitted that he'd lost the ability to gauge the worth of the music the band had recorded.

"I can't even tell if it's good any more," he said. "I mean, there are days I feel like this is the greatest thing we've ever done, and there are days that I'm like, 'This is just going to die in the water.'"

In fact, Kiedis seemed more interested in talking about hip-hop's new shit stirrer, Eminem, than his band's upcoming long-player. His interest in the rapper was perfectly logical: if there was any band that knew something about the wrath of the censor and how negative an impact that cultural conservatism can have on your image and career, it was the Red Hot Chili Peppers.

"Eminem's lyrics are as funny as ever," Kiedis told a Scottish reporter. "The thing that cracked me up most wasn't intentional, but it was the amount of times he says 'me'. Talk about acquired situational narcissism – he has it in spades."

Kiedis wasn't the only Chili Pepper having trouble working out whether their new record was brilliant or boring. Frusciante – along with the rest of the band – was dragged away on an overseas promotional tour for their album, even before *By The Way*'s final mix was complete.

I spoke with Frusciante not long after this strange time when he would have to politely excuse himself from interviews in order to listen to mixes that he had downloaded on his computer. Even for this mellow Californicator, his frustration was obvious. "I feel it's the best record we've made," he assured me, "but there was a point where I was in Europe and they'd send mixes through an ISDN line and I'd give my comments and they would change stuff and send the mix back. I was very all over the place. I was uncentred.

"Years ago I didn't care," he continued, "[because then] all I did was play my guitar. But now with all my backing vocals and playing other instruments, I'm more involved."

More involved was a hefty understatement; the album was John Frusciante's baby.

Neither Kiedis nor Frusciante should have been too concerned. When the first single, *By The Way*'s title track, was given a worldwide radio premiere on May 27, the day before its official release, the response was overwhelmingly positive. It seemed as though the *Californication* lovefest was set to continue. It was a confirmation that Frusciante's return to the Peppers brotherhood was very much the right move for band, management, label and their collective bank managers.

"It's as if the band looked back at its collection of hits," *Billboard* wrote of the lead single, "then tossed the best elements of each into one eyeball-popping composition. " 'By The Way'," they continued, "is the musical equivalent of that high school dude who wore stripes, patterns and polka dots and somehow managed to look cool."

"The Red Hot Chili Peppers return with their most adventurous, loosest single in years," reported *BPI Entertainment News Wire*, "a manic outing that chains together sweet, melodic verses with a head-banging lead to the chorus, then a pure, runaway pop hook."

And the track was a radio hit. By mid-June it had reached number 55 on the *Billboard* Hot 100 and number 12 on the Mainstream Rock Tracks chart. It reached number nine on *Billboard*'s Modern Rock Tracks chart. It coincided with the band celebrating (chamomile teas all round) an unprecedented 13 year run on the Modern Rock Tracks chart, a hit-making stretch that began with 1989's 'Knock Me Down'. If that wasn't enough, the quartet had now scored 19 Top 10 hits in the Modern Rock Tracks chart, which placed them fourth behind U2, Pearl Jam and R.E.M. In some ways it was a shame that the band had dried out, because they had plenty to celebrate.

What they did, instead, was head to the Garage in North London. There they played to 400 punters, which was one of their smallest audiences since their Grand Rapids "homecoming" in 1984, when Flea flashed the crowd and they were chased out of town. This "secret" club show was received like the second coming – and the band clearly loved the idea of rocking such a stripped-back gig. Playing low-key shows such as these was an idea that arena acts like The Rolling Stones had warmed to during recent world jaunts. You could pack the stadiums for the cash and the flash, and then play the occasional club show to hone your chops and actually see your audience. Flea celebrated by dyeing his hair electric blue; he and Kiedis were so ready that they had dispensed with their shirts even before hitting the stage.

Leading off with 'By The Way', which would soon become the regular opening number for their shows, the Californian four worked their way through a solid bracket of new tracks, as well as a wild 'Give It Away' and a soulful take on 'I Could Have Lied'. Then Frusciante stepped forward for his own tearaway take on UK band Sweet's glam rock standard, 'Fox On The Run' – the audience repaid his local knowledge by chanting his name. Flea and Kiedis looked on like benevolent older brothers, which in many ways they were. The

Peppers closed the show with 'Under The Bridge', which UK popsters All Saints had recently covered, badly, even though the royalty cheques provided the band with some comfort.

The show was the hottest ticket in London, in more ways than one. "Sweat dripped off the walls, never mind the group's bare, gleaming torsos," wrote *The Times*' David Sinclair, who went on to ponder the band's "distinct homoerotic undercurrent" and bemoan how the new wave of funk-rock fusionists, such as nu-metal knuckleheads Limp Bizkit, couldn't match the Chili Peppers in any number of ways. "Thank goodness they are back," he concluded, "to show the rest of them how it should be done."

The band were in cracking form, which didn't necessarily help their support acts. At Dublin's Lansdowne Road, Frusciante favourites New Order tried to cope with the 40,000-plus crowd's general indifference. "Tell yer dads you saw us," snarled frontman Bernard Sumner, before exiting. Pop-metal belter Andrew WK suffered the same treatment in London's Wembley Arena on June 26. He was booed and jeered and then used as the target for a few half-empty beer bottles.

But with actress Gwyneth Paltrow looking on, the Peppers bounded onstage in London like homecoming heroes. Flea even walked across the stage on his hands. "I love England and your pies and mash and your Echo & The Bunnymen and your soldiers in red with big hats standing guard," he declared before running out of breath.

"The Peppers are comprised of three hyperactive frontmen and an animal drummer," surmised *The Times*' David Sinclair, back for his second Peppers helping. "They were on astounding form."

The Guardian's Alexis Petridis was equally impressed. "Approaching their forties, surrounded by reductive progeny, the Chili Peppers seem suddenly interested in ageing with dignity." Both writers gave the show a four-star review.

The band were on a natural high by the time they returned Stateside – and the album hadn't even been released yet.

As with their previous three long-players, *By The Way* does run too long at 16 tracks and 68 minutes. The Chili Peppers remain a group sorely in need of an editor. And the album doesn't share the vague thematic link that binds its predecessor – Kiedis' notion of the "Californication" of the universe. But the band had never released such a solid, diverse and melodic set of tunes. This was an album where the tattooed four moved beyond punk-funk and embraced their inner pop band.

Mind you, you wouldn't know it from the title track, which starts the record with an old-school Chili jam. Flea's slap-happy bass kicks in 30 seconds into 'By The Way', swiftly followed by one of Kiedis' trademark scattergun sex-and-sin raps about skinning, turning tricks and making leeway. It's as typical a Chili Peppers song as you were likely to hear on *By The Way*, an album that would confuse some die-hards but also open up the 20-year-old quartet to an entirely new audience.

'Universally Speaking' was the Chili Peppers' first step in a very pop direction. Kiedis did his best to pull off a legitimate croon while Frusciante's sun-kissed harmonies swirled behind him. And rather than throw in a bassbin-rumbling Flea solo or a squealing guitar, the song was propelled by subtle strings and keyboards. Kiedis then headed back under the bridge with 'This Is The Place', another of the band's very LA-inspired scenarios.

In a voice loaded down with sorrow and regret, Kiedis sings of a place where junkies gather and time becomes meaningless. But these few minutes of rock *noir* were more about restraint than an ejaculation of sheer noise. That was also the case with 'Dosed', one of many broken-hearted ballads on the album, where the once bulletproof Kiedis sang of his inability to disappear within himself while, in the background, another of Frusciante's crystalline guitar figures waltzes sadly, echoing Kiedis' melancholy lyric.

Of course it would be criminally negligent of the Californicators to completely suppress their powerhouse engine room of Flea and Smith. They funked up the not entirely satisfying 'Can't Stop' and several other tracks on *By The Way*. But by letting Frusciante run amok with synths and mellotrons and voices – mostly overdubbed towards the end of the Rick Rubin-guided recording – the band had become (in the well-chosen words of *Rolling Stone*) "the alt-rock Aerosmith (minus the screeching and beseeching power ballads), creators of music that could be at once credible and commercial." As strange as it would have seemed 10 years earlier, the Chili Peppers were now a pop band.

The sweet hooks and eminently hummable harmonies flowed through *By The Way* like a river of sound. 'Zephyr Song', one of the album's many singles, was possibly the lightest, airiest song the band had ever cut, with a ridiculous lyric to boot, but it was no less joyous because of that. 'I Could Die For You' was a strummed-guitar-and-strings ballad, lifted above the maudlin by another aching confession from Kiedis and some guitar work from Frusciante that he declared to be among the best of his career. Equally light and tuneful was the acoustic led 'Cabron', though speculation about the exact meaning of the title has proved inconclusive. Some Spanish/Mexican speakers insist it is street slang for "asshole" while others define it more literally as Spanish for "cuckold", a man whose wife has cheated on him. Either way, it's an insult of some sort.

But judging by the downbeat tone of 'I Could Die For You' and 'Dosed', there was clearly trouble in paradise. It turned out that Kiedis had broken up with Logan during the recording of the album. While he was finally ready to commit himself to one person – apart from his dog, Buster – she wasn't ready for a family. Kiedis was heartbroken, and it showed in his writing.

On 'Midnight' he regrets the passing of the familiar. It's another tune powered by a gentle melody and Beach Boys-worthy harmonies. This was the type of vulnerability rarely displayed by a guy whose idea of male-female relations used to be about as well-considered and sensitive as "party on your pussy". Maturity can often be the curse of rock'n'roll (take the now cuddly, chat-show-ready Rod Stewart, for starters), but it brought out an intriguingly adult side to The Red Hot Chili Peppers, even if it meant that their vocalist was hurting both in song and in private.

In much the same way that Frusciante's musical concept of the album – with a little encouragement from Rubin – morphed from punk to pop during its writing, the tone of Kiedis' lyrics shifted considerably during the record's evolution. In his Hollywood Hills home, writing lyrics while sitting in front of an enormous feature window with panoramic views of the LA basin, Kiedis had set out to compose a sweet batch of love song lyrics. Then things changed.

"I was madly in love with life and music and everything," he said of his mindset during the early phases of the record. "I was just connecting with the cosmos. There were times that my heart was so incredibly open to feeling all of the love in the universe that I felt like writing about it."

Kiedis' big love for life and music (and his girlfriend, clearly) soured considerably when his relationship with Logan ended. You could hear his discontent most strongly during 'Dosed', but it was all over the record.

When they were still coupled during 2002, Kiedis had told *Penthouse* magazine that Logan was very much his soulmate. He had extremely high hopes for their relationship. "What I want," he confessed, "is a companion who knows me and knows all sides of me and is that friend I can be myself around. Every night I go to bed I get into the same position with my girlfriend [and] it feels like the first time we've ever been in that position because it feels so good. To me, it's even a better feeling than being out at the club going, 'I wonder about this girl, I wonder about that girl.'

"Yeah, it's great having such a multitude of sexual experiences," Kiedis admitted, "[but] I'm lucky I still have an interest in sex."

But by the time of early interviews to promote the record, Kiedis let it slip that his dream of slowing down and maybe spending the rest of his life with Logan was over. He even admitted that his lovelife was in a slump since their split, which was a major revelation from the self-proclaimed Sir Psycho Sexy.

"I wanted to move in the direction of a family," he explained to Ian Winwood of *Kerrang*, "which for me is easy because I've found myself and I've found what I want to do, [whereas] she's sort of in the process of finding out who she is and trying to make her mark creatively. So we were at different points in our lives, unfortunately."

To some extent, the cause of their break-up was the usual stuff of rock'n'roll lives: in order to live with and love a performer, you need to understand the stop-start nature of their lives and the potential lure of the many temptations to be found on the road. Logan wasn't prepared to live their life in segments, with gaping six-month pauses while the band was touring, doing promotion or recording. Having children with Kiedis would have made the periods of separation that much harder. It was the same type of conflict that had caused Flea and his wife Loesha to split in 1990, likewise Chad Smith and his wife Maria.

"It wasn't easy," an obviously upset Kiedis told Australia's *Juice* magazine in July 2002. "She had a hard time accepting my job, really. She got pissed at me all the time because people gave me so much attention – she couldn't go for that one bit. And God forbid if I happened to know a girl's name and said hello. I'm getting anguish for the next 24 hours. That's way too much to take. I don't have a girl-friend now."

"I never fell out of love with her," he told another writer. "We're just not together. It wasn't a 'confused, what's going on, tragedy' break-up. It was kind of a 'it's time to go on a new path' break-up." Always on the lookout for inspiration, Kiedis found the heartache he was feeling a useful cue for his sometimes clumsy, occasionally teary lyrics.

Not the kind of man to miss the chance of getting his name in print, Kiedis' father even bought into the discussion of his son's love life. When *The Grand Rapid Press'* Jill Kipnis spoke with him about *By The Way*, Dammett figured that you could tell which lyrics his son had written before and after the split. "Fortunately the songs aren't about drugs any more," the occasional actor added.

When it came to matters of love and sex, Kiedis was in the enviable – but nonetheless confusing – situation of many rock stars. Due to his star status, too many people, especially women, considered the guy either unapproachable or unattainable. And those that did approach him, were, well, not the type of women the 40-year-old was seeking.

Kiedis readily admitted that women did throw themselves at him, but that held little allure for him any more. "It's like that classic state-ment that Groucho Marx encapsulated: if someone's going to give themselves up that easily, I'm not going to join that club."

The flipside was that there were successful females to whom Kiedis was drawn, but he was reluctant to approach them. "There are women whose art I admire," he said in the same interview, "and therefore I want to meet them and maybe have a chance of getting to know them. But I wouldn't want to just fuck them because they're famous."

Maybe Kiedis was suffering the downside of the sexual boasts he made when the band was loud, proud, snotty and virtually unknown. It takes a long time to live down such claims as that in *Freaky Styley*'s 'Nevermind', way back in 1985: They call me the Swan, he announces before threatening to love all the women to death with his magic wand. And his boast in 'Out In LA' about lining up 100 women and fucking them all didn't even bear thinking about.

But not only had Kiedis lost a partner, he and the band had also been losing friends, including Gloria Scott, someone very close to the band.

A grey-haired, straight-talking former drug counsellor from Venice Beach who'd survived her own toxic dependency, Scott had helped Kiedis and others deal with their addictions. When they found out she was suffering from cancer, the Peppers staged a benefit show for her at the Hollywood Palladium on March 1, 2001, helped out by Neil Young & Crazy Horse and the omnipresent Thelonious Monster (Perry Farrell was the DJ). As Scott's illness became terminal, they relocated her to an expensive apartment with a sweeping view of the Pacific Ocean and picked up the tab for the rent. It was there that she eventually passed away.

By The Way's soul-stirring closer, 'Venice Queen', was the band's musical tribute to the woman, a sort of moody rock'n'roll elegy. During the six-minute-long track, which has been acknowledged as one of the band's best-ever songs, Kiedis' voice cuts through a moaning synthesiser and mournful bass and drums, as he sang a simple farewell to his Venice Queen, intoning poignant rhymes that climax, inevitably, with . . . we miss her, before Frusciante's voice kicked in behind him. It was a poignant close to the album and a mark of how far Kiedis had developed as a word-man.

"I always found Anthony's lyrics interesting," said producer Rubin, "but it seems like they have gone from interesting abstract lyrics to personal, heartfelt lyrics. And I think that's because he's not telling a sex story but conveying a real emotional experience."

Scott's death hit Kiedis hard. During the last year he couldn't even count the number of times he'd found himself crying. He cried even as he wrote the lyrics to 'Venice Queen'. "Part of it," he explained, "was because I miss her but part of it was because it feels so good to sing about someone who meant so much to me. I'm good at losing," he sighed. "It's one of my specialties."

These heavy emotions also permeated the track 'This Is The Place', another Kiedis ode to Los Angeles. Not only was the song a meditation on the fast and facile side of the city, it was also a rumination on his very Hollywood upbringing, when he and Dammett prowled the city like two horny bachelors on a very long, lost weekend. Kiedis made his point very clearly by referring to his father's promiscuity and expressing his unwillingness to follow in his footsteps. He was casting a keen, sharp eye over his life up to now. Though the poetry wasn't rich with nuance or metaphor, his feelings ran very deep.

'Dosed' was a more interior lyric, clearly written about Kiedis' break-up with Logan. But listen up, because it also nodded to the *noir* fiction that he and Frusciante had been soaking up over the past few years. While away from the Peppers, Kiedis and Frusciante had been gorging on Dashiell Hammett and Raymond Chandler, two expert chroniclers of life in the City of Angels. "I think in the last three years both John and I fell in love with that whole genre," he told writer Peter Murphy.

Parts of the track 'Dosed' ponder the beauty of Kiedis' former partner, but the song also told a second story, about a murder. "It's about loving someone so much that you actually kill them, even though I've never had a murderous instinct in me," he said. "The verses are kind of strictly about relationships. Then the chorus, even though I don't say it specifically, it's about killing someone you love."

The title track was another of the band's odes to their hometown, as well as being an attempt at "rock'n'roll *noir*". It was a song Kiedis described as being about "the colour of any given night in the Los Angeles basin". It described a typical street scene, "from a crime in a parking garage to a sexy little girl named Annie singing songs to some guy who she's got a crush on. It's an atmospheric lyric," he reasoned.

But ultimately *By The Way* was about love and loss: the band's love for the city, Kiedis' loss of his former girlfriend, their affection for Gloria Scott, even Frusciante and Kiedis' love for the writing of Hammett and Chandler. Then there was what Kiedis described as "the spirit of universal love and the spirit of God" that coursed through the track 'Don't Forget Me' and much of the rest of the album.

"That energy is everywhere," he explained. "It doesn't turn its back on people because they're fuckups, losers and dope fiends. For me, that beauty has always been there, even when I was dying."

"Greetings from the dimension of invisible shapes and colours," the band wrote in the waffly press release that accompanied *By The Way* when it hit stores. "The music on this record has expanded our space and made us bigger. Thank you for listening and being exactly where and who you are."

Chad Smith summed up *By The Way* in much more lucid terms. "It's very honest, raw, emotional music . . . it's a very dynamic, rich and lush album. Probably the best collection of Chili Peppers songs we've ever put out."

Rolling Stone agreed. In his four-star review, writer Tom Moon nailed the gradual makeover that the Chili Peppers had been undergoing, especially with their two most recent albums and Frusciante's return. "They swim around in the same inviting Southern Californian waters that inspired The Beach Boys," wrote Moon, who 13 years earlier had been an advocate of the *Mother's Milk* album, "and discover that the incandescent hook can say as much as, if not more than, the testosterone-driven backbeat".

The New York Times noted a lengthy checklist of musical influences on the album, mentioning The Strokes, No Doubt, Fugazi and The Beatles. "But the feeling," wrote Kelefa Sanneh, "is one of casual exploration, not desperate reinvention."

While still writing them off as "a hopeless funk band", Paul Rees of hard rock bible *Kerrang!* enthused at the way the Chili Peppers brought The Beatles, cheesy electronica, The Beach Boys, ska, Tex-Mex, mellotrons, synths, Fifties rock'n'roll and Sixties surf pop to the party. "[*By The Way* is] also everything The Red Hot Chili Peppers of *BloodSugarSexMagik* vintage could never have been: sombre, soothing, lovely, lilting, frequently beautiful and wholly uplifting. By Christ, you find yourself thinking time and time again, they're good."

The *LA Weekly* was equally turned on, calling the album "perhaps their boldest and greatest achievement yet. It is a diverse and complex pop masterwork that evokes Southern California and particularly Los Angeles, as only a handful of previous records has done."

In a nod to Robert Hilburn's put-down of the band almost 20 years earlier, the *Weekly*'s John Albert qualified his observations. "[If you were] so audacious to mention their latest disc in the same category as a hallowed masterpiece like The Beach Boys' *Pet Sounds* you'll get laughed out of the used-record/graphic-novel store. But the truth is, the Chili Peppers' latest release is one of the most interesting and creative new records around and arguably belongs in the pantheon of great Los Angeles albums with the work of The Beach Boys, The Doors, The Flesheaters, X and others."

After 20 years, one of modern rock's definitive LA bands had finally made a definitive LA album. And Flea would be seriously chuffed to see his group ranked with X, one of his most-loved bands.

The response in the UK was equally emphatic. *The Times*' David Sinclair chipped in again. "Diehard fans of the group may find this album a little too genteel, but it is a tremendous achievement for this long-standing band to make such a bold stylistic leap forward." Writing in the *Daily Mirror*, Gavin Martin also declared *By The Way* a success. "[It's] the most mature, sophisticated and varied album of their career . . . the Red Hot Chili Peppers are miles ahead of all the young metal rap outfits like Sum 41 and Blink 182 that have grown up in their shadow."

The Daily Telegraph's David Cheal was also won over. "They may not do the funk-metal thing with quite as much heavyosity as they used to . . . but this is overwhelmingly another triumph, a seductive fusion of power, melody, harmony and torque, tension and release."

Even the Japanese press bought into the hugfest. "*By The Way* picks up where *Californication* left off," observed *The Daily Yomiuri*'s Dave Hilson, "completing the Peppers' journey from testosterone-driven funk rock to a sound as mellow and smooth as the west coast beaches where the foursome frolicked in their youth."

Entertainment Weekly neatly summed up the band's 20-year transition from feral punks to pop craftsmen. "Not content with being the un-official party hosts of the skate-punk generation, they want each album to show off as much of their brains as they do their bodies. No longer the dangerous kids on the block, the Chili Peppers have settled for a less provocative fate: professional craftsmen, with or without their shirts."

Naturally, there were a few dissenting voices, such as *The Scotsman*'s Fiona Shepherd, who called the album "frustratingly average". She even suggested that they'd borrowed from Britpop heroes Coldplay for the arrangement of the closing 'Venice Queen'.

The Toronto Star's Ben Rayner admired the fact that the band had realised that it was their songs, not their "wiggly punk-funk jams" that had sustained their loyal fanbase, but he still missed the old Chili Peppers. "One actually wishes the band would rouse itself and write another stupid ditty about Magic Johnson," he declared in his review. Writing in the *Sunday Telegram*, Craig S Semon figured the album should be renamed *Buyer Beware*. "The album is easily one of the most unwelcome musical makeovers in recent memory for a once cutting-edge band."

Kiedis already had a response for the few critics who'd felt the band had drifted too far from the testosterone-powered raunch of *Mother's Milk* and *BloodSugarSexMagik*. "There's no need for us to play anything we already played," he said. "I think we innately and intuitively know that. [It's] like feeling that you don't want to backtrack when you're driving somewhere, even if you forgot your keys. It's like, 'Fuck it, let's just keep going straight and we'll find a way to get in when we get there.'"

The positive press was great; it wasn't as if the Chili Peppers had problems when it came to having their egos stroked. But what about the record-buying public: had they moved on? Was their second coming with *Californication* a fluke? They would find out on July 9, when the album hit the shelves.

All was in place for the release of *By The Way*: the reviews had been great, the band – especially Kiedis – had spilled their guts in dozens of pre-release interviews, and radio had jumped all over the lead single. But the band's label, Warner Bros, wanted to ensure saturation exposure in time for the release, while at the same time steering fans away from websites that encouraged unauthorised downloading that filtered sales away from the band (and, of course, lost their record company revenue). Warners' plan was to launch the "A Song A Day" campaign, which kicked into action on June 21. With the participation of more than 150 US radio stations and such high-impact web portals as MTV.com, VH1.com, Windowsmedia.com, Apple.com and several other sites, the label leaked one album track a day, along with an interview with the band where they talked up the song of the day, leading conveniently to the album's July 9 release. The songs could even be downloaded to cell phones and two-way pagers, ensuring that Warners had the band's entire digital fanbase stitched up. America On Line (AOL) also bought into "A Song A Day", declaring the Peppers their Artist Of The Month. They streamed an interview and a performance by the band, sold an MP3 of the album's first single for less than a dollar, and offered on-line punters the chance to see the band play in Japan in November. Virtually anyone who logged onto the Internet during June had no way of avoiding the Red Hot Chili Peppers. For those who were technophobic, Warners set up high-profile campaigns with major retail record chains across the USA.

By The Way debuted at number two in the US on release, selling

281,948 copies, which was around 93,000 more than first week sales for *Californication*. The album's competition for that week was a mixed bag – there was the acid-addled space of the Flaming Lips' *Yoshimi Battles The Pink Robots*; *Dreamland*, a self-indulgent album of covers from sometimes Led Zep belter Robert Plant, and the heavily hyped garage rock of Australia's The Vines, who dropped their debut album, *Highly Evolved*, which reached the number 11 spot on the US album chart. But both The Vines and the Peppers were helped by what one industry observer believed to be a "price war" on CDs. Taking note of the low-price-tag-assisted success of the debut album from R&B rookie Ashanti, which sold over 500,000 copies on its release in April, with a selling price of $8.99, The Vines were flogging their album at $7.99, almost half the typical CD price, while one chain was selling *By The Way* for as low as $9.99.

On a global level, the album shifted 1.8 million copies in its first week, debuting at number one in a dozen countries, including England, Australia, Germany, Ireland, Norway, Sweden, Holland and Switzerland. It was double platinum within its first week of release in Ireland and platinum in Canada, Italy, New Zealand, Australia, Japan, Switzerland and Indonesia. With the response to the record almost as universally positive as the feedback for *Californication*, it was time to get back to their second home, the road.

But just as they had done with their surprise club gig in the UK the month before, the band, their Q Prime managers Cliff Bernstein and Peter Mensch, and Warner Bros had plans to shake things up a little when it came to promoting the record in North America. It was the perfect way to break up the usual pattern of recording/promotion/touring, which can turn from a novelty to a grind quicker than you can say "multi-platinum".

So the US launch of *By The Way* took place on New York's Ellis Island, once the entry point for millions of immigrants. Sponsored by rock radio station K-Rock, it was titled the "Pep Rally". On a sticky, steamy Tuesday in early July, the band – despite Kiedis' complaints of feeling hoarse several songs in – barrelled through a set of hits and new tracks, while about 900 fortunate fans ignored the few sprinkles of rain and a ban on alcohol to take in what the *New York Post* declared "one of the top concerts of the year". The location of the gig wasn't chosen at random; it was designed to reinject a little life into lower Manhattan after the 9/11 disaster – and money raised from the show went to the Twin Towers Fund.

The Peppers were now officially warmed up. They could kiss the next 18 months of their lives goodbye.

The *By The Way* tour lacked the high-profile one-shots of *Californication*; there were no Woodstock or Red Square shows this time around. Instead, the band looked at a map of the world and figured, "Why not?" and then set out to visit virtually every city that had a record store and/or an arena. They globe-trotted through Europe, South America, Japan, Singapore, Thailand, New Zealand and virtually every inch of North America. In the 12 months between November 2002 and 2003, they played 57 US dates, performing for more than 650,000 punters and raking in almost $27 million. They were competing with James Taylor and Jimmy Buffett for an audience share, as well as Metallica and 50 Cent.

The Australian leg of the tour took place only a month after the horrific Bali disaster, where 200 Westerners and locals were burned alive by terrorist bombs in a Kuta nightspot. Whereas many acts – Paul McCartney included – cancelled Australian tour plans in the wake of Bali, the Peppers played on. They drew 30,000 punters to their outdoor show at the Sydney Football Stadium – a rare event, Sydney being at the mercy of rigid noise pollution controls and constantly complaining (and influential) inner-city residents. The band were in rare form; and when Flea delivered the usual instruction for everyone (willing females included) to "take off your shirt and swing it over your head like a helicopter", during an encore of 'Me And My Friends', the sight was truly remarkable. Healing was sorely needed after the Bali bombing, and the Peppers provided just that.

One of the rare downbeat notes in the *By The Way* tour was the electrocution death of a fan, 26-year-old Ashley Faris, during a show at the Verizon Wireless Amphitheater in Charlotte, North Carolina. Between the opening set from Snoop Dogg – finally Flea had gotten his way and secured an African/American hip-hopper as support – and the Chili Peppers, Faris had been walking barefoot on a wet stairway when he received a fatal shock.

Flea ruminated on the accident the next day, during one of his regular Fleamails. "I don't know what went wrong," he wrote, "but the guy went to have fun at a concert and never came home. Bless his heart. Whoever it is he has been let in on the big secret. He is probably having a great time right now. My heart and my prayers go out to the person's loved ones."

By May 2003 the Peppers were back in New York, headlining at Madison Square Garden, the ground zero for only the biggest and best in the city that never sleeps. The show's reviews were uniformly rapturous. "The band came to Madison Square Garden for an extraordinary two-hour show," declared the *New York Times'* Kelefa Sanneh, "full of wildly inventive playing and – even better – lovely songs."

Rolling Stone's David Fricke was equally enthused, speculating that the band's rhythm section was so tight that they should cut their own instrumental album. He also cited *BloodSugar* as "the standard by which most rap-metal still fails miserably". As for their broad selection of covers – 'London Calling', Funkadelic's 'Cosmic Slop', the Velvet Underground's 'Ride Into The Sun' – it was proof for Fricke that the Peppers circa 2003 possessed a "now encyclopedic range as a pop band".

It had taken almost 20 years, one death, several reinventions, many burn-outs and sackings, plus endless rises and falls, but the Red Hot Chili Peppers could now stake a claim to being one of the biggest bands on the planet, even if they weren't exactly the radical outfit they'd envisaged 20 years earlier.

ENDING

"Hopefully we can look back and have a laugh at what knuckleheads we were."

THROUGHOUT 2003 and well into 2004, the Red Hot Chili Peppers continued to do what came naturally – touring and selling records. As the buzz gradually started to fade on *By The Way*, the band's second best-of – their first with Warners – appeared on November 18, 2003, alongside a companion DVD, *Live At Slane Castle*, an Irish show in front of 80,000 sweaty, screaming fans. *The Red Hot Chili Peppers' Greatest Hits* was a useful reminder of the consistent hitmakers that they'd become since moving labels for the *BloodSugarSexMagik* album. Of the album's 16 tracks, only two new Rick Rubin productions ('Fortune Faded' and 'Save The Population') were remotely unfamiliar. And such cuts as 'Scar Tissue', 'Under The Bridge', 'Californication' and 'Soul To Squeeze' had become rock radio standards, instantly recognisable, immensely hummable – and in some cases, deeply soulful – career-making songs. By January, the album had been certified platinum in 12 countries, gold in 15 others, including the USA. 'Fortune Faded' was a hit single; *Live At Slane Castle* was a massive Christmas season DVD all around the world.

And the Peppers kept rolling, touring Europe, yet again, throughout April 2004 and then England in June – with three shows in London's Hyde Park on June 19, 20 and 25 – as the band officially turned 20 years old. Somewhere near 100,000 fans turned out for each of their London shows, the results of which ended up on *The Red Hot Chili Peppers Live in Hyde Park* album. James Brown warmed up the huge crowds, while the Peppers threw in off-the-cuff covers of Donna Summer's 'I Feel Love' and Joy Division's 'Transmission'. Chad Smith celebrated by re-forming his old band, Toby Redd, for a one-off club show at the Hot Rocks Cafe in Warren, Michigan. For once, Smith could actually eyeball the crowd, rather than just look out at a sea of heads.

The rest of the band, meanwhile, were fending off rumours that they'd been approached to play at the May 2004 wedding of Prince Fredrik of Denmark, who was a big fan. The Peppers had now graduated from social rejects to royal insiders.

The success of *Greatest Hits* proved how ubiquitous the band's music had become. They crossed over most modern radio formats – classic rock, modern rock, alternative rock, "heritage" rock – while their best-known songs were essentials for film soundtracks, TV shows, virtually anywhere commercial music was played and heard. All that was missing were muzak versions of 'Scar Tissue' and 'Under The Bridge', which surely couldn't be too far in the future.

John Frusciante, meanwhile, continued to explore the outer edges of rock'n'roll with another first-rate solo album, *Shadows Collide With People*, which came out in February 2004. But that was merely the beginning of an outpouring of music from Frusciante. Between June 2004 and February 2005 he released six solo albums: *The Will To Death*, *Automatic Writing* (under the Ataxia tag), *DCEP*, *Inside Of Emptiness*, *A Sphere In The Heart Of Silence* and *Curtains*. Although *Shadows* – the most accessible set of the bunch – was released by Warners, the others appeared through Record Collection, a label designed to handle the "indie" side of Warners.

As for Anthony Kiedis, he teamed up with veteran rock writer Larry "Ratso" Sloman to pen his tell-all life (and near-death) story, *Scar Tissue*, which hit the shelves during October 2004.

The Chili Peppers' days as a cutting-edge outfit at the intersection of hip-hop, funk and punk were as distant a memory as Chad Smith's hairline. Their asterisk band logo was almost as recognisable as that of many computer or automobile brands. But the wealth, security and dedicated fanbase that the band had amassed over 20 years made that sacrifice seem acceptable. And, unlike the band, their fans had actually become younger: the average punter at a Chili Pepper show during their *By The Way* tour was even more youthful than the band's most junior member, John Frusciante, who was born in 1970.

Unlike any other band this side of U2, the Chili Peppers had been reborn, several times over. Many predicted the end of the band when Hillel Slovak OD'd and died in 1988; they bounced back with *Mother's Milk* and then *BloodSugarSexMagik*. Just when it seemed that their core audience had moved on to the abrasive, black T-shirt clad moanings of nu-metal, the Peppers released *Californication* and the good time boys had their second coming. The massive sales and positive critical response to *By The Way* proved that they had a few more rides left on the rock'n'roll gravy train. The band that tried to kill themselves more than once simply refused to die.

Of course there were those, such as embittered former producer Andy Gill, who felt that the band had sold their soul years ago in the pursuit of commercial reward. When I asked his opinion of the band's more recent output, he replied: "I don't think it's as passionate, [but] obviously they've become a more polished outfit."

There was no question that the band's sound had softened, even if their torsos remained as hard as ever. Or as Lindy Goetz would put it, "Today they're Chrysler – when I first met them, they were Hyundai." But mainstream audiences aren't renowned for their critical insight or their sense of history: they simply dig the songs, so the records keep selling. *The Red Hot Chili Peppers' Greatest Hits* was a runaway smash, remaining one of the planet's biggest records as 2003 ticked over into 2004. And there's a fair chance that most of those who bought that best-of already owned the parent albums – *BloodSugarSexMagik*, *One Hot Minute*, *Californication* and *By The Way* – from which the songs had been culled. And while promoting their greatest hits, the band spoke excitedly of even more fresh recordings with Rick Rubin.

Not that their virtually unparalleled success – few American bands could touch the Peppers' hot streak since 1991 – erased their wayward pasts. Kiedis remains the recovering junkie son of a drug dealer; Flea is still as emotionally fragile as ever; Smith can hold a beat much steadier than he could hang onto a relationship; and Frusciante's wilderness years as an addict re-emerge in virtually every public conversation that the guitarist buys into. Outside of the band, the four aren't the most successful human beings on the planet, even though Flea and Smith's efforts as parents far surpass their attempts at relationships.

"He's a good kid," Flea's father, Mick, assured me.

"Hopefully we can look back and have a laugh at what knuckleheads we were," Kiedis figured in 2003. "I have no regrets or shame or guilt about who we were at the time, because that's who we were supposed to be. Something you just have to experience and hope that you don't hurt too many people along the way."

As with most superstar acts, they've climbed over – or buried, in

Hillel Slovak's tragic case – many bodies in their climb to the top. But when they connect on stage as The Red Hot Chili Peppers, there is a chemistry between the four that is, to their millions of fans, truly magical. And even as three of the band moved into their forties, the raw physicality of their live performances are undeniable, if a tad mechanical, while the polish that Rick Rubin brings to their music helps them achieve the most difficult of things: generating songs that pass both the critical and commercial once-over.

The band may have headed into a rare period of hibernation through early 2005, but they give no indication that they'd be slowing down soon. And why should they? This band offers them the security that their off-stage lives rarely could, so why not keep recording and playing.

And that is in spite of the fact that Kiedis is a strangely bland frontman, who lacks the evangelical qualities of a Bono, or Michael Stipe's personal and political convictions. Kiedis was described to me as a "cipher" by former guitarist Jack Sherman, who admitted that he still barely knew the singer after spending a year working alongside him. "He's the archetype of this vicious, ambitious type," Sherman said. "I don't know if there's a person down there. Maybe he really is running on some heavy fuel."

Sherman told me of a recent encounter with Flea, which proved how elusive Kiedis really is. "He said to me, 'God, I don't even know if I know him and he's my best friend.'"

Kiedis might have been born in the midwest, but he will remain the quintessential Californian, sun-blessed and gym-toned, opting to charm with a goofy grin rather than deliver profound statements. Even his lyrical preoccupations – personal redemption, lust and libido, personal "issues" – are the stuff of the west coast, where materialism and store-bought spirituality rule. He's never wanted to change the world – hell, for many years he and his fellow Peppers were simply hoping to sleep with most of it. But even in their darkest moments, The Red Hot Chili Peppers have never claimed to be about anything but the best possible time, ideally for the longest possible time. And in a 21st century world that seems hell-bent on destroying itself, rock fans need all the relief they can buy, which suggests that there's plenty of juice left yet in these occasionally lewd, heavily tattooed and totally renewed Californicators.

Cast of Characters

Mick Balzary – Flea's father is a semi-retired consultant, living in south-eastern Australia.

Keith "Tree" Barry – Flea's long-time friend runs the Silverlake Music Conservatory in LA.

Michael Beinhorn – after producing *The Uplift Mofo Party Plan* and *Mother's Milk*, he worked with Aerosmith, Marilyn Manson, Soundgarden and Hole. He produced Korn's *Untouchables* in 2002.

Addie Brik – Hillel Slovak's girlfriend is now a singer-songwriter, based in London; her 2004 album was called *Loved Hungry*.

George Clinton – Mr Funkadelic was busted in December 2003 for possession of crack cocaine.

Blackie Dammett – Anthony Kiedis' father now runs Rockinfreakapotamus, the Peppers' official fan club.

Andy Gill – the producer of Peppers debut LP is still London-based; he has produced records for Bis, Boss Hog, Michael Hutchence and the Stranglers. The original Gang of Four played their first gig for 24 years in London in January 2005.

Lindy Goetz – the former Peppers manager is now a semi-retired music industry consultant (and keen vegetable grower) living near Santa Barbara, California.

Rob Gordon – erstwhile Peppers A&R manager now runs WhatAreRecords, the label of jazz great Maceo Parker, out of Boulder, Colorado.

Jack Irons – he recovered from 1988 breakdown and drummed for Pearl Jam from 1995 to 1998 and released his solo debut, *Attention Dimension*, in June 2004.

Dave Jerden – the engineer/mixer/producer who worked on *The Red Hot Chili Peppers* and *Mother's Milk* went on to work with Anthrax, Alice In Chains, The Offspring and Jane's Addiction. He produced and mixed Dropbox's 2004 self-titled debut.

Arik Marshall – after being fired from the Peppers he went on to play guitar for Moloko, Macy Gray and Weapon Of Choice; he's now the guitarist in Macy Gray's touring band.

Cliff Martinez – post-Peppers he produced soundtracks (*Sex, Lies & Videotape, Narc, Traffic*) and now lives in Calibassis, California; his latest soundtrack is *Havoc*.

DeWayne "Blackbyrd" McKnight – returned to George Clinton's P-Funk Allstars after being sacked from the Chili Peppers. Played on 1990's *P-Funk*

All Stars Live, 1994's *Dope Dogs* and 1995's *Hydraulic Funk*, amongst others. Still playing with Clinton.

Dave Navarro – he joined the re-formed (and now defunct, yet again) Jane's Addiction; their last album *Strays*, was released in 2003.

DH Peligro – one-time Peppers drummer currently fronts LA-based band Peligro.

Marisa Pouw – Flea's long-time girlfriend was last seen on screen in 2000's *Risk*.

Rick Rubin – the über-producer recently bought the Houdini Mansion, where the Peppers recorded *BloodSugarSexMagik*; his most recent production was Slipknot's *Vol 3: The Subliminal Verses*. He made his recording debut with the track 'Fade Out/In', which appeared on the 2003 soundtrack *Daredevil*.

Jack Sherman – played with Bob Dylan, George Clinton, Peter Case and Feargal Sharkey after being sacked from the Peppers in 1985. Currently living in Savannah, Georgia.

Ione Skye – married and then divorced Beastie Boy Adam Horowitz after splitting with Anthony Kiedis; last seen on screen in 2001's *Southlander: Diary Of A Desperate Musician*.

James Slovak – Hillel's brother is still living in Los Angeles; in 1999 he compiled and published *Behind The Sun*, a book of his brother's artwork and diary entries.

Jesse Tobias – is living in Melbourne, Australia with wife Angie Hart; they play in a duo called Splendid.

Loesha Zeviar – still living in California and sharing parenting duties of Clara Balzary with Flea.

Acknowledgements

Many Thanks To These Good People, Without Whom, etc: Diana Gonsalves, Chris Charlesworth, Melissa Whitelaw, Norm Lurie, Maureen Lamberti, Chris Cuffaro, Michael Dwyer, Ian Watson, Jennifer Fontaine, Val McIver, Rick Gershon, Michael Beinhorn, James Slovak, Larissa Friend, Dr David W Balok and all at Fairfax High School, Mick Balzary, Anton Corbijn, Andy Gill, Robert Wilonsky, Lindy Goetz, Dave Jerden, Steve Roeser, Kevin Flaherty, John Watson, Keith "Tree" Barry and all at Silverlake Conservatory of Music, Graham Spillard, Drew Carolan, Rob Gordon, Cliff Martinez, Robert Hilburn, Aaron Wilhelm, Susan Krieger, Maggie Reinhart, Steffo Mitakides, Addie Brik, Vicky Vogiatzoglou, Gary Panter, Spit Stix, David Meikle, Rodney Bingenheimer, Harvey Kubernik, Kim Fowley, Jack Sherman, Sylvia Massy Shivy, the chipper staff at Mount Sinai Memorial Park and Amoeba Records, plus all at the NSW State Library. Oh, and to the unsuspecting couple in Room 78 of the Chateau Marmont – sorry about that.

Sources

Anon, "Chili Peppers Too Hot As Would-be Concert Goers Mix It Up On The Street", *The Associated Press*, January 21, 1988

Anon, "Shrink – Antwan the Swan of the Red Hot Chili Peppers Under The Lamp", *Melody Maker,* July 23, 1988

Anon, "Two Members Of Red Hot Chili Peppers Arrested Following Attack On Student", *The Associated Press*, March 16, 1990

Anon, "Rock Band Members Plead To Assault Charge", *The Associated Press,* August 10, 1990

Anon, "Woodstock Revisited", *Grand Rapids Press*, April 24, 1994

Anon, "People In The News", *Associated Press*, September 5, 1994

Anon, "Rapper Just Loves Himself And That's Why Peppers Have Hots For Him", *Scottish Daily Record,* May 24, 2002

Anon, "Contest 'Gets A Little Humiliating', Says Red Hot Chili Peppers' Frontman", *The Toronto Sun*, August 9, 2002

Anon, "Blood! Sugar! Sex! + Spontaneous Ejaculation" Australian *Rolling Stone,* December 2002

Anon, Live review, *Houston Chronicle*, December 13, 1985

Anon, "An In–depth Interview with Anthony Kiedis", *Vibe*, March 2003

Anon, "Jack Irons: This Inner Life", *Modern Drummer*

Albert, John, "Sons of the City", *LA Weekly*, December 6-12, 2002

Aledort, Andy, "John Frusciante, Freak Patrol Reporting for Duty", *Guitar World*

Arnold, Gina, Live Review, *Rolling Stone*, February 20, 1992

Babisi, Suzan, "Tony! Tony! Tony! Bennett The Ultimate In Cool And Suave", *Los Angeles Daily News*, October 24, 1993

Bennett, Tina, "Synergy Rules at ESPN Action Sports Awards", *The Press-Enterprise*, April 18, 2002

Bream, Jon, "Woodstock Diary", *Star-Tribune*, August 15, 1994

Burk, Greg, "Droning Man: Cliff Martinez: The Buzz", *LA Weekly*, October 3-9, 2003

Caudle, Todd, "Chili Peppers Boil With Intensity/ High Energy Band Heats Up A Chilly Evening in Denver", *Colorado Springs Gazette Telegraph*, December 18, 1989

Caudle, Todd, "Bands' Triple Punch Leaves Nowhere To Hide: Denver Crowd Nearly Out Of Control", *Colorado Springs Gazette Telegraph*, December 16, 1991

Cheney, Peter, "MuchMusic Rockin' TV's Socks Off", *Toronto Star*, November 23, 1991

Christensen, Thor, "Peppers Turn Blender Up A Couple Of Notches", *Milwaukee Journal*, October 23, 1991

Clerk, Carol, "Peace Corpse", *Melody Maker*, May 21, 1988

Clode, Sam, "All Fired Up", *Juice*, July 2002

Cohan, John, "In The Studio With The RHCP's Drummer And Producer", *Drum Magazine*, May/June 2002

Connell, Christopher, "Administration Pulls Radio Spot Featuring Convicted Singer", *The Associated Press*, January 7, 1994

Dafoe, Chris, Album review, *The Globe And Mail*, December 10, 1987

Danielsen, Shane, "Chili Reception", *Sydney Morning Herald*, October 9, 1992

Deckard, Linda, "Lollapalooza Gross Nears $20 Million In Two Months", *Amusement Business*, September 21, 1992

DeVault, Russ, "The Joy, Sadness Of Mother's Milk", *Atlanta Journal And Constitution*, December 1, 1989

di Perna, Alan, "Red Hot And Bothered", *Guitar World*, 1995

di Perna, Alan, "Getting Better All the Time", *Guitar Magazine*, August 2002

di Perna, Alan, "Magic John: Frusciante Channels Spirits on His New Solo Album", *Guitar World* Acoustic #43

Dougan, John, "Punk Music" (www.allmusic.com)

Edwards, Gavin, "Are We Not Men? We Are Peppers!" *Rolling Stone*, June 2000

Engleheart, Murray, "RHCP Wipe The Slate Clean", *CD Now*, 1999

Ericson, Pernilla, *OKEJ Magazine*, July 1999

Foege, Alec, "Chili Peppers Grow Up To Be Sensitive White Males", *Rolling Stone*, November 1995

Fort, Marc, "We Got The Funk In Austin: Peppers, Fishbone Drop A Bomb On Receptive Audiences", *Austin American-Statesman*, December 10, 1991

Franklin, Charlotte, "Days Like These", *Sunday Life*, January 11, 2004

Fricke, David, "The Red Hot Chili Peppers", *Rolling Stone*, June 25, 1992

Gonzalez, John D, "Chili Peppers May Have Evolved, But The Music Is Still Spicy", *Grand Rapids Press*, December 30, 1990

Gonzalez, John D, "It Could Be Years Before Chili Peppers Play Here", *Grand Rapids Press*, October 25, 1991

Gonzalez, John D, "Red Hot Chili Peppers Deserve A Chance Here", *Grand Rapids Press*, November 1, 1991

Gonzalez, John D, "Chili Peppers Still Red Hot, But Seasoned By Time", *Grand Rapids Press*, November 17, 1991

Gonzalez, John D, "Kiedis, Peppers, Fans All Red Hot", *Grand Rapids Press*, November 21, 1991

Gonzalez, John D, "Charts Show The Chili Peppers Are Red Hot", *Grand Rapids Press*, July 19, 1992

Gore, Joe, "Inside The Peppermill: Dave Navarro And Flea Reinvent The Chilis", *Guitar Player*, April 1, 1995

Grobel, Lawrence, "Buster, No! Buster, Sit Down!", *Penthouse*, 2002

Gundersen, Edna, "Funk's Red Hot Ticket: Sex Fuels Chili Peppers Musical Fire", *USA Today*, July 16, 1992

Harrington, Richard, "The Medium Is The Mayhem; Red Hot Chili Peppers, Rocking Their Socks Off", *The Washington Post*, May 13, 1990

Healy, James, Album review, *The Omaha World-Herald*, November 1, 1987

Hoekstra, Dave, "Chili Peppers Headline A Very Hot Dance Show", *Chicago Sun-Times*, April 15, 1988

Howell, Peter, "The Peppers May Be Hot, But Their Pals Are On Fire", *Toronto Star*, March 7, 1996

Ikenberg, Tamara, "Playing With Fire: Red Hot Chili Peppers Like To Stir Things Up By Mixing Fun, Funk And Feeling", *NY Times News Service*, February 2, 1996

Jenkins, Mark, "Chili Peppers' Milk Tastes Of Yesterday", *The Washington Post*, November 17, 1989

Johnson, Dean, "Woodstock: Superstar Acts Provide Superb Final Performances", *Boston Herald*, August 15, 1994

Kiedis, Anthony, "Whole Lotta Love", *Details for Men*, July 1992

Kim, Jae-Ha, "Red Hot Chili Peppers Retool, Hit The Road", *Chicago Sun-Times*, December 24, 1989

Kipnis, Jill, "Red Hot Chili Peppers' 'By the Way' Due in July From Warner", *Billboard*, June 22, 2002

Lanham, Tom, "Smug And Rude Are The Boys In The Nude", *San Francisco Chronicle*, January 12, 1986

Liner notes for 2003 reissue of *The Red Hot Chili Peppers* CD

Liner notes for *Freaky Styley*, reissued by EMI 2003

Liveten, Sharon, "New Album, Tour – Chilis Bounce Back After Guitarist's Death", *Los Angeles Times*, September 10, 1989

Lloyd, Robert, "This Ain't No Juilliard!", *LA Weekly*, October 4-10, 2002

MacSmith, James & Sams, Christine, "Rock Brothers Go From Shed Hot To Red Hot", *Sun Herald*, July 14, 2002

Magnuson, Ann, "To Live And Die In LA", *Spin*, August 1999

Manelis, Michele, "Californication", *Juice*, Yearbook 1999

Marvel, Mark, "Anthony Kiedis Of the Red Hot Chili Peppers", *Interview*, October 1994

McDonnell, Evelyn, "Talent In Action", *Billboard*, June 2, 1990

McLeod, Harriet, "Parliament/Funkadelic George Clinton Plays Funk, Whole Funk And Nothing But The Funk", *Richmond Times-Dispatch*, February 10, 1993

Mitchell, Rick, "Funk Lives/New Material And New Fans: George Clinton Is Having Fun", *Houston Chronicle*, November 17, 1989

Moon, Tom, "Medium Hot: Rock's Loutish Love Thugs Trade P-Funk for Tunes", *Rolling Stone*, July 25, 2002

Morris, Chris, "Red Hot Chili Peppers' 'Magik' Touch", *Billboard*, September 28, 1991

Morris, Chris, "Ex-Chili Pepper Jack Sherman Sues Band", *Billboard*, March 27, 1993

Morris, Chris, "Frusciante Steps Out With American Set", *Billboard*, October 1, 1994

Myers, Caren, "Red Hot Chili Peppers – The Spice Is Right", *Melody Maker*, February 17, 1990

Neely, Kim, "Lollapalooza '92", *Rolling Stone*, September 17, 1992

Neely, Kim, "Flea of the Red Hot Chili Peppers", *Rolling Stone*, November 17, 1994

Neely, Kim, "Sir Psycho Sexy: The Rolling Stone Interview with Anthony Kiedis of the Red Hot Chili Peppers", *Rolling Stone*, May 1994

Nelson, Artie, "Space Cadet", *Raw* magazine #163, 1994

New Rolling Stone Encyclopedia of Rock & Roll, The, Fireside 1995

Petridis, Alexis, "Pop – Red Hot Chili Peppers – London Arena", *The Guardian*, June 28, 2002

Pettigrew, Jason, "Red Hot Chili Peppers Funkin' Up the Milky Way", *Alternative Press*, November 1989

Racine, Marty, "Chili Peppers Keep Hot Taste For Life", *Houston Chronicle*, September 30, 1989

Reynolds, Simon, "Magicians Followed But Not Chaste", *London Observer*, September 29, 1991

Roeser, Steve, "Stand By Me (And My Friends)", *Goldmine*, August 7, 1992

Roeser, Steve, "Infinite Zero: The Record World of Henry Rollins and Rick Rubin", *Goldmine*, January 16, 1996

Rosen, Craig, "It's A Travelling Woodstock", *St Petersburg Times*, June 29, 1992

Roth, Bennett, "Star's Past Too Red Hot", *Houston Chronicle*, January 8, 1994

Rotondi, James, "John Frusciante: Goodbye Chili Winds, Hello 4th Dimension", *Guitar Player*, January 1, 1995

Rotondi, James, "Till I Reach The Higher Ground", *Guitar Player*, November 1997

Russell, Deborah, "Old Track Is New Hit For Chili Peppers", *Billboard*, November 28, 1992

Scott, Jane, "Rockers Rattle Music Hall's Walls", *The Plain Dealer*, October 28, 1991

Serba, John, "Return of Red Hots", *Grand Rapids Press*, April 21, 2002

Simpson, Dave, *The Guardian*, February 14, 2003

Sinclair, David, "Bad-Boy Heroes Of Sock 'N' Roll", *The Times*, September 23, 1995

Sinclair, David, "The Red Hot Way Of Life", *The Times*, June 3, 2002

Sinclair, David, "Red Hot Chili Peppers London Arena", *The Times*, June 28, 2002

Slovak, James, *Behind the Sun: The Diary and Art of Hillel Slovak*, Slim Skinny Publications, 1999

Smith, Mat, "Phallus Or Fallacy", *Melody Maker*, March 12, 1988

Smith, Russell, "Punkadelic Sensations: Red Hot Chili Peppers Go For Punk-Funk Fringe", *The Dallas Morning News*, December 10, 1985

Smith, Russell, "The Alarm Delivers A Red-Hot Show For Dallas Fans", *The Dallas Morning News*, December 15, 1987

Snider, Eric, Album review, *St Petersburg Times*, November 1, 1987

Snider, Eric, "Peppers To Unleash Their Energy At Jannus Landing Series", *St Petersburg Times*, December 8, 1989

Snyder, Michael, "Chili Peppers Heat Up The I-Beam", *San Francisco Chronicle,* January 9, 1985

Stegall, Tim, "Fear's Lee Ving: Confessions and Misinformation", *Austin Chronicle*

Stout, Gene, "Well-Rested Peppers Promise A Red Hot Show At The Key Arena", *Seattle Post-Intelligencer*, April 12, 1996

Stubbe, Britt, "No Drugs, Yes Religion", *Oor* Magazine, June 29, 2002

Sullivan, Jim, "A Night Of Mayhem In Pepperland", *The Boston Globe*, November 4, 1991

Sullivan, Jim, "MTV Has Fun With Obsessive Fans", *The Boston Globe*, April 8, 1992

Sullivan, Kate, "Icons", *Spin*, August 2002

Sutcliffe, Phil, "The Band That Tried to Kill Themselves", Q, 1999

Tan, Theresa, *Etc Magazine*

The Uplift Mofo Party Plan liner notes; reissued by EMI 2003

Thomas, Brett, "Glitterati", *Sun Herald*, May 17, 1992

Thompson, Dave, *Red Hot Chili Peppers*, St Martin's Press, 1993

Toltz, Mel, "Blood Sugar", Australian *Rolling Stone*, April 1993

Unterberger, Richie, "British Punk" (www.allmusic.com)

Unterberger, Richie, "American Punk Rock" (www.allmusic.com)

Wall, Mick, "Anthony's Sex Files", *Kerrang*, Issue #673, 1990

Whalen, Kathi, "Red Hot Chili Peppers", *The Washington Post*, November 20, 1989

Wiederhorn, Jon, "Secret Sauce", *MTV*, 2002

Wild, David, "Red Hot & New", *Rolling Stone*, July 8, 2002

Williams, John, "The Red Hot Chili Peppers Q&A", *Jam!*

Williams, Mary, "Kiedis Gives It All Away For Chili Peppers' New Album",
   Daily Brun, March 11, 2002

Wilonsky, Robert, *New Times*, Los Angeles, 1996

Winwood, Ian, "The Young Ones", *Kerrang* #911

Winwood, Ian, "Older. Wiser. Stronger." Australian *Kerrang!*, Volume 1,
   Issue 8

Wooldridge, Simon, *Juice*, December 1999

Selective Discography

Albums, CDs

This discography lists all albums readily available commercially. For details of limited edition releases, boxed sets, etc., go to: www.allmusic.com

The Red Hot Chili Peppers
August 1984
True Men Don't Kill Coyotes/Baby Appeal/Buckle Down/Get Up And Jump/Why Don't You Love Me/Green Heaven/Mommy Where's Daddy/Out In LA/Police Helicopter/You Always Sing The Same/Grand Pappy Du Plenty

March 2003
Remastered Version – Bonus Tracks:
Get Up And Jump (Demo)/Police Helicopter (Demo)/Out In LA (Demo)/Green Heaven (Demo)/What It Is (aka Nina's Song) (Demo)

Freaky Styley
September 1985
Jungleman/Hollywood (Africa)/American Ghost Dance/If You Want Me To Stay/Nevermind/Freaky Styley/Blackeyed Blonde/The Brothers Cup/Battleship/Lovin' And Touchin'/Catholic School Girls Rule/Sex Rap/Thirty Dirty Birds/Yertle The Turtle

March 2003
Remastered Version – Bonus Tracks:
Nevermind (Demo)/Sex Rap (Demo)/Freaky Styley (Orig. Instrumental Long Version)/Millionaires Against Hunger (B-side from Taste The Pain)

The Uplift Mofo Party Plan
September 1987
Fight Like A Brave/Funky Crime/Me And My Friends/Backwoods/Skinny Sweaty Man/Behind The Sun/Subterranean Homesick Blues/Special Secret Song Inside*/No Chump Love Sucker/Walkin' On Down The Road/Love Trilogy/Organic Anti-Beat Box Band

* Renamed 'Party On Your P***y' in Re-issue

364

March 2003
Remastered Version – Bonus Tracks:
Behind The Sun (Instrumental Demo)/Me And My Friends (Instrumental Demo)

Mother's Milk
August 1989
Good Time Boys/Higher Ground/Subway To Venus/Magic Johnson/
Nobody Weird Like Me/Knock Me Down/Taste The Pain/Stone Cold
Bush/Fire/Pretty Little Ditty/Punk Rock Classic/Sexy Mexican Maid/
Johnny, Kick A Hole In The Sky

March 2003
Remastered Version – Bonus Tracks:
Song That Made Us What We Are Today (Demo)/Knock Me Down
(Original Long Version)/Sexy Mexican Maid (Original Long Version)/
Salute To Kareem (Demo w/guitar track)/Castles Made Of Sand (Live
21/11/89)/Crosstown Traffic (Live 21/11/89)

BloodSugarSexMagik
September 1991
The Power Of Equality/If You Have To Ask/Breaking The Girl/Funky
Monks/Suck My Kiss/I Could Have Lied/Mellowship Slinky In B Major/
The Righteous & The Wicked/Give It Away/BloodSugarSexMagik/
Under The Bridge/Naked In The Rain/Apache Rose Peacock/
The Greeting Song/My Lovely Man/Sir Psycho Sexy/They're Red Hot

One Hot Minute
September 1995
Warped/Aeroplane/Deep Kick/My Friends/Coffee Shop/Pea/One Big
Mob/Walkabout/Tearjerker/One Hot Minute/Falling Into Grace/Shallow
Be Thy Game/Transcending

Californication
June 1999
Around The World/Parallel Universe/Scar Tissue/Otherside/Get On Top/
Californication/Easily/Porcelain/Emit Remmus/I Like Dirt/This Velvet
Glove/Savior/Purple Stain/Right On Time/Road Trippin'

By The Way
July 2002
By The Way/Universally Speaking/This Is The Place/Dosed/Don't Forget
Me/The Zephyr Song/Can't Stop/I Could Die For You/Midnight/
Throw Away Your Television/Cabron/Tear/On Mercury/Minor
Thing/Warm Tape/Venice Queen

Red Hot Chili Peppers Live in Hyde Park
August 2004
Intro/Can't Stop/Around The World/Scar Tissue/By The Way/Fortune Faded/I Feel Love/Otherside/Easily/Universally Speaking/Get On Top/Brandy/Don't Forget Me/Rolling Sly Stone/Throw Away Your Television/Leverage Of Space/Purple Stain/The Zephyr Song/Californication/Right On Time/Parallel Universe/Drum Homage Medley/Under The Bridge/Black Cross/Flea's Trumpet Treated By John/Give It Away

Compilation Albums

What Hits!?
November 1992
Higher Ground/Fight Like A Brave/Behind The Sun/Me & My Friends/Backwoods/True Men Don't Kill Coyotes/Fire/Get Up And Jump/Knock Me Down/Under The Bridge/Show Me Your Soul/If You Want Me To Stay/Hollywood/Jungle Man/The Brothers Cup/Taste The Pain/Catholic School Girls Rule/Johnny, Kick A Hole In The Sky

Out In LA
November 1994
Higher Ground (12" Vocal Mix)/Hollywood (Africa) (Extended Dance Mix)/If You Want Me To Stay (Pink Mustang Mix)/Behind The Sun (Ben Grosse Remix)/Castles Made Of Sand (Live)/Special Secret Song Inside (Live)/F.U. (Live)/Get Up And Jump (Demo Version)/Out In LA (Demo Version)/Green Heaven (Demo Version)/Police Helicopter (Demo Version)/Nevermind (Demo Version)/Sex Rap (Demo Version)/Blues For Meister/You Always Sing The Same/Stranded/Flea Fly/What It Is/Deck The Halls

The Best Of The Red Hot Chili Peppers
June 1998
Behind the Sun/Johnny, Kick A Hole In The Sky/Me And My Friends/Fire/True Men Don't Kill Coyotes/Higher Ground/Knock Me Down/Fight Like A Brave/Taste The Pain/If You Want Me To Stay

Greatest Hits
November 2003
Under The Bridge/Give It Away/Californication/Scar Tissue/Soul To Squeeze/Otherside/Suck My Kiss/By The Way/Parallel Universe/Breaking The Girl/My Friends/ Higher Ground/Universally Speaking/Road Trippin'/Fortune Faded/Save The Population

Videos/DVDs

Psychedelic Sexfunk Live From Heaven
June 1990
Stone Cold Bush/Sexy Mexican Maid/Good Time Boys/Star-Spangled
Banner/Pretty Little Ditty/Knock Me Down/Nevermind/Magic Johnson/
Subway To Venus

Positive Mental Octopus
June 1990
Taste The Pain/Higher Ground/Knock Me Down/Fight Like A Brave/Fire/
Catholic School Girls Rule/Jungle Man/True Men Don't Kill Coyotes

Funky Monks
November 1991
Suck My Kiss/Funky Monks/Sikamikanico/Sir Psycho Sexy/Fela's Cock/
Breaking The Girl/Mellowship Slinky In B Major/Soul To Squeeze/Give It
Away/Apache Rose Peacock/They're Red Hot/My Lovely Man/Under
The Bridge

What Hits!?
November 1992
Behind The Sun/Under The Bridge/Show Me Your Soul/Taste The Pain/
Higher Ground/Knock Me Down/Fight Like A Brave/Jungle Man/
True Men Don't Kill Coyotes/Catholic School Girls Rule/Fire (Live)/
Stone Cold Bush (Live)/Special Secret Song Inside (Live)/Subway To Venus
(Live)

Off The Map
December 2001
Around The World/Give It Away/Usually Just A T-Shirt #3/Scar Tissue/
Suck My Kiss/If You Have To Ask/Subterranean Homesick Blues/
Otherside/Blackeyed Blonde/Pea/BloodSugarSexMagik/Easily/What Is
Soul?/Fire/Californication/Right On Time/Under The Bridge/Me And
My Friends/Skinny Sweaty Man (Live)/I Could Have Lied (Live)/Parallel
Universe (Live)/Sir Psycho Sexy (Live)/Search And Destroy (Live)
Plus pre-show backstage footage/interview footage

Greatest Hits
November 2003
Disk 1 – CD
Under The Bridge/Give It Away/Californication/Scar Tissue/Soul To
Squeeze/Otherside/Suck My Kiss/By The Way/Parallel Universe/Breaking

The Girl/My Friends/Higher Ground/Universally Speaking/Road Trippin'/Fortune Faded/Save The Population

Disk 2 – Videos
Higher Ground/Suck My Kiss/Give It Away/Under The Bridge/Soul To Squeeze/Aeroplane/My Friends/Around The World/Scar Tissue/Otherside/Californication/Road Trippin'/By The Way/The Zephyr Song/Can't Stop/Universally Speaking

Live At Slane Castle
November 2003
By The Way/Scar Tissue/Around The World/Universally Speaking/Parallel Universe/Zephyr Song/Throw Away Your Television/Havana Affair/Otherside/Purple Stain/Don't Forget Me/Right On Time/Can't Stop/Venice Queen/Give It Away/Californication/Under The Bridge/Power Of Equality

Index

11/05 (56755)

JEFF APTER is an Australian-based music writer, who has been reporting on popular culture for the past 15 years. He spent five years as the Music Editor at Australian *Rolling Stone*, and his work has also appeared in the *Sydney Morning Herald*, *Juice*, *Juke*, *Rhythms*, *No Depression*, *The West Australian*, *GQ*, *The Bulletin* and numerous other magazines, newspapers and web sites. This is his second book. His first, *Tomorrow Never Knows: The Silverchair Story*, was published in May 2003, and a third, *Never Enough: The Story of The Cure*, is due in late 2005. He lives in Sydney.